Themes in Social Anthropology
edited by David Turton and Marilyn Strathern

The appropriation
of nature

Themes in Social Anthropology

Buddhism in Life
The anthropological study of religion and the Sinhalese
practice of Buddhism
Martin Southwold

Sacrifice in Africa
A structuralist approach
Luc de Heusch

Initiation
Jean S. La Fontaine

Tim Ingold

The appropriation of nature

Essays on human ecology
and social relations

Manchester University Press

Copyright © Tim Ingold 1986

Published by Manchester University Press,
Oxford Road, Manchester M13 9PL, UK

British Library cataloguing in publication data
Ingold, Tim
    The appropriation of nature. — (Themes
    in social anthropology)
    1. Hunting and gathering societies
    I. Title   II. Series
    307.7'72   GN388

ISBN 0 7190 1862 5 *cased*

Typeset in Hong Kong
by Best-set Typesetter Ltd
Printed and bound in Great Britain by
Biddles Ltd, Guildford and King's Lynn

Contents

To C. T. Ingold

Acknowledgements

This book owes its inception to a suggestion from David Turton, and it would never have been written had it not been for the generosity of the University of Manchester in granting me sabbatical leave for the academic session 1984–5, and of my colleagues in the Department of Social Anthropology who covered my teaching and administrative responsibilities during my absence. My thanks to all.

The chapters consist of separate essays, each of which has its own history. They therefore call for separate acknowledgement, and I shall go through them in turn.

Chapter 1 bears a slight relationship to a paper originally presented some years ago at a conference held in Cambridge on Economic Archaeology, since published as 'The hunter and his spear: notes on the cultural mediation of social and ecological systems' (in *Economic Archaeology*, eds. A. Sheridan and G. N. Bailey, BAR International Series 96, Oxford 1981). The prominence given in the present version to the ideas of J. J. Gibson results from my very recent encounter with his work, which I believe to be of outstanding significance for ecological anthropology. I have to thank Ed Reed for drawing Gibson's writings to my attention. Lesley Haviland taught me a few things about how best to introduce the themes of this book, though I have certainly not gone as far as she would have liked in expunging the word 'man' as a collective term for the human species.

Chapter 2 began life as a paper which was read to anthropology seminars at the Universities of Oxford and Kent. It was subsequently rewritten in its entirety, and presented as the Malinowski Memorial Lecture for 1982, at the London School of Economics and Political Science. The lecture was published in the journal *Man* (N.S.) **18**: 1–20, 1983. I am grateful to the editor of *Man*, and to the Royal Anthropological Institute, for permission to reprint it in this volume. I have made only minor, cosmetic alterations.

Chapter 3 was written in spring 1985, and part of it was presented to the anthropology seminar of the Research School of Pacific Studies, Australian National University. Besides the participants in that seminar, a great many people have helped me with ideas for subsequent revision, particularly Bill McGrew, Ed Reed, Vernon Reynolds and Charles Reed.

Chapter 4 was written during the same period, and has since been considerably revised in the light of extremely helpful comments from Geza Teleki, Bill McGrew, Karen Endicott, Gisli Palsson, Bruce Winterhalder, Vernon Reynolds and Hitoshi Watanabe. The chapter also bears the imprint of a memorable evening spent with Junichiro Itani and his colleagues at the University of Kyoto.

Chapter 5 'grew' out of the previous one, and was completed on a flight from Manchester to Sydney in July 1985. A shortened version was presented to seminars at the Research School of Pacific Studies, Australian National University; the School of Social Sciences, Deakin University; the Department of Anthropology and Sociology, University of Queensland; and the Department of Prehistory, University of New England. I have benefited from the comments of participants in all these seminars.

Chapter 6 was originally written for the Third International Conference on Hunter–Gatherers, held at Bad–Homburg, West Germany, in June 1983. I am grateful for funds from the Social Science Research Council (U.K.) and the Maison des Sciences de l'Homme (Paris) which enabled me to attend the conference. The paper has since been considerably revised and expanded with the help of critical comments from many of the participants at that conference: I would like to mention, in particular, Les Hiatt, Ed Wilmsen, Harvey Feit, David Turner and Michael Asch. Since the conference I also received valuable comments and criticisms from Nic Peterson, Alan Barnard, Dick Werbner, David Turton, and from participants in a seminar held at the Centre for Arctic Cultural Research, University of Umeå, in March 1985. The essay, in its present form, represents my first attempt to tackle the ethnographic material on Aboriginal Australia, a field of which I was previously largely ignorant. A Visiting Fellowship at the Department of Prehistory and Anthropology, Australian National University, financed by a grant from the University of London Australian Studies Centre, enabled me to spend six weeks in the summer of 1985 totally immersed in Australian ethnography. I should like to thank all those – especially Nic Peterson – who contributed to my 'Australian education'.

Parts of Chapter 7 are based on an earlier paper, 'Time, social relationships and the exploitation of animals: anthropological reflections on prehistory' (In *Animals in Archaeology vol. 3: Early herders and their flocks*, eds. Juliet Clutton-Brock and Caroline Grigson, BAR International Series 202, Oxford 1984). I should also acknowledge the seminal work of

Tommy Carlstein, which has a major bearing on this chapter.

The paper included here as Chapter 8 was originally written for the Third International Conference on Food Conservation held at Levroux, France, in November 1980. I should like to thank the organizers of the conference, and especially Alain Testart and François Sigaut, for their encouragement and assistance. I am also grateful for financial support from the Maison des Sciences de l'Homme (Paris) and the Social Science Research Council (U.K.) which enabled me to attend. The proceedings of the conference have recently appeared as a magnificent two-part work edited by Marceau Gast, François Sigaut and Corinne Beutler (*Les techniques de conservation des grains à long terme*, Vol. 3, Éditions du Centre National de la Recherche Scientifique, Paris 1985). The same original version of the paper was also presented in November 1980 to the archaeology seminar at the University of Southampton, where I benefited from a provocative exchange with Lewis Binford. It has since been revised for publication in the journal *Man* (N.S.) **18**: 553–71, 1983, in the light of comments from Clive Gamble, Geoff Bailey, Robin Torrence, Barbara Bender, James Woodburn and David Turton. I am grateful to the editor of *Man*, and to the Royal Anthropological Institute, for permission to reprint the published version here, with very minor modifications.

Chapter 9 is a completely recast and rewritten version of a paper by the same title originally presented at the Second International Conference on Hunting and Gathering Societies held at Laval University, Quebec, in September 1980. I am grateful to the Maison des Sciences de l'Homme (Paris) for funds which enabled me to attend the conference.

Chapter 10 was written in January 1985, and has been presented to seminars at the Department of Anthropology, University of Cambridge; the Department of Ethnology, University of Helsinki; and the Centre for Arctic Cultural Research, University of Umeå. At Cambridge I received valuable criticisms from Caroline Humphrey and Keith Hart. I am extremely grateful to Hitoshi Watanabe, Dick Werbner, David Riches and Paul Baxter, who all read and commented on the manuscript.

Finally, I owe my greatest debt of thanks to my wife Anna, and to Christopher, Nicholas and Jonathan, who had to put up with a sometimes absent-minded and irritable father, and who persistently advised him not to overwork.

T. I.
January 1986

1

Prologue: concerning the hunter, and his spear.

I

My concern, in the essays that make up this volume, is with the material conditions of social life. This is a field to which many and various theoretical paradigms have laid claim, each competing for its share of anthropological attention. Labels abound, such as cultural ecology, cultural materialism, neo-Marxism, neofunctionalism, and a host of other concoctions designed to advertise the 'born-again' condition of their adherents. Much of the debate and argument surrounding these alternatives centres on the juxtaposition of four grand terms – environment, technology, society and culture – and the connections between them. We enclose our terms in boxes with arrows going this way or that, or sometimes in all directions at once (see, for example, Cohen 1974: 65). Depending upon the source of inspiration, there is talk of selective pressure, dialectical process, or a labyrinth of 'multiple feedback loops'. Colossal, polyhyphenated, multi-systemic monsters stalk the pages of this debate: there are techno-environmental and sociocultural systems, somehow exchanging heads and tails with socio-environments and techno-cultural complexes. It is all very confusing, and not a little imprecise. I think it best, in the circumstances, to abandon these monsters to their fate, and to start again by considering what is apparently the simplest of situations, in which are nevertheless condensed all the essential ingredients of our inquiry.

Let us imagine, then, a human hunter, armed with a spear, out in pursuit of game. He is of course an individual organism, the occupant of an environment that includes the animal he brings down. But he also belongs to a social group, or a band, amongst whose members the products of his hunting will eventually be distributed. Though in possession of certain bodily equipment, head and hands, arms and legs, he augments their effect through the attachment of an artefact – the spear – which he has designed and constructed himself. But in its use, he brings to bear the knowledge and experience of past generations, handed down as an accumulating tradition. Encompassed in this elementary situation are therefore all four of the components of anthropological system building to which we have just alluded: environment, society, technology, culture. There is no better way to begin than by examining the import of each of these in turn. First on our agenda is...

The environment

It may seem obvious, but is often forgotten, that an environment can only be defined relative to a being or beings whose environment it is, whether a single individual, a local or regional population, or an entire species. 'No animal', as Gibson puts it, 'could exist without an environment surrounding it. Equally...an environment implies an animal (or at least an organism) to be surrounded' (1979: 8). Thus an uninhabited planet, such as was the earth before the dawn of life, was a world, but not an environment. For an individual organism, the environment normally comprises three components: the non-living or abiotic world, the world of other species, and the world of conspecifics. These worlds do not, in themselves, make up a system; what they offer to the surrounded individual is rather a set of possibilities, or *affordances*, to use Gibson's term (1979: 127). The same objects, whether living or non-living, will afford quite different things to different individuals, depending on the nature of their project: for example a tree affords movement to a squirrel, but places of rest to a bird. The organization of environmental possibilities into a coherent system has its source *within* the individual, being a projection of its own internal organization onto the world outside its body. (Lewontin 1982: 160). But that world is, of course, finite in extent, so that there are outer limits on what it will afford which naturally constrain the realization of the objectives of the organism or organisms surrounded.

Defined as a set of affordances, an environment exists just as well for the insect predator, whose project is presumably governed by instinct, as it does for the self-conscious human hunter. For both, animal prey afford eating. Yet it has been said that for the unintelligent organism, 'there cannot be any such thing as an "environment"' (von Glasersfeld 1976: 216). In what sense, then, can an environment exist for intelligent human beings, but not for putatively unintelligent insects? To this we answer: as a set of essences rather than affordances, as a landscape or habitat rather than a niche, whose constituent objects are defined in terms of composition rather than function, in terms – that is – of what they are made of rather than what can be done with them. We observers can of course regard the environment of the insect in this way, but the animal itself does not. What it perceives are not objects as such, but the affordances of objects, already organized for the execution of a received project. We humans, on the other hand, find ourselves in an environment consisting of raw materials that have yet to be organized in accordance with a project of our own devising. We perceive an essential disjunction between ourselves, the organizers, and this inherently resistant material. In shaping the world to our design, there is a sense in which we 'make' it even if we do not physically modify it: thus our environment is factitious although not necessarily artificial. The disjunction between making and modification is the central theme of our discussion in Chapter 3, but some exemplification is appropriate at this point.

Suppose that I find a stone, and wonder whether I might use it as a missile, for hammering, or perhaps as a pendulum bob or paperweight. For none of these purposes need the stone be modified. But the tiny insect hiding behind the stone never perceived its 'stoniness'; it simply perceived concealment, and responded accordingly. Likewise the hunter's environment includes animals, which may or may not be regarded as edible. The insect predator, on the other hand, perceives only food. It discriminates things that afford eating from things that do not, but it does not recognize 'the animal'. In Chapter 4 I develop a contrast between hunting and predation, and correspondingly between gathering and foraging, which ultimately hinges on this difference. The gatherer–hunter is a self-conscious agent, confronting a world of plants and animals from which he or she selects those that will furnish suitable raw materials for consumption. The forager–predator, to the contrary, merely responds to the presence of environmental objects that are perceived to afford eating. It is when we say that the environment comprises stones rather than missiles or hammers, caves rather than shelters, plants and animals rather than food, air rather than breathing space, trees rather than ladders and ground rather than platforms, that we are treating it in a fashion exclusive to ourselves. Such an environment of essences (the habitat) does not, in itself, specify either how it is to be exploited, or to what degree of intensity. That is for us to decide.

I mentioned a moment ago that for an individual organism, unless reared in isolation, one component of the environment consists of other individuals of the same species. The sum of these individuals, together with their interrelations, constitute the next item on our agenda...

The society

The problem of what are, and are not, to be regarded as social relations is a recurrent theme of the essays that follow. We can provide a lead into the problem by posing this question: if the environment of an animal includes its conspecifics, how – if at all – can we distinguish between its social relations and its ecological relations? Ecology, according to a widely accepted definition, is the study of the interrelations between organisms and their environments (Odum 1975: 1–4). Is sociology, then, a branch of ecology, dealing with the *subset* of interrelations between organisms and their *conspecific* environments? Arguably, for any one individual in society, other individuals are ecological objects that furnish a set of affordances richer and more elaborate than anything else on offer, and indeed the whole field of social behaviour might be supposed to rest upon the perception (or misperception) of what these others afford (Gibson 1979: 135). To be sure, to us humans other humans do not afford eating, except under somewhat exceptional circumstances! But there are plenty of species of insects and fish which regularly eat their own kind. And even if we disregard such instances, all sorts of other possibilities may be furnished by the presence of conspecifics, many of which – being reciprocally available to every party in the interaction – come under the general rubric of 'co-operation'. Indeed a case may be made for treating all intraspecific co-operation as a kind of tool use: as for example when one chimpanzee 'uses' another to bring it food, through positive inducement or threat (Hall 1963: 479). Though the use and manufacture of tools is the subject of a separate essay (Chapter 3), the question of whether social interaction and tool-using are the same or different warrants a brief consideration here.

Let me return to the hunter and his spear. We do not doubt that the spear is a tool – in Gibson's language it is a large, pointed and elongated object that affords piercing (1979: 133). Now suppose that the hunter is not alone, but that he works in consort with others who have perhaps lured or driven the game towards a location where he waits in readiness to strike. Would we not have an equal right to regard these others as objects which afford the possibility of direct encounter with prey? Rather more obvious examples of using other humans as tools come from the field of circus acrobatics, where they are employed for climbing, swinging, supporting, and a host of other purposes. Such acts seem to us to represent the most perfect form of co-operation, yet they are distinguished from the co-operation of everyday life only by the precision with which the parts of the multiple-bodied apparatus are co-ordinated, and by its practised rather than improvised nature. If society, then, is the field in which the individuals of a population reciprocally use one another, as they would use tools, in the pursuit of their goals, it must follow that the content of social relations is exclusively instrumental. In Chapter 2, I argue that this is an inevitable implication of current sociobiological definitions of society, which take the essence of sociality to lie in co-operative organization, whether among insects, human or non-human primates, or any other order of animals.

Yet to include fellow humans alongside piercing projectiles and animal prey within the set of affordances that constitute an environmental niche for the individual hunter is to treat them as physical objects, mere organisms. It is certainly possible to comprehend, within a general ecological framework of organism–environment interrelations, the cooperative interactions whereby one organism harnesses the technical capacities of one or more conspecifics to its own project, and *vice versa*. But the hunter's colleagues are not just environmental objects; they are, like himself, *intentional subjects*, or persons in the strict sense. Moreover the effectiveness of their co-operation depends upon their commitment to a common purpose, and in Chapter 5 I try to show that in such common commitment lies the essence of the relation we call sharing. As a relation between persons as subjects, this is fundamentally distinct from the association and interaction of physical organisms that biologists consider to be social. And if we follow anthropological usage in reserving the concept of the social for intersubjective relations of this kind, we have a clear basis for *separating* the respective domains of social and ecological relations, instead of regarding the former as a subset of the latter. But this does mean having to reject the commonly held view that the difference between social and ecological relations is that the first are intraspecific and the second interspecific. It is rather the case that intraspecific relations, at least as far as human beings are concerned, have both a social and an ecological aspect: social in so far as they exist between persons (wilful subjects), ecological in so far as they exist between things (organic objects). Thus sharing and co-operation fall on either side of this distinction, and in Chapter 6 I argue that the same applies to the concepts of tenure and territoriality. The distinction pertains, furthermore, to the category of inter- as well as intraspecific relations, with hunting on one side and predation on the other, the former as socially directed action on the natural world, the latter as an ecological reaction, *within* the natural world, between the organism and its environment.

In brief, hunting, sharing and tenure are all ways in which nature is caught up in the framework of human (social) relations; predation, co-operation and territoriality are all ways in which human beings are caught up in the framework of natural (ecological) relations. Both sets of relations, however, are mediated or conducted by instruments, and this brings us to the third term on our agenda...

The technology

Returning once more to our example of the hunter and his spear, our first observation must be that the spear itself, however elegant its construction, forms but a small part of the hunter's equipment. Far more important is his knowledge about the different species of animals available to him, where they may be located, how they reproduce, and how they may best be approached and captured. And again, for those kinds of hunting that involve the co-operation of a number of people, an effective allocation of tasks among the participants may be more crucial for the success of the hunt than the sophistication of their material equipment. The adaptive repertoire of the hunter must therefore be broadened to include such immaterial factors as skills, organizational techniques, and knowledge about the natural world and the way it behaves. Indeed the primary reference of the concept of technology is to knowledge and skill, and not to instruments made and used. Unintelligent animals frequently use tools, and may even modify objects to render them more efficient in use, but they do not have a technology in the form of a systematic, symbolically-encoded body of knowledge that may be applied in practice and transmitted through teaching. Technology in this sense is *internal* to individuals, carried in their imaginations, but *external* to the material world of organisms, existing only on the level of ideas.

Tools, on the other hand, are both material objects and – in so far as they are detachable from the bodies of users – *external* to individuals. In use, however, they extend the body, to such a degree that when – say – the hunter thrusts a spear into his victim, he directly feels the resistance offered by the prey rather than that offered to his hand by the shaft of the spear. 'This *capacity to attach something to the body* suggests that the boundary between the animal and the environment is not fixed at the surface of the skin but can shift' (Gibson 1979: 41). More generally, the elements of 'material culture' could be regarded interchangeably as parts of an environment to which individuals are constrained to adapt, and as parts of a composite apparatus of adaptation, that includes the bodily equipment of its users. 'The Eskimo's igloo', Geertz remarks, 'can be seen as a most important cultural weapon in his resourceful struggle against the arctic climate, or it can be seen as a, to him, highly relevant feature of the physical landscape within which he is set and in terms of which he must adapt' (1963: 9). A moment's reflection, however, will show that the same could apply to almost any component of the physical world in which an individual lives and moves, whether or not constructed or modified by human agency, that could be harnessed to the realization of his project. A natural cave can afford shelter from the elements, just as well as can an igloo, yet it is as surely a part of the given landscape. That landscape, however, which is the *setting* for the individual's activities, is an environment of essences rather than affordances, a habitat rather than a niche. This he confronts, and struggles to organize through the imposition of form and meaning. Thus does the cave become a shelter, and the hollow dome of snow and ice a dwelling.

The difference between the two ways of regarding the tool does not, therefore, hinge directly on whether it is placed on the side of the organism or on the side of the environment. It depends, rather, on how we define the environment itself. As a set of affordances, the environment joins the tool in extending the range of activity of the surrounded individual; it is – as Marx long ago observed – one enormous tool-house (1930: 171), furnishing all the requisite means of production and reproduction, or simply of survival. But if we were to subtract the technological project that assigns to every object its particular function, in terms of which each becomes useful for one purpose or another, these erstwhile instruments would revert – alongside all other environmental objects – to their primordial status as things in a landscape, confronting the organizing subject rather than extending its organized activity. What was food for the hunter becomes a certain species of animal, what was his spear becomes a long, pointed stick, and what was his house becomes a construction of earth, timber, skins or other material. Now as objects of the essential environment, no functional relationship exists between these things; it requires the project of a user to bring them into any kind of relationship at all – such as between things that afford eating, killing and shelter respectively. It follows that such relationships, between tools and the environments in which they are deployed, cannot be considered in isolation from the technologists, the society of individuals who *use* the tools.

In his classic exposition of the procedures of cultural ecology, Steward lays down as a first step the analysis of 'the interrelationship of productive technology and environment' (1955: 40). As our argument implies, and as Steward himself recognized, this interrelationship is predicated upon the 'culturally prescribed ways' in which a given environment is utilized in acts of production. Though it would appear from this that culture underwrites the environment–technology relationship, Steward proceeds to invert the entire argument, converting the cultural premises of production into its cultural consequences. 'Technology and environment', he declares, 'prescribe that certain things must be done in certain ways', and the constellation of these ways of doing things makes up what he calls the *cultural core* (1955: 37, 41). To be sure, if you want to succeed in hunting an antelope with a spear, you need to know how to go about it. But antelopes do not prescribe that they should be hunted; no more do pointed sticks prescribe that they should be used as weapons in the chase. Steward could only treat culture as technologically and environmentally prescribed by ignoring (or taking for granted) the cultural prescription of given environmental objects as resources to be exploited and as instruments for use. Sahlins puts the point in a nutshell: in Steward's cultural ecology, he writes, 'the activity of production is . . . culturally deconstituted, to make way for the constitution of culture by

the activity of production' (1976: 101). His remark serves to introduce the
final term on our agenda, namely. . .

The culture

With regard to humanity, are there two ecologies or just one? Looking at
human beings as individual organisms, or in aggregate as populations, we
could study their interrelations with the environment in precisely the
same way as do ecologists whose concern is with non-human species. Yet
Steward, for one, insisted that such *biological* ecology was quite separate
from *cultural* ecology, the latter dealing with the questions 'of how
culture is affected by its adaptation to the environment' (1955: 31).
Steward's view was partially conditioned by a tendency, common at the
time, to treat culture not merely as a 'superorganic' product of the
symbolic faculty unique to mankind, but as a 'superorganism' with a life
of its own, over and above those of its individual constituents:

Man enters the ecological scene. . .not merely as another organism which is
related to other organisms in terms of his physical characteristics. He introduces
the super-organic factor of culture, which also affects and is affected by the total
web of life. (1955: 31)

Cultural ecology, then, was to be understood as the study of the
interrelations between this cultural superorganism and its environment,
whereas human biological ecology studies the environmental relations of
individual organisms. Moreover, by virtue of the transcription to the
superorganic domain of all culturally transmitted attributes, the constitution of human individuals came to be regarded as residually *non*-cultural,
or genetic, so that their relations with the environment were assumed to
be mediated exclusively by genetically constructed attributes.

We would be inclined to reject out of hand the 'two ecologies' view, as
the product of a spurious superorganicism that quite unjustifiably reifies
the abstraction of culture. There is, of course, no such beast. It is not even
true, as is so often blandly and clumsily asserted, that '*Homo sapiens* is
the only species which has evolved techniques for producing its own
subsistence non-genetically' (Ellen 1982: 91). For it is a well-established
fact that not only among non-human primates, but also more widely in the
animal kingdom, a substantial proportion of subsistence-related behaviour is learned. Whether it is encoded symbolically, and therefore
transmissible by teaching, is another matter: the ability to *represent*
technical procedures may indeed be unique to our species – although in
Chapter 2 I argue that such representations are at best partial or
incomplete. It is absolutely vital that we abandon the simplistic dichotomy between the instinctive and the symbolic, and as a corollary, that we

do not confuse the symbolic organization of experience characteristic of human culture with the non-genetic modes of behavioural transmission common to man and many other animals. Even our human hunter, if the occasion so demanded, would be hard put to explain how he was able to cast his spear in just the right way, in just the right place and at just the right time, to make a kill. It is a matter of having the knack, acquired through example and practice. That is to say, it manifests a practical rather than symbolic intelligence; and no one who has observed – say – the hunting of wolves could claim that such intelligence is an exclusively human prerogative.

As a culture-bearing organism, a human being is no less confined to the *biological* ecological scene than his non-human animal counterparts, relating as he does to other such organisms in terms of characteristics that are based on a combination of genetic and traditional, learning transmitted instructions. Yet Steward was right to claim that man introduces something else, and subsequent critics are wrong in thinking that the whole of human life may be embraced within a single framework of ecological analysis. The element that is missing from such analysis is consciousness, and its introduction has profound implications for the study of adaptation since it brings the selection of behavioural instructions under the control and direction of intentional agency. Human beings, in short, are selectors of their cultural attributes, not merely objects of selection. And to understand their patterns of adaptation, we have to know something about their purposes. A persistent theme throughout the following essays is that the purposes of human agents have their source in the intersubjective domain, that is in the field of social relations that lies beyond rather than within the general field of ecological relations. We would agree with Steward, then, that something more is required than a human ecology of organism–environment relations; not however another ecology in which cultures substitute for organisms, but an anthropology of relations among human beings as persons. Only within the context of a conjunction of systems of relations of both kinds, ecological and social, can we specify the objectives and conditions of cultural adaptation.

II

In the dichotomy between social and ecological relations, and the problem of understanding the reciprocal interplay between them, lies our field of inquiry in this book. It leads us, at every juncture, to insist upon upholding the distinction between material interactions, in which one organism – through its behaviour – affects the state of one or more others or of inanimate objects in its environment, and the intentional control of these interactions by wilful social subjects. In Chapter 2 I show how this distinction underlies quite different senses of work, as expenditure of effort (the 'work' of the body), and as purposive labouring activity (the 'work' that *I* do). The same distinction appears in our discussion of tool-making in Chapter 3, where the true artefact is characterized not merely as the outcome of constructive behaviour, in which an organism modifies an external environmental object so as to render it more effective in use, but as the material expression of a design that already existed in the mind of the subject and that governed the construction process. Moreover, just as the *making* of artefacts is distinguished from *constructive* behaviour, so also is the *appropriation* of natural resources distinguished from *extractive* behaviour, both distinctions exemplifying the more fundamental dichotomy between *production* and *execution*. These points are elaborated in Chapters 4 and 5, and are extended in the latter to cover the definition of *co-operation* as a form of intraspecific interaction.

Summarizing: construction, extraction and co-operation are all com-pounded from behavioural executions directed by an animal organism towards, respectively, inanimate objects, plants and animals of other species, and conspecifics. And their intentional regulation amounts, in the same order, to making, appropriation, and sharing. In this subjection of material reactions to purposive control lies the essence of what is commonly seen as man's 'mastery', not only of his environment, but also over his own nature. But are human beings unique in this regard? It is a question we cannot avoid, yet one to which we are unable at present to give an unequivocal answer. In Chapter 4 I explore the consequences of viewing production as an index of the distinctiveness of mankind, whereas in Chapter 2 I put the contrary view: that although the prior representation of an end to be achieved may depend upon a uniquely human cognitive capacity, this is not a precondition for the conscious direction of conduct, so that non-human animals may be producers too. The problem here turns on difficult philosophical issues about the nature of intentionality, which insistently demand attention even though they tax our competence. It is surely better that they be raised, at the cost of exposing contradictions in our approach, than that they be ignored in the hope that they will thereby go away.

Further problems, however, attend the definition of humanity itself. It might be agreed that there is more to making than construction, more to appropriation than extraction, and more to sharing than co-operation, and that these differences serve to establish a critical evolutionary rubicon. Philosophers, more concerned with exploring the implications of the rubicon than with ascertaining the objective properties of the species *Homo sapiens*, are inclined to identify the essence of humanity with whatever falls beyond, from which it follows by definition that any animal that makes, appropriates and shares must be human. Supposing that there were convincing evidence to prove that chimpanzees do all these things too, the philosophers' response would be to affirm the essential humanity of chimpanzees rather than to seek an alternative definition of man. But such a response would obviously not satisfy biologists, who are concerned to establish the factors that set the hominid lineage on an evolutionary course divergent from those leading to contemporary non-human primate species. The lesson to be learned here is that if there was a fundamental rubicon to be crossed, marked by some threshold in the evolution of consciousness, there is no *a priori* reason why the crossing could not have been made in the phylogenetic history of other species besides our own. Should we discover that such is the case, this might dent the image we cherish of our own supremacy in the animal kingdom, but it would in no way reduce the significance of the rubicon, nor would it lessen the real differences in both morphology and behaviour that separate *Homo sapiens* from other putatively intelligent species.

Though the mastery over nature epitomized in the concept of appropriation has classically been reserved for man, as a diagnostic criterion it has tended to slide from the human/non-human distinction onto a quite different one, distinguishing human *pastoralists and cultivators* from *hunters and gatherers*, human and non-human alike. Human hunter–gatherers, it is commonly assumed, have yet to bend nature to their purposes, remaining wholly caught up within a framework of material relations; and for this reason their activities have frequently been regarded as an ideally suited subject for exclusively ecological analysis. Thus, hunters and gatherers are supposed not to produce their food, but only to forage for it just as other animals do. They are supposed under certain circumstances to exhibit territorial behaviour, again like other animals, but not to engage the components of their environment in relations of tenure, as do agriculturalists and pastoralists with regard to land and livestock respectively. Whereas food-producing, herd-owning pastoralists have been called nomadic, the movements of hunters and gatherers in foraging over a common range are seen as mere wandering, akin to the wandering of animals. And finally, whereas agriculturalists and pastoralists are credited with emergent, institutionalized social orders loosely designated as 'tribal', the societies of hunters and gatherers – known only as 'bands' – are considered to be no more than local population aggregates founded on co-operative interaction, comparable in this respect to the social groups of non-human animals.

In the central chapters of this book, I set out to challenge these assumptions about hunters and gatherers, in an attempt both to recapture the essence of their humanity, and to isolate what truly distinguishes their modes of production and subsistence from agriculture and pastoralism. Chapter 5, for example, shows how hunting may be viewed as a form of production, in that it entails the appropriation – if not the transformation – of natural resources. The argument parallels that of Chapter 3, which examines the sense in which tools may be made without the constructive modification of environmental objects. Again, in Chapter 6 I explore the forms of tenure that are to be found in hunting and gathering societies, showing how they differ from the agricultural tenure of land. Chapter 7 incorporates a comparison of the nomadic movements of hunter–gatherers with the various forms of pastoral nomadism. Lastly, in Chapter 9, I turn to the question of what might qualify, in hunting and gathering societies, as the true evolutionary precursor of 'the tribe'.

In developing my ideas on these topics, I found it necessary to rethink the notion of appropriation itself, and to abandon what now appears to be an oversimplified dichotomy between extraction as the removal of resources from the environment for human use, and appropriation as the conversion of these resources into objects of property, such that they come to embody the relations between persons in society. Extraction and appropriation seemed to contrast as interspecific, ecological relations, to intraspecific, social relations. In one of the earliest written essays to be included in this volume, reprinted here as Chapter 8, I propose that we should distinguish between three kinds of labour – extractive, constructive and appropriative – arguing that the last of these is uniquely characteristic of agricultural and pastoral economies, whereas the first two are common also to economies based on hunting and gathering. I have since realized that the food-procurement activities of hunter–gatherers are not merely extractive, and that 'use-removal', when intentionally performed, has an essential social aspect. I refer to this aspect as *concrete* appropriation, by which I mean the actual 'taking hold' of resources by a social subject. This is how hunting exceeds predation, and how gathering exceeds foraging: in each pair the first term stands to the second as appropriative action (social) to extractive behaviour (ecological). To make something an object of property, on the other hand, is a matter of *abstract* appropriation, for property is an abstract concept, and the relations it implies are part of the idealized regulative order that anthropologists habitually call 'social structure'. Chapter 9 deals specifically with the forms that property can take in hunting and gathering societies; in land, instruments and garnered produce.

The final essay in our collection (Chapter 10) is rather different, both in its substance and in its arguments, from all the others. A direct spin-off from my earlier work on circumboreal reindeer hunting and pastoralism, it draws more heavily than other chapters on ethnographic material, and takes as its subject the way the people themselves understand their relationships with the animals on which they depend for subsistence. These animals can sometimes be regarded as persons, no different from human persons except in their outer garb; so that what we might see – say in hunting – as a confrontation between subjects and objects, or persons and things, they would see as an encounter between persons, and therefore just as much a part of social life as the encounters that take place entirely within the human domain. What really connects this essay with its predecessors, however, is the theme of human 'mastery'. The pastoral householder sees himself, or is seen to be, the master of his domestic animals, a relation of domination that is clearly manifested in acts of sacrifice. But there are masters in hunting societies too, non-human (mythic) guardians who control the wild species just as human guardians control their domestic herds. The former, like the latter, must periodically slaughter animals to ensure world renewal. When, as is commonly believed, the animal guardian 'presents' a beast for a particular hunter to kill, he is making a 'sacrifice' in which the hunter performs the immolation. Thus all the elements of sacrifice are prefigured in the beliefs and rituals of the hunt, and it requires no more than a transfer of mastery from non-human to human persons to bring them out. On the secular level, of course, this transfer is what we recognize as domestication.

Although united by a set of common themes, each of the chapters in this book is a self-contained essay, which may if desired be read and understood on its own. I have arranged them in an order that I think brings out most effectively the connections between them, nevertheless the order is somewhat arbitrary and the reader need not feel constrained to follow it. The essays have been written at different times over the last five years, a period that spans the gap between the publication of my study of reindeer hunting and pastoral economies and their transformations (Ingold 1980) and the completion of a large-scale theoretical work on evolutionary theory in anthropology, biology and history (Ingold 1986). They reflect fairly accurately the development of my interests over that period, from rather specific issues concerning the social and ecological aspects of hunter–gatherer and pastoral modes of subsistence, to very general questions about the differences between human beings and other animals, and their evolutionary implications. Naturally, my views have not remained unchanged in the course of this development, nor have they come finally to rest upon some ultimate and immutable paradigm. There are, for this reason, many inconsistencies between (if not within) the arguments of separate essays, some of which I have already mentioned. Thus I maintain in one that non-human animals produce, in another that only humans do; in one that resource appropriation is restricted to agriculturalists and pastoralists, in another that it is common to hunters and gatherers. Rather than trying to iron out these inconsistencies, at the

risk of destroying the internal coherence of each essay, I have thought it
preferable to leave them more or less as they stand, so that readers can
judge for themselves the merits and faults of alternative arguments.
Nothing is to be gained by papering over the differences. For my part,
there are several vital issues that I simply do not know how best to
resolve; all we can do is to try out the alternatives and see where they
lead us.

These essays are offered, then, as a set of explorations, or rather of
experiments, all of which address the central theme of the appropriation
of nature, but from different angles. Though no prior familiarity with the
subject is assumed, the book is *not* intended as a general review of the
field of ecological anthropology, and should not be read as such. Many
excellent reviews are already available, of which the most outstanding are
by Bennett (1976), Hardesty (1977) and Ellen (1982). My aim has been to
introduce some conceptual clarity into previously grey areas, and thereby
to break new theoretical ground; it has not been to provide a comprehen-
sive recapitulation of achievements to date. My citations from existing
literature have been guided by this aim. Moreover I have felt under no
obligation to keep within the disciplinary bounds of social or cultural
anthropology, as demarcated by one or another school of thought.
Anthropology, for me, is the study of humanity, and anything that furthers
our understanding of what makes us human is pertinent to our project. I
have wilfully trespassed onto ground normally trodden by ecologists and
evolutionary biologists, psychologists and philosophers, and prehistoric
archaeologists, and I hope that what I have to say will interest them as
much as fellow anthropologists. The scope of our inquiry is admittedly
vast, perhaps limitless, yet it is all contained in that one elementary
situation with which I began: of the hunter, and his spear!

References for Chapter 1

Bennett, J. W. 1976 *The ecological transition: cultural anthropology and human
    adaptation*. New York: Pergamon Press.
Cohen, Y. A. 1974 Culture as adaptation. In *Man in adaptation: the cultural
    present* (second edition), ed. Y. A. Cohen. Chicago: Aldine.
Ellen, R. 1982 *Environment, subsistence and system: the ecology of small-scale
    social formations*. Cambridge University Press.
Geertz, C. 1963 *Agricultural involution, the process of ecological change in
    Indonesia*. Berkeley: University of California Press.
Gibson, J. J. 1979 *The ecological approach to visual perception*. Boston: Houghton
    Mifflin.
Glasersfeld, E. von. 1976 The development of language as purposive behaviour. In
    Origins and evolution of language and speech, eds. H. B. Steklis, S. R. Harnad
    and J. Lancaster. New York Academy of Sciences.

Hall, K. 1963 Tool-using performances as indicators of behavioural adaptability. *Current Anthropology* **4**: 479–94.

Hardesty, D. L. 1977 *Ecological anthropology*. New York: Wiley.

Ingold, T. 1980 *Hunters, pastoralists and ranchers*. Cambridge University Press.

Ingold, T. 1986 *Evolution and social life*. Cambridge University Press.

Lewontin, R. C. 1982 Organism and environment. In *Learning, development and culture*, ed. H. C. Plotkin. Chichester: John Wiley.

Odum, E. P. 1975 *Ecology* (second edition). New York: Holt, Rinehart and Winston.

Sahlins, M. D. 1976 *Culture and practical reason*. University of Chicago Press.

Steward, J. H. 1955 *Theory of culture change*. Urbana: University of Illinois Press.

2

The architect and the bee: reflections on the work of animals and men

I should like to put to you a simple question. It is: do animals work? The answer is anything but simple, as is evident from the response of a psychologist to my question. He said: human beings work, animals just behave. And so we are led directly to an examination of the criteria by which man may be distinguished from other animals, not forgetting, of course, that man *is* an animal. We have to consider, too, how the concept of work or labour[1] might be separated from the notion of behaviour, and whether the former entails some, all or none of the distinguishing marks of humanity. Perhaps I have made it clear already how my little question throws into relief the very foundations of the study of man. Conceived in this broadest sense, anthropology concerns itself with just one segment of the world of living things, a particular species product of evolution. And yet the social or cultural anthropologist claims as the object of his inquiry a distinctive *domain* of life, variously conceived by such curiously hybrid terms as superorganic, psychosocial, extrasomatic and socio-cultural[2], all of which are intended to convey its irreducibility to the physical or biological conditions of existence. The identification of the study of this domain as a branch of the study of man rests upon an assumption at the core of our discipline: that the social or cultural dimension of existence has come into being through an event or series of events in the phylogenetic history of the human species. This could be called 'the doctrine of emergence'. My purpose in presenting you with an admittedly rhetorical question is to open up this doctrine for some critical inspection, and eventually to qualify the vision of evolution that it evokes.

Let me begin with the celebrated story about the architect and the bee. The narrator is Marx, and his concern is to establish a form of labour which, he says, is 'peculiar to the human species':

A spider carries on operations resembling those of the weaver, and many a human architect is put to shame by the skill with which a bee constructs her cell. But what

from the very first distinguishes the most incompetent architect from the best of
bees, is that the architect has built a cell in his head before he constructs it in wax.
(Marx 1930: 169–70)

Here the peculiarity of human labour rests on the capacity to construct, in
the imagination, a model or blueprint of the task to be performed, prior to
its performance. How, then, are we to comprehend the activity of animals,
which are supposed to lack this capacity? Marx dismisses the issue with
an aside that goes to the heart of our problem. 'We are not here
concerned', he writes, 'with those primitive and instinctive forms of
labour which we share with other animals'. But is the opposite of
'instinctive' behaviour, whatever that may mean, activity that is guided by
a conscious blueprint? It would appear not. Rather, in Marx's terms, it is
activity directed by *purposive will* or intent, which is manifested in the
attention devoted to the task in hand. In what follows, I wish to suggest
that the exercise of will and the pursuit of purpose do not depend upon
the symbolic construction of the procedures by which that purpose is to
be realized in practice. Whether or not activity is purposive, and whether
it follows a genetically or a culturally coded template, are separate
questions. The recognition of this separation, I contend, has major
implications for the way we think about both social and biological
evolution.

I

In its most general, physical sense, work refers to any expenditure of
energy. And as the biologist will point out, for any organism – plant or
animal – 'it requires work [in this sense] just to keep alive' (Harrison 1979:
37). This statement is almost a tautology, for when is a piece of matter
said to be alive? Only, answered Schrödinger, 'when it goes on "doing
something", moving, exchanging material with its environment, and so
forth' (1945:70). Perhaps, then, we should first ask: do plants work? To
this we would be inclined to answer that they 'just grow'. Do animals,
then, 'just grow'? Speaking as an animal myself, I would reply categorical-
ly in the negative. From personal experience, I know that bodily growth,
maintenance and reproduction depend upon the performance of a great
many activities which have to do, directly or indirectly, with the procurement of subsistence. Unable to synthesize their own food, animals must
usually move about in order to obtain it, and in all but the most
rudimentary animals this movement is not random but directed (Thorpe
1974: 39–40).

Yet we have still not progressed beyond a Cartesian view of animal
existence. For Descartes, animals (excluding man) were automata, which

'did not act from knowledge, but only from the disposition of their organs'
(Descartes 1911 I: 116, see Midgley 1978: 210–11). Now it might be said
of human beings, too, that work is conducted by the organs of our bodies.
But confronted with the biologist's observation that my body is 'working'
(expending energy) even when I am asleep or reclining after a meal, my
response would be that *I* am not the same as my body. And it is precisely
at this juncture that our problems begin. At what point do *I*, as the wilful
subject in command of certain physical faculties, enter the work process?
Implicit in this question is some notion of a division within the body itself,
between what could crudely be called a 'maintenance part' and an
'executive part'. The former contains such essential life-supporting
organs as the heart, lungs and digestive system, whose functioning is
more or less automatic, and required by the fact that the body – unlike an
inanimate machine – is involved in a perpetual process of internal
self-reconstruction (Monod 1972: 21). The latter contains the instruments
of detection and implementation, sense organs and limbs (Popper 1972:
273), which together provide us with the bodily means to relate to our
external environment. My existence as a subject obviously depends upon
the functioning of the maintenance part. The executive part, however,
depends for its operation on *purposive direction*. I, the subject, stand
between the two parts: sustained by one, I wield the other.

But this is to speak only for myself and my conspecifics. What of other
species? Are we, like Descartes, to regard all animals apart from
ourselves as mindless automata, as beings without will? This, curiously
enough, was Marx's view (Marx 1964b: 102), and it was on this basis that
he was able to class domestic animals alongside the most primitive tools
as *instruments* of human labour (1930: 171–2, see Ingold 1980: 88). For a
living being to be treated as instrument rather than agent of production,
all intentionality must be suppressed or denied (Cohen 1978: 43–4). It
becomes no more than a physical object, a thing. Some today would
extend this view of animal existence even to human beings, conceived as
instrumental devices for the replication of their genes under that grand
master, natural selection (Dawkins 1976: 21). Accordingly, it is supposed
that the hiatus between mind and brain can in principle be closed, that
our experience of volition is merely a cover for our ignorance of the
immensely complex physico-chemical interactions that actually govern
behaviour. E. O. Wilson concludes his *Sociobiology* with the bleak pre-
monition that a millennium of 'total knowledge' will arrive in a hundred
years, after which our subjective selves will be condemned to eternal
exile. By that time, the mind will have been 'torn down' and reconstructed
as the circuitry of neurons (1980: 6, 300–1). Considering that the central
nervous system in man 'contains from one to ten billion neurons
interconnected by means of about a hundred times as many synapses'

(Monod 1972: 138), Wilson's prophecy may seem somewhat premature. Yet however long the code might take to crack, and even if the attainment of total knowledge were to recede to infinity, mechanistic monism obliges us to recognize that the Cartesian dichotomy between mind and body is ultimately an illusion, albeit one we cannot live without (Monod 1972: 148).

The fallacy of this view lies in its supposition that reality is coterminous with the arbitrarily restricted domain of phenomena that can be handled by the methods of natural science. These methods hinge on the postulate that an objectified 'nature' constitutes the final arbiter of true knowledge. Clearly, this postulate excludes any consideration of the world of subjective experience, yet we have no reason to conclude that such experience is hence illusory. Neurophysiology can explain a great deal about the mechanisms of thought and action, but nothing at all about our experience of thinking and doing (Thorpe 1974: 330). There would be no need to dwell on the mechanistic fallacy for an anthropological audience, well aware of the limitations of the natural science paradigm in the study of man (Barnes 1979: 25), were it not for an odd attitude that continues to prevail amongst anthropologists with regard to animals. As observers of man we are especially privileged, for being human beings ourselves we are able to enter into the experience of the people we are studying to an extent impossible for the ethologist wishing to study the behaviour of – say – geese, rats or even chimpanzees (Weber 1947: 104, though see Huxley 1962, cited in Callan 1970: 46). But it would be quite wrong to conclude from our inability to penetrate the experience of other species that we are uniquely endowed with subjective will.[3]

I take as axiomatic the dualistic premise, underlying the entire corpus of Marx's writings on the human condition, that man's corporeal existence as an integral part of the natural world constitutes both the precondition for, and the instrument of, his conscious purpose or intentionality in acting upon it. Where I differ is in extending this axiom to the animal kingdom in general. The absurdity of the extreme Cartesian view that all animals save man are but natural machines has been succinctly put by Midgley: 'if it were true, there would have been a quite advanced point in animal evolution when parents who were merely unconscious objects suddenly had a child who was a fully conscious subject' (1978: 217). The only position compatible with the theory of evolution is that the development of consciousness has proceeded alongside that of the organic structures with which it corresponds (Thorpe 1974: 319–21), and consequently that it is present with varying degrees of elaboration and complexity at least in all higher animals. Thus I have argued elsewhere, *contra* Marx, that the domestic animal in the service of man constitutes labour itself rather than its instrument, and hence that the relationship

between man and animal is in this case not a technical but a social one
(Ingold 1980: 88).

The notions of purpose and intent, consciousness and will, which up to
now I have used rather indiscriminately, require some elaboration. I do
not mean to imply, by my use of these terms, the possession or deployment of the intellectual faculty of reason. Volition, for example, can refer
either to a formal process of rational choice, or to the intentionality of an
action. These are by no means the same, and it is the latter meaning that I
wish to convey. An action that embodies intent or purpose is one that is
consciously directed. There is a systematic bias in our own, so-called
'western' ideology that leads us to see all purposive action as the outcome
of intellectual deliberation by autonomous individuals, each acting in
pursuit of his own self-interest. It is perhaps for this reason that the terms
we have to denote intent (such as 'deliberate') extend simultaneously to
formal decision-making (such as 'deliberation'). Consequently, too, we
find it difficult to comprehend the intentionality of action by animals
which, rightly or wrongly, are thought not to possess the power of reason.

II

The next step in my argument is to relate the intentionality or purposive-
ness of activity to the dimension of existence we call *social*. This term has
been used in such an ambiguous fashion that I believe it now constitutes a
major impediment in the attempt to connect up the perspectives of
biology and anthropology. To clarify the issues, let me first explain what I
do *not* mean by 'social'. Here's Radcliffe-Brown, in a rare moment of
charm:

> For a preliminary definition of social phenomena it seems sufficiently clear that
> what we have to deal with are relations of association between individual
> organisms. In a hive of bees there are relations of association of the queen, the
> workers and the drones. There is the association of animals in a herd, of a mother-
> cat and her kittens. These are social phenomena... (1952: 189)

This, of course, is pure Spencerian utilitarianism. Society is constituted
by a myriad of interactions between a plurality of discrete individuals,
co-operating in diverse ways to their mutual advantage. Thus conceived,
social relations have an exclusively instrumental content: society is the
means, the life of each individual the end (Dumont 1970: 44). It is not
without significance that Radcliffe-Brown draws his examples from the
animal kingdom, for it is precisely this view of the social that underlies
current ethological usage. Just as the order of nature is conceived in the
image of civil society, so the latter is construed to rest upon a natural
foundation (Sahlins 1976b: 101–7). Lorenz, for example, considers the

absolute baseline of social evolution to be what he calls the 'anonymous flock', such as a shoal of fish, inside which 'there is no structure of any kind...but just a huge collection of like elements' (1966: 123). More usually, some form of internal differentiation is posited, but the emphasis remains on patterns of association within an aggregate of organisms: 'sociality means group-living' (Alexander 1974: 326). Wilson, in *Socio-biology*, defines society as 'a group of individuals belonging to the same species and organized in a co-operative manner' (1980: 7, 322). The attraction of such definitions is that they seem to be applicable just as well – say – to insect colonies as to human communities, and therefore to offer the prospect of a unified theory of social evolution.

This unification is achieved by treating the social as an aspect of what is called 'behaviour'. Though I have so far avoided this term, we must now pause to consider its significance. Originally extended from the domain of human conduct to that of physico-chemical reactions, its present usage represents a reverse extension from the inanimate to the animate world of beasts and men (Ardener 1973). The implications of this extension are twofold. First, behaviour suggests activity that is either essentially random or naturally determined, albeit by mechanisms as yet unknown. Secondly, as a corollary, behaviour implies activity devoid of control by a knowing subject. If there is freedom in the behaviour of individuals, it is an illusory freedom akin to that of molecules in a gas, subject to statistical rather than mechanical laws (Bidney 1963: 31–2). Thus to study social action as a system of behaviour is to treat that action *as if* it were undirected by conscious purpose: actions are carried out, behaviour is merely emitted (Weber 1947: 88–90, Levine 1975: 165–6, Reynolds 1976: xv, 242–3). We are left with a description of the activities of animals and men which makes them appear constantly to be 'going through the motions' without actually *doing* anything. The reality of life thereby dissolves in an endless series of performances. Whether the script is thought to be coded in culture or in genes, or in some combination of the two, the director's seat is occupied by – well, by whom?

The answer can only be Nature, omnipresent and personified, using her monadic creations as instruments in the implementation of a cosmic design. Visualized in her latest pseudo-Darwinian guise, she is construed to achieve her purposes through the ruthless application of the principle of natural selection. I do not want at this stage to be deflected into an extended critique of sociobiology, but I should at least point out the absurdity of treating natural selection as natural *direction*. Wilson refers to 'the pervasive role of natural selection in *shaping* all classes of traits in organisms', which for him is the 'central dogma of evolutionary biology' (1980: 15, my emphasis). Dogma it may be, but Darwinian it is not. Selection, as we well know, does not shape anything, it tinkers with forms already in existence. Moreover, the pressures of selection impinging on a population of organisms are a function of what those organisms are seeking to *do* in their environment. Taken on its own, the environment specifies neither the manner nor the intensity of its exploitation, and hence exerts no selective pressure at all (Monod 1972: 121, see Sahlins 1976a: 208–9). Wilson's notion that certain environmental factors 'tend to induce social evolution' (1980: 23) is thus not only sociological nonsense, it is biological nonsense too.

The view of society that I wish to present here is precisely opposed to the one I have just outlined. Far from the social being an aspect of the instrumental behaviour by which a natural purpose is implemented, I assert that the natural world furnishes a set of instruments for the execution of a social purpose. Let me indicate a few of the implications of this contrast.

First of all it entails a different notion of objectivity (Lienhardt 1964: 4), signifying not a denial of the subjective world but an entry into it, not an exclusive concern with the concrete, empirical manifestations of purpose but a concern to understand the purposes of others by making them one's own, not observation but participation (see Habermas 1979: 136–7, Midgley 1978: 225–6). The essence of sociality, in this latter sense, lies in the awareness of self as the predicate of one's relation to others or to the collectivity, or what Dumont (1970: 39–42) calls sociological apperception. In other words, being social implies not co-operation but *consciousness* (Crook 1980: 30–1), the establishment of a dimension of intersubjectivity which is not reducible to the association and interaction between individuals defined in objective (organic or physical) terms. We might return at this point to Radcliffe-Brown, who insisted on the distinction between the individual *qua* organism and the person, defined as 'a complex of social relationships' with others. Magnificently contradicting his initial conception of the social, which I cited a moment ago, he goes on to assert in Durkheimian vein that persons, and not individuals, are the units out of which a society is composed (Radcliffe-Brown 1952: 193–4).[4] The entire edifice of social anthropology is constructed on this contradiction, like a building raised upon the line of a geological fault.

A second implication of the contrast I have drawn in the meaning of the social is that there is no evolutionary continuity between what biologists generally regard as social behaviour in animals, and those systems of social relations identified by anthropologists, within which subjects are located as conscious agents (Bock 1980: 149). The latter have their existence on an entirely distinct plane of reality. Consider, for example, the extraordinarily elaborate organization of a hive of bees (von Frisch 1950). A single hive contains some sixty thousand individuals, co-operating on the basis of a complex differentiation of functions. Moreover, honey bees possess one of the most remarkable systems of communication yet discovered in the animal kingdom, a dance movement whereby 'workers' can signal the precise direction of flight from the hive to any particular feeding place. By the criteria of association, co-operation and communication, an ethologist would have no hesitation in regarding the organization of bees as social. But equally, an anthropologist would – in *his* terms – not hesitate to deny their sociality. This denial can only properly rest on the supposition, which everyone seems to accept, that the behaviour of bees is entirely preprogrammed and reflexive, and is not directed by conscious intent. Most anthropologists, of course, differ from those students of insect societies who aspire to pronounce on the human predicament, for as a rule they do not expect their theories to apply to bees, but only to the architects of human culture. It is therefore fairly easy for them to disregard the semantic ambiguities that attend the concept of society. We can all agree that human beings are social, without having to worry too much about whether this implies associative interaction or intersubjectivity, co-operation or consciousness, instrument or purpose.

The problems begin when we come to ask what is *not* social. For example, taking the first term of each of the above pairs of oppositions, we could conclude that our time is divided up into social and non-social episodes, according to whether we act alone or in consort. Adopting the same idea, some observers of primate behaviour have attempted to measure the sociality of various species by the percentage of their time devoted to 'social interaction', as opposed to solitary pursuits (Davis *et al.* 1968, Teleki 1981: 310–11). But if we regard the social domain as the locus of conscious intent, then any action directed by that intent must be social in character, irrespective of whether it is conducted on an individual or on a collective basis. This latter consideration has to do with the practical arrangements by which particular tasks are implemented, with *how* they are done. Social relations, on the contrary, constitute the persons *who* are carrying them out, and direct their purposes. The forms of association and co-operation comprised by the organization of work, which one view equates with the social, are in the other view systematically opposed to it: as material relations to social relations. The upshot of this second view, the one I adopt, is that '*not all relations between men are social*' (Cohen 1978: 93).[5]

We are now in a position to resolve what Wilson sees as the 'paradox' of social evolution. Comparing the colonial invertebrates, the social insects, the non-human mammals and man, he asserts that the progression from 'more primitive and older forms of life to more advanced and recent ones' is accompanied by a retrogression in 'the key properties of social existence', by which he means the scale, cohesiveness and complexity of organization. Yet man is unique in having reversed this 'down-ward trend' in social evolution, a fact which – for Wilson – represents 'the culminating mystery of all biology' (1980: 179–82). Once it is recognized that the supposed downward trend is associated with the development of social consciousness, in a domain of reality distinct from the material domain of biological phenomena, the mystery disappears. At one end of the scale, every individual is but a part of an extraordinarily complex, genetically programmed apparatus, and the relations described as social are those between its elements. At the other end, we are dealing with relations between conscious agents in respect of their control and use of the material apparatus of production, including its genetically fashioned component. It is precisely the confusion between these two sorts of relations that engenders those facile analogies, to which we are so accustomed, between beehives and ancient empires. As regards the 'downward trend', it can reasonably be argued that the elaborate or-ganization that is found among certain insects would be impossible among animals with a more evolved social consciousness, since its achievement would depend upon such subordination of will to a dominant purpose as is found only at an advanced stage in the evolution of human society (see Midgley 1978: 146).

Now there is a popular argument, though one decidedly unpopular in anthropology, which holds that the actions of men, and indeed those of other animals, are directed by more or less innate physiological drives. This contention is obviously incompatible with the view I am advancing here, that the source of intent lies in a distinct social domain. And yet it would be absurd to deny that, as human beings, we are all subject to certain sensations and emotions. We *do* have a nature, and one that in several respects is not so different from that of many other animal species. This, of course, was a point on which Malinowski insisted. Where he erred was in regarding this nature as a set of impulses, antecedent to the actions which were supposed to lead to their satisfaction (Malinowski 1944: 77). Our emotions and feelings are real enough, but they constitute qualities of action itself, not internal impulses that spark it off. Terms such as pleasure, pain, aggression, fear, and so on refer to the manner in which activities are conducted, that is to the way they are experienced both by the self and by others – for I am as much the witness of my actions as those who are, so to speak, on the 'receiving end' of them (Ryle 1949: 88). Work is emotional as well as physical, if indeed the two can be separated at all, and both attributes characterize the implementation of purpose, not the purpose that is to be implemented. In other words, emotion or feeling is the animator of social intent. Marx called it 'passion', regarded as 'the essential force of man energetically bent on its object' (1964a: 182).

Having separated the purpose of action from the manner of its conduct, the way is open for us to relate human nature to morality. We are moral beings because, whilst acting as conscious subjects, we act with feeling. A man who acted precisely in accordance with the dictates of his society, but whose actions were not animated by feeling, would be regarded as amoral – we might say 'inhuman' (Kantorowicz 1958: 46–7). The emotional energy that imparts a moral charge to social action has a foundation in human nature; that is to say it rests on certain innate potentialities which are of course open, in that they can be realized in any number of ways, depending upon the cultural context. I am therefore prepared to go along with ethologists such as Lorenz, in so far as they argue that morality derives part of its force from what are rather crudely called 'instincts' (Lorenz 1966: 219). Where I differ quite radically is in insisting that, far from serving to regulate impulses which derive from the same innate source, morality inheres in actions whose source is essentially *social*. It follows from what I have said that natural feelings and emotions do not oppose but rather inform the rational pursuit of purpose. The idea of an evolutionary struggle between instinct and reason, in which the latter gradually gains the upper hand, is quite misguided, since 'these are not parallel terms' (Midgley 1978: 332).[6]

It is important to stress that our recognition of the innate component of moral conduct in no way compromises our assertion of the autonomy of the social. To inquire into the rationality of action is not the same as to inquire into its morality, for the latter is not just a matter of what we do but of how we do it, of the quality of feeling that our nature imparts to it. Some confusion on this point appears to underlie the banishment of human nature from structural anthropology, which has consequently yielded an account of social existence remarkable for its aridity. Indeed it might be said that, since Malinowski, we have suffered a prolonged drought. Shakespeare puts us back on the right track when, in *Othello*, he has Iago declare that 'our bodies are our gardens to the which our wills are gardeners'. Otherwise put: from our nature spring the powers, both physical and emotional, that bear a social purpose into eventual fruition.

III

Let me recapitulate. I began with the remark of a psychologist, who contrasted the work of men with the behaviour of animals. I have shown that, implicit in the distinction between work and behaviour, is the premise that the former is directed by a knowing subject. In other words, work implies consciousness and purpose. The wilful subject, in turn, is constituted by his relations with others: hence consciousness and social existence are but two perspectives on the person, from the inside looking 'outwards', and from the outside looking 'inwards'. In short, social being is consubstantial with consciousness.

We recall Marx's famous dictum that 'it is not the consciousness of men that determines their existence, but their social existence that determines their consciousness' (1970: 21). As Avineri has rightly remarked, 'the worst that can be said about this...sentence is that it is tautological' (1971: 76). Yet some odd constructions have been placed upon it. One of these has it that consciousness is not a predicate of social being but an epiphenomenon of some social reality located at a deeper, invisible level. The search has been on for some time now, especially in France, for 'unconscious structures' of social life which are supposed to underlie conscious experience (Godelier 1972: xix, 260). This appears to be guided by two basic misconceptions: the first is that the unconscious is equivalent to the non-intentional or unwilled; the second is the identification of social consciousness with the conscious model of society – of the reality with its symbolic representation. Marx's point was that social relations *constitute* the conscious, wilful subject and are not wilfully designed by subjects whose consciousness is somehow given in advance, as though individuals had an independent, subjective existence outside of, and opposed to society.[7] Historically, people have not made up societies, rather societies have made up people. We do not deal, in the study of social evolution, with a series of inventions or 'socifacts' (Bidney 1953: 130, Reynolds 1976: 65, Harré 1979: 18), nor does the design of social relations issue from a preconstituted unconscious (Lévi-Strauss 1968: 58–9, Laughlin and d'Aquili 1974: 150). The mind, whether conscious or unconscious, is not a property of individuals *in vacuo*, a mysterious ghost in the bodily machine (Ryle 1949) within whose recesses we might hope to find the hidden secrets of social structure. It exists in the very system of intersubjective relations that *is* social structure, and unfolds right before our eyes in purposive action. That human beings, by virtue of their faculty of symbolic thought, are capable of representing and reflecting upon their conscious experience, albeit in a partial and distorted way, is another matter altogether, to which I shall return.

It should be clear from the earlier part of my argument that everything I have just said about consciousness and sociality, barring the last point concerning its symbolic representation, applies not only to man but much more widely in the animal kingdom. So here I would have to disagree with my psychologist friend. If work implies purposive action, then some animals work too – though not all (I think we may reasonably exclude insects and other invertebrates). When animals act as conscious subjects they must – in my terms – be *social*, though I must stress once again that what I have in mind here is quite different from what ethologists and sociobiologists mean by social behaviour. The fact that in many species such behaviour is genetically programmed in no way infringes upon the exercise of conscious purpose, for as I have shown, nature furnishes the instruments and powers – including material relations of association and co-operation – for executing the purpose of socially constituted subjects. In man these instruments and powers are extended and partially replaced by culturally fashioned attributes, nevertheless our greatest technological achievements pale beside the physiological complexity of the human body. My general contention, then, is that the subjective existence of the higher animals, including man, is located on a level of reality we call social, which is not reducible to the physical domain of nature. The problem of evolution is to discover the dynamic, reciprocal interplay between the social and physical domains of life without treating either one as directly derivative of the other. The link between the two domains lies in purposive activity that affects the state of the physical world, in other words in social production, work.

In the consciously directed work of extracting and consuming their food, animals act on nature to bring about a continuous flow of materials and energy from their environment into their own bodies, to the point at which it may be organically assimilated. This flow is a precondition for their growth, maintenance and reproduction. These latter processes are going on in nature, and represent production in its ecological rather than social sense (Ingold 1979: 274–7). Thus social production effects changes in the state of the physical world of which the producers are equally a part, and on which their subjective existence depends.

The distinction I am drawing is between socially directed action *on* the physical world and ecological reaction *in* the physical world. On one side of the boundary fall the extraction and consumption of food; on the other fall growth, maintenance and reproduction. Now it is clear that this boundary marks the point at which – to speak as the subject – it is *I* who am working, rather than just the organs of my body. Consequently, too, it marks off the division between what I earlier called the 'maintenance' and 'executive' parts of the body – between vital organs whose functioning is automatic, and the bodily instruments whose operation depends on purposive direction. In contending that this dualism applies generally among higher animals I am also challenging an assumption central to anthropological orthodoxy: that animal existence is 'purely' organic or ecological, whereas human existence is 'purely' social or cultural. My argument, to the contrary, is that there are distinct physical and social domains to both animal and human existence, and that anthropology has tended to mistake 'the disjunction between [these] domains...for a temporal leap from one domain to the other, supposedly separating man from the animals' (Ingold 1979: 273). You will perhaps recognize this leap, possibly gradated into a series of steps, from the 'doctrine of emergence' to which I referred in the very first paragraph.

IV

In the final part of this essay I should like to turn my attention from work itself to a consideration of its instruments. First, though, a word about the so-called 'forces' of production, which up to now have been very vaguely conceived. It is commonplace in the literature to find the forces presented as an inventory of tools and material equipment appropriate to some ill-defined 'level of development'. Two points need to be made about this. First, it takes more than tools to do a job. Put a spear into my untutored hand, and I would be no more capable of hunting than without it. If equipment were destroyed but knowledge of its construction and use retained, then one could always start afresh with a new set of tools. Keep the equipment and destroy the knowledge, and one is left with nothing but a heap of useless museum scrap (Cohen 1978: 41–2, see also Popper 1972: 107–8). Secondly, spears do not hunt. That is to say, technical instruments conduct, but do not constitute, socially directed activity. It is absurd to regard as a 'force' something that, by itself, is practically inert. How, then, should the 'forces' be regarded? I would suggest that there are two kinds of force, that correspond to the two kinds of production I have identified: social and ecological. Thus, instead of an opposition between 'forces' and 'relations' of production, we should think in terms of the interplay of two *systems* of *relations* existing on distinct, social and physical levels of reality. The Marxian dialectic can then be rephrased as one between the forces of social action and those of ecological reaction, emanating from each of these levels. The intensity of what, in Darwinian theory, are called 'selective pressures' is a function of the degree of strain between these two sets of potentially contradictory forces (Ingold 1981). The pressures are at their peak where social production is up against the limits of ecosystemic functioning, or in other words, of reproduction in the physical world.

Bearing in mind, then, that the instruments of production are not to be confused with the forces they conduct, we can proceed to a comparison of the instruments of man with those of other animals. For the sake of argument, I shall adopt the undoubtedly oversimplified view that the instruments of animals, whether they be a part of the body such as the teeth of the beaver, or separate from it such as the web of the spider, are both constructed and operated in accordance with an innate programme.[8] Men, by contrast, fashion tools and use them by cultural design. Never-theless, human instruments are not exclusively cultural. The hand, for example, is markedly ineffective without tools to extend it, but the arm, the wrist, the hand and the tool it holds together constitute a *composite instrument*, only one component of which is culturally fashioned. Likewise, although our jaws and teeth can work on certain foods only after they have been processed by cultural technique, we cannot eat without them. Moreover, to operate these bodily, executive instruments we do not need to carry the equivalent of an instruction manual in the imagination, although in theory we would be capable of constructing such a manual. The fact that we do not in no way reduces the intentionality of the acts of consumption in which the jaws and teeth are used. Unlike the subsequent maintenance processes of digestion, where 'intentionality lapses' (Cohen 1978: 55), eating is something we do on purpose – indeed it is one of the supreme expressions of conscious sociality.

Perhaps these observations suffice to dispel the notion that the cultural design and use of tools is a precondition for purposive labour (Engels 1934: 34, see Ingold 1979: 280). If it is argued that, say, the beaver's action in felling trees is non-purposive because he does it with his teeth, whereas man employs an axe, we would have to conclude – in direct contradiction to experience – that our action in eating is non-purposive too. So what, if anything, really distinguishes the beaver's felling with teeth and man's felling with the axe?

Lewis Henry Morgan, an authority of his day on the American beaver, believed that this animal possesses a capacity for rational thought differing only in degree from that of man (1868: 252). Today we have good reason to reject this belief, but this gives us no grounds whatever for doubting the intentionality of the beaver's action. Man is not uniquely purposive, but he is unique to the extent that he carries a conscious, symbolic representation of the *procedures* by which his purpose is to be executed. This might include both a plan for the construction of the axe itself, and a set of instructions for its use in tree cutting. I wish to suggest, however, that the symbolic representation is at best only a partial one. Anyone, with a bit of practice, can learn how to swing an axe, without having to form a complete intellectual construct of his capability. Undoubtedly the woodsman does carry in his head an image of the notch that he will carve in the tree and of its evolving shape and direction, and before every blow, he lines up his axe with the intended cut. Yet in the instant of the swing, a marvellously sophisticated apparatus of bodily control comes into operation to co-ordinate the man's vision with the muscles of his trunk and limbs, 'guiding' the blade to its intended target (Bateson 1972: 317). Watching him at work, we judge the accuracy of each blow as a mark of the woodsman's skill. But the demonstration of competence neither attests to, nor depends on, the existence in his mind of a symbolic blueprint for the operation of the composite apparatus, comprising both body and tool, which he applies to his task. The converse argument, of course, is that technical knowledge does not necessarily confer competence. As Ryle (1949) long ago pointed out, to 'know that' is not necessarily to 'know how': a good theoretician can be a poor practitioner.

It is commonly supposed that the intelligent performance of some act depends upon two successive operations. One has first to plan out in the mind what is to be done, 'and then to put one's plan into practice. You will recall the architect who, in Marx's story, builds 'a cell in his head before he constructs it in wax' (or concrete). And yet Marx pointedly compared the *most incompetent* architect with the *best* of bees. To have con-structed a building in the imagination before constructing it in concrete is, as we know from countless disasters, no guarantee that it will not fall down. The general point, as Ryle showed, is that 'efficient practice precedes the theory of it' (1949: 31). However, I wish to argue further that this point applies not only in a logical but also in a developmental sense.

In non-human animals, practice is conducted through procedures that are largely or wholly innate. In man, practice is never conducted through procedures that are wholly cultural, but always through a combination of genetically and culturally transmitted capabilities which, throughout human evolution, have been most intricately conjoined (Dobzhansky 1962: 75). Cultural adaptation cannot therefore have begun where organic adaptation left off (Caspari 1961: 274, Geertz 1965). I am inclined, rather, towards a gradualistic view of the development of culture, according to which man has acquired a progressively more inclusive, though still far from complete knowledge of the technical operations activated by his purpose. As I have shown, such knowledge is not a prerequisite for social production. In the developmental sense, the representation of technique in the imagination *followed* rather than preceded the operations repre-sented. For example, as Haldane (1956: 9) once suggested, our flint-chipping hominid ancestors may have been setting tools in stone for any length of time before they began to design them in their minds. For much of our evolutionary history, technology as a corpus of knowledge must have followed one step behind technique as a body of practice.

Yet this argument does imply some kind of threshold, consequent upon a certain degree of development of the symbolic faculty, very probably associated with the appearance of language (Kitahara-Frisch 1980: 217–21). The reflexive property of human language enables the speaker to explore, in thought, the conscious representations he has formed of his practical activity, and by the logical manipulation of concepts, to generate alternative procedures appropriate to the execution of *new* projects. Symbolic thought may thus be detached from the immediate context of action, shaping practice rather than merely expressing it (Reynolds 1976: 182; Crook 1980: 140). To return to the image of the architect: one does not need a conceptual model to build a house, nor even to build it well. But only when one has constructed such a model does it become possible to design and build houses of different kinds. From that point on, practice follows one step behind technology, rather than the other way around.

Two of the key features of cultural (as opposed to organic) adaptation stem from this reversal. The first is that innovation involves conscious creativity rather than trial and error; the second is that the tempo of adaptation is increased by several orders of magnitude (Durham 1976: 100–1). Moreover, possessed of a symbolic faculty, human beings can model not only their own procedures but also those that they observe elsewhere in the animal kingdom. In this way the specialized capabilities of a range of species may be rolled into the generalized capability of one species. We should not forget, though, that the representation – whether of human or animal operations – is only partial, and that we remain constrained by the nature of our bodily instruments, whatever we may attach to them. Nothing illustrates these limitations more clearly than the sad history of man's earlier attempts to fly. Having constructed a pair of wings on the basis of a plan modelled on the observation of birds, and affixed them to his arms, the would-be flyer plummets to the earth. For not only was the model constructed in ignorance of the principles of aerodynamics on which flight depends, but also the executive apparatus of the flyer's body is quite inadequate to perform the intended feat.

Throughout my discussion, I have regarded technology as a corpus of knowledge, representing the procedures which mediate or conduct the force of social action upon the physical world.[9] Even though that physical world may, to a great extent, be 'engineered' by human action, we should not confuse the artificial result with the instrumental means, as in the notion of 'techno-environment' (Harris 1968: 4). Moreover we may generalize from technology, as one part or aspect of a larger symbolic system, to culture as a whole, to argue that *culture serves to translate a social purpose into practical effectiveness.* This implies a rejection not only of the crude materialism that locates human purposes in the world of nature, but also the kind of idealism that so inverts agent and instrument as to suppose that persons are the instruments of cultural purpose rather than culture the instrument of social purpose.[10] Words and symbols can convey meanings in a culture, and spears can be used to kill game, but words and symbols cannot think or talk any more than spears can hunt (Ingold 1981). Just as language comprises a 'system of cognitive instruments... for use in the service of thought' (Piaget and Inhelder 1969: 87), so the material tool-kit provides us with a set of instruments for practical action. But *culture, divorced from social purpose, is practically inert.* To be activated, it must bear the intent of the hunter of game or the speaker of language, and the source of intent (as opposed to referential significance) lies in the domain of the social.

All this requires us to make an absolute distinction between the social and the cultural, just as technology must be distinguished from its environmental object. Consequently, too, we must not confuse the processes of social evolution and cultural adaptation. Culture mediates or transmits the force of social action on the physical world, and is conditioned by pressures born of the tension between social and ecological forces. These same pressures condition the evolution of the executive organs of the body whose operation is amplified by the cultural equipment. Cultural and organic adaptation are closely interdependent and are analogous in so far as both proceed through variation under selection (Durham 1976, Ingold 1979). But as I pointed out earlier on in this essay, the criteria of selection are not given by the environment alone but depend upon what members of the subject population are seeking to do in it. If the social domain is the source of their purpose, it follows logically that society *cannot* evolve through a process of adaptation. For the concept of adaptation, unless combined with a demonstrable principle of selection, loses all significance: without it, anything that exists and therefore functions is, *ipso facto*, adapted (Godelier 1972: xxxiv). Only by regarding social structure as a set of instrumental responses to extra-social, natural or hedonistic impulses can it be placed alongside culture as the object of a selective process.[11]

With Malinowski, I take culture to be, in essence, 'an instrumental apparatus' (1944: 150),[12] though I part company with him in locating the purpose of action in a subjective social consciousness rather than an objective human nature. Yet my separation of the social and the cultural, once orthodox in social anthropology, rings hollow today. Thus Sahlins writes scornfully of the 'arbitrary differentiation of "culture" from "social system" in the British school, as if social relations were not also composed and organized by meaning' (1976a: 117). Sahlins's objections bring us back once more to the story of the architect and the bee.

Recall that the architect, who here stands for cultural man, has built a cell in his head before constructing it in wax. From this Marx infers that 'the labour process ends in the creation of something which, when the process began, already existed in the worker's imagination...in an ideal form' (1930: 170). And this seems tantamount to the assertion, central to Sahlins's thesis, that the objectives of work are symbolically constituted – that purposive action is governed by an autonomous cultural logic. Yet the entire thrust of Marx's argument is entirely to the contrary. As Sahlins shows, Marx gets both himself and his readers thoroughly entangled in a circular attempt to transform "the pre-existent image of production into its objective consequence' (1976a: 153). What I have tried to show is that

Marx is wrong, as indeed is Sahlins too, in supposing that the pre-existent image or model is a condition for production. Animals produce as conscious, purposive agents without holding such a model; and if men act to a cultural blueprint, the representation is incomplete. In other words, consciousness is a precondition for production, the conscious model is not. Social relations, constituting consciousness, invest action with purpose, and in that sense give it meaning. But this does not make them mean in the sense of referring symbolically to another reality: they *are* the reality.[13] The fault lies in thinking of production as a number of discrete, finite processes, each with a beginning and an ending. Men (and other animals) produce, even as they live, continuously – if not without temporary interruptions. Production, and the meaning of production, must therefore be understood *intransitively*, not as a transitive relation of image to object. Thus in order to locate culture, we should ask not 'what is being produced?' but 'how are people producing?' The images and artefacts of culture neither initiate nor conclude production; they are the vehicles by which it is carried on.

V

It is now time to draw together the strands of this essay. My problem has been to resolve an age-old dichotomy in our views of human existence, between whose poles anthropology has oscillated – as Sahlins graphically puts it – 'like a prisoner pacing between the farthest walls of his cell' (1976a: 55). One view begins with man as an organic part of nature, an individual human being, interacting materially with other components of his natural environment. In its Malinowskian version, this view treats the social as an aspect of culture, which in turn is thought to consist of a set of conditioned, instrumental behaviours for the fulfilment of purposes that necessarily lie outside society, in the realm of nature. For socio-biology, social behaviour is similarly the instrument of a natural design, though the instrumental apparatus is here largely genetically rather than culturally coded. Against this can be set the opposite view, which focuses on human experience as the product of involvement in a collectivity conceived not as an aggregate of individuals but as an ordered system of relations with an independent logic, and existing on a level of reality that is set apart from nature. Whereas the first view comprehends society and culture together as functional extensions of the human organism, the second treats the 'sociocultural system' as though it had a life of its own – analogous to, rather than extending, that of the organism – of which system human beings are merely the instrumental supports. Between these two views, it has been asserted, there is no room for compromise (Sahlins 1976a: 55).

Fortunately there is no need for compromise, as we have the key that will release the prisoner from his cell. It lies in the separation of the social, as the source of conscious intent, from the instruments and powers that constitute culture. The latter can then be connected up with those instruments and powers that are located in human nature. All purposive action is conducted by an intimate conjunction of both innate and cultural vectors, whose relative contributions vary (Thorpe 1974: 167). In man the strength of the cultural vector may outweigh that of the natural, in animals it is obviously the other way around, *but the purpose remains*. Together both vectors provide us with the equipment to act socially upon the physical world. By 'demoting' culture from purpose to instrument I do not for a moment mean to question its indispensability. Without culture, as Geertz (1965) remarks, we would be 'incomplete and unfinished animals'. Nevertheless, I believe it is essential that we should distinguish between the body of cultural knowledge and the subjective consciousness of those who use it.[14]

It is a remarkable fact that both the cultural anthropologist and the sociobiologist, glaring at one another from the opposite corners of their cell, are together trapped by certain common misconceptions. The first is that both invert agent and instrument: for one the social is the instrument of culture; fór the other it is the instrument of nature. Hence the prisoners' dilemma, for having opposed natural to cultural determination it appears that we can but opt for one or the other. I have argued, to the contrary, that both nature and culture – operating in conjunction – furnish instruments for the execution of social purpose. Instinct is neither the locus of purpose nor the antithesis of cultural reason, for both genetic and cultural programmes – like computer programmes – encode the *mechanisms* through which rational purpose operates to achieve its effects (Thorpe 1974: 329–30, Popper 1972: 224–5).

The second misconception shared by both cultural anthropology and sociobiology is that animal existence is purely physical or organic. Cultural anthropologists assert human uniqueness and evolutionary discontinuity through various versions of the 'doctrine of emergence' (Kroeber 1917, Spuhler 1959). Sociobiologists, on the contrary, deny such uniqueness and stress evolutionary continuity by tracing culture to a genetic template.[15] Both adopt a thoroughly mechanistic view of animals other than man. The failure to appreciate the distinct social domain of animal experience has allowed the biology of evolution to be written up to now as though this domain did not exist. Consequently, human social action is comprehended from an evolutionary perspective by grafting on the social as an extension of man's organic nature. My intention is quite different. It is to suggest a synthesis of biological and anthropological approaches to the problem of evolution which is flawed neither by biological reductionism nor by anthropocentric delusions of grandeur and ascendancy. Accordingly, we should account for the continuity of the evolutionary process not by locating it on a purely physical level but by showing how the pressures conditioning the adaptation of both organic and cultural forms are generated by an underlying, reciprocal interplay between systems located in quite separate social and physical domains of existence. Man not only acts on nature, he is also a part of it (Giddens 1979: 161). My approach implies that the same goes for those animals whose action is demonstrably governed by conscious purpose.

Perhaps I may conclude by affirming the vision of anthropology which lies behind all I have argued, as the study not just of mankind as a whole but of the Whole Man. He is to be conceived as an unusual kind of animal, not merely a bearer of culture but a creature of flesh and blood, of emotions and feelings, who acts purposefully and creatively on his environment through the instruments available to him in order to achieve concrete, practical results. The idea is hardly novel, for it was precisely this vision of man, and of anthropology, which informed the work of that great anthropologist to whose memory this essay is dedicated – Bronislaw Malinowski.

Notes to Chapter 2

1 In approaching the definition of work, I should point out that I am concerned with the use of the term as a concept in analysis, and not with its classificatory significance as an item of everyday discourse in our own or any other society. For this reason I shall disregard the semantic subtleties of the distinction between work and labour (Firth 1979: 178–9), and use the terms more or less interchangeably.

2 See, for example, Kroeber (1917), Steward (1955: 31), Huxley (1956), White (1959), Harris (1968: 241).

3 As Lorenz has written:
  'It is in principle impossible to make any scientifically legitimate assertion about the subjective experiences of animals... However, similarities and analogies in the nervous processes of animals and men are sufficiently great to justify the conclusion that higher animals do indeed have subjective experiences which are qualitatively different but in essence akin to our own' (1966: 180).
  Indeed to argue otherwise would be blatantly anthropocentric. It is no accident that the same rhetoric is used today about animals to extol the qualities of common humanity as was used a century ago about 'savages' to extol the virtues of European civilization.

4 Following the original publication of this paper, Cheater (1985) has disputed my claim that Radcliffe-Brown's view of the social was self-contradictory. For my response see Ingold (1985).

5 In Chapter 5, I argue with regard to hunting and gathering societies that the

distinction between material and social relations underlies that between co-operation and sharing. One implication, explored in Chapter 9, is that bands – which are constituted by co-operative or associative relations – cannot be treated as the evolutionary precursors of tribes. For the concept of tribe signals a specific form of social consciousness that rests on a principle of segmentary exclusion, derived from the negation of the principle of inclusive incorporation manifested in sharing.

6   Though agreeing with Midgley on this point, I do not agree with her general argument that 'just in proportion as automatic skills drop off at higher levels of evolution, innately determined general desires become more necessary' (1978: 333). In this view, the hereditary component of behaviour transfers in the course of evolution from the specification of techniques to the specification of objectives, from means to ends, which may then – in man – be pursued through the exercise of rational intelligence. My view, to the contrary, is that the transfer is from ends to means, from objectives to instruments, which may then be put in the service of a social rationality.

7   The same point is made, still more forcefully, in the sixth of Marx's *Theses on Feuerbach*: 'The human essence is no abstraction inherent in each single individual. In its reality it is the ensemble of social relations' (Marx and Engels 1977: 122).

8   I thus ignore reported cases of serendipitous or learned patterns of tool-making and tool-using in the animal kingdom. Whether or not man is in fact unique in his ability to construct and operate tools by cultural design, though it may influence the conception of our difference as a species, does not affect the structure of my argument. The issue of tool-making is considered separately in Chapter 3.

9   'Man's contact with nature has never been direct; it has always been mediated through knowledge structures via his senses and his intellect' (Moscovici 1976: 145).

10 This is the sort of inversion that leads everyday life to be regarded as a spectacle put on for the benefit of an other-cultural observer; a symbolic enactment in which people are nothing other than the roles they play, and 'practices are no more than "executions", stage parts, performances of scores, or the implementing of plans' (Bourdieu 1977: 96).

11 See for example, Ruyle (1973: 204): 'Social structures may themselves be subject to positive or negative selective pressures depending on the degree to which they facilitate the satisfaction of individual needs or desires'.

12 But when Malinowski elsewhere describes culture as 'the organized, implemented and purposeful behavior of man' (1944: 203) he is classically confusing the instrument with the force of purposive action it conducts. In a recent paper, Salzman (1981: 243) commits a similar error. Having defined culture, much as I do, as 'equipment which *enables* various forms of orientation, organization and action', he proceeds to regard it as 'a force in its own right' which has 'a determining impact, if a partial one, upon human action'. Enabling equipment determines not the purpose of action, but the way it is carried on.

13 Compare Sahlins, who criticizes Marx for apprehending the symbolic (domain

of culture) as 'the model of a given [social] system in consciousness, while ignoring that the system so symbolized is *itself symbolic*' (1976a: 139, original emphasis). Sahlins conflates culture and society by equating both meanings of meaning – the transitive one of reference and the intransitive one of intent – with the symbolic.

14   This distinction bears comparison with, but is not identical to, that made by Popper (1972) between 'second' and 'third worlds'.

15   In the words of Wilson: 'The genes hold culture on a leash' (1978: 167). This is apparently one of his favourite metaphors, for he has gone on to formalize it as the 'leash principle', and has even suggested ways by which the length of the 'leash' might be measured (Lumsden and Wilson 1981: 13).

References for Chapter 2

Alexander, R. D. 1974 The evolution of social behavior. *Annual Review of Ecology and Systematics* **5**: 325–83.

Ardener, E. 1973 Behaviour: a social anthropological criticism. *Journal of the Anthropological Society of Oxford* **4**: 152–4.

Avineri, S. 1971 *The social and political thought of Karl Marx.* Cambridge University Press.

Barnes, J. A. 1979 *Who should know what?* Harmondsworth, Middx.: Penguin.

Bateson, G. 1972 *Steps to an ecology of mind.* New York: Ballantine.

Bidney, D. 1953 *Theoretical anthropology.* New York: Columbia University Press.

Bidney, D. 1963 The varieties of human freedom. In *The concept of freedom in anthropology*, ed. D. Bidney. The Hague: Mouton.

Bock, K. 1980 *Human nature and history: a response to sociobiology.* New York: Columbia University Press.

Bourdieu, P. 1977 *Outline of a theory of practice.* Cambridge University Press.

Callan, H. 1970 *Ethology and society: towards an anthropological* view. Oxford University Press.

Caspari, E. W. 1961 Some genetic implications of human evolution. In *Social life of early man*, ed. S. L. Washburn. Chicago: Aldine.

Cheater, A. P. 1985 The sociality of animals. *Man* (N.S.) **20**: 743–4.

Cohen, G. A. 1978 *Karl Marx's theory of history: a defence.* Oxford University Press.

Crook, J. H. 1980 *The evolution of human consciousness.* Oxford University Press.

Davis, R. T., R. W. Leary, M. D. C. Smith and R. F. Thompson 1968 Species differences in the gross behaviour of nonhuman primates. *Behaviour* **31**(3,4): 326–38.

Dawkins, R. 1976 *The selfish gene.* Oxford University Press.

Descartes, R. 1911 *The philosophical works of Descartes*, 2 vols. (trans. E. S. Haldane and G. R. T. Ross). Cambridge University Press.

Dobzhansky, T. 1962 *Mankind evolving.* New Haven, Conn.: Yale University Press.

Dumont, L. 1970 *Homo hierarchicus.* London: Weidenfeld and Nicolson.

Durham, W. H. 1976 The adaptive significance of cultural behavior.*Human Ecology* **4**: 89–121.

Engels, F. 1934 *Dialectics of nature.* Moscow: Progress.

Firth, R. 1979 Work and value: reflections on ideas of Karl Marx. In *Social anthropology of work*, ed. S. Wallman (A.S.A. monogr. 19). London: Academic Press.

Frisch, K. von 1950 *Bees: their vision, chemical sense and language.* Ithaca, NY: Cornell University Press.

Geertz, C. 1965 The impact of the concept of culture on the concept of man. In *New views of man*, ed. J. R. Platt. University of Chicago Press.

Giddens, A. 1979 *Central problems in social theory.* London: Macmillan.

Godelier, M. 1972 *Rationality and irrationality in economics.* London: New Left Books.

Habermas, J. 1979 *Communication and the evolution of society.* London: Heinemann.

Haldane, J. B. S. 1956 The argument from animals to men: an examination of its validity for anthropology. *Journal of the Royal Anthropological Institute* **36**: 1–14.

Harré, R. 1979 *Social being.* Oxford: Blackwell.

Harris, M. 1968 *The rise of anthropological theory.* New York: Crowell.

Harrison, G. A. 1979 Views from three other disciplines: biological anthropology. In *Social anthropology of work*, ed. S. Wallman (A.S.A. monogr. 19). London: Academic Press.

Huxley, J. S. 1956 Evolution, cultural and biological. In *Current anthropology*, ed. W. L. Thomas. University of Chicago Press.

Huxley, J. S. 1962 Higher and lower organization in evolution. *Journal of the Royal College of Surgeons of Edinburgh* **7**: 163–79.

Ingold, T. 1979 The social and ecological relations of culture-bearing organisms: an essay in evolutionary dynamics. In *Social and ecological systems*, eds. P. C. Burnham and R. F. Ellen (A.S.A. monogr. 18). London: Academic Press.

Ingold, T. 1980 *Hunters, pastoralists and ranchers.* Cambridge University Press.

Ingold, T. 1981 The hunter and his spear: notes on the cultural mediation of social and ecological systems. In *Economic archaeology*, eds. A. Sheridan and G. Bailey. BAR International Series 96, Oxford.

Ingold, T. 1985 The sociality of animals: response to Cheater. *Man* (N.S.) **20**: 744–6.

Kantorowicz, H. 1958 *The definition of law* (ed. A. H. Campbell). Cambridge University Press.

Kitahara-Frisch, J. 1980 Symbolizing technology as a key to human evolution. In *Symbol as sense*, eds. M. L. Foster and S. H. Brandes. London: Academic Press.

Kroeber, A. L. 1917 The superorganic. *American Anthropologist* **19**(2): 163–213.

Laughlin, C. D. Jr. and E. G. d'Aquili 1974 *Biogenetic structuralism.* New York: Columbia University Press.

Levine, D. P. and L. S. Levine 1975 Social theory and social action. *Economy and Society* **4**: 162–93.

Lévi-Strauss, C. 1968 *Structural Anthropology.* Harmondsworth, Middx.: Penguin.

Lienhardt, R. G. 1964 On the concept of objectivity in social anthropology. *Journal of the Royal Anthropological Institute* **94**: 1–10.

Lorenz, K. 1966 *On aggression.* London: Methuen.

Lumsden, C. J. and E. O. Wilson 1981 *Genes, mind and culture.* Cambridge, Mass.: Harvard University Press.

Malinowski, B. 1944 *A scientific theory of culture, and other essays.* Chapel Hill: University of North Carolina Press.

Marx, K. 1930 *Capital.* London: Dent.

Marx, K. 1964a *Economic and philosophical manuscripts of 1844.* New York: International Publishers.

Marx, K. 1964b *Pre-capitalist economic formations* (ed. E. J. Hobsbawm). London: Lawrence and Wishart.

Marx, K. 1970 *A contribution to the critique of political economy* (preface). Moscow: Progress.

Marx, K. and F. Engels 1977 *The German ideology* (ed. C. J. Arthur). London: Lawrence and Wishart.

Midgley, M. 1978 *Beast and man: the roots of human nature.* Ithaca, NY: Cornell University Press.

Monod, J. 1972 *Chance and necessity.* Glasgow: Collins.

Morgan, L. H. 1868 *The American beaver and his works.* Philadelphia: Lippincott.

Moscovici, S. 1976 *Society against nature.* Brighton: Harvester Press.

Piaget, J. and B. Inhelder 1969 *The psychology of the child.* London: Routledge and Kegan Paul.

Popper, K. R. 1972 *Objective knowledge: an evolutionary approach.* Oxford University Press.

Radcliffe-Brown, A. R. 1952 *Structure and function in primitive society.* London: Cohen and West.

Reynolds, V. 1976 *The biology of human action.* Reading: W. H. Freeman.

Ruyle, E. E. 1973 Genetic and cultural pools: some suggestions for a unified theory of biocultural evolution. *Human Ecology* 1: 201–15.

Ryle, G. 1949 *The concept of mind.* London: Hutchinson.

Sahlins, M. D. 1976a *Culture and practical reason.* University of Chicago Press.

Sahlins, M. D. 1976b *The use and abuse of biology.* London: Tavistock.

Salzman, P. C. 1981 Culture as enhabilmentis. In *The structure of folk models*, eds. L. Holy and M. Stuchlik (A.S.A. monogr. 20). London: Academic Press.

Schrödinger, E. 1945 *What is life?* Cambridge University Press.

Spuhler, J. N. (ed.) 1959 *The evolution of man's capacity for culture.* Detroit: Wayne State University Press.

Steward, J. H. 1955 *Theory of culture change.* Urbana: University of Illinois Press.

Teleki, G. 1981 The omnivorous diet and eclectic feeding habits of chimpanzees in Gombe National Park, Tanzania. In *Omnivorous primates: gathering and hunting in human evolution*, eds. R. S. O. Harding and G. Teleki. New York: Columbia University Press.

Thorpe, W. H. 1974 *Animal nature and human nature.* London: Methuen.

Weber, M. 1947 *The theory of social and economic organization.* New York: Free Press.

White, L. A. 1959 The concept of culture. *American Anthropologist* **61**: 227–51.

Wilson, E. O. 1978 *On human nature.* Cambridge, Mass.: Harvard University Press.

Wilson, E. O. 1980 *Sociobiology* (abridged edition). Cambridge, Mass.: Harvard University Press.

3

Tools and *Homo faber*: construction and the authorship of design

The specialization of the hand – this implies the tool, and the tool implies specific human activity, the transforming reaction of man on nature, production. Animals in the narrower sense also have tools, but only as limbs of their bodies: the ant, the bee, the beaver; animals also produce, but their productive effect on surrounding nature, in relation to nature, amounts to nothing at all. Man alone has succeeded in impressing his stamp on nature . . .
(Engels 1934: 34)

Plans and products

Human beings are the only animals to possess tools, and yet, says Engels, non-human animals do also – in a sense. Human beings alone produce, yet he admits that other animals do also – in a sense. Like so many writers since, acutely aware of the difficulty of reconciling the continuity of the evolutionary process with the apparent uniqueness and supremacy of mankind, Engels wanted to have it both ways. A century later, we are a great deal more knowledgeable about the technical and cognitive capabilities of non-human animals, yet when it comes to the specification of what is or is not a tool, or what does or does not constitute production, we are no less confused or equivocal than was Engels. My intention in the present essay is to try to sort out at least some of this confusion, by isolating the specific senses of tool use and manufacture which entail a 'transforming reaction *on* nature' as opposed to those which involve nothing more than the mediation of interactions *within* the natural world. Central to my argument is the distinction between *constructive performance* and *self-conscious design*. I shall show that the preconditions for man's transformation of the environment should be sought in the evolution of the ability to plan, and therefore that the planned deployment of unmodified instruments, or of the body itself, bears a much closer relation to the specifically human mode of tool-making than does the manufacture of instruments by non-human animals which are presumed incapable of forming in advance a conceptual representation of the object to be constructed.

Engels himself was convinced that rational planning was of the essence of productive activity (Venable 1975: 66). It comes as no surprise, then, to find him declaring almost in the same breath that this is what finally distinguishes man from other animals, and yet that – in a sense – all animals are capable of planning to various degrees. In his uncompleted essay on 'The part played by labour in the transition from ape to man', he has these comments to offer on the subject:

> Animals exert a lasting effect on their environment unintentionally and.... accidentally. The further removed men are from animals, however, the more their effect on nature assumes the character of premeditated, planned action directed towards definite preconceived ends...
>
> It goes without saying that it would not occur to us to dispute the ability of animals to act in a planned, premeditated fashion. On the contrary, a planned mode of action exists in embryo wherever protoplasm, living albumen, exists and reacts... There is something of the planned action in the way insect-eating plants capture their prey, although they do it quite unconsciously. In animals the capacity for conscious, planned action is proportional to the development of the nervous system, and among mammals it attains a fairly high level... But all the planned action of all animals has never succeeded in impressing the stamp of their will upon the earth. That was left for man. (1934: 178–9)

If planning implies premeditation, the construction in the imagination of a desired future state in advance of its material realization, to describe the predatory behaviour of the insectivorous plant as 'planned action' is patent nonsense. The plant has no imagination, and quite how it can 'unconsciously' premeditate is not entirely clear! It is all too evident from this passage that Engels has blundered into the fallacy of attributing the end-directedness or *teleonomy* of animal and plant behaviour to its *teleological* conformity to a set of prior intentions. It is of course a characteristic of all living organisms that each is 'endowed with a purpose or project' (Monod 1972: 20). But the crowning achievement of Darwinian theory was to have shown how the process of variation under natural selection can account for the evolution of design in living nature in the *absence* of a designer. There exists no conception of the project of the plant, save in the mind of the observing naturalist, and the same goes at least for all 'lower' animals in which the functions of consciousness are but poorly developed.

In relation to non-human animals, one should therefore substitute the phrase 'teleonomic performance' for Engels's notion of the 'planned mode of action'. And if we are prepared to allow such performance as an instance of production, then of course we may admit that these animals, and even plants, produce. But this does mean having to extend the concept of production to cover what would normally be regarded as behaviour rather than action, that is conduct undirected by the prior intention of a knowing subject, in which the individual figures as the executor but not as the originator of design. By the same token, it becomes clear that the question of whether or not the tool – in Engels's words – 'implies specific human activity' turns on the issue of intentionality, rather than on the criterion of the detachability of the instrument from the body of the user. It is not the case, as Engels suggests, that the instruments of non-human animals are invariably attached to the body, and in due course I shall be citing some examples to the contrary. The philosopher Henri Bergson, who for reasons like those of Engels advocated the definition of man as *Homo faber*, makes the same mistake:

> Now, does an unintelligent animal also possess tools or machines? Yes, certainly, but here the instrument forms a part of the body that uses it; and, corresponding to this instrument, there is an *instinct* that knows how to use it. (1911: 146)

For Bergson the notion of instinct was constituted by its opposition to 'intelligence', the latter consisting essentially in 'the faculty of manufacturing artificial objects'. This faculty is equated with the capacity to invent, that is to author one's own mechanical project. 'Invention', Bergson wrote, 'becomes complete when it is materialized in a manufactured instrument' (1911: 145). What crucially separates intelligence from instinct, then, is not the externality of the product but the *priority of the plan*. If unintelligent animals have tools, their construction and use is governed by innate templates of which the possessors are more or less unaware. Only those tools whose fabrication conforms to rational, intelligent design are *artificial*. The tools of *Homo faber* are artefacts, those of other animal species are not.

Following a precedent set by Lotka (1945: 188) it has become commonplace to describe the artificial products of human industry as 'extra- (or exo-) somatic'. This notion can, however, be understood in two quite different senses, and their common confusion perpetuates the error, noted above in the remarks of Engels and Bergson, of inferring the presence of intelligent design from the construction and use of detached tools. In one sense, the dividing line between the somatic and the extra-somatic is drawn at the boundary of the individual organism. Thus a tool such as an axe is extrasomatic, the hand that holds it is somatic – a part of the user's body. Extrasomatic instruments are defined in this sense as objects anatomically separate from the body, which nevertheless serve as its functional extensions (Medawar 1957: 139). In the other sense, however, the opposition somatic/extrasomatic corresponds to one between the physical world of organisms and the cultural world of ideas and symbols: hence the extrasomatic aspect of the axe lies not in its anatomical detachment from the body but in the ideal 'conception of its nature and use' that pre-exists in the mind of the user, whilst its somatic aspect lies in the bodily movements actually entailed in behaviour governed by this conception (White 1959: 12–16). In the first sense, then, it is the material object that is 'exteriorized', in the second sense it is the ideal plan. It cannot be assumed that the execution of plans necessarily yields detached objects, for in certain respects the human body is itself an artefact, a medium for the expression of cultural form as in coiffure, tattooing and sacrification (Wilson 1980: 104). Nor can it be assumed that the fabrication of detached objects necessarily presupposes an ideal plan. The hive is no more attached to the body of the bee than is the house to the body of the human architect. But as Marx long ago pointed out, the essential difference between them is that the architect has initially 'built a cell in his head' whereas the bee has not (1930: 169–70). If the completed house is, in the first sense, an extrasomatic object, the imaginary house 'in his head' is, in the second sense, its extrasomatic aspect.

'Man', wrote Leslie White, 'so incorporates tools into his life, psychically as well as mechanically, that they become *inner* realities to him as well as things in the external world' (1959: 74). The human tool leads a double existence, as an objective instrument and as a corresponding subjective conception. The totality of these conceptions and their interrelations, located in men's minds, constitutes a *technology*. It is vital that we should not confuse the technology with the assemblage of material equipment recovered from a particular context. Archaeologists do not dig up technologies from prehistoric sites, they dig up their material expression in the form of artefacts, leaving us to guess how they were made and used. A technology consists, in the first place, of a *corpus of knowledge* that individuals carry in their heads, and transmit by formal, symbolically encoded instruction. Even if all artefacts were destroyed, so long as there were no breach in the continuity of transmission the technology would remain intact, and from it a replacement set of artefacts could be constructed. To be sure, knowledge is technology only in one of its aspects, namely as models *for* rather than *of*, or as instructions rather than representations (Geertz 1966: 7–8). Yet the very same practical orientation to the material world that converts knowledge into technology simultaneously furnishes the constituents of that world with a corresponding set of images, thereby converting objects into artefacts. That is why the net-trap of the human hunter is an artefact whereas the web of the spider is not, and why the human house is an artefact whereas the beehive is not. The difference in each case, as Sahlins notes, lies not so much in the physical form, scale or efficiency of the instruments taken by themselves, but in 'the instrument–user relation'. 'Anthropologists', he goes on to declare, 'are only satisfied by the extratechnological observation that in invention and use the human instrument expresses "conscious ingenuity" (symboling), the insect's tool, inherited physiology ("instinct")' (1972: 79). But however valid this observation may be, we cannot concur that it is 'extratechnological'. For technology is nothing if not precisely that 'conscious ingenuity', expressed in the instrument, which Sahlins reserves for man.

At this point the objection might be raised that the web is just as much 'spider-made', and the hive as much 'bee-made', as is the human trap or house 'man-made': in all these cases form and function is being imposed on raw material, through the application of forces *exterior* to the objects constructed (Monod 1972: 21). In this way they may be distinguished from living organisms which 'just grow' as a result of spontaneous morphogenetic processes. But the distinction rests entirely on where we choose to draw the boundaries of the organism. Compare the spider's web and the snail's shell. One, we commonly say, is made; the other grows. It is reasonable to suppose, however, that both web and shell are the outcomes of processes that are ultimately under genetic control, hence the former is as much an expression of the spider's genotype as is the latter of the snail's genotype. Thus spider and web together compose one and the same phenotype, whose boundaries in this case encompass but do not coincide with those of the animal's body. On these grounds, Dawkins (1982: 198–200) brings all so-called animal artefacts under the rubric of his concept of the 'extended phenotype', connoting the sum of phenotypic effects of a given genotype that are extrasomatic in the sense of lying outside the body of the individual gene-carrier. If we grant the essential unity of the whole phenotype, it makes no more sense to attribute to design the construction of the extended phenotype than it does so to attribute the construction of that part of the phenotype which remains internal to the soma. Neither process depends upon the prior existence of an ideal plan, and if we recoil from calling the spider an artefact for *this* reason, we must also deny artificial status to the web. Let us say that the spider *executes* the web but not that he *makes* it; or in other words that his behaviour serves to reveal or 'write out' a structure of which he is not the author – one indeed which *has no* author.

It must nevertheless be admitted that a good deal of animal tool behaviour is based on tradition transmitted by observational learning rather than on genetically fixed prescriptions, yet does not require the symbolic articulation of maker's or user's knowledge in the form of a technology. Thus it is far too simple to erect a 'great evolutionary divide' between the instinctive and the symbolic (Sahlins 1972: 80). For this leaves out the entire field of behaviour that is *not* instinctive (in that it will not be manifested by individuals deprived of contact with conspecifics at crucial moments of ontogenetic development), but which is still executed in the absence of self-conscious design. Moreover this field *overlaps* the boundary between human and non-human animals: there is no doubt that much human constructive behaviour, usually called 'cultural' merely because it is learned, is not preceded by a 'picture in the mind'; or in Alexander's (1964) terms, it is *unselfconscious*. The individual executor of tradition, in an 'unselfconscious system', is according to Alexander not the author of his work, any more than is the spider of its web, but merely an agent in its realization (1964: 58). And if the prior conception of the object in the mind of an author is a condition for its categorization as an artefact, then clearly the products of unselfconscious construction do not qualify, even if the constructors are human. In short, the distinction between instinct and learning, as modes of transmission of behavioural instructions, does not coincide with that between the innate and the artificial as characterizations of behavioural products, and neither suffices to isolate the specifically human. The former distinction is too broad, lumping human activity along with that of very many other social species, far removed from man in the scale of nature. The latter, on the other hand, is too narrow, isolating only a specific class of human constructions rather than separating all the constructions of man from all those of other animals. But it is the symbolic imagination, unique to mankind, which ultimately makes possible the *invention* of tools, and the transmission of discoveries not through imitative learning but through *formal tuition*. At issue here is the relative priority of practice and theory, or technique and technology: only when the latter overtakes and proceeds to govern the former do we enter into the production of artefacts. And the result is the cumulative or progressive growth of knowledge which is surely an undeniable feature of human history (White 1942: 371).

What is a tool?

Bearing these general considerations in mind, let me now review some possible approaches to the problem of defining the tool. A simple illustration will help to focus our discussion. Suppose that I am thirsty, and that before me stands on unopened bottle of beer. In order to quench my thirst I have first to remove the top. Here are three possible ways in which I might proceed:

1 Fortunately, I have a bottle-opener. Gripping it in my hand, with a swift and skilful movement I can easily lever off the top.
2 Having searched my pockets in vain for an opener, I pick up a nearby stone of suitable shape and size, and attempt to remove the top by repeated blows to the edge.
3 I am stranded in a place where neither stones nor any other suf-

ficiently hard objects are to be found. In desperation I endeavour to wrench off the top of the bottle with my teeth.

Now in all three scenarios we are concerned with an end-directed act performed by the same agent, myself, towards the same object, the bottle. Moreover, unless we believe in miracles of spoon-bending, or analogously that bottle tops can conveniently be caused to dislodge themselves by a barrage of concentrated mental attention, some apparatus must be interposed between agent and object that serves to translate the intention of the former into a change in the physical state of the latter. That is to say, besides an object to work *on*, I must have something to work *with* (Cohen 1978: 32). In the first scenario that thing may be identified as the opener, which we would normally have no hesitation in regarding as a simple tool. In the second case it is the stone, which may seem like a tool in use, but is quite unremarkable outside this specific context. Finally, in the third scenario I have no instruments to draw on save those of my own body, primarily the teeth. Yet if this lack of extra-corporeal equipment leaves me somewhat disabled, the disability is slight compared with what I would experience if – say – my hands had been amputated after an accident. This observation should suffice to demonstrate that in the first two scenarios, opener and stone do not compose the totality of the instrumental apparatus, for in each case the object forms part of a composite instrument which includes at the very least the hand and the musculature of the arm.

In the broadest sense, we could equate tools with the general category of what Marx calls 'instruments of labour'. According to his definition, 'the instrument of labour is a thing, or a complex of things, which the worker interposes between himself and the subject matter of his labour, and one which serves as the conductor of his activity' (1930: 171). For elementary subsistence tasks such as gathering fruit, 'man's bodily organs suffice him as the instruments of labour', but more commonly these are supplemented by objects supplied from the natural environment. 'Thus', Marx wryly comments 'nature becomes an instrument of his activities, . . . adding a cubit and more to his stature, scripture notwithstanding'. Not only, then, do we find that all labouring activity is *ipso facto* tool-using, but also we have to admit that everything in nature – including the human body – is a potential tool, to the extent that the earth itself, in Marx's words, is man's 'primitive tool-house' as well as his store of provisions. Moreover, if we are prepared to widen the notion of instrument to cover 'all such objects as are necessary for carrying on the labour process', as Marx in all seriousness suggests, then among them would be the very air we breathe and the ground we stand upon (1930: 173).[1] But whilst from this point of view the definition of the instrument seems so broad as to be virtually meaningless, from another it seems overly exclusive. For in the specific context which I have just cited, Marx is adamant that labour is purposive activity guided by an intention which 'when the process began, already existed in the worker's imagination, already existed in an ideal form' (1930: 170). Thus an object becomes an instrument only when harnessed to the intentional project of an agent. Where there is no prior representation of an end there can be no instrumental means, no tools.

In the example with which I began, the opener, the stone, and my teeth would all qualify as instruments of labour in Marx's sense, since it is assumed that my action is based on rational deliberation about means and ends. But if I use my teeth only occasionally and exceptionally for opening bottles, I use them habitually, several times a day, to cut and grind the food I eat. So do a lot of other animals, which we would not normally credit with the ability to construct and articulate prior intentions. Are we to conclude that teeth cease to be instruments at the point when the mental image of the completed act fades out? The conclusion is surely absurd, for whether preceded by the image or not, eating is an end-directed performance which adopts the teeth as means: *technically*, the addition or subtraction of the image makes no difference to the behaviour. And indeed, in another context, Marx seems quite prepared to admit as instruments any organs used by living things for the purposes of survival and reproduction, including the instruments of self-conscious human agents – distinguished by their artificiality – as just one subset of the more general class of 'productive organs':

Darwin has aroused our interest in the history of natural technology, that is to say in the origin of the organs of plants and animals as productive instruments utilized for the life purposes of these creatures. Does not the history of the origin of the productive organs of men in society...deserve equal attention? (Marx 1930: 392 n.2)

He goes on to point out, acknowledging Vico, that the crucial difference between these two kinds of history is that the latter consists of works *authored* by man. But both are histories of instruments, and to validate the comparison it is necessary to widen the definition of the instrument to include *any object that, harnessed to the specific project of a living being, is turned to account in its realization.*

The difficulties with such a broad conception become apparent as soon as we wish to isolate a restricted domain of 'tool-using behaviour', which would not simply be coterminous with the entire field of teleonomic performances. The solution most commonly adopted, particularly in studies of animal behaviour, is to limit the class of tools to instruments external to, and detachable from, the body of the user. The following definition by Warren is typical:

A tool is any object extraneous to the bodily equipment of an animal that serves as a functional extension of the organism, permitting it to enlarge the range of its movements or to increase their efficiency in manipulating the environment. (1976: 407)[2]

No longer can my teeth be counted as tools for bottle-opening, but the stone and the opener both qualify. We would not attribute the same intentionality to the solitary digger wasp that uses a pebble to tamp earth over its underground nest, nor to the woodpecker finch that uses a stick as a probe for insects (van Lawick-Goodall 1970: 197–8). But both the pebble and the stick would be admitted, on Warren's definition, as tools. On the other hand the wasp's mandibles which it uses for holding the pebble, and the protrusile tongue of the true woodpecker which is also an effective insect probe, would both be excluded, along with my teeth.

But even this definition may turn out to be too broad for the declared purpose of separating tool-using from non-tool-using behaviour. We might agree, for instance, that the ladder is a tool: propped up against the trunk of a tree it permits an enlargement of the range of vertical movement, enabling us to recover fruit from the upper branches. By the some token, however, the trunk itself can serve as a tool with a ladder function if we can climb it unaided, as the chimpanzee does as a matter of course in its foraging. Before long, it appears that any feature of the environment on which the animal stands or to which it clings can be regarded as a tool for assisting its passage to wherever it desires to go next. Then all movement is tool use, and whatever stands between and connects the individual to its goal is potentially a tool. Expressly in order to counter objections such as these, Beck has recently come up with a rather more elaborate definition of tool use:

. . . the external employment of an unattached environmental object to alter more efficiently the form, position, or condition of another object, another organism, or the user itself when the user holds or carries the tool during or just prior to use and is responsible for the proper and effective orientation of the tool. (1980: 10)

The final clause of this definition is designed to close the loophole illustrated above in the case of tree-climbing, for the trunk is neither carried nor oriented by the climber. However, it further requires us to exclude the use of all objects with a fixed attachment to the substrate – that is, which are either lying on or rooted in the ground.

Strict adherence to these criteria brings its own difficulties. The animals, as Beck himself is forced to admit (1980: 133), 'seem not to respect our categories', so that a bird may just as well impale insects *with* sticks as *on* sticks, and a chimpanzee desiring to open a thick-skinned fruit to reach its edible contents may just as well pound food *with* a stone (hammer) as *on* a stone (anvil).[3] Is there any good reason for viewing these as fundamentally different kinds of behaviour, and for admitting only the former technique in each pair as proper tool use? Parker and Gibson, drawing on a Piagetian framework of developmental psychology, argue that there are valid grounds for doing so, recognizing 'true tool use' – as against simpler forms of 'prototool use' – by the employment of 'one detached object (not a part of the animal's anatomy) to change the state of another object' (1979: 371). But if, following J. J. Gibson, tools are to be regarded as 'detached objects of a very special sort', being 'graspable, portable, manipulatable, and usually rigid' (1979: 40), we would have to exclude every form of animal architecture, such as nests, dens, burrows and hives; as well as fixed facilities such as traps and webs. Many would consider this an unreasonable and arbitrary restriction (Lancaster 1968a: 60; Reed 1985: 91–2, 96). Moreover the distinction between detached and attached environmental objects is not entirely free from ambiguity. Gibson characterizes the former in terms of the formal topological criterion of complete surface closure, such that 'the detached object can be moved without breaking or rupturing the continuity of any surface'. Yet he goes on to note, parenthetically, that whilst 'a tree is an attached object in the environment of animals since it is rooted in the ground like a house with foundations... it is a detached object, a whole organism, when considered as a plant with roots between soil particles' (Gibson 1979: 34).

When it comes to human tool use the difficulties multiply. Consider the plough. On Beck's criteria the plough is not a tool because it is supported by the earth, even though the farmer is responsible for its orientation. It is not a detached object, in Gibson's terms, because its movement breaks the surface of the ground. Yet therein lies its very function: a plough that failed to rupture the substrate would be useless! Still more surprising is Beck's conclusion that the rifle is not a tool. This is evidently because, although held and aimed by the hunter, it is put together from exotic materials and does not therefore qualify like the bow and arrow as an 'environmental object'. We would not perhaps find these results so odd were it not for our commonsense understanding that both rifle and plough, like the bottle-opener but *unlike* the stone, are tools by virtue of their very construction. And because they are tools, we suppose, their use must be tool use. By the same logic the use of the unmodified stone, which is *not* a constructed object and therefore not a tool in this sense, cannot qualify as tool use. An example of this kind of reasoning is to be found in a paper by Gruber (1969), who defines the 'true tool' as a modified object whose manufacture involves a 'certain degree of difficulty or sophistication', of which only human beings are thought capable. He goes on to restrict tool using proper to the *use of true tools*, a restriction that automatically excludes all cases of so-called tool using among non-human animals (1969: 577).

Now it is essential to recognize that this is to approach the definition of tool use from quite another angle. Instead of starting from the project of a user, classing as a tool anything that happens to facilitate its implementation (subject to the restrictions about externality, portability and orientation set out above), we start from the tool itself as an object already endowed with form and function, classing as tool use all behaviour that discharges the functions of the tool (as bottle-opening discharges the function of the opener, or as ploughing discharges the function of the plough). There is of course a difference, as Moscovici notes, 'between picking up a stone or breaking off a branch in self-defence, and handling a tool as a carpenter handles a hammer or a pair of pliers. The stone or the branch is not a tool until it is used as such' (1976: 53). But it is worth considering the rather intriguing borderline case, by no means uncommon, which occurs in situations when we use in an *ad hoc* fashion implements constructed for one purpose in order to do something completely different. For example, having mislaid my opener, I might lever off the top of the bottle with the blade of a pocket-knife. The knife is a tool on the criterion of its construction, so in one sense to use it in any capacity whatever would be tool use. On the other hand, its function is to cut and not to lever, and if it happens to be serviceable for removing bottle tops, the same could be said of the unmodified stone, or even of my teeth, neither of which are tools *for opening* until used as such.

I propose to adopt a very handy set of terms, originally suggested in quite another context by Gould and Vrba (1982), to sort out ambiguities of this kind. Compare the stone, the knife and the opener as implements for bottle-opening. All three are *apt* for the purpose; this character of suitability may be defined as *aptation*. But only the opener has been specifically shaped for its current use, so that its employment can be regarded as a discharge of *function*. It is, in the most literal sense, an *ad*apted object. The knife, though also an adapted object, was not shaped for bottle-opening, and is therefore being *co-opted* to a project different from the one for which it arose as an adaptation, but which fortuitously endowed it with appropriate properties. In its use as a lever, it renders an *effect* but does not discharge a function. The stone, used as a hammer, likewise renders an effect, and is co-opted rather than constructed for the project in hand. The useful properties of both knife and stone, in the context of bottle opening, are not adaptations but *exaptations*, in that they have arisen for purely contingent reasons that have nothing whatever to do with efficiency in opening bottles. But unlike both the opener and the knife, the stone not only lacks a function in bottle opening, it lacks any function at all. The knife, at least, can discharge a function in cutting. The stone, which in its 'raw' state is not *adapted for* anything, can only deliver effects.

In the course of organic evolution, it very often happens that morphological features which have originated as adaptations through the operation of natural selection turn out to have fitness-enhancing effects quite unrelated to the specific conditions that promoted their emergence, effects which are subsequently augmented through further adaptive modification, so that the ancestral feature comes to acquire an entirely new and different function. Thus, as Jacob puts it, 'evolution makes a wing from a leg or a part of an ear from a piece of jaw' (1977: 1164). Adaptation, then, proceeds from a foundation in exaptation. There is every reason to believe that what applies to morphological features also applies to the evolution of behaviour patterns, and more specifically, to the emergence of tool-using in animal populations. For example, patterns of agonistic display or redirected aggression involving the brandishing of sticks or stones could have had the coincidental and beneficial environmental effect of improving access to food (Hall 1963), an effect that would be subsequently reinforced through adaptive modification of the original behavioural programme such as to bring sticks or stones into regular use as instruments of foraging. As the effect of the behaviour becomes its function, so the objects manipulated become tools, and their manipulation tool use. Thus Alcock speculates that 'most examples of the use of tools *could* have had their origin in the novel use of a pre-existing behaviour pattern. These behaviour patterns may have been performed in a way that more or less accidentally involved the use of objects as tools in special situations' (1972: 466). In other words, tool use may evolve through the co-option of innate behavioural programmes in projects for which they were not already adapted, but for which they are fortuitously and peculiarly apt.

Now the same argument can be generalized to cover the constructive modification not only of morphology and behaviour, but also of external objects. That is to say, such objects once harnessed as tools may deliver useful effects, unanticipated in their genesis, which could be further enhanced through adaptations of the objects themselves, converting those effects into their embodied functions in just the same way as with the adaptation of originally co-opted body parts. Starting with instruments *co-opted* for a project (whose relevant features were *exaptations*), we end with instrument *constructed* for a project (whose relevant features are *adaptations*). The essential distinction between using tools in tasks for which they are constructed, and in tasks for which they are co-opted, is equally applicable to corporeal as to extra-corporeal objects. For example, to employ teeth for eating would be an instance of the former, to use them in bottle opening, or for carrying things when the hands are full, would be an instance of the latter.[4] The co-option of bodily instruments, for use in ways quite contrary to the normal and spontaneous modes of everyday life for which they are adapted, is the stock in trade of the acrobat or circus clown who – for example – holds things with his feet whilst walking on his hands. And that apparently functionless appendage, the mammalian tail, can be co-opted for a whole host of projects, from swatting flies to raking in otherwise inaccessible food (Reynolds 1981: 155–7). Again for those ungulates that possess them, pointed horns are as good for scratching as sticks held in the mouth, though neither horns nor sticks are adapted for the purpose (van Lawick-Goodall 1970: 205–7, Beck 1980: 36–7). Moreover the contrast between construction and co-option is indifferent to the criterion of whether or not the object, if external to the body, is carried and oriented by the user. A tree trunk, liberally supplied with horizontal branches, is easy to climb, and so can be co-opted for my project in reaching fruit (in the context of which the branches are *ex*aptations). Alternatively I could construct a ladder, which is functionally *ad*apted for climbing. In that case, of course, I carry it to the spot and set it up immediately prior to use. But I could equally well have modified the tree trunk by drilling holes and driving in pegs as footholds (in lieu of branches). In so doing I would have converted the trunk into a constructed tool with a ladder function: unlike branches, pegs are *made for* climbing.[5]

Making things and using them

Far more crucial and more troublesome than these questions concerning the externality and orientation of tools is the issue of intentionality. The trouble arises because of the rather imprecise way in which we customarily employ the notion of tool-*making*. Strictly speaking, as I have already argued, we should only say that a tool is made when it qualifies as an artefact, self-consciously authored by an agent in whose mind there pre-exists an image of the final product. In the absence of such an image, the tool may be *executed* but not made. However, most definitions hinge upon the criterion of the constructive modification of the object, and carry no stipulation about subjective intentionality – although this is often inferred or implied. Thus according to McGrew and his collaborators (1979: 189), tool-making is 'the modification of an inanimate object so that it is used more efficiently as a tool', and Beck (1980: 11–12) proposes an almost identical formulation. Likewise for Oswalt, the distinction between tools that are made and those that are not 'is based on whether or not the form is modified by man before it is used' (1973: 35). At a bare minimum, modification consists in the *detachment* of one environmental object from another (or from the substrate), such as in breaking off a branch. Further removal of material from an unattached object, as in stripping leaves from the severed branch, entails a *subtraction* or *reduction* process. A more complex tool may be fashioned by the addition or combination of previously unconnected objects, through what Oswalt calls a *multiplication process*, and involving a *conjunctive principle* (such as lashing) by which the parts are held together. Lastly, amplifications of design may lead to a fundamental restructuring or *reshaping* of material (Oswalt 1973: 19–20, Beck 1980: 105).

Now of course it is not only man who modifies forms in all of these ways; witness the bee, the spider and the beaver. The hive, the web and the lodge are all constructed objects, the evolution of whose adaptive properties can be put down to the operation of natural selection on innate behavioural predispositions. On the strength of the objects alone, we would have no more valid reason to attribute human constructions to intelligent design (Pumphrey 1953: 233).[6] Just because a form is modified for use we cannot conclude that it has been *made*; hence our distinction between construction and co-option cannot be simply identified with one between the presence or absence of tool-making. They are, in fact, separate distinctions, which in combination yield four possibilities:

1 Use of self-consciously constructed objects.
2 Use of self-consciously co-opted objects.
3 Use of unselfconsciously constructed objects.
4 Use of unselfconsciously co-opted objects.

The bottle-opener and all other detachable human artefacts, in the discharge of their proper functions, fall in category 1. So do artificial limbs, false teeth, and other substitutes for somatic organs, which may be more or less permanently affixed and are thus, in a sense, internal to the body. Of the objects in this category, we are in no doubt that they are made. The pebble used by the digger wasp in building its nest, and the stick used by the woodpecker finch to probe for insects, undoubtedly fall in category 4; they just as certainly are *not* made. But what about the objects in categories 2 and 3? How are we to comprehend things harnessed to a prior intention without adaptive modification, and things adaptively modified in the absence of a prior intention?

The confusion engendered by these awkward categories can be rather nicely illustrated by referring to a distinction, suggested by Oswalt, between artefacts and what he calls 'naturefacts':

Objects extracted from their natural setting and subsequently used without modification will be termed *naturefacts*... *Artefacts* are forms created by withdrawing materials from their natural setting and modifying them in trifling or remarkable ways... All forms made and used are artefacts; all forms used, but not made, are naturefacts. (1973: 14–17, 35)

Both kinds of tool, in Oswalt's terminology, are distinguished from the natural organs of the user's body, which he calls 'anatomical aids' (1973: 29). At face value, the naturefact/artefact opposition appears to correspond to ours between co-opted and constructed objects. Nothing is suggested about planning or self-conscious design. By and large, Oswalt tells us, non-human animals use naturefacts, however he is quite prepared – at least in one context – to admit into this category the pebble of the digger wasp, although its use is entirely governed by instinct (1973: 14–15). But a subsequent statement flatly contradicts this position:

...another discovery completed the background for all future technological developments; it was the momentous step of removing a natural form from its setting for a planned purpose. *Use-removal* was a critical innovation because it gave rise to the employment of naturefacts...(1973: 18)

What Oswalt calls use-removal *for a planned purpose* corresponds to our *self-conscious* co-option (category 2). And if planning is a precondition for the employment of objects as naturefacts, all unselfconsciously co-opted objects like the wasp's pebble in our category 4 must be excluded. By contrast the unmodified stone. which I deliberately select for use in opening a bottle would qualify as a true naturefact.

There is a similar ambiguity in Oswalt's conception of the artefact. According to the definition he provides, an object has only to be modified for use in order to qualify. Yet he asserts elsewhere that when the earliest men, having previously obtained their food largely through the use of anatomical aids enhanced by naturefacts, began in addition to fashion simple artefacts, 'foresight and planning were involved' (1973: 169–70). How can the construction and use of artefacts be specifically symptomatic of planning, when the latter is also deemed essential to the employment of naturefacts? If, on the other hand, both artefacts and naturefacts are taken to imply foresight, how are we to classify the many cases of animal tool use, and construction, where conscious intentionality is presumed to be lacking? These problems can be very simply resolved by separating out the criterion of constructive modification from that of self-conscious design. Since 'facts' are literally things that are *made*, not so much through the physical alteration of objects in the external world as through the establishment of a relation between these objects and a corresponding set of *ideas* in the mind of an agent (Bohm 1980: 142), I would be inclined to reserve Oswalt's terms for our categories 1 and 2. The artefact, then, is a self-consciously constructed object, the naturefact a self-consciously co-opted object. Indeed the latter term is peculiarly apt to express the way a thing can become a tool simply by the agent's attending to it, from the moment when he sees in it a potential solution to a known technical problem. Thus in my mind's eye the stone has become a bottle-opener even before I pick it up to use it.

In Marxian terms, the stone is a *use-value*, belonging to the class of 'articles capable of satisfying wants of one kind or another' (Marx 1930: 169). Marx distinguished between two kinds of use-values: those which are 'naturally given', having merely to be severed 'from their immediate connection with their environment'; and those which – although 'materially supplied by nature' – are intentionally modified, 'adapted to human wants by a change of form'. According to his definitions, only the latter qualify as *products* (1930: 171–3). And yet the unmodified stone, as naturally given, is no more than an object in the landscape, one constituent of what in Chapter 1 we introduced as the environment of essences. It is *not* naturally given for bottle opening or for anything else, becoming so only in so far as it is incorporated into the project of a user. It has to be *made* into a bottle-opener, if not through deliberate construction, then through deliberate co-option. Marx's two kinds of use-value therefore correspond to our categories of naturefacts and artefacts respectively. And if production is equated with making, both kinds must be counted as products. The point I wish to emphasize here is that tools may be made, in a sense, *without any modification of physical objects at all*. One has only to supply each object with a *conception* of its nature and use, or to place it in what White called its extrasomatic context.

Suppose that I encounter a man engaged in some constructive activity, and that upon inquiry he is able to give me a full account of the object he expects to produce, together with instructions about how to proceed. In theory I would be able to go away and construct an identical object, without ever having seen the result of the man's labour. I think we can truthfully claim that this is something of which no other animal is capable. There is no doubt that the man's activity qualifies in our terms as *making*, but is it *tool*-making? Three possibilities can be envisaged:

1 The product is destined for direct consumption (as in cookery).
2 The product will be 'consumed' through wear and tear in use as an instrument for producing something else.
3 The product satisfies ends of a non-utilitarian nature (such as display), but is an enduring object like an ornament, which may later be co-opted as an instrument for producing something else.

The dish which the cook prepares, since it involves the intentional transformation of raw material according to a set of explicit cultural rules, can reasonably be regarded as artificial. But it would be absurd to call it a tool. Not all artefacts, then, are tools, just as not all tools are artefacts.

Ornaments too, almost by definition, are non-tools: they are designed *not* to be used, and would cease to qualify as ornaments from the moment when they are co-opted for use for some purpose for which they were not designed. A silver cup, designed for display as a trophy, is not meant for use as a drinking vessel, and would lose its status if it appeared on the table alongside regular cups and glasses, becoming a 'mere tool'. Conversely, of course, tools can become ornaments when the intention to use them lapses, as with the antique cup, once in regular service, now in a museum cabinet.

Thus out of the possibilities listed above, only the second can be regarded as an instance of tool-making. What this shows is that whilst *making* implies the existence of an image of a desired future state, *tool*-making requires that this image – of the completed object – be subsumed under yet another, as it were one step prior, which envisages the state to be brought about through its use. If either of these images is blanked out, we have making but not tool-making; if both are blanked out we no longer have making at all but mere execution. To indicate this result formally, let T stand for the constructed object, with T' its ideal representation; and let S stand for the state to be achieved through use, with S' its ideal representation. Then in true tool-making:

$$S' \subset T' \to T \supset S$$

Beginning with S' ('the open bottle') we derive T' ('the bottle-opener'), on the basis of which we construct T (the opener), subsequently used to realize S (to open the bottle). The essential point is that S' should *precede* and *underwrite* the material realization of T' as T. If it does not, this realization is not tool-making, even though the object T may at a later time be deliberately co-opted to a project in which it acquires a tool function. It is then 'made' as a tool in the co-option, not in the construction, through the fitting of the prefashioned object to a conception founded on a projected future use, which was not present at the time of its original construction. Thus we have two separate stages:

$$\text{Construction:} \qquad T_1' \to T$$
$$\|$$
$$\text{Co-option:} \qquad S' \subset T_2' \to T \supset S$$

Here, although both the construction and the co-option are self-conscious, only the latter – which involves no physical modification of the made object – makes of it a tool.

Concluding his discussion of modes of animal tool manufacture, Beck notes that the characterization of behaviour as such is largely founded on its temporal precedence over acts in which the modified object is put to use. If a chimpanzee breaks off a branch from a tree, whether out of annoyance, through sheer gusto, or simply by accident, and then after waving it about for a moment simply discards it, we would hardly infer that he had constructed a tool. If, however, he goes on to use the branch to reach fruit or to lever open a box, the observer is inclined to report the same behaviour in breaking it off as an instance of elementary tool construction. But did he do it *in order* to be able to reach fruit? Not necessarily, for as Beck continues:

intentionality is not always implied and in several cases seems, by the length of the intervening interval, to be counterindicated. In many cases, however, the interval is short and behavior flows smoothly and directly from manufacture to use. Intentionality is a reasonable inference in such instances. (1980: 115)

The temporal horizon of the chimpanzee is short, so that we could not expect the detachment of an object to have been motivated by a conception of its future use when that use does not follow almost immediately afterwards. And if it was not so motivated, the detachment – though conceivably a form of manufacture – was not *tool* manufacture.

But with man the situation is different. As White (1942) long ago stressed, in a pioneering comparison of tool use by man and non-human primates, human intentions do not evaporate in the moment they are conceived but may be suspended indefinitely in the continuum of time, caught in the mesh of an enduring matrix of significant symbols. From the time-lag between construction and use we can infer nothing about the form of intentionality. The fact that the use of an object long postdated its construction does not mean that the image that underwrote the construction (the concept of make) was not itself underwritten by a conception of its mode of use, or that the latter merely governed its subsequent co-option. If the observed interval is a long one, two interpretations are possible, indicated schematically below:

Interpretation A

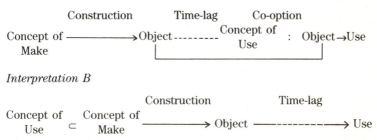

Interpretation B

According to interpretation A, successive stages of construction and co-option are separated by a time-lag, so that there is *no* such long temporal separation between the concept of use and its realization.

According to interpretation B, the concept of use *precedes* the concept of make, so that the time-lag necessarily intervenes before its realization; but by the same token the process of construction qualifies as tool-making. With man both interpretations are possible, but with the chimpanzee we would be limited to interpretation A.

The search for a definition of man

The technical capabilities of non-human animals have been a constant source of embarrassment to those seeking to define the essence of man on the basis of his industry (Alcock 1972: 471). First it was claimed that humans alone *use* tools, until animals were found that did the same – indeed of all classes of animals, only among amphibians and reptiles are there no reported instances of tool use (Beck 1980: 21). Then it was claimed that only man *makes* tools, until the animals again proved our equals – though once again with amphibians and reptiles as the inexplicable exceptions. Nowadays, however, many students of human and animal behaviour confidently declare that they have at last discovered an unassailable rubicon: man, it is said, is the only animal who *uses tools to make tools* (Oakley 1962: 187, Gruber 1969: 577, Warren 1976: 412, Beck 1980: 218). Ashley Montagu goes even further:

Man is not defined as a tool-making animal. He's defined as an animal that makes tools with which to make other tools on which he becomes continuously dependent. All these three are requirements of this definition of man. (1976: 328)

No doubt this holds, in a sense. But without a clear definition of what constitutes tool-making (or tool-using, for that matter) it does not mean very much. What is more, so long as we remain satisfied with the usual ethological definition of tool manufacture as any *modification* process by which an external object becomes adapted for use, it is simply not true that man is the only animal to make or use tools to make other tools. Surely the beaver, at least, does this as well when he builds his dam and lodge.

If the tool is any object, internal or external to the body, harnessed instrumentally to a given project, then it is perfectly obvious that to make a tool is *ipso facto* to use another one, so that there is simply no difference between making tools and using tools to make tools. The animal which, rather than relying on bodily instruments, first constructs or co-opts an *external* object to construct another object is of course doing something more, but the whole process may be entirely unselfconscious and even instinctive. It is not unreasonable to regard the nest of the digger wasp as a tool, and we know that the wasp is 'programmed' to co-opt a pebble for use in its construction. We are justified in regarding the pebble also as a tool, not because its co-option was governed by an intention regarding its future use, but because the co-option behaviour is embedded within the same teleonomic performance that ends with the completion of the nest, its programme having evolved through natural selection as one component of a total adaptive complex. When it comes to the question of why, in one species, the adaptive response to some environmental condition should take the form of a stereotyped behaviour pattern, whilst in another the same condition is coped with through the development of a specialized morphological feature, we can offer no clear answer.

One argument, advanced by Alcock (1972: 472), is that tool-using behaviour tends to evolve in species which have recently invaded ecological niches radically different from those occupied by other members of the genus to which they belong, and that – faced with competition from species already established in these niches – such behaviour compensates for their comparative lack of appropriate morphological equipment. But as Beck has reasonably objected, one could just as well argue that a morphological feature develops to compensate for the lack of appropriate behaviour patterns, as *vice versa* (1980: 186). Does the stick-using behaviour of the woodpecker finch, in probing for insects, substitute for its lack of a protrusile tongue, or does the protrusile tongue of the woodpecker substitute for the absence of behaviour involving the use of probing tools? Be that as it may, the evident adaptive equivalence of innate morphological and behavioural traits at once gives the lie to the long-cherished assumption that the use, and more particularly the constructive modification, of external objects as tools is indicative of relatively more advanced cognitive capacities in the species concerned, placing them in some sense closer to our human selves. The assumption was effectively demolished in a now classic paper by Hall (1963), who demonstrated that in the general context of animal evolution, instances definable as tool use or modification represent specialized behavioural adaptations whose resemblance to human tool-using and making is purely superficial and fortuitous. The wasp that uses a tool to build its nest is neither more intelligent nor more adaptable than the wasp that does not.[7]

To what, then, should we turn in order to discover the proper antecedents of human constructional capacities? Not to behaviour patterns distinguished by their involvement of external, material objects; but to the ability to place the repertoire of behaviours – whether innate or learned – under the control of a body of concepts, through which may be realized the intention of an agent. This is what Reynolds (1981: 150) calls the *instrumental modality of action*, which appears as tool use when it employs 'peripheral effectors to create external effects that have been predicted from conceptually stored information'. Within this modality, the crucial variable lies in the peripherality of the instruments (or effectors) employed. The ape can manipulate parts of its own body to form conceptually-controlled configurations that can be used instrumentally, as for example the configurations of the hand used in communicative signalling. Humans are capable of this, but in addition they can similarly manipulate external objects, resulting in 'image-driven productions that remain after their makers have ceased to operate on them'. The manufacture of artificial instruments is therefore the logical culmination of a process to which Reynolds refers as 'the distalward migration of iconic motor control', requiring 'the incorporation of programs that control the extensions of the body into instrumental programs that already control the body itself' (1981: 163).

If Reynolds's argument is accepted, human tool-making represents one extreme of an evolutionary continuum on which significant transitional instances are exemplified by the ability of some contemporary non-human primates to co-opt their bodily equipment in conformity with an internal image; instances that, according to conventional behavioural definitions, would not qualify even as tool use, let alone as tool-making. Clearly, the error in such definitions lies in their focus upon the properties of products rather than upon the priority of plans. If we are to come anywhere near to identifying the foundations of what is *human* in tool-making, we must start from the intentionality that precedes it, rather than from the constructed nature of the result. As Hallowell has written:

Tool-making at the human level implies an act performed in the present which cannot be dissociated from a purposeful use of the object at some future time... Tool-making is *psychologically* much more complicated than tool using. Among other things, we would have to assume [if an ape could make tools] that the ape possessed a capacity for 'self-awareness', and that he could somehow represent himself in some future time to himself... But a far more important point of difference is that a man does not just make a tool; quite apart from any technological knowledge involved, he *shapes* it, and for this he must have some image in the mind which necessitates intrinsic representative processes. (1956: 98–9)

What Hallowell calls 'shaping', as something that goes beyond 'making', corresponds to what we call making as going beyond execution: where the former exceeds the latter is in the prior construction of the mental image, that is, in the *authorship of design*. This is exactly how, in the classic Weberian conception, action exceeds behaviour (Weber 1947: 88). As with all action, so conceived, tool-making is a self-conscious process that depends upon the subject's ability to reflect upon his own existence in the dimension of time.

Similarly, if using tools to make tools adds anything that is not necessarily entailed in *any* tool-making activity (which must involve tool use of a kind), it should lie in the *self-conscious co-option* of what we have called naturefacts, specifically for use in the self-conscious *construction* of artificial instruments. Arguably, the appearance of stone artefacts bearing all the hallmarks of formal design provides the first conclusive evidence of the deliberate co-option of secondary tools, since unlike organic materials such as wood or bone, stone cannot be worked with bodily instruments unaided by objects as or more resistant to modification – that is, as a rule, by other stones co-opted for the purpose (Kitahara-Frisch 1978: 104). To be precise, then, we should substitute for the phrase 'using tools to make tools' the self-conscious co-option of naturefacts (such as stone pebbles) for artefact production, as in the following formula:

$$\text{Co-option}$$
$$S' \subset T_1' \subset T_2' \xrightarrow{\hspace{2cm}} T_2 \supset T_1 \supset S,$$

where T_1 is the artefact to be produced (a tool for realizing end-state S), and T_2 the co-opted naturefact. Likewise the phrase 'making tools to make tools' would be replaced by the same formula, but substituting construction for co-option in the image–object relation T_2'–T_2. Note, however, that this formula expressly *excludes* cases when a tool is constructed or co-opted for use in a task that is not itself constructive, but which yields a product that happens to come in handy for another, subsequent project for which it was not designed. In other words, the construction or co-option of T_2 must be preceded not only by a conception of its use in making T_1, but also by a conception of the use of T_1 in realizing S – and by virtue of which T_1 qualifies as a tool. In his imagination, then, the subject must picture himself two steps ahead of the task in hand. The hunter, selecting a stone with which to sharpen the point of his spear, already has in mind the use of the spear in killing game.

There is no denying that the logical operations represented by the left-hand side of the above formula involve a degree of reflexivity far beyond the capacity of any being not endowed with what Cassirer (1944: 33) calls 'symbolic imagination and intelligence'. The singular ability of human beings, who *are* thus endowed, is to convert their own subjective conceptions of the world into objects of reflection, from whose exploration in thought it is possible to derive the principles for generating novel conceptions corresponding to no already existing state. In application, these principles constitute a technology for actualizing such conceptions, that is, for the construction of an artificial environment. Standing in a patch of virgin forest a man may visualize a house and fields, and set to work to build his farm, but not without first having conceived and made the necessary tools for the job. Moreover, whereas the unselfconscious constructor, human or non-human, can only execute the equipment for a *given* project, according to received instructions genetically inherited or acquired through observational learning, the self-conscious tool-maker can design and build the equipment for *any* project – often enough by deliberately copying the innate equipment of other animals. 'An animal', as Marx long ago observed, 'forms things in accordance with the standards and need of the species to which it belongs, whilst man knows how to produce in accordance with the standard of every species' (1964: 113–14).

One of the first to recognize the reflexivity of human tool-making was Bergson, who regarded as the fundamental characteristic of an intelligence unique to man the faculty of making tools to make tools, '*and of indefinitely varying the manufacture*'. What he called instinct, to the contrary, involves 'nothing but the utilization of a specific instrument for a specific object' (Bergson 1911: 146–7). To the human intellect, the world of nature does not appear as it does to an instinct, already organized (like the body of which it forms an extension) for the execution of a given project, but simply as disorganized raw material which may be turned to account for any purpose whatever. That is why Bergson chose to characterize the instruments constructed and used by intelligent design – or as we would say, self-consciously – as *unorganized* rather than *organized*, meaning that the principles of their organization are in no wise intrinsic to the material. Today we would express the same contrast by the opposition between the *arbitrary* and the *iconic*, where the former term denotes the absence of any 'necessary relation between the form of the final product and the original material' (Holloway 1969: 401). The tool that is truly artificial is one that is 'called up' not by the presence of an environmental object, but by an entirely independent conception in the mind of the subject. Thus in his distinction between the unorganized instruments of mankind and the organized instruments of other animals, Bergson anticipated a much more modern definition of that which is distinctively *human* in culture, or more specifically in tool-making, namely what Holloway calls 'the *imposition of arbitrary form upon the environment*' (1969: 395).

Bergson's *Homo faber* is therefore also, and necessarily, *Homo cogitans*, the man who thinks before he works. We need but add the qualification that *real* men, for much of the time, do not act like this, and indeed normal social life would probably be impossible if they did. To claim that men are distinguished from other animals by a unique cognitive capacity is not to assume that this capacity is engaged more than intermittently in the governance of conduct (rather than, for example, in reflecting upon it after the event). However, in our formula for reflexive tool-making, the left-hand side truly epitomizes the competence of *Homo cogitans*, the right-hand side that of *Homo faber*. The former focuses on *symbolic intelligence* as the foundation for human *technology*, the latter focuses on *practical adaptability* as the crux of human *technique*. Thus:

Homo cogitans	*Homo faber*
$S' \subset T_1' \subset T_2' \quad\longrightarrow$	$T_2 \supset T_1 \supset S$
Symbolic intelligence	Practical adaptability
Technology	Technique

Moreover as the locus of intelligent design is the brain, so the principal somatic instrument of constructive adaptability is the hand. Characterizing human tools in the *Grundrisse*, Marx specifies both components; thus tools are '*organs of the human brain, created by the human hand*; the power of knowledge, objectified' (1973: 706). As a definition of artificially manufactured instruments, this would be hard to beat (Heyer 1982: 93).

Is man a product of culture?

The interdependent development, in human evolution, of tools, the brains that designed them, and the hands that shaped them, is nowadays well established. It has become almost a cliché to say that biological man is not just the producer of culture but its product (Geertz 1965: 42). Yet over a century ago, and barely five years after the publication of Darwin's *The Descent of Man*, the same point was being made by Engels. For its time, his essay of 1876 on 'the transition from ape to man' must rank as first-class anthropological speculation, whose originality subsequent commentators have been somewhat reluctant to recognize. One recent advocate, however, has gone so far as to claim that the essay 'is a brilliant scientific anticipation of what is now thought . . . to be the likely pattern of early human evolution' (Woolfson 1982: 3). But if he got the pattern roughly right, his explanation of the mechanism by which it came about is almost completely wrong. For Engels, everything hinged on *labour*, so that 'in a sense, we have to say that labour created man himself' (1934: 170). It is quite clear from his subsequent remarks that this sense rests entirely on the assumption that the special qualities acquired by an individual through the use of his bodily organs will be passed on by physical inheritance to offspring (Venable 1975: 69–73). Like virtually everyone else at that time, Darwin included, Engels accepted as a matter of course the doctrine of the inheritance of acquired characteristics. In particular, he believed that newly acquired dietary habits would produce heritable changes in the chemical composition of the blood, and that the diversity of substances entering the body – following from an increasingly omnivorous diet – constituted 'the chemical premises for the transition to man' (1934: 175–6).

Consider the chain of reasoning by which he connects tool-making with the enlargement of the brain. 'In the proper sense of the word', he declares, 'labour begins with the making of tools'. What were the first tools? Hunting (and fishing) implements. What does this indicate? The adoption of a meat diet. And the meat diet, besides 'giving bodily strength and independence to man in the making', more importantly 'had its greatest effect on the brain, which now received a far richer flow of the materials necessary for its nourishment and development, and which, therefore, could develop more rapidly and perfectly from generation to generation' (1934: 176). Human evolution, then, appeared to Engels as an extended body-building exercise, in which each generation augments the accumulated achievement of its predecessors, playing its part in a total process of development. In like vein, he maintained that the human hand has reached its presently 'high degree of perefection' by dint of the efforts of past generations in striving to master new and ever more complicated operations. Through constant exercise, muscles, ligaments and (more slowly) bones undergo special development, and every improvement in finesse is inherited. Thus when Engels pronounced that 'the hand is not only the organ of labour, *it is also the product of labour*', he meant it to be taken quite literally (1934: 172). If the pianist's strong fingers can be put down to the effects of practice continued from an early age, man's opposable thumb and precision grip are the results of practice continued from the days of his earliest ancestors.

In hindsight, it is easy to see that Engels's entire argument concerning the concurrent development of natural and artificial organs in human evolution rests on a failure to comprehend the essence of the distinction between them. It is that so-called 'Lamarckian inheritance' is precisely what characterizes the transmission of artificial *as opposed to* innate equipment (Steadman 1979: 129–30). Both the hand and the axe are organs of labour, the latter is also its product, the former is not. We could certainly say of the artificially manufactured instrument that it builds on the accumulated experience of previous generations in adapting to new circumstances through consciously induced modification. But that is not how the human body was built.[8] Perhaps we should not chide Engels overmuch for an error that was common to the greatest minds of his day. Rather more worrying is the fact that contemporary literature is full of pronouncements on what Dobzhansky (1963) called the 'cultural direction of human evolution' which do not differ in substance from what we read in Engels. At best, such pronouncements are a highly disingenuous shorthand for what is actually going on; at worst they are simply wrong. Here is one glaring example:

The diversity and intricacy of man's manual activities gradually modified the bone structure of his hands and the nerves and muscles exercised when seizing prey, a tool or a piece of food... The human brain was begotten by the human hand – or, more precisely, by hunting. (Moscovici 1976: 56)

Scarcely less misleading is Washburn's assertion, with regard to the impact of tool using and making on human evolution, that 'each behavioral stage was both cause and effect of biological change in bones and brain' (1960: 75).

The trouble with such statements lies in their fostering of the impression that tool use and manufacture generate anatomical modification in just the same way that brain and hand combine in the generation of tools. Nothing could be further from the truth. The human body has reached its present form as a result of a process of variation under natural selection, which did not cease to operate with the advent of culture. But in no branch of nature are the conditions of selection for a population of organisms given by the environment alone; rather these conditions are constituted by the manner in which the components of the environment are harnessed to the teleonomic projects of the organisms themselves. In other words, the effective environment of selection for a population depends on what the individuals of the population are organized to do in it (Waddington 1960: 400–1). Selective pressures favoured the development of the woodpecker's protrusile tongue *because* its project was to probe for insects in the crevices of trees. Put another bird, with a different project, in the same environment, and quite another set of pressures will be operative. Natural selection thus constitutes a kind of feedback nexus whereby the organism, through its behaviour, 'elects' the premises of its own adaptation. How is it, then, with a being that already possesses an embryonic capacity to solve problems of *specific* adaptation through the *artificial* selection, and subsequent implementation, of conceptual variants – that is, through self-conscious design? Limiting the cultural to the artificial, we could say of such a being that its project is culture, and that in the adoption of this project, selective pressures inevitably swing in favour of bodily modifications – notably of the brain and hand, as instruments of design and implementation respectively – which enhance generalized adaptability. But it makes no more sense to say that man, through his cultural behaviour, created his hand and brain than it does to say that the woodpecker, through its insect-probing behaviour, created its long tongue. Man's work, his labouring activity, may certainly have established the conditions for the further adaptive modification of his somatic attributes, determining which variations were to be 'notched up' in the course of natural selection, but it *did not bring the modification about.*

The co-discoverer of natural selection, A. R. Wallace, was the first to suggest that because of man's capacity to adapt to diverse circumstances through the design of artefacts, selection would tend to favour a one-way advance in the generalized faculty of intellect. In *The Descent of Man*, Darwin merely reiterated Wallace's argument, though he could not accept – as Wallace had done, and as we do today – that the intelligence of supposedly 'primitive' folk is on a level with that of the most 'civilized' nations (Wallace 1870: 302–31, Darwin 1874: 195–224). The argument ran that individuals who were 'more sagacious' (as Darwin was wont to say), having bigger and better brains, could design more ingenious tools, which would confer on their users a reproductive advantage. This in turn would ensure the differential preservation, in future generations, of intelligence-enhancing variations, leading to yet further advances in technology and technique, and so on through mutual reinforcement – or what Wilson has recently called 'autocatalysis' (1978: 84–5). Contemporary elaborations of the interconnectedness of the innate and the artificial during the formative period of human evolution, or in the process of what is now called 'hominization', have added little to the original argument. However, whether the dependence *for survival* on tools purposefully made and used, which is sometimes claimed as the hallmark of the specifically 'human' level of culture (Mann 1972: 382), has been the sole or even the principal condition behind the evolution of intelligence, is a matter of some dispute. It could well be, as Humphrey (1976) has suggested, that the crucial selective test lies in the individual's ability to manipulate not the inanimate objects of his environment but *other individuals* in his social group, and to cope with the demands of an ever-shifting configuration of relations with conspecifics. In short, rather than having anything very much to do with the construction and use of tools, or with strategies of subsistence (Parker and Gibson 1979: 370), the key to the evolution of intelligence may reside in the pressures of sociality.

Tool-making and language

Now it is clear that the modifications of the hominid brain that laid the foundations for symbolic intelligence cannot be dissociated from those which gave rise to the principal vehicle of that intelligence – namely propositional language. Hence any discussion of the relation between tool-making and intelligence must inevitably draw us into the problem of its relation to language. This is a large and fascinating topic, which can only be summarily dealt with in the present essay. The question it raises can be simply put as follows: do the intellectual operations represented by the left-hand side of our formula for reflexive tool-making presuppose a language capacity unique to mankind? Are we to agree, with Révész, that 'since conscious purpose and the invention of tools are based on mental processes that require linguistic fixation, we are justified in identifying *Homo faber* with *Homo loquens*' (1956: 93)? Many have argued that this is so, in other words that language is the essential instrument of conception, without which it would be impossible to envisage ends in advance of their realization. As long ago as 1927, de Laguna doubted whether the art of tool-making, necessitating conceptual thought, 'could have been developed by men who had not yet learned to speak' (1927: 218). Her views have been echoed more recently by Oakley, the outstanding modern advocate of a definition of man as *the* tool-making primate. Man, Oakley maintains, is basically an artist according to the Aristotelian definition of art which 'consists in the conception of the result to be produced before its realization in the material' (1954: 14). Moreover,

It is extraordinarily difficult, if not impossible, to think effectively, to plan, or to invent, without the use of words or equivalent symbols. Most of our constructive thinking is done in unsounded words. (1954: 18)

Oakley goes on to suggest that the repertoire of verbal symbols, indeed language itself, is a 'tool which had to be invented'. Here he undoubtedly over-steps the mark: for if language is used, it is certainly not made, being founded on convention rather than invention (Wagner 1975: 51). Indeed, natural languages constitute the epitome of what is *non*-artificial in culture, standing in this sense opposed to such formal symbolic systems as mathematics.

It could further be objected that the internal image preceding the realization of the artefact may be purely pictorial, and may equally precede any attempt to put it into words. Furthermore, tool techniques could have been informally transmitted for any length of time merely through visual observation and imitation (Hewes 1973a: 8). Yet linguistic description must be an essential part of the transmission of design by *teaching*, enabling the novice equipped with a set of verbal directions to make a tool of a given type without having previously encountered anything of the kind (Wilson 1980: 145–6). The capacity to pass on technical traditions through intentional linguistic instruction must, as Guilmet (1977: 43) notes, have instigated a major change in hominid tool-making, towards greater regularity and conformity to ideal patterns. It may be, then, that the major contribution of language to tool-making lies not in invention but in the *standardization* of arbitrary design rules, allowing for the accurate replication of highly differentiated artificial assemblages (Isaac 1976). It is difficult, Hallowell writes,

to imagine how the manufacture of tools, and the development of tool-making traditions could have arisen at a protocultural stage at which the mechanism of

social transmission was exclusively observational learning and at which communication was mediated by signs rather than through any form of symbolic
representation. (1962: 248)

More to the point, perhaps, it is difficult to see how, without symbolic
communication, tool traditions could assume the cumulative and progressive character, with each successive generation actively augmenting
received knowledge through fresh discovery, that appears to us to be
unique to the history of human works.

Admittedly, non-human animals have been known to hit upon new
techniques, and the novelties can diffuse through a local population by
imitative learning – supporting claims that these animals have 'social
customs' or 'behaviour dialects'. That most of the evidence for such
so-called cultural variation comes from studies of monkeys and apes,
particularly chimpanzees (McGrew and Tutin 1978), may simply reflect a
biased expectation on the part of observers who assume that if learning-
transmitted patterns of tool construction are not unique to man, they
must be shared at most by those few non-human species whose level of
intelligence comes closest to our own. Reed, for example, maintains that
learned techniques of construction, which he calls 'cultural', are limited to
'a few kinds of primates and perhaps elephants', and that all other
instances of constructive behaviour are entirely instinctive (1985: 97). Yet
Jones and Kamil (1973) have described the serendipitous acquisition and
dissemination, through imitation, of a behavioural sequence involving
tool construction and use among captive blue jays. There is no reason to
believe that this example is in any way exceptional. Indeed in an attack on
what he sees as 'chimpocentric' bias in cognitive ethology, Beck (1982)
has argued that the learned behaviour of herring gulls in dropping
molluscs on rocks to break the shells and gain access to the edible
contents is every bit as sophisticated as the reported tool techniques of
chimpanzees. There is a world of difference, however, between the
origination of technique through accident or blind variation, and through
inventive insight; and between its dissemination through observational
learning and through teaching. Every innovation, in the former case,
remains as a disconnected trait, passively acquired, rather than being
integrated into a coherent and developing technological tradition.
Invention and teaching, by contrast, involve the symbolic articulation of
makers' and users' knowledge, that is, of a technology. And Beck's herring
gulls are no more capable of this than are chimpanzees, amongst which,
as White put it, 'one generation is no further advanced than its pre-
decessor' (1942: 371).

Another argument for the relation between language and tool-making,
rather than supposing that the one – in providing a medium for invention

and teaching – is a prerequisite for the other, posits that both are the con-
cordant derivatives of a single, more fundamental cognitive mechanism
(Holloway 1969: 404). Proponents of this view point to what appear to be
close analogies between the processes involved in the production of tools
and in the production of utterances. For example, tool-making is said
to share all the 'design features' identified by Hockett as unique to
human language – notably *displacement, reflexiveness* and *prevarication*
(Hockett 1963). The first is exemplified by the capacity both to talk about,
and to make tools for use in, environments remote in space and time from
those which presently surround the subject, and indeed which he may
never have encountered. The second consists both in speaking about
what is spoken, and in making tools to make tools (Kitahara-Frisch 1978:
105–6). Linguistic prevarication, the production of utterances whose
meaning is founded upon deception or illusion, has its analogue in the
production of those tools we call toys – objects with which we *pretend* to
change the world. At another level, it is suggested that as words are
combined according to syntactical rules to produce unique utterances, so
a 'vocabulary' of motor operations may be combined, in a similarly rule-
governed way, to produce unique tool forms (Holloway 1969: 402). 'There
exists', as Montagu suggests, 'a grammar of tool-making in much the same
sense that there exists a grammar of language and of speech'; between
them there is 'a certain isomorphism' indicative of some common derivation (1976: 269–70). But Montagu errs in identifying the mental analogue
of the tool as the word. If the grammatical isomorphism holds, then tools
correspond to complete utterances, and elementary motor events to
spoken words (see also Lieberman 1975: 165–70).

The pronounced lateralization of the human brain lends additional
weight to the connection between language and tool-making, since the
latter depends on manual skills whose underlying neural programmes,
just like those underlying the effective production of speech, are principally localized in the dominant hemisphere. Moreover, a lesion in this
area of the brain can affect motor skills in just the same way as it affects
speaking: the patient can produce and recognize individual words or
perform elementary motor acts, but cannot put them together into
coherent, structured sequences to yield complete utterances or skilled
performances. All this suggests that the ultimate 'deep structure' wherein
are enshrined the universal properties of human language is really a
'fundamental capacity to acquire and utilize complex patterned sequences', which finds expression equally in tool manipulation as in
speech (Hewes 1973b: 109). 'In the long course of hominization', Hewes
suggests, 'it is the evolutionary growth in this kind of syntactic capacity
that has been so important, and not its separate manifestations in technology and language' (1973b: 109–10). This leads him to propose that the

original propositional language operated through manual gestures rather than spoken words, since such language would employ the same 'gestural–visual' channel as is employed in the construction and use of tools – both involving patterned sequences of hand movements in the generation of a product. Only as a result of subsequent cognitive enhancement, unrelated specifically to language, were conditions established for the cross-modal transfer from the gestural–visual channel to the vocal–auditory channel employed in speech.

This is a controversial theory, which comes close to treating tool-use and language-use not merely as analogous but as identical phenomena. At the other extreme are views which hold that there is no particular connection between language and tool behaviour at all. Though undeniably, language may have given a certain impetus to technological development, it is argued that the conditions that favoured the emergence of language lay not in man's relations to objects of the external world, but in his relations to fellow subjects. 'It seems to us', write Steklis and Harnad, 'that the source of insights as to language-origins is more likely to be in the dialogue between man and man than between man and tool' (1976: 450). According to this view, language did not evolve as a means for the identification of *things*, or for attaching concepts to objects as in their self-conscious co-option for use. That is to say, its original function was not – as Lancaster (1968b: 456) has argued – one of *naming* or environmental reference, allowing humans to communicate information about raw materials, or about animal or plant resources, that may be of strategic value in the conduct of co-operative foraging activities. Its primary significance lay rather in the identification of *persons*, of the self *vis-à-vis* the other, 'I' as against 'you', 'us' as against 'them'. In short, far from emerging as an adjunct to the organization of work, or as a tool for practical co-operation, language developed as an instrument for the negotiation of personal identity – that is, for the management of inter-subjectivity.[9] This view is of course consistent with the idea, presented at the end of the previous section, that the challenges posed by social living, and not by the physical environment, established an initial selective bias in favour of the development of the advanced cognitive capacities in which the facility of language is based. Only subsequently, with the elaboration of tool traditions that language made possible, would tool-use and manufacture have become significant spurs to the further evolution of intelligence (Beck 1980: 246).

The human transformation of nature

To draw our discussion to a close, I should like to return once more to Engels, and to the problem with which I began: in what sense can we say that man, through his labour and his tools, has worked a *transformation* on his environment? Here is Engels at his most emphatic:

In short, the animal merely *uses* its environment, and brings about changes in it simply by its presence; man by his changes makes it serve his ends, *masters* it. This is the final, essential distinction between man and other animals, and once again it is labour that brings about this distinction. (1934: 179–80)

Now when he comes to give concrete examples of such mastery, Engels invariably turns to the activities of plant and animal husbandry, to agriculture and pastoralism. 'The animal', he writes, 'destroys the vegetation of a locality without realizing what it is doing. Man destroys it in order to sow field crops on the soil thus released, or to plant trees or vines which he knows will yield many times the amount planted' (1934: 178). Moreover through selective breeding man has changed certain animal and plant species beyond recognition, and through the importation of domestic breeds he has so altered the fauna and flora of entire continents 'that the consequences of his activity can disappear only with the general extinction of the terrestrial globe' (1934: 34). Not that nature fails to take its revenge: thus Engels bemoans the long-term effects of agricultural clearance and deforestation in desiccating the landscape. Yet he is optimistic that through the advance of scientific knowledge, and its rational application, we may control even the more remote consequences of our present activities. In the last resort, then, our mastery over nature consists – no more and no less – 'in the fact that we have the advantage over all other creatures of being able to learn its laws and apply them correctly' (1934: 180).

This is an advantage, presumably, shared by all men. But in opposing non-human animals, which do not deliberately modify their environment, to human agriculturalists and pastoralists who do, Engels completely leaves out of account the condition of mankind for the greater part of his existence on this earth – namely, as a hunter and gatherer. Are hunters and gatherers to be regarded as the masters of their environment, or do they merely 'use' it? Of course they make and use tools, often of considerable complexity and sophistication. Moreover they possess an intimate knowledge of the natural world, in many respects unrivalled even by western science (Laughlin 1968: 314–15). However in its practical application, this knowledge is used not to reconstruct the world, but to draw a subsistence from an essentially *unmodified* environment.[10] The activities of hunters and gatherers have not, by and large, had the intended environmental consequences which Engels perceives to flow from human 'mastery', that is from *production* in the specific sense reserved for man:

The most that the animal can achieve is to *collect*; man *produces*, he prepares the means of life, in the widest sense of the words, which without him nature would not have produced. This makes impossible any unqualified transference of the laws of life in animal societies to human society. (1934: 308)[11]

According to this formulation, the collector merely takes for his liveli-hood what resoures nature has to offer, rather than intervening directly in the process of their reproduction. As the archaeologist V. G. Childe was later to write, in terms immediately reminiscent of Engels, with food production men became 'active partners with nature instead of parasites on nature' (1942: 55). Yet Childe's concern was to delimit the rubicon that divides not man from other animals, but 'neolithic' men and their suc-cessors from 'palaeolithic' hunters and gatherers, representing the stages of 'barbarism' and 'savagery' respectively. Ever since then, it has been customary to assert that only pastoralists and agriculturalists literally *produce* their food, and that hunters and gatherers – for all their humanity, knowledge and expertise – are but food-*collectors*. The origins of production, it is commonly supposed, do not lie in the inception of tool-making, rather they are to be found in the domestication of plants and animals, or more generally, in the constructive modification of the environment.

Now throughout our discussion of tool-making we have emphasized the need to distinguish between, on the one hand, the authorship of plans, and on the other, the adaptive modification of environmental objects. It is the failure to recognize precisely the same distinction that has led to the ambiguities noted above in the conception of man's mastery over nature. Do we say that mastery lies in the rational application of technological knowledge, in self-conscious planning? Then hunters and gatherers are masters, even though they do not seek to construct an artificial environ-ment. Do we say that mastery lies in the alteration of the environment, so that its ecologically productive potential may be harnessed more efficiently to given needs? Then hunters and gatherers are not masters but users, whereas human agriculturalists join company with certain species of attine ants, which quite instinctively intervene in the reproduction of their food resources by executing operations formally identical to those of cultivation (Reed 1977: 15–17). Of course the difference between the human farmer and the ant, just as that between the human architect and the bee, is that the former begins work with an idea already established in his imagination of the nature of the end-result. Like the architect's house, the farmer's field is artificial, *engineered* by human action.

How, then, should we comprehend the environment of the hunter–gatherer, which although bent to his purpose is not especially modified for it? Recall the stone that, according to our earlier example, is har-nessed in its 'natural' state to my purpose of bottle opening. Likewise the environment of the hunter–gatherer *is not constructed but co-opted, it is not artificial but 'natureficial'*. Human foragers are to be distinguished from their non-human counterparts in so far as their world does not initially appear to them 'ready-made', in terms of the opportunities afforded for the execution of a received project, but rather confronts them as a set of generalized potentials waiting to be organized in accordance with a project of their own design. They must therefore begin by *making* their world, imposing an arbitrary ordering of concepts, constitutive of 'culture', upon objects in the landscape, constitutive of 'nature' (Ellen 1982: 252–3). But in making the world, supplying every object with a concept of its use (thereby turning it into a use-value), they do not physically *change* it – not at least to any radical extent. From the fact that they do not, we would be mistaken to infer that they are subservient to natural laws to a degree that agriculturalists and pastoralists have overcome. For to conclude, *it is in the self-conscious co-option of unmodified nature, whether internal or external to the body, that man's original mastery resides.*

Notes to Chapter 3

1   In this broad sense, instruments are equivalent to what Gibson (1979: 127) calls the *affordances* of an environment, that which 'it *offers* the animal, what it *provides* or *furnishes*, either for good or ill'. Thus 'air affords breathing'; whilst a 'horizontal, flat, extended, rigid surface affords support'. Such a surface, commonly called a ground or floor, is 'stand-on-able, . . . walk-on-able and run-over-able' (Gibson 1979: 127, 130–1). The earth, as Marx wrote in similar vein, 'provides the worker with the platform for all his operations' (1930: 173).

2   According to McGrew, Tutin and Baldwin (1979: 189), a tool is to be defined as 'a detached, inanimate object used to facilitate acquisition of a goal'. Likewise for van Lawick-Goodall (1970: 195), the tool is 'an external object [used] as a functional extension of mouth or beak, hand or claw, in the attainment of an immediate goal'. In another formulation, by Alcock, 'tool-using involves the manipulation of an inanimate object, not internally manufactured, with the effect of improving the animal's efficiency in altering the position or form of some separate object' (1972: 464). The most elaborate definition of tool-using in this genre, provided by Beck (1980: 10), is cited below (see p. 48).
    Adopting a somewhat different approach, Reed agrees that tools are external to the body of the user, but argues that their most salient characteristic is that they function as 'secondary energy traps' – that is, as aids for acquiring or conserving energy on behalf of an organism which is itself a 'primary energy trap'. But if all tools are secondary traps, not all such traps are tools: for example the cart is a tool, the domestic horse that pulls it is not, yet the latter functions as a secondary energy trap since its power lies at the disposal of its human master. Focusing on the function of both animate and inanimate objects as secondary energy traps, the subsidiary distinction

between tools and non-tools seems unimportant, since all such objects 'provide means for utilization or conservation of energy which would not have been available to a particular animal were it limited to the use of its own body without the additional help of the external object' (Reed 1977: 13–14; 1985).

3   Fascinating evidence for the use of stones as hammers and anvils by free-ranging chimpanzees is provided by Sugiyama and Koman (1979: 516–18), and by Boesch and Boesch (1982).

4   From filmed observations made among the Aboriginal people of Yuendumu, Central Australia, Barrett has reported the use of teeth not only for mastication but also for the non-masticatory purposes of holding, peeling, stripping, gripping, sharpening and fighting (Barrett 1977: 20–1).

5   See Menzel (1972; 1973) and McGrew *et al.* (1975) for a remarkable blow-by-blow account of the apparent invention, elaboration and dissemination of the ladder as an escape technique among chimpanzees in a naturalistic enclosure. By these means, the animals confounded human attempts to keep them confined by ringing standing tree trunks with electric shock wires.

6   Knowing that human tools *are* the products of an advanced intelligence rather than an instinct, we can of course seek evidence for its evolution by examining changes in the design properties of these tools. Employing Piagetian epistemology, Wynn (1979; 1981) has compared the geometrical form of stone tools constructed and used almost two million years ago by Oldowan hominids with those of Acheulean man from about 300,000 B.P. He concludes that whereas the former manifest no more than a pre-operational intelligence, also typical of modern apes, the latter demonstrate a fully operational intelligence equivalent to that of contemporary humans. On the basis of these results he argues that the evolution of intelligence became significant in human evolution only after about 1.6 million years ago, but that the intellectual abilities of modern man were reached much earlier than previously thought.

7   Van Lawick Goodall makes the same point through another example: 'The larva of the ant-lion (Cicindelidae spp.) which flings grains of sand to knock struggling insects further into its funnel-shaped pit is no more "gifted" than is the larva of the dragonfly (Anisoptera spp.) which has developed a hinged, elongated labium which it shoots out to grasp a passing prey. One has evolved a behavioural mechanism which performs a similar function to the structural mechanism of the other' (1970: 244).

8   I exclude from consideration here those aspects in which the body can itself be treated as an artefact. The case of body decoration has already been mentioned; perhaps more significant is the surgical replacement or reconstruction of limbs and other somatic organs. The totally artificial human fortunately remains – at least for the foreseeable future – a subject of science fiction rather than the real world.

9   This point is taken up again in Chapter 5.

10 An exception to this rule, perhaps of greater import than we are inclined to admit, is the deliberate use of fire by hunter–gatherers, in order to maintain a productive vegetation cover attractive to favoured species of prey (Lewis 1982). This kind of planned, long-range modification must of course be distinguished from the unintended, though possibly beneficial consequences of fires

lit for immediate extractive purposes such as flushing out game or signalling, which have been allowed to spread unchecked (Oakley 1962: 183). Only in the former case is it appropriate to speak, with Jones, of 'fire-stick farming' (Jones 1969, Gould 1971), or of the construction of an artificial environment.

11 Elsewhere, in *The German Ideology*, Marx and Engels similarly take production to be the essential hallmark of human activity. Men, they say, 'begin to distinguish themselves from animals as soon as they begin to *produce* their means of subsistence, a step which is conditioned by their physical organization. By producing their means of subsistence men are indirectly producing their actual material life' (1977: 42). But in this they come close to insinuating that hunters and gatherers, by their very nature, are not yet proper representatives of mankind!

References for Chapter 3

Alcock, J. 1972 The evolution of the use of tools by feeding animals. *Evolution* **26**: 464–73.

Alexander, C. 1964 *Notes on the synthesis of form.* Cambridge, Mass.: Harvard University Press.

Barrett, M. J. 1977 Masticatory and non-masticatory uses of teeth. In *Stone tools as cultural markers: change, evolution and complexity,* ed. R.V.S. Wright. Canberra: Australian Institute of Aboriginal Studies.

Beck, B. B. 1980 *Animal tool behavior: the use and manufacture of tools by animals.* New York: Garland STPM Press.

Beck, B. B. 1982 Chimpocentrism: bias in cognitive ethology. *Journal of Human Evolution* **11**: 3–17.

Bergson, H. 1911 *Creative evolution.* London: Macmillan.

Boesch, C. and H. Boesch 1982 Optimization of nut-cracking with natural hammers by wild chimpanzees. *Behaviour* **83**: 265–86.

Bohm, D. 1980 *Wholeness and the implicate order.* London: Routledge and Kegan Paul.

Cassirer, E. 1944 *An essay on man.* New Haven, Conn.: Yale University Press.

Childe, V. G. 1942 *What happened in history.* Harmondsworth, Middx.: Penguin.

Cohen, G. A. 1978 *Karl Marx's theory of history: a defence.* Oxford University Press.

Darwin, C. 1874 *The descent of man and selection in relation to sex* (second edition). London: John Murray.

Dawkins, R. 1982 *The extended phenotype: the gene as the unit of selection.* San Francisco: W. H. Freeman.

de Laguna, G. A. 1927 *Speech: its function and development.* New Haven, Conn.: Yale University Press.

Dobzhansky, T. 1963 Cultural direction of human evolution. *Human Biology* **35**: 311–16.

Ellen, R. F. 1962 *Environment, subsistence and system: the ecology of small-scale social formations.* Cambridge University Press.

Engels, F. 1934 *Dialectics of nature.* Moscow: Progress.

Geertz, C. 1965 The transition to humanity. In *Horizons of anthropology,* ed. S. Tax.

London: Allen and Unwin.

Geertz, C. 1966 Religion as a cultural system. In *Anthropological approaches to the study of religion*, ed. M. Banton (A.S.A. monogr. 3). London: Tavistock.

Gibson, J. J. 1979 *The ecological approach to visual perception*. Boston: Houghton Mifflin.

Gould, R. A. 1971 Uses and effects of fire among the Western Desert aborigines of Australia. *Mankind* **8**: 14–24.

Gould, S. J. and E. S. Vrba 1982 Exaptation – a missing term in the science of form. *Paleobiology* **8**: 4–15.

Gruber, A. 1969 A functional definition of primate tool-making. *Man* (N.S.) **4**: 573–9.

Guilmet, G. 1977 The evolution of tool-using and tool-making behaviour. *Man* (N.S.) **12**: 33–47.

Hall, K. 1963 Tool-using performances as indicators of behavioral adaptability. *Current Anthropology* **4**: 479–94.

Hallowell, A. I. 1956 The structural and functional dimensions of human existence. *Quarterly Review of Biology* **31**: 88–101.

Hallowell, A. I. 1962 The protocultural foundations of human adaptation. In *Social life of early man*, ed. S. L. Washburn. London: Methuen.

Harnad, S., H. Steklis, and J. Lancaster (eds.) 1976 *Origins and evolution of language and speech*. New York Academy of Sciences.

Hewes, G. 1973a Primate communication and the gestural origin of language. *Current Anthropology* **14**: 5–12.

Hewes, G. 1973b An explicit formulation of the relationship between tool-using, tool-making, and the emergence of language. *Visible Language* **7**: 101–27.

Heyer, P. 1982 *Nature, human nature and society: Marx, Darwin and the human sciences*. Westport, Conn.: Greenwood Press.

Hockett, C. F. 1963 The problem of universals in language. In *Universals of language*, ed. J. H. Greenberg. Cambridge, Mass.: M.I.T. Press.

Holloway, R. L. 1969 Culture, a *human* domain. *Current Anthropology* **10**: 395–412.

Humphrey, N. 1976 The social function of intellect. In *Growing points in ethology*, eds. P. Bateson and R. Hinde. Cambridge University Press.

Isaac, G. 1976 Stages of cultural elaboration in the Pleistocene: possible archaeological indicators of the development of language capabilities. In *Origins and evolution of language and speech*, eds. S. Harnad, H. Steklis and J. Lancaster. New York Academy of Sciences.

Jacob, F. 1977 Evolution and tinkering. *Science* **196**: 1161–6.

Jones, R. 1969 Fire-stick farming. *Australian Natural History* **16**: 224–8.

Jones, T. B. and A. C. Kamil 1973 Tool-making and tool-using in the northern blue jay. *Science* **180**: 1076–8.

Kitahara-Frisch, J. 1978 Stone tools as indicators of linguistic abilities in early man. *Annals of the Japan Association for Philosophy of Science* **5**: 101–9.

Lancaster, J. 1968a On the evolution of tool-using behavior. *American Anthropologist* **70**: 56–66.

Lancaster, J. 1968b Primate communication systems and the emergence of human language. In *Primates – studies in adaptation and variability*, ed. P. Jay. New York: Holt, Rinehart and Winston.

Laughlin, W. S. 1968 Hunting: an integrating biobehavior system and its evolutionary importance. In *Man the hunter*, eds. R. B. Lee and I. DeVore. Chicago: Aldine.

Lewis, H. T. 1982 Fire technology and resource management in aboriginal North America and Australia. In *Resource managers: North American and Australian hunter–gatherers*, eds. N. M. Williams and E. S. Hunn (AAAS Selected Symposium 67). Boulder, Colorado: Westview Press.

Lieberman, P. 1975 *On the origins of language*. New York: Macmillan.

Lotka, A. J. 1945 The law of evolution as a maximal principle. *Human Biology* **17**: 167–94.

McGrew, W. C. and C. E. G. Tutin 1978 Evidence for a social custom in wild chimpanzees. *Man* (N.S.) **13**: 234–51.

McGrew, W. C., C. E. G. Tutin and P. J. Baldwin 1979 Chimpanzees, tools and termites: cross cultural comparisons of Senegal, Tanzania and Rio Muni. *Man* (N.S.) **14**: 185–214.

McGrew, W. C., C. E. G. Tutin and P. S. Midgett, Jr. 1975 Tool use in a group of captive chimpanzees, I: Escape. *Zeitschrift für Tierpsychologie* **37**: 145–62.

Mann, A. 1972 Hominid and cultural origins. *Man* (N.S.) **7**: 379–96.

Marx, K. 1930 *Capital*. London: Dent.

Marx, K. 1964 *Economic and political manuscripts of 1844*. New York: International Publishers.

Marx, K. 1973 *Grundrisse*. Harmondsworth, Middx.: Penguin.

Marx, K. and F. Engels 1977 *The German ideology*, ed. C. J. Arthur. London: Lawrence and Wishart.

Medawar, P. B. 1957 *The uniqueness of the individual*. London: Methuen.

Menzel, E. W. 1972 Spontaneous invention of ladders in a group of young chimpanzees. *Folia Primatologica* **17**: 87–106.

Menzel, E. W. 1973 Further observations on the use of ladders in a group of young chimpanzees. *Folia Primatologica* **19**: 450–7.

Monod, J. 1972 *Chance and necessity*. London: Collins.

Montagu, A. 1976 Tool-making, hunting and the origins of language. In *Origins and evolution of language and speech*, eds. S. Harnad, H. Steklis and J. Lancaster. New York Academy of Sciences.

Moscovici, S. 1976 *Society against nature*. Brighton: Harvester Press.

Oakley, K. P. 1954 Skill as a human possession. In *A History of technology, I: From early times to the fall of ancient empires*, eds. C. Singer, E. J. Holmyard and A. R. Hall. Oxford University Press.

Oakley, K. P. 1962 On man's use of fire, with comments on tool-making and hunting. In *Social life of early man*, ed. S. L. Washburn. London: Methuen.

Oswalt, W. 1973 *Habitat and technology*. New York: Holt, Rinehart and Winston.

Parker, S. T. and K. Gibson 1979 A developmental model for the evolution of language and intelligence in early hominids. *The Behavioural and Brain Sciences* **2**: 367–408.

Pumphrey, R. J. 1953 The origin of language. *Acta Psychologica* **9**: 219–39.

Reed, C. A. 1977 The origins of agriculture: prologue. In *The Origins of agriculture*, ed. C. A. Reed. The Hague: Mouton.

Reed, C. A. 1985 Energy-traps and tools. In *Hominid evolution: past, present and future*, ed. P. V. Tobias. New York: Alan R. Liss.

Révész, G. 1956 *The origins and prehistory of language.* London: Longmans, Green.

Reynolds, P. C. 1981 *On the evolution of human behavior: the argument from animals to man.* Berkeley: University of California Press.

Sahlins, M. D. 1972 *Stone age economics.* Chicago: Aldine.

Steadman, P. 1979 *The evolution of designs: biological analogy in architecture and the applied arts.* Cambridge University Press.

Steklis, H. and S. Harnad 1976 From hand to mouth: some critical stages in the evolution of language. In *Origins and evolution of language and speech,* eds. S. Harnad, H. Steklis and J. Lancaster. New York Academy of Sciences.

Sugiyama, Y. and J. Koman 1979 Tool-using and -making behavior in wild chimpanzees at Bossou, Guinea. *Primates* **20**: 513–24.

van Lawick-Goodall, J. 1970 Tool-using in primates and other vertebrates. *Advances in the Study of Behavior* **3**: 195–249.

Venable, V. 1975 *Human nature: the Marxian view.* Gloucester, Mass.: Peter Smith.

Waddington, C. H. 1960 Evolutionary adaptation. In *Evolution after Darwin, I: the evolution of life,* ed. S. Tax. University of Chicago Press.

Wagner, R. 1975 *The invention of culture.* Englewood Cliffs, NJ: Prentice-Hall.

Wallace, A. R. 1870 *Contributions to the theory of natural selection.* London: Macmillan.

Warren, J. 1976 Tool use in mammals. In *Evolution of brain and behavior in vertebrates,* eds. R. Masterson, M. Bitterman, C. Campbell and N. Hotton. Hillsdale, NJ: Erlbaum.

Washburn, S. L. 1960 Tools and human evolution. *Scientific American* **203**(3): 63–75.

Weber, M. 1947 *The theory of social and economic organization.* New York: Free Press.

White, L. A. 1942 On the use of tools by primates. *Journal of Comparative Psychology* **34**: 369–74.

White, L. A. 1959 *The evolution of culture.* New York: McGraw-Hill.

Wilson, E. O. 1978 *On human nature.* Cambridge, Mass.: Harvard University Press.

Wilson, P. J. 1980 *Man, the promising primate.* New Haven, Conn.: Yale University Press.

Woolfson, C. 1982 *The labour theory of culture: a re-examination of Engels's theory of human origins.* London: Routledge and Kegan Paul.

Wynn, T. 1979 The intelligence of later Acheulean hominids. *Man* (N.S.) **14**: 371–91.

Wynn, T. 1981 The intelligence of Olduwan hominids. *Journal of Human Evolution* **10**: 529–41.

4

Gatherer–hunter, forager–predator: modes of subsistence in human evolution

'Cultural Man has been on earth for some 2,000,000 years; for over 99 per cent of this period he has lived as a hunter–gatherer' (Lee and DeVore 1968: 3). These opening words of the celebrated symposium on *Man the Hunter* conceal, with a flourish of confident rhetoric, a yawning uncertainty about what a life of hunting and gathering actually entails. It is not merely that during all periods of history, men and women must have done other things with their time besides hunting and gathering, nor that we representatives of the residual one per cent sometimes hunt and gather too. For even as categories denoting types of activity, the terms 'hunting' and 'gathering' are fraught with ambiguity. Until we reach agreement on what these terms mean, there can be no basis for reasoned comparison of the modes of life and subsistence either of humans and non-human animals, or of early humans and the greater part of contemporary mankind that is supposed to have progressed beyond the 'hunter–gatherer' stage. In this essay I shall take a step in this direction by reviewing some of the attempts, in recent anthropological and ethological literature, to define hunting and gathering, along with the host of contingent terms including collecting, trapping, fishing, and more particularly, foraging and predation. The conclusion to which I move is that whilst the latter pair of terms may be used to describe extractive behaviour throughout the animal kingdom, hunting and gathering – as terms conventionally reserved for human subsistence activities – imply something more. Commonly indicated by the manufacture and use of tools, this additional component consists in reality in the *subjective intentionality* that is brought to bear on the procurement process, and by virtue of which it is lifted from the sphere of extractive behaviour to that of appropriative action. Hunting and gathering, in short, do not merely denote mechanical executions, triggered by environmental stimuli, of a received behavioural programme (whether innate or learned), but repre-

sent alternating phases in that continuous task which, for the hunter–
gatherers, is no less than *life itself*.

Types of activity and types of produce

The first point to note is that hunting and gathering refer, in the first place,
to what people do rather than to what they eat; that is to patterns of
conduct rather than nutrition (Teleki 1975: 127–8). According to the types
of food consumed, human beings (or other animals) may at times be
herbivores, carnivores or omnivores. Although there are obvious corres-
pondences between gathering and herbivorous diet, and between hunting
and carnivorous diet, these are by no means exact, and the two sets of
terms should not be confused (Galdikas and Teleki 1981: 242). Our
problems do not, however, end there; for food procurement activities may
be classified either in terms of *how* they are conducted, or in terms of
what they yield for consumption. Of the repertoire of labels in conventional use, some (like 'gathering') connote practical operations of particular kinds, regardless of what is obtained; others (like 'fishing')
categorize activities according to the kinds of things they are expected to
yield, regardless of the operations involved; and still others (like
'hunting') tend to carry both types of connotation simultaneously.

One of the first to attempt a systematic classification of subsistence
activities was Murdock, who used it as a basis for coding societies in his
Ethnographic Atlas. The first three types were: (1) 'gathering of wild
plants and small land fauna'; (2) 'hunting, including trapping and
fowling'; (3) 'fishing, including shellfishing and the pursuit of large
aquatic animals' (Murdock 1967: 154). Evidently, small animals are
included under the objects of gathering on the grounds that the operations entailed in their procurement do not differ essentially from those
entailed in the procurement of plants: they can be *collected*, whereas
hunting involves an element of *pursuit*. But on this very criterion, the
collection of shellfish, and the pursuit of large sea-mammals, which
Murdock brings under fishing, should be classed with gathering and
hunting respectively. A set of revised definitions which purport to overcome these anomalies has since been proposed by Lee, reflecting a broad
consensus arising out of the *Man the Hunter* symposium: '*Gathering* –
collecting of wild plants, small land fauna and shellfish; *Hunting* – pursuit
of land and sea mammals; *Fishing* – obtaining fish by any technique' (Lee
1968: 41–2, see also Friedl 1975: 12).

These definitions serve to focus the contrast between gathering and
hunting on the behavioural opposition of collection *versus* pursuit. But
once we turn to the contrast between hunting and fishing, everything
appears to depend upon the class of animal obtained. Any activity that

yields fish is to be regarded as fishing, irrespective of whether they are caught in nets or by hook and line, speared under water or shot with arrows, or washed up onto mudflats and collected (Struever, in Lee and DeVore 1968: 92). Thus the harvesting of shellfish, and the capture of sea-mammals, are both excluded from fishing not because they entail operations of collection and pursuit respectively, but because neither molluscs and crustaceans nor mammals are, taxonomically speaking, proper fish.[1] Sandwiched between gathering (a particular kind of operation for procuring anything) and fishing (any operation for procuring a particular kind of thing), the definition of hunting is necessarily composite – it is the pursuit (rather than collection) of mammals (rather than fish).

Comparing Murdock's category of hunting 'including trapping and fowling' with Lee's – 'pursuit of land and sea mammals' – it is obvious that in tidying up the definitions a great deal has been left out. On the one hand there is the pursuit of animals that do not fall into the taxonomic orders of either mammals or fish, most notably the larger birds and reptiles. On the other hand, there is the entire field of trapping, netting and snaring activities, often involving the use of fixed facilities. Both omissions stem from the compromise nature of the definition. Thus if hunting were to join fishing (in its original sense of catching fish) as one component term in a systematic classification of activities based on the taxonomic status of what is obtained rather than on the pattern of procurement procedures, then it would have to be redefined as the procurement of mammals by *any* technique – whether of pursuit, trapping or collection. Gathering likewise should be redefined as the procurement of plants *only*, and additional terms would have to be introduced to cover the procurement of birds ('fowling'), reptiles, and all other animal orders excluding fish. But in a classification of food-getting activities based consistently on behavioural or technical criteria, hunting would become the procurement of any animal large and mobile enough to require pursuit, whilst the category of fishing, in such a classification, would have no place at all. Some fish-yielding activities would be included under gathering (as collection), some under hunting (as pursuit), but the majority would be included under a third category of *entrapment*: the use of nets, snares or traps to obtain animals of any kind.[2] In this context, the notion of fishing is meaningful only in an extended sense, referring to activities whose technical nature is constrained by the invisibility of the object sought right up to the moment of extraction (Palsson 1982: 210). For one whose point of view remains above water level, this constraint usually applies when catching not only fish but also a range of other aquatic animals, all of which are rarely seen until caught. But it can apply, as well, to the procurement of many land-dwelling animals which, remaining unseen, can be trapped but not pursued.

Gathering, collecting and foraging

Let us see whether it is not possible to arrive at rather more precise characterizations of hunting and gathering, as procurement procedures, quite apart from what they happen to yield. I shall begin with gathering. The usual connotations of this term are twofold: firstly, the picking or digging up from the substrate, or the plucking from bushes or trees, of virtually immobile, small items; and secondly the concentration of these items, formerly dispersed in the environment, into an aggregate that is physically intact – most commonly secured in some kind of container. There are two other terms in common use whose meanings overlap with those of gathering, namely collecting and foraging. Collecting shares with gathering (but not foraging) the specific connotation of aggregate formation, and often substitutes for gathering as in the phrase 'hunting and collecting'. Very commonly, however, it is employed in a general sense to cover all activities involved in the procurement of uncultivated foodstuffs, as when 'food collection' (by hunter–gatherers) is conventionally opposed to 'food production' (by agriculturalists and pastoralists).

Foraging, likewise, has both a specific and a general reference. Specifically, it implies an additional element of search or movement from one food source to another, but not necessarily the aggregation of extracted produce which is an essential feature of gathering and collecting. More generally, foraging has come into widespread use as a convenient shorthand for 'hunting and gathering', with the advantage of being neutral as regards both the relative importance of one or the other activity, the respective contributions of animal and plant foods, and the sex of the procurer. Thus for Winterhalder, foraging includes 'hunting, trapping, netting, snaring, gathering or other techniques' (1981a: 16). Lee (1980) has gone so far as to propose the notion of a 'foraging mode of production', finding other labels (such as 'the hunting and gathering mode of production') excessively cumbersome. Binford also employs the notion of foraging in this general sense, but contrasts it with collecting on the grounds that whereas foragers take food on encounter to satisfy immediate daily needs, collectors have 'logistically organized food-procurement strategies' involving aggregation and storage (Binford 1983: 339–46). Hunn and Williams, however, feel that to speak of human hunter–gatherers as foragers is to underestimate their capabilities. '"Foragers"', they claim, 'calls to mind dull-witted ungulates grazing their way through a field of daisies' (1982: 8)! There may indeed be more to gathering than foraging, but we shall not discover it by caricaturing the ways of non-human animals.

It is nevertheless true that 'gathering' has tended to be restricted in its (mainly anthropological) usage to human procurement activities, whereas both 'collecting' and 'foraging' have been much more widely applied in studies of animal behaviour and ecology. In comparing the subsistence patterns of human and non-human primates, Teleki reserves 'gathering' for appropriate human activity, and recommends that 'collecting' be retained as a parallel term to denote equivalent behaviour among monkeys and apes. The term was deliberately adopted in preference to 'foraging', which had previously been proposed (1973: 42), since the latter can also be applied to the search and pursuit of a mobile quarry. On similar grounds he distinguishes between human 'hunting', and 'predation' by non-human primates; thus the counterpart of the human *gatherer– hunter* is the primate *collector–predator* (Teleki 1975: 129). I shall return shortly to the distinction between hunting and predation, which for us has a quite different significance. As far as Teleki is concerned the terms gathering and collecting, and hunting and predation, 'are generically similar in meaning. Whether or not the food-getting activities of monkeys and apes differ sufficiently from those of men to warrant independent terminological identity...needs still to be resolved' (1975: 129). His conclusions are that, by and large, the differences are more on the side of hunting/predation than of gathering/collecting, and that their effect is to modify the proportion of all food procurement activities devoted to the harvesting of stationary resources, rather than to change their essential nature. In other words, gathering by humans is just like collecting by apes, except that – because of an expansion of predatory activities made possible by a weapon technology – it typically accounts for only some 75 per cent or less of overall food intake, compared with figures in the region of 95 to 99 per cent among chimpanzees and baboons (Teleki 1975: 137).

Isaac and Crader (1981: 102–3 fn. 23) object to Teleki's use of the term 'collection' with reference to non-human primate subsistence patterns. Following the standard dictionary definition, they point out that collecting, like gathering, implies the assembly, aggregation or concentration of objects into one place. We should not therefore describe as a gatherer/ collector the animal that feeds as it moves, for the description is apt only when produce is accumulated and 'brought back' for later consumption at some central point. Accordingly, Isaac and Crader define gathering as 'acquisition with postponed consumption' (1981: 88). This is something that humans normally do, although they may also eat some of what they obtain on the spot.[3] Here is an example, from Gould's description of subsistence behaviour among the Aborigines of the Australian Western Desert:

Staples...are always collected by the women in such large quantities that they must be transported in bulk inside wooden bowls back to camp rather than being consumed at the place where they are collected. It is common to see Aborigines eating occasional fruits or berries as they forage, but staples are always brought to camp, firstly because they are too abundant to be consumed entirely in such 'snacks' and, secondly, because most staples require further processing by the women. (1969: 261)

In this example, and following Isaac and Crader's definition, only the staples carried in the bowls have been gathered or collected, and *not* the fruits and berries consumed as snacks.

Many non-human animals also gather in this sense, for example, beavers, squirrels and ants. But on the whole, non-human primates do not:

Clearly it is only in the stomachs of chimpanzees that most of their food is collected. The problem is our lack of a word that specifically distinguishes peripatetic selective feeding, which is what chimpanzees do, from gathering with postponed consumption, which is so characteristic of humans...(Isaac and Crader 1981: 102–3)

There are two points here, one substantive, the other terminological. The first is that among primates, gathering really is distinctively human, and is conditional upon a technology of carriers and containers which non-human primates lack. The importance of the latter cannot be over-estimated, for without such devices for holding and transporting foodstuffs, it would have been impossible to bring enough back to the home base to warrant their subsequent redistribution (Isaac 1978: 102). The second point is that collecting is a misleading label for activities which involve the extraction of immobile items but *not* their aggregation or transport prior to consumption. 'Foraging', as we have already noted, does not share this latter connotation with gathering and collecting, and is perhaps, after all, the better term.

In a recent work, Tanner has employed the notion of foraging in just this sense, and explicitly contrasts it with gathering. She links the contrast, moreover, with the long-term dependence of young humans on adult providers, and with the fact that the aggregation of foodstuffs in gathering has specific regard for their future distribution:

Foraging is on-the-spot collection and consumption of plant food and presumes that, after weaning, the young individual is on its own. In contrast, gathering involves collecting and carrying quantities for later consumption by more than one individual; it is compatible with extended dependence of the young (1981: 140).

Far from being essentially continuous with non-human primate foraging, gathering constitutes in Tanner's view a fundamental innovation – 'a new way of exploiting plant food with tools' (1981: 139).

Apes, of course, also use tools in their foraging, so that the major additions to the tool-kit, marking the transition from foraging to gathering, were devices for carrying rather than extraction. Nevertheless the digging stick, as an extractive implement, must have facilitated a major enlargement in the range of foods available for consumption – particularly stuff 'embedded in a solid matrix such as the earth, which had to be penetrated or excavated in order to free it' (Parker and Gibson 1979: 371). There is an obvious connection between the use of tools in digging and especially in carrying, and bipedal locomotion. Since the tools themselves would generally have been made from organic materials such as wood, skin or fibre, none of which preserves well, we have no proof of their antiquity, but it is entirely plausible that they may have long predated the earliest tools for hunting. However, where the manufacture of tools required the use of other (non-corporeal) tools, the latter must, as a rule, have been harder and more durable than the former: thus skin or fibre may be worked with wood or bone, but in the absence of metal, wood and bone can only be worked with stone. A population whose equipment for extraction and transport was of perishable raw material may still have depended on a stone technology (Testart 1981: 192–3).

It appears, then, 'that food gathering is a more novel and original behaviour in hominid history than predation or small-game hunting. It requires some technology as well as a sense of purpose...' (Campbell 1979: 295). To recognize the distinctiveness and priority of human gathering is at once to cast doubt on the deep-rooted assumption that it was in the adoption of a hunting mode of subsistence that man's evolutionary pathway diverged from that of other primates. Arguing along the same lines, Zihlman asserts that 'gathering and not hunting was the initial food-getting behaviour that distinguished ape from human... Furthermore, rather than a leading force, hunting must have emerged late in human evolutionary history from a technological and social base in gathering' (1981: 93). Like Tanner, Zihlman adopts Teleki's distinction between human hunting and non-human primate predation, such that hunting proper involves the use of tools to kill animals larger than the hunter, whereas predation – as practised for example by baboons and chimpanzees – involves the killing of relatively small animals by hands and teeth, unaided by extrasomatic equipment (Zihlman 1981: 108–9, Tanner 1981: 80–1, see Teleki 1975: 139). The suggestion, then, is that the first and most critical transition in subsistence-pattern marking the process of hominization was from forager–predator to *gatherer*–predator, and not to forager–*hunter*. Hence it was gathering that subsequently set the stage for the emergence of hunting from predation, perhaps by furnishing significant technological inputs. As the digging stick may have developed from the ape's termite-probing stick, so – Zihlman speculates – the wooden spear or club may have developed from the digging stick, fishing and hunting nets from carrying bags, and stone tools for cutting and pounding meat from those used in plant food preparation (Zihlman 1981: 109).

This is not the only line of attack on the orthodoxy epitomized in Laughlin's forthright assertion that 'hunting is the master behaviour pattern of the human species' (1968: 304). Another approach, instead of substituting gathering for hunting as the key to human uniqueness, emphasizes the similarities and continuities between the subsistence patterns of human hunter–gatherers and those of non-human primates. Thus for Teleki, what really tells is the mounting evidence of predatory behaviour among monkeys and apes, on the basis of which we would have as good a reason to launch a career for 'chimpanzee-the-hunter' or 'baboon-the-hunter', as for 'man-the-hunter' who, just like the baboon and chimpanzee, actually gets most of his food from gathering (Teleki 1975: 127).[4] It is suggested that hunting, far from setting mankind on a divergent course, has an ancient history within the primate order, beginning with the eating of small insects, progressing through the capture of larger insects to predation on small vertebrates, as a prelude to the pursuit and capture of larger mammals (Harding 1981: 200). But this suggestion is founded upon an elementary confusion between the procurement and consumption of faunal resources and the technical operations of predation. If it is true that among primates, 'the collection of insects . . . may involve motor patterns exactly like those performed while collecting grass seeds' (Harding and Teleki 1981: 5), the fact that the former yields animal food does not make it any less like gathering, or any more appropriate as an antecedent for hunting activities which involve operations of a quite different kind. There is rather more justification, perhaps, for seeing a link between primate predation on small mammals and the human hunting of larger ones. But the differences remain striking, and there is equal justification for Zihlman's argument that the distinctive features of human hunting have their origin in gathering. The most reasonable conclusion, perhaps, is that human hunting rests on a synthesis of motor patterns derived from non-human primate predation, with technical and intellectual capacities which developed in the course of the transition from pre-human foraging (exemplified by contemporary chimpanzees) to human gathering. Particularly noteworthy in this regard is the fact that tool-using, which is held to be distinctive of human hunting, is equally distinctive of the foraging activities of chimpanzees which never, apparently, use tools in predation (Boesch and Boesch 1982: 284–5).[5]

The current reassessment of the part played by gathering in the process of hominization is of course prompted by the realization that about half of the members of any population of early humans would have been females, who probably contributed a good deal more than half of the food supply (Hunn and Williams 1982: 8). 'Man the hunter' was always supposed to have been not only human but also male; thus the same arguments that were developed to set humans above and apart from their primate ancestors were also invoked to set men above and apart from women, especially in strength, skill and intellect. To place 'woman the gatherer' at the cutting edge of hominization is to reverse this order of dominance, whilst preserving the distinction; whereas to downplay the distinctiveness of human subsistence patterns is not to concede any particular precedence to either sex.[6] However the issue of the relative priority of gathering and hunting is only linked to that of the origin of sex and gender distinctions by virtue of the common assumption that by and large, men hunt and women gather (Friedl 1975: 16). Yet in many, if not most, hunter–gatherer societies, men do a substantial amount of gathering themselves, whilst the assumption that only men normally hunt has been seriously undermined by at least one recent study of a society (the Agta of the Philippines) in which women are frequent hunters of big game animals (Estioko-Griffin and Griffin 1981). In certain respects the Agta seem atypical, for example in their dependence for plant food on the produce of neighbouring cultivators acquired in exchange for meat from killed game, and in the absence from their environment of large carnivores that in other regions can make hunting a rather dangerous business. But the pursuit of small mobile animals by women is much more widely reported, although its extent has been obscured by a systematic observers' bias towards regarding such pursuit, which would usually be classed as 'hunting' if performed by men, as mere 'gathering' or 'collecting' if performed by women (Endicott n.d.: 6–7).[7] In view of these considerations, it is surely advisable to keep clearly separate the questions of how the food procurement activities of men differ (if at all) from those of women, and of how the activities of humans (male and female) differ from those of non-human primates. My concern, in this essay, remains with the latter question alone.

Hunting and predation

Let me now return to the problem of how hunting, as a procurement procedure, is to be precisely characterized. We have already noted the element of pursuit, and it is this, rather than the connotation of searching for something, that makes the idea of plant-hunting apparently so incongruous. 'Plants', as Laughlin observes, 'do not run away nor do they turn and attack. They can be approached at any time from any direction, and they do not need to be trapped, speared, clubbed, or pursued on foot until they are exhausted' (1968: 318). The work of extraction, moreover, can be interrupted at will, and the pace is set by the forager. The same, of course, goes for the procurement of many kinds of animal, such as insects and other invertebrates, most of which naturally occur in 'small packages', and have to be collected in quantity if they are to make a significant contribution to the food supply (Zihlman 1981: 95). That is why hunting cannot be equated with the extraction of faunal resources. It is all very well to imagine man the hunter, fleet of foot and armed with club, spear or bow and arrow, as lovingly depicted in countless 'artist's impressions' of our ancient ancestors, setting off in hot pursuit of mobile big-game, but hardly of grubs or snails! But granted that the procurement of the latter should be classed along with the procurement of plants as gathering or collecting (McGrew 1981: 45), there remains a substantial field of extractive behaviour between this extreme, and the other extreme of ·hunting large land or sea fauna with weapons.

Chimpanzees, when presented with an immediate opportunity (but apparently rarely otherwise) will stalk, pursue, capture, kill and consume mobile prey such as arboreal monkeys and small ungulates (McGrew 1981: 42–3, Takahata *et al.* 1984). Quite a lot of the meat consumed by human hunter–gatherers is also of relatively small or juvenile animals obtained in a similarly casual and spontaneous way, without the use of any equipment beyond what a person might happen to be carrying at the time (Watanabe 1985: 9). A digging stick, for example, can be turned to account as a club, should the need arise, though in many cases the victim can be grabbed with bare hands and stunned by beating against hard ground or rock. Unless the prey is completely immobile, such as nestling birds, instances of this kind are a far cry from simple gathering or collecting. Small animals will not necessarily consent to being picked up or plucked from a stationary position, but must be pursued and captured, just like larger ones (Endicott n.d.: 9). And yet on account of the brevity and fortuity of the extraction process, and the lack of specialized equipment, it does not seem quite to amount to what we are inclined to regard, albeit intuitively, as 'true hunting' (Hunn and Williams 1982: 8).

Teleki places all such behaviour involving pursuit and capture, when performed by non-human primates, into his category of 'predation'. Drawing on data from Silberbauer's study of G/wi bushmen (Silberbauer 1972), he notes that much of their meat intake comes from kills of small game, and that there is a striking similarity between the list of species taken in this size range (yielding less than about 16 kg of meat per kill) and the list of those taken by predatory baboons. But he goes on to infer that, among groups such as the G/wi, 'this regular emphasis on small game, much of which is collected or trapped, brings the hunting component of human subsistence closer to the predator component of monkey and ape subsistence' (Teleki 1975: 137). The convergence, however, is not real but an artefact of deceptive categories. Teleki contrives to reduce the component of human subsistence derived from hunting (rather than gathering) by *excluding* the procurement of small game, most of which is *included* in estimates of the component of non-human subsistence derived from predation (rather than collecting). We have already observed how the inclusion of all small-game procurement under the rubric of gathering obscures the substantial contribution of human females in this field of activity, and the same distortion is evident here. The trouble is that having reserved the notion of predation for non-human activities, and having taken on board the standard anthropological definition of hunting as the pursuit of *large* animals, Teleki is left without a category to accommodate the pursuit and capture of small prey by humans. Within the terms of the hunting/gathering dichotomy, what is not hunted must be gathered;[8] and the resulting designation as gathering of much of what would count as predation by non-human primates has to be disguised behind a one-sided emphasis on the extent to which small game is 'collected or trapped'. That human hunters should derive, from kills of big game, a proportion of total food intake close to that derived by chimpanzees or baboons from kills of small game is, of course, purely coincidental, given that big-game hunting adds to the human resource base rather than substituting for small-game procurement.

One way around these difficulties would simply be to define predation as the procurement of small, mobile animals by pursuit and capture *irrespective* of whether conducted by man or other animals. Hunting, then, would contrast as the procurement of large game through the use of specialized extrasomatic implements, and as such would be uniquely human (Campbell 1979: 294–5). Likewise the extraction of stationary resources for consumption 'on the spot' may be regarded as foraging, whether by humans or non-humans, whereas gathering as defined above – which also depends on the use of implements – similarly stands out as a human accomplishment. Hunting and gathering are, in these terms, essential aspects of a mode of subsistence distinctive of our species, but this does not mean that foraging and predation dwindled and eventually ceased in the process of hominization. Indeed, evidence from contemporary hunter–gatherer groups points decisively to the contrary. Predation and foraging appear to go on side by side with hunting and gathering; though we should add that whether or not kills of mobile game are brought back for later consumption in the camp is to some extent independent of their size. The concurrence of gathering and foraging is well illustrated by the following observations of Woodburn, on the Hadza of Tanzania:

Whatever the type of vegetable food, a large proportion is eaten where it is gathered. Berries are quickly and easily collected and are eaten raw.... Only the food which remains after the women and children have satisfied their hunger is brought back to camp. (1968: 51)

Hadza men, likewise, 'satisfy their hunger at the place where food is obtained', whether the kill is of a large animal or a small one. And the concurrence of hunting and predation is nicely indicated in Gould's remark, of the Western Desert Aborigines, that 'men hunt for large game, usually collecting lizards and other edibles more or less incidentally along the way' (1969: 262). Although adults engage in both foraging and predation, we might venture the generalization that in human communities they are the particular province of *children*, who have neither reached the age and maturity when they can engage in hunting proper, nor assumed responsibilities towards domestic dependants which necessitate gathering for future redistribution (for examples recounted from the memory of a !Kung San woman, see Shostak 1981: 94–5, 101–2).

Even if our categorical distinctions are revised as I have just suggested, they still seem clumsy. For they imply that procurement of big game is not at the same time an instance of predation, and that extraction of immobile resources for postponed consumption is not equally an instance of foraging, implications that play havoc with established ecological usage. It would be far more consistent to recognize hunting and gathering as *special forms* of predation and foraging, whose common diagnostic feature is the use of implements (for immobilizing prey and carrying produce respectively). There is, however, an additional feature of hunting which has not yet been mentioned, and which is of the utmost importance. Whereas the predatory sequence of pursuit and capture begins at the moment when the predator detects the presence of a potential victim, hunting can begin long before with the onset of an intentional *search* for signs of prey, or with the phase of what Laughlin (1968: 307–8) calls 'scanning'. To be sure, the pursuit itself may be prolonged and deliberative, even when performed by non-human primates. Chimpanzees, according to Teleki, can stalk a quarry for over an hour, and are prepared to chase it for a distance of one hundred metres or more, both stalk and chase being undertaken in a 'deliberate and controlled manner' often involving 'complex strategies and manoeuvres to isolate and corner the targeted individual' (1975: 149). But they do not, so far as is known, purposefully seek out, investigate or monitor possibilities for pursuit, taking it up only when, in the course of normal travel through their range, the opportunity happens to present itself.[9]

Thus chimpanzee predation is *spontaneous*, by which we mean that the intention to procure the animal resource does not precede but succeeds the instant of initial encounter. In other words, the ape becomes a predator *from that point when the animal presents itself as an object of attention*. Human hunting, by contrast, is not spontaneous but *projective*; that is to say, the intention to procure game precedes the encounter with prey.[10] The Aborigine hunter, interrupting his search for large game to pursue and kill a lizard that chances to cross his path, remains a hunter of game but confronts the lizard only as a predator. The encounter that the hunter seeks need not of course be a direct, visual one; thus he may in the first instance be casting about for signs (sounds, smells, markings, tracks, spoor) that may alert him to an animal's presence or direct him to its whereabouts. As soon as such signs are located, the phase of search or scan ends and the phase of pursuit (stalking if the encounter is indirect, chasing if it is direct) is initiated – terminating either with successful capture or with the escape of the prey (Winterhalder 1981b: 68). All effective predation entails pursuit and capture, but only when these are preceded by deliberate search can we speak of hunting. A simple example will serve to illustrate the distinction. Imagine that I meet someone on the path, and on inquiry as to his purposes, he merely replies that he is going on his way. Later, I hear that he has brought down an animal, whose tracks he happened to cross *en route*. Had he not been travelling that particular way, at that particular time, no kill would have been made. Are we to conclude, in retrospect, that when I met the man on the path he was actually hunting? Of course not, because at that time he had no intention or expectation of procuring game. Had he had such an intention, he would have replied to my initial inquiry that he was, indeed, out hunting.

Thus the essence of hunting lies in the prior intention that motivates the search for game, the essence of predation lies in the behavioural events of pursuit and capture, sparked off by the presence, in the immediate environment, of a target animal or its signs.[11] And if there can be predation without hunting, in the form of responses spontaneously triggered by an environmental object in the absence of any prior intention, there can also be hunting without predation, when the intention to procure game remains unfulfilled. Suppose, to return to our example, that the man told me he was hunting, but that as it turned out, he subsequently returned empty-handed. In this case, *no predation occurred*. Yet it would be as absurd to conclude that since nothing was obtained, he cannot after all have been hunting, as it would have been to conclude (in the opposite instance) that because a kill was made, he must have been hunting. In short, we can no more infer hunting intentions from observations of predatory behaviour than deny such intentions when the appropriate behaviour is not observed to follow.

Purposive action and extractive behaviour

Our discussion of the distinction between predation and hunting prompts us to inquire whether the same considerations could be adduced to support the distinction between foraging (in the restricted sense of extracting immobile items) and gathering. There is, here, both a similarity and a difference. The similarity is that gathering exceeds foraging, as hunting exceeds predation, in so far as it involves a temporal extension beyond the immediate situation of extraction. The difference is that whereas with hunting this extension *precedes* the extractive situation, with gathering it *follows on*. One does not begin to gather until the resource has been located, yet the activity only qualifies as gathering because it is motivated by an intention to distribute the produce for consumption by dependants at a later time. The contrast might be summarized schematically as in the diagram.

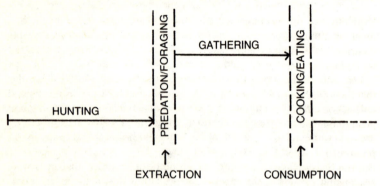

Here, extraction (the withdrawal of produce from the environmental 'store' constituted by living plants and animals) and consumption (the returning of produce to the store constituted by living human bodies) punctuate the temporal flow of purposive activity into phases of hunting (fulfilled in extraction) and gathering (fulfilled in consumption).

Yet in this model, the distinction between hunting and gathering is independent of the nature of the extractive process itself. One hunts for food, and subsequently collects it, irrespective of whether the items concerned are mobile or stationary, or of whether or not extraction entails pursuit. With plants it does not; however McGrew notes that one of the crucial advances that must have set hominid females beyond anything represented by contemporary non-human primates lay 'in the increasing ability to predict, detect, and remember the locations of [mainly plant] food sources', and concomitantly, in the ability '*to travel purposefully to feeding sites* (rather than to forage opportunistically)' (1981: 59, my emphasis).[12] Such purposive travel can hardly be described by the concept of gathering, but in emphasizing the element of deliberate scanning, it makes perfectly good sense to say that one is 'hunting for plants'. And when Meehan refers to the most industrious gatherers of shellfish among the Anbarra, a coastal group of Australian Aborigines, as 'very good hunters' (1977: 367), this is not a perverse inconsistency, but simply a recognition of the fact that individuals who bring back the most produce are also the most eager and enthusiastic when it comes to seeking it out:

> To speak of women 'hunting' shellfish, yams or goannas is not as incongruous as it sounds, especially when one has had the good fortune to observe them on the scent of a new patch of yams, a rich bed of the 'fat' bivalve *Tapes hiantina*, or a young goanna's burrow. Much of the tension, excitement and expectation of the traditional hunt is present. (Meehan 1982: 119)

Evidently the procurement of plants or shellfish, just like the procurement of mobile game, may be *projective*, and in this respect may be contrasted with spontaneous acts of either predation or foraging, whether by human or non-human primates.

Just as both immobile and mobile resources may be hunted, meaning that the intention to procure them precedes their discovery, so also both – unless consumed on the spot – must be gathered, that is, recovered for postponed consumption at a central point or home base. Laughlin (1968: 309–11) refers to this, in the context of animal procurement, as the final phase of *retrieval*, following that of immobilization (killing or capture). But the phase is surely no part of hunting. Indeed with the exception of scavenging or meat-robbing from other predators (Morris and Goodall 1977), it makes no more sense to say that one is 'hunting' animals that are already dead than it does to say that one is 'gathering' plants that have yet to be discovered. The retrieval or 'bringing back' of kills is a matter not of hunting but of collecting, just as is the recovery of plant food. It is motivated, in both cases, by an intention to distribute the food, more or less widely according to circumstance. If the notion of 'gathering kills' sounds odd or inappropriate, it is only because the initial aggregation or concentration of material has already occurred in the living animal, so that no further work of aggregation is needed in order to allow for distribution.

When it comes to the characterization of the extractive moment itself, rather than the hunting it concludes and the gathering it initiates, we have to return once more to the behavioural opposition between predation and foraging. Teleki actually isolates three stages in full predation, namely pursuit, capture and consumption (1975: 148). In our model, consumption is excluded from predatory extraction, on the grounds that if prey have been killed, predation has occurred regardless of the extent to which the kills are consumed, if at all. Thus the lion is a predator even when (as reported among the G/wi bushmen) it is driven from its kill by human hunters who rob the meat (Silberbauer 1981: 216); though having said that, we should note that predation and consumption can overlap in the event that the victim dies whilst being eaten. Restricting predation, then, to the two stages of pursuit and capture, it is evident that the latter stage is behaviourally equivalent to the grasping of immobile resources; indeed we call it capture only because it has been preceded by a chase or stalk. Therefore foraging (still using the term in its most specific sense) represents the limiting case where pursuit time is reduced to zero. There exists a continuum between this extreme, and the other where pursuit can last for hours or even days. We might be tempted to include under foraging the procurement not only of completely stationary resources like plants, but also those whose procurement involves very brief pursuit of the kind that might better be called 'seizure'. In seizures, according to Teleki, 'distances covered can usually be measured at a metre or two, and elapsed time in seconds' (1975: 149). Granted that seizure represents an intermediate behavioural form between the mere 'picking up' of immobile items and the lengthy pursuit by chase or stalk of fully mobile ones, just where we choose to divide the continuum is arbitrary. A pursuit time that may seem significant in the context of resource extraction by non-human primates could appear negligible in the context of human predation on big game, which can be of much greater duration, so that small-game procurement unequivocally classed as predation by, say, chimpanzees or baboons tends to be relegated to the residual category of foraging when practised by humans. We have already seen how this inconsistency can distort the comparison between non-human and human predation, by artificially reducing the predatory component in human extractive behaviour.

A word should be said here about trapping, which, like foraging, involves negligible pursuit time. This saving, however, is offset by the costs of setting and maintaining the traps (Winterhalder 1981b: 82 fn. 1). Trapping is distinguished from normal predation in so far as the preliminaries to capture are not carried out immediately beforehand, but rather on a separate occasion. Where capture flows directly on from pursuit (else the operation fails), it flows only indirectly from the laying of traps which are triggered by the movements of the prey themselves. Thus hunting is divided into two phases: the scan for locations, and the subsequent travel to trapping sites to check for kills. The total sequence could therefore be diagrammed as in the following figure. If the first phase is discounted, the subsequent phases of purposive travel to extraction sites, and removal for postponed consumption, are exactly as they would be for the procurement of predictable and immobile resources such as plants. But on account of the first phase, the operation is altogether more complex, requiring a much greater degree of foresight. Since the search for sites and setting of traps is governed by an intention to procure game,

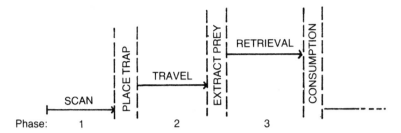

this initial phase is – so to speak – 'embedded' in the total process of hunting. The trapper does not set out with the expectation of an immediate return on arrival at his destination, but with a view to possible returns in the future. He may, nevertheless, run the first two phases together by checking old traps and setting new ones (or resetting the old) on the same trip.

To conclude, let me return to the question of technology. We have seen that a diagnostic feature of human hunting and gathering is the regular manufacture and use of tools, both for extraction (implements and facilities) and for transport (carriers and containers). Yet this is but an outward symptom of a much more fundamental capacity: that is to harness the range of available behaviour patterns to the realization of an intentional project, already construed in the mind of an agent. We use the terms 'foraging' and 'predation' to denote patterns of extractive behaviour, which may be both compared and contrasted with the patterns of constructive behaviour engaged in tool-making (see Chapter 3). The degree to which these patterns are innate or learned is irrelevant to our present concerns. The important point is that just as tools may be constructed in the absence of a prior image, so also may food be extracted without any purposive direction by an intending subject. The spider constructs (or executes) its web, and as a predator, it captures insects. But it does not *hunt* insects any more than it *makes* its web. Man, to the contrary, is a hunter of game for the same reason that he is a maker of tools: because of the teleological conformity of his extractive or constructive performances to a design of his own; something that requires a developed self-consciousness and a corresponding awareness of time past and future. From this point of view, it does not suffice to identify hunting or gathering on the basis of overt behavioural criteria, such as the use of external instruments, the pursuit of mobile prey, or the collection of stationary food items. For it is, we insist, *the intentional component of action that transforms the forager–predator into a gatherer–hunter.* In the essay that follows, we shall see that this point has a fundamental bearing on the questions first, of what is meant by 'production', and secondly, of whether there is anything distinctive about hunter–gatherer social relations.

Notes to Chapter 4

1 From a survey of fishing-related terminologies in a number of different languages, Leap finds that fishing is almost invariably described not as an activity in its own right, as distinct from hunting, but as a kind of hunting which happens to yield fish (Leap 1977: 256–7).

2 Ellen (1982: 128) distinguishes four basic types of technique for the procurement of 'non-domesticated' resources. These are: '1. gathering of vegetable species; 2. collecting of animal species and their products (small game, insects, honey,. . .); 3. fishing; 4. hunting and trapping.' The rather idiosyncratic distinction offered here between gathering and collecting evidently rests on the criterion of yield, as does the notion of fishing. But hunting and trapping are types of operation; thus all fishing must come under the rubrics of either hunting/trapping or collection.

3 Lee (1969: 74) has noted that one feature of the economy of hunting and gathering groups such as the Kalahari bushmen is that 'the relation between the production and consumption of food is immediate in space and time'. This does not mean, however, that the food is literally consumed on the spot, but only that consumption occurs within about 48 hours of procurement, and that produce is not distributed beyond the confines of the local group or camp. Thus food is still acquired for postponed consumption, later that day or on the next, back at the site of residence. In stressing the immediacy of consumption relative to human economies involving extensive surplus accumulation and exchange circuits, we should not underestimate (as does Teleki 1975: 140) the contrast with the economy of non-human primates, by comparison with which the consumption of food gathered by humans is considerably delayed (Isaac 1978: 92–3).

4 The validity of Teleki's observations on chimpanzee predation has, however, been seriously questioned by Reynolds, who believes that the high frequency of predation among the chimpanzees of Gombe Reserve, where Teleki conducted his fieldwork, may have been the result of an artificial feeding situation (Reynolds 1975).

5 There is, in fact, just one published report on tool use in chimpanzee predation, in which a rock was hurled during an attack on bush pigs (Plooij 1978).

6 Galdikas and Teleki (1981), citing data on wild chimpanzees and orang-utans, suggest that an incipient division of labour by sex exists among all pongids, in which the predatory pursuit of small vertebrates is left to males. The specialization is not absolute: 'chimpanzee females occasionally hunt game and males certainly spend considerable time collecting insects'. However, this lack of complete specialization is also true of most human hunter–gatherer populations (1981: 245).

7 Such biases may be reflected in native categorizations as well. The Miskito Indians of Nicaragua, for example, claim that the edible parts of small game – of the sort that might be procured by women – represent 'flesh' but not hunted

'meat' (Nietschmann 1972: 55). And the Niuans of Polynesia celebrate the hunting of big fish, but smaller fish procured by women are said to have been merely 'picked up' like shellfish (Kirch and Dye 1979: 65).

8   Watanabe (1985: 9) has shown how the element of small-game procurement by early man has been systematically disregarded since it cannot be accommodated within the hunting/gathering dichotomy.

9   'So far as is known' is the operative phrase here. Even if chimpanzee predation were premeditated, it would be difficult for the observer to recognize the animal's intentions, or to tell whether it is monitoring pursuit possibilities or merely going about its normal business. Appearances may be misleading.

10 I am not sure whether these are the best possible terms. What I have called spontaneous predation is most commonly described in the literature as 'opportunistic'. Endicott, for example, defines *opportunistic hunting* as the procurement of game 'as opportunity presents itself, without the use of specialized hunting weapons, but rather with tools used primarily for other purposes, such as digging'. She contrasts this to *intensive hunting*: 'the intentional pursuit of game, usually with specialized weapons made and carried specifically for killing game' (Endicott n.d.: 10). I have not adopted these terms because they have also been used, by myself and others (e.g. Bailey 1981), to refer to the application or non-application of some principle of planned conservation or husbandry in resource exploitation. Much human hunting which would qualify as opportunistic in this regard, involving no such principle, is certainly not spontaneous as we define it here.

11 Even if it is agreed that non-human primates are predators in this sense, but not hunters, a serious problem arises in relation to the larger social carnivores. From Kruuk's study of the spotted hyena, for example, we learn that 'zebra-hunting hyena packs can be recognized as such by the observer long before they have selected a quarry – they are setting out to hunt zebra rather than any other prey' (Krunk 1972: 180). On the strength of this description we would have to admit hyenas as projective hunters. I am not sure how this problem should be resolved, whether simply by dropping the exclusively human connotation of hunting, or by refining the notion of intentionality in a way that would discriminate (somehow) between human and non-human animal projection.

12 Not that this ability is entirely lacking in pongid populations. Wrangham writies that the chimpanzees of Gombe reserve 'were capable of returning to known food sources precisely and by economical routes, apparently from any direction. This was an important skill. . . . My subjective impression was that a chimpanzee noticed and remembered enough about the environment on his daily travels for his best feeding strategy to be a reliance on the knowledge so gained' (1977: 532–3).

References for Chapter 4

Bailey, G. N. 1981 Concepts of resource exploitation: continuity and discontinuity in palaeoeconomy. *World Archaeology* **13**: 1–15.

Binford, L. R. 1983 *Working at archaeology*. London: Academic Press.

Boesch, C. and H. Boesch 1982 Optimisation of nut-cracking with natural hammers by wild chimpanzees. *Behaviour* **83**: 265–86.

Campbell, B. 1979 Ecological factors and social organization in human evolution. In *Primate ecology and human origins: ecological influences on social organization*, eds. I. S. Bernstein and E. O. Smith. New York: Garland STPM Press.

Ellen, R. 1982 *Environment, subsistence and system.* Cambridge University Press.

Endicott, K. (n.d.) Food-getting, sharing, and status in immediate-return foraging societies. Unpublished paper.

Estioko-Griffin, A. and P. B. Griffin 1981 Woman the hunter: the Agta. In *Woman the gatherer*, ed. F. Dahlberg. New Haven, Conn.: Yale University Press.

Friedl, E. 1975 *Women and men: an anthropologist's view.* New York: Holt, Rinehart and Winston.

Galdikas, B. M. and G. Teleki 1981 Variations in subsistence activities of female and male pongids: new perspectives on the origins of hominid labor division. *Current Anthropology* **22**: 241–56.

Gould, R. A. 1969 Subsistence behaviour among the western desert Aborigines of Australia. *Oceania* **39**: 253–74.

Harding, R.S.O. 1981 An order of omnivores: non-human primate diets in the wild. In *Omnivorous primates: gathering and hunting in human evolution*, eds. R.S.O. Harding and G. Teleki. New York: Columbia University Press.

Harding, R.S.O. and G. Teleki 1981 Introduction. In *Omnivorous primates: gathering and hunting in human evolution*, eds. R.S.O. Harding and G. Teleki. New York: Columbia University Press.

Hunn, E. S. and N. M. Williams 1982 Introduction. In *Resource managers: North American and Australian hunter–gatherers*, eds. N. M. Williams and E. S. Hunn (AAAS Selected Symposium 67). Boulder, Colorado: Westview Press.

Isaac, G. L. 1978 The food-sharing behavior of protohuman hominids. *Scientific American* **238**(4): 90–108.

Isaac, G. L. and D. C. Crader 1981 To what extent were early hominids carnivorous? An archaeological perspective. In *Omnivorous primates: gathering and hunting in human evolution*, eds. R.S.O. Harding and G. Teleki. New York: Columbia University Press.

Kirch, P. V. and T. S. Dye 1979 Ethno-archaeology and the development of Polynesian fishing strategies. *Journal of the Polynesian Society* **88**: 53–76.

Kruuk, H. 1972 *The spotted hyena: a study of predation and social behavior.* University of Chicago Press.

Laughlin, W. S. 1968 Hunting: an integrating biobehavior system and its evolutionary importance. In *Man the hunter*, eds. R. B. Lee and I. DeVore. Chicago: Aldine.

Leap, W. L. 1977 Maritime subsistence in anthropological perspective: a statement of priorities. In *Those who live from the sea: a study in maritime anthropology*, ed. M. Estellie Smith. St. Paul: West Publishing Co.

Lee, R. B. 1968 What hunters do for a living, or, how to make out on scarce resources. In *Man the hunter*, eds. R. B. Lee and I. DeVore. Chicago: Aldine.

Lee, R. B. 1969 Kung bushman subsistence: an input-output analysis. In *Contribu-*

. *tions to anthropology: ecological essays*, ed. D. Damas. Bulletin 230. Ottawa: National Museums of Canada.

Lee, R. B. 1980 Existe-t-il un mode de production 'fourrageur'? *Anthropologie et Sociétés* **4**: 59–74.

Lee, R. B. and I. DeVore 1968 Problems in the study of hunters and gatherers. In *Man the hunter*, eds. R. B. Lee and I. DeVore. Chicago: Aldine.

Lee, R. B. and I. DeVore (eds.) 1968 *Man the hunter*. Chicago: Aldine.

McGrew, W. C. 1981 The female chimpanzee as a human evolutionary prototype. In *Woman the gatherer*, ed. F. Dahlberg. New Haven, Conn.: Yale University Press.

Meehan, B. 1977 Hunters by the seashore. *Journal of Human Evolution* **6**: 363–70.

Meehan, B. 1982 *Shell bed to shell midden*. Canberra: Australian Institute of Aboriginal Studies.

Morris, K. and J. Goodall 1977 Competition for meat between chimpanzees and baboons of the Gombe national park. *Folia Primatologica* **28**: 109–21.

Murdock, G. P. 1967 Ethnographic Atlas: a summary. *Ethnology* **6**: 109–236.

Nietschmann, B. 1972 Hunting and fishing focus among the Miskito Indians, Eastern Nicaragua. *Human Ecology* **1**: 41–67.

Palsson, G. 1982 *Representations and reality: cognitive models and social relations among the fishermen of Sandgerdi, Iceland*. Unpublished Ph.D. thesis, University of Manchester.

Parker, S. T. and K. R. Gibson 1979 A developmental model for the evolution of language and intelligence in early hominids. *The Behavioural and Brain Sciences* **2**: 367–408.

Plooij, F. X. 1978 Tool-use during chimpanzees' bushpig hunt. *Carnivore* **1**: 103–6.

Reynolds, V. 1975 How wild are the Gombe chimpanzees? *Man* (N.S.) **10**: 123–5.

Shostak, M. 1981 *Nisa: the life and words of a !Kung woman*. Harmondsworth, Middx.: Penguin.

Silberbauer, G. B. 1972 The G/wi bushmen. In *Hunters and gatherers today*, ed. M. G. Bicchieri. New York: Holt, Rinehart and Winston.

Silberbauer, G. B. 1981 *Hunter and habitat in the Central Kalahari desert*. Cambridge University Press.

Takahata, Y., T. Hasegawa and T. Nishida 1984 Chimpanzee predation in the Mahale mountains from August 1979 to May 1982. *International Journal of Primatology* **5**: 213–33.

Tanner, N. M. 1981 *On becoming human*. Cambridge University Press.

Teleki, G. 1973 The omnivorous chimpanzee. *Scientific American* **228**(1): 32–42.

Teleki, G. 1975 Primate subsistence patterns: collector–predators and gatherer–hunters. *Journal of Human Evolution* **4**: 125–84.

Testart, A. 1981 Pour une typologie des chasseurs–cueilleurs. *Anthropologie et Sociétés* **5**(2): 177–221.

Watanabe, H. 1985 The chopper–chopping tool complex of Eastern Asia: an ethnoarchaeological–ecological reexamination. *Journal of Anthropological Archaeology* **4**: 1–18.

Winterhalder, B. 1981a Optimal foraging strategies and hunter–gatherer research in anthropology: theory and models. In *Hunter–gatherer foraging strategies*, eds. B. Winterhalder and E. A. Smith. University of Chicago Press.

Winterhalder, B. 1981b Foraging strategies in the boreal forest: an analysis of Cree hunting and gathering. In *Hunter–gatherer foraging strategies*, eds. B. Winterhalder and E. A. Smith. University of Chicago Press.

Woodburn, J. 1968 An introduction to Hadza ecology. In *Man the hunter*, eds. R. B. Lee and I. DeVore. Chicago: Aldine.

Wrangham, R. W. 1977 Feeding behaviour of chimpanzees in Gombe National Park, Tanzania. In *Primate ecology: studies of feeding and ranging behaviour in lemurs, monkeys and apes*, ed. T. H. Clutton-Brock. London: Academic Press.

Zihlman, A. L. 1981 Women as shapers of the human adaptation. In *Woman the gatherer*, ed. F. Dahlberg. New Haven, Conn.: Yale University Press.

5

Extraction, appropriation and co-operation: the constituents of human hunting.

> The slaughter and consumption of a deer by a lion armed only with claws and by hunters armed with bows and arrows or shotguns and speaking to each other while they hunt are, ecologically speaking, transactions of the same general type. In both there is a material exchange between predator and prey populations. (Rappaport 1971: 242)

My concern in this essay is with the meaning of production, particularly as an index of the distinctiveness of mankind. Focusing on the comparison between human hunters and non-human predators, I aim to demonstrate that although when viewed from an ecological perspective their interactions with prey are indeed of the same general kind, *socially* speaking they are quite different, and that to grasp the difference is also to pinpoint the essence of production. The argument is presented in two major sections. In the first, the dichotomy between hunting and predation is shown to rest on a more fundamental opposition between appropriative action and extractive behaviour; and this leads us to reject those views that equate hunting with a subsistence technique or its enactment. As a mode of appropriation, hunting cannot be reduced to the mechanical working of a system of forces, under the governance of certain technical rules, since it consists essentially in the putting to use of this system by an agent – the hunter. To relocate the hunter at the creative centre of the labour process is also, and necessarily, to bring into the account the form of the social relations that constitute him as an intentional subject. In the second part of this essay we show that these relations, among hunters, are of sharing, understood not as a pattern of manifest behaviour, nor as a culturally imposed rule, but as an experience of mutual interpersonal involvement. We go on to establish an opposition between sharing and co-operation, placing the latter on the side of the forces rather than the social relations of hunting – that is, as an aspect of predation. As predation stands to hunting, so co-operation stands to sharing: in each pair the first term denotes a *material* process of interaction between individual organisms, either of the same species (co-operation) or of different species (predation); the second denotes a *social* process through which the resources of nature are engaged in the course of intersubjective life. Given the dual character, material and social, of relations both among men and between men and their animal prey, we conclude that the boundary between social and ecological domains of human existence does not coincide with that between intraspecific and interspecific associations but rather corresponds to the limits of the intentional control of action.

I

Hunting as production

Men, according to Marx and Engels, 'begin to distinguish themselves from animals as soon as they begin to *produce* their means of subsistence' (1977: 42). Do hunters, then, produce their food? The conventional answer is that they do not, but that in a general sense, they 'collect' it. Surely theirs is an extractive economy no different, in essence, from that of all other animals that must extract their food from an unmodified environment in order to survive and reproduce. Are we to conclude, in consequence, that for the greater part of his history, man has remained the prisoner of his organic nature, destined to perform within the limitations of his own animality? It seems as though we are caught on the horns of a dilemma: either we deny the hunters their humanity, or we discover production in every branch of animal life. My own attempts to resolve the dilemma led me, initially, to the latter extreme. Distinguishing what I called 'economic' from 'ecological' production, I identified the former as work performed, or effort expended, in the extraction from the surrounding environment, and subsequent consumption, of the means of subsistence (Ingold 1979: 274–6). Quite obviously, human hunters are expenders of subsistence effort, and if this is what is meant by production, then they are producers too. They are also producers in the ecological sense, which refers in general to the bodily processes of growth and maintenance that are going on *within* living organisms, fuelled by energy derived from food ingested, or in the case of plants, synthesized (Odum 1975: 65–6).[1]

But if human beings must eat in order to grow, the same goes for all other animals down to the most lowly invertebrates, and even for certain insectivorous plants. Are we seriously to regard the predatory behaviour of the plant as a form of economic production? Engels, incidentally, was inclined to think so, on account of its goal-directed or (as we should now say) teleonomic character. 'There is something of the planned action', he wrote, 'in the way insect-eating plants capture their prey, although they do it quite unconsciously' (1934: 179). That is to say, the plant is endowed with a specific behavioural project, but it is not one which it has designed itself, or of which it has any knowledge at all. When, on other occasions, Engels reserves production for man, he is quite explicit that it is action *wilfully* performed by an agent in fulfilment of an intended purpose. Then the plant is not a producer, save in the ecological sense (it grows), but the human hunter undoubtedly is. Yet if there were nothing more to hunting than the behaviour patterns manifested as pursuit, capture and consumption, would we not have to infer, say, that the ladybird is a 'hunter' of aphids just as much as is man a hunter of large mammals, and that the activity of the one has as good a right to be considered a form of economic production as that of the other? Supposing (at least for the sake of argument) that the ladybird's predation is not at all under conscious control, the inference cannot be correct. But again, starting from this supposition, if there were nothing more to hunting than predatory behaviour, we would end up having to deny the intentionality of human food procurement activity, at least in so far as it involves non-cultivated resources. And this is no more credible than attributing intentionality to ladybirds!

In the light of our discussion in the previous essay (Chapter 4), the solution to the dilemma is plain to see; so plain, indeed, that my initial failure to perceive it seems inexcusable. Quite simply, *hunting and predation are not the same* (and likewise, gathering or collecting is not the same as foraging). There *is* more to hunting than predation, namely the intention of the subject who experiences the activity as *something he does*, in person. Unlike ladybirds, men carry the responsibility for their hunting; it is a responsibility, moreover, that is founded in their mutual involvement with others in a social collectivity. For this reason, hunting qualifies as a form of social action, as production. We are justified, then, in affirming that hunters *do* produce their means of subsistence, even though the behaviour patterns involved in extraction bear comparison with those of non-human predators which do not. The transition to humanity, as Faris has argued, was marked not so much by the appearance of new types of subsistence behaviour as by 'the *emergence of* [self-] *consciousness* – the objectification of work' (1975: 236). Thus the man who succeeds in bringing down game is both a hunter and a predator, so that his conduct must be understood simultaneously at two distinct levels. At one level he is an organic individual, a human being naturally endowed with certain instruments and powers, and as such he encounters individual organisms of other species – his potential prey. What we call predation is an *interaction* between one biological organism (which in this case, happens to be human) and one or more others, resulting in the death of the latter, and most usually their conversion into food for ingestion by the former. This interaction pertains to the *ecological* domain of organism–environment relations, and is wholly contained *within* the natural world. On the other level, however, our man is an intentional agent, a person, to whom nature appears as a world apart, the medium in which he inscribes his work. As a hunter, he encounters the things of this world, including the animals he intends to kill, as subject to objects: the encounter, therefore, is not interactive but *dialectical*. This is to recognize hunting, in contradistinction to predation, as action directed *on* the natural world rather than interaction within it, and attributable to a purpose, inherently social, that transcends it.

With this distinction in mind, we might turn to that celebrated passage in *Capital*, where Marx describes the labour process as one

in which man, through his own activity, initiates, regulates, and controls the material reactions between himself and nature. He confronts nature as one of her own forces, setting in motion arms and legs, head and hands, in order to appropriate nature's productions in a form suitable to his own wants. (1930: 169)

Supposing our man to be a hunter, is this a description of his hunting or his predation? As one of nature's forces he is of course an individual organism possessed of certain somatic equipment. But he does *not*, in this capacity, 'confront nature', any more than does the ladybird or the insectivorous plant. What he confronts are other components of the natural environment, such as animals of select prey species, which are opportune to his project. Thus the 'material reactions' of which Marx speaks are going on not between man and nature but within the world of nature between the human organism and its prey. They add up to a process of *extraction*, by the organism of raw materials from its environment, but not to one of *appropriation*, by the wilful subject of natural things. I must myself plead guilty of confusing the two, when having defined economic production as action directed *on* nature, and serving to remove *from* nature the material means of subsistence, I extended the concept to cover all extractive processes in the animal kingdom (Ingold 1979: 275). Clearly the physical world of nature cannot be apprehended as such, let alone confronted and appropriated, save by a consciousness to some degree emancipated from it.

Now it is just such a consciousness that, by virtue of its emancipation, can initiate, regulate and control the interactions of natural bodies. Man, the *intending subject*, confronts the world of objects, and the nature confronted includes his own. He it is who puts the instrumental apparatus of his body to work, engaging it in interactions with other such bodies in order to secure from the environment the materials and energy on which life depends. Thus, hidden in Marx's description of the labour process are two quite different things, namely (1) the physical work of the body, involving movement and expenditure of effort, whose consequence is the extraction, from the natural environment, of raw materials for consumption; and (2) the intentional *putting* to work of the body *in order* to appropriate raw materials in a desired form. If the work entails the killing of animals for food, then the first of these is predation, which is a form of extractive behaviour, and the second is hunting, which is a form of appropriative action. As a predator the ladybird is a part of nature, 'one of her own forces' as Marx would say, and we can readily observe the movements of its body in killing and eating aphids. We could make similar observations of human beings killing and eating game. But as a *hunter* man brings these movements under the direction of his purpose, which he seeks to realize 'in the nature that exists apart from himself' (Marx 1930: 170). Hence we can redefine the essence of hunting, or more generally of the production of subsistence from an unmodified environment, as *the subjection of an extractive process to intentional control*. The gist of our argument up to this point is summarized diagrammatically in Figure 5.1.

If hunting is accepted as a form of production, what becomes of the notion that 'food-producing' is limited to the operations of plant cultivation and animal husbandry? The apparent paradox here, that

Figure 5.1 Social and material dimensions of human subsistence activity.

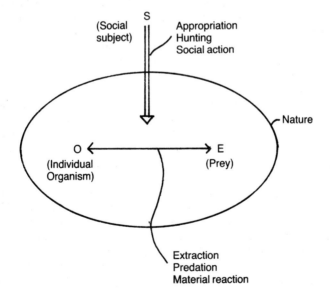

hunters produce their food without 'producing' it, goes back to an ambiguity that has its precise analogue, in the field of tool provision, in the confusion of 'making' and 'construction'. We saw in Chapter 3 how tools could be *made*, without any physical modification of environmental objects, when their selection and removal is governed by an intention concerning possible future use. The modification of objects to render them more efficient in the discharge of instrumental functions is what we called *construction*, but not all constructive processes in nature are intentionally governed. Now the equivalent terms to making and construction, in the field of subsistence procurement, are *appropriation* and *transformation* respectively . In cultivation, the environment (or a patch of it) is transformed so as to improve its efficiency in yielding food. The human farmer does this intentionally, thereby creating an artificial environment, but certain insects are known to execute equivalent operations quite unintentionally. Moreover food can be appropriated, as by the hunter, without transforming the natural environment, when its extraction for consumption is *purposive*. Thus hunting, the intentional regulation of an *extractive* (rather than transformative) process, is the logical counterpart of the self-conscious *co-option* (rather than construction) of tools, which likewise involves planned removal for use.

Now consider the following definition of production proposed by Cook: 'the process by which the members of a society appropriate and transform natural resources to satisfy their needs and wants' (1973: 31). As with making and construction, appropriation is one thing, transformation quite another. Lumping them together under the rubric of production, Cook comes up with the extraordinary assertion that '*sapiens* is the only species which produces its own means of subsistence by directly manipulating and transforming the physical environment through organized social activity' (1973: 41). It may be that *sapiens* alone is a producer of food, but it is certainly not the only species to manipulate its environment in ways that increase its edible yield, nor need such manipulation form a necessary part of productive activity. If it were, the status of hunters as representatives of modern man would again be thrown into question. Cook's definition of production might be compared with another, widely accepted definition proposed by Godelier, which explicitly *includes* the operations of hunting, gathering and fishing, in which objects for consumption are merely 'found' rather than physically transformed as in agriculture, craft and industry. 'Production', Godelier writes, 'is the totality of the operations aimed at procuring for a society the material means of existence' (1972: 263). Granted that procurement does not necessarily involve the transformation of nature, are we to regard it as a matter of appropriation, or is Godelier merely referring to the behavioural operations of extraction?

It should first be recalled that objects in the landscape, though 'naturally given', are *not* immediately given as 'articles capable of satisfying wants', that is as use-values (Marx 1930: 169–70). They become so through the attachment to them, by the subject, of an idea of their potential utility. Thus the components of the natural world are to be regarded as 'resources' only in so far as they are harnessed to an intentional project. 'There are', Godelier writes, 'no resources as such', for their exploitation

presupposes a certain awareness of the properties of the 'objects' and of their necessary relations under certain 'conditions', and the application of a body of technique which 'uses' these necessities in order to produce an expected result. (1972: 264)

Does this 'awareness' make the exploitation of natural resources tantamount to their appropriation? We have defined production as appropriative action; but in his initial formulation of the constituent structures of the economic system, Godelier keeps production and appropriation quite distinct. Both are said to be governed by rules or norms, however whilst the rules of production are *technical* (implying in the case of hunting a detailed 'ethnoscientific' knowledge of the natural history of animals) those of appropriation are quasi-*jural*, defining the 'rights' that members of a society exercise in relation to means of production and products (Godelier 1972: 269).

Now this opposition, between technical and jural rules, is commonly mapped onto another, derived from the Marxian paradigm, between 'forces of production' and 'relations of production', which coupled together, constitute the totality known as the 'mode of production'. The forces, to cite Godelier again, include 'the material and *intellectual* means that the members of a society implement, within the different "labour" processes, in order to work upon nature'; whilst the relations define people's rights of 'access to resources and to control of the means of production', allocate 'the labour force of a society's members among the different labour processes', and determine 'the social form of redistribution of the product of individual or collective labour' (Godelier 1978: 763). Put more simply, in the structure of the relations of production lie the answers to the questions: who controls what? who does what? who gets what? Godelier places particular emphasis on the point that both forces and relations are grounded in what he calls *idéel* elements, namely images or representations in the mind, codified in language, which precede and underwrite their material expression. Thus the 'intellectual means' included in the forces comprise the knowledge of how to make and use the material instruments of production, in other words they constitute a *technology*. And if the human tool leads a double life, as a subjective

conception and a corresponding material artefact, the same applies –
according to Godelier – to the social relation which exists simultaneously
'both outside of man's thought and within it...[as] a material and an
idéel reality' (1978: 767, compare White 1959: 74.)

What happens, in this scheme of things, to the concept of hunting? In
delineating what he calls the 'foraging mode of production', Lee follows
Godelier in classing with the productive forces such tools as hunting
weapons, the human musculature needed to operate them, and the
knowledge and skill required to apply them effectively. Relations of
production, in the foraging mode, characteristically include generalized
access to resources, individual possession of tools, sexual division of
labour, and sharing of produce (Lee 1980: 61–5, see also Leacock and Lee
1982: 7–9). However a mode of production, Lee insists, is not the same
thing as a mode of subsistence: 'For example, hunting and gathering do
not constitute, in themselves, a mode of production; these two activities
simply represent productive techniques, or together, a system of
production' (1980: 61). Hunting, then, is unequivocally placed, alongside
gathering, in the domain of the productive forces. Social relations, and the
appropriative movements which they govern, simply play no part in it at
all. Ellen has more recently made the same point, defining the *subsistence
technique* as 'a combination of material artifacts (tools and machines)
and the knowledge required to make and use them', and the *mode of subsistence* as a range of such techniques employed by a single population. This concept, he continues, 'operates at the level of technical
relations of production [and] indicates little about the *social* relations of
production', which require information of a quite different kind for their
proper characterization. Included in Ellen's list of 'basic types' of
subsistence technique, involving the procurement of non-domesticated
resources, are: gathering, collecting, fishing, hunting and trapping (Ellen
1982: 128).

Regarded as a technique, in the sense of the definition just cited,
hunting is not something that hunters do, but rather comprises what they
use (equipment) and know (technology). This is rather like saying that
cookery consists of recipe books and kitchen utensils, but not what the
cook gets up to in the course of preparing meals. The difference between
technique and conduct, whether in hunting or cookery, might be viewed
merely as one between a programme and its enactment, instructions
codified and followed, script and performance. But this would be
tantamount to the reduction of practical action to a sequence of
behavioural executions, *revealing* certain techniques, yet embracing
nothing more than what is already prefigured in the *idéel* technological
system. A strictly analogous kind of reduction may be adduced from the
field of structural linguistics, where following Saussure (1959: 13–15),

speaking (*la parole*) is regarded as a chain of discrete and spontaneous 'psychophysical' utterances, emitted by individuals, which successively reveal the terms and relations of a given system of linguistic signs (*la langue*). Between this system and its overt behavioural manifestations, however, there is no room for the *intentionality* of the speaker, that is for his purpose in saying what he does. Thus a conspicuous inadequacy of Saussurian linguistics, as Bourdieu has pointed out, lies 'in its inability to conceive of speech and more generally of practice other than as *execution*' (1977: 24). Now the *idéel* components of procurement technology are disclosed in subsistence behaviour, just as the elements of *langue* are disclosed in the events of *parole*. And if we were to treat hunting as nothing but the execution of technique, our understanding would be impoverished in precisely the same way as when we treat speaking as nothing but the emission of utterances. What is missing, in both cases, is the intentionality of the agent, which uses technology and language as its vehicles in hunting and speaking respectively, and by virtue of which the conduct qualifies as social action, or production, rather than as individual behavioural execution.

Let me return for a moment to Godelier's formulation of the structure of production. It consists, he explains, in the combination of three essential factors: resources (R), instruments of labour (I) and men (M) (1972: 264). But what do these men bring into production? Not, apparently, their purpose. Rather, M stands for the labour-power which may be delivered by the human body when put to work, and the skill and knowledge which underwrite the manufacture and use of the material instruments (I). Together, I and M make up a system of productive forces: thus in hunting I might include weapons, and M a set of operating instructions carried in men's heads, as well as the armature of their bodies. Now recalling our earlier discussion of the constituents of the labour process, it is necessary to distinguish between the mechanical work of the body (possibly extended by extrasomatic instruments) and the intentional *putting* to work of the bodily apparatus. If hunting, then, is understood to be no more than the engagement of the body (M), extended by instruments (I), with environmental objects (R), that is if it is seen as but the functioning of a system of forces, it cannot be anything but extractive behaviour, and as such equivalent to predation. One could just as well substitute for M a mechanical robot, suitably programmed with a device for homing in upon and dispatching certain types of prey. Say I were to construct such a robot and to set it in motion, would we describe as hunting the robot's operation or my operating of it?

Our answer is that I hunt, by putting the machine to work, whilst the working of the machine is covered by the concept of predation. The example may seem far-fetched, but it serves to demonstrate my basic point, which is that *a view of hunting as the mechanical operation of a system of productive forces leaves out the person of the hunter*. To find him again, we have to redefine our terms. Godelier's formula for production as a combination of resources, instruments and men can be retained, but only by changing the values of I and M. We would include in the class of instruments (I) the entire gamut of productive forces, *including* the apparatus and techniques of the body (or the robot, in our example, that replaces them) which in Godelier's formula come under the category of 'men' (M). But men bring into production not only their bodies and their skills but also their intentions, and it is these that we class under M rather than I. In other words, M stands not for the individual but for the person, in his capacity as an *agent* of production. This is no more than to rephrase Marx's listing of the elementary factors of the labour process: 'first, purposive activity, or the labour itself; secondly, its subject matter; and thirdly, its instruments' (Marx 1930: 170). Moreover, only by introducing agency into production does it make sense to speak of the forces as instrumental *conductors* of activity, interposed between persons and resources. The machine, left to tick over in the absence of an operator, can exert a physical force on its surroundings, but only when harnessed to the project of an agent, when *used*, can it conduct action (Cohen 1978: 42–4).

Once the hunter is brought back into hunting, it is no longer possible to restrict the latter to the execution of subsistence technique, nor can we continue to disregard the social relations that constitute the hunter as a person. For the same reason, production cannot be divorced from appropriation. This point has latterly been appreciated by Godelier himself, who now recognizes the labour process in production as *concrete* appropriation, and distinguishes it from the *abstract* appropriation jurally conceived as a system of rules concerning rights to property. The forms of concrete appropriation, Godelier writes, 'are always social, whether individual or collective; and they take the form of what we call hunting, gathering, fishing [etc.]...In our society, we call these activities "labour" and we term the organized development of each of these activities the "labour process"' (1979: 139–40). Behind the distinction between concrete and abstract appropriation is a much more fundamental issue concerning the nature of social relations. On the one hand they may be conceived, in the classic mould of structural anthropology, as relations between parts and positions in an ideal, regulative order, such as a kinship system, whole ultimate locus is in men's minds. When Godelier speaks of the *idéel* aspect of social relations, as part of the content of consciousness, he has in mind an order of this kind. To the extent that these relations specify the rights to material means formally enjoyed by occupants of the positions they define, they constitute a system of abstract appropriation. On the other hand, there are the social relations between real persons as living, acting and intending subjects; relations that continually evolve in the course of intersubjective life. No man exists, as a wilful agent, except within a field of relations of this kind which, enfolded in practical consciousness, unfolds in the purposive action it presents. Where such action is directed upon the material world, it is a form of concrete appropriation.

So long as social relations are understood only in the first of the above two senses, as part of the *cognized* order of rules which in their totality are commonly known as culture, they must necessarily be withdrawn from action, as indeed must consciousness, which becomes a mere container for *idéel* elements. Hence the separation of appropriation from production, and the reduction of the latter to behavioural execution. But if we identify consciousness with the purposive movement or flow of intentionality that adopts culture as its vehicle, then it must perforce lie at the very heart of action, as must the *real* social relations that consciousness enfolds. It is through such action, at once productive and appropriative, that social relations are brought to bear upon nature, which is consequently 'caught up' in the social process, or in a sense, 'humanized', This is surely what Marx meant in his somewhat cryptic comment that 'history itself is a *real* part of *natural history* – of nature developing into man' (1964: 143). The history he has in mind is not some kind of extension of the biological process of hominization, but one in which man *makes himself* through his dialectical confrontation with nature in the work of production. It is a history, then, of human beings as *subjects*; and through its appropriative engagement in such history, nature acquires a *human* past. For 'natural history', we should read the 'human history of nature' rather than the 'natural history of man' (Moscovici 1976: x; Schmidt 1971: 76–8).

Let me return to the particular instance of hunting, which we have contrasted to predation as production to execution, action to behaviour, appropriation to extraction. We can now recognize hunting as a process whereby hunters mutually create and recreate *one another*, through the medium of their encounter with prey. Each hunt, therefore, is not an isolated act, but is one moment in a continuous historical movement, whose dynamic lies in the interplay between the social world in which, as persons, the hunters find themselves, and the physical world that provides the wherewithal for their existence as organic individuals. Cut out from this total process, acts of hunting reduce to events of predation, each of which – as we have seen – is an elementary interaction between the human organism and other animate objects in its environment. Whereas hunting pertains to the human history of nature, predation is quite evidently an aspect of the natural history of man, and as such can be understood in terms that are exclusively ecological. In other words, if hunting engages nature in human relations, predation engages man in natural relations. Ecologists, of course, often speak of predation as an association between local populations or entire species, but the association is statistically compounded from a large number of unit interactions, just as the population is compounded from a large number of discrete individuals. The effect of the predatory association is to secure the biological reproduction of the human population, which is a necessary condition for the continuity of social life. But this social life is not reserved for periods of 'time off' from food-procurement activity. A man lives socially even as he hunts, since his intentions are constituted by his involvement with, and responsibility for, other persons. From the perspective of the whole, mankind confronts nature in hunting as a collective subject, whilst interacting with the environment in predation as a collection of objects.

I hope that I have now made it absolutely clear why, if the labour process is to be characterized as one of hunting, it *cannot* be described as a predatory interaction mediated by certain natural and artificial instruments. It is simply not enough to give an account of the kind an animal ecologist or ethologist might provide, detailing the behaviour emitted and the physical changes effected in predator and prey. We have rather to grasp the quality of the hunter's purposes, and to do this it is necessary to penetrate the social or intersubjective context of their formation. To suggest as I have done that there is anything distinctive about the social relations of hunters has usually been to court accusations of having indulged in a now thoroughly discredited 'techno-ecological' determinism, or of having failed to maintain the proper distinction between modes of subsistence and modes of production (for example, Ellen 1982: 175). The very notion of the 'hunting society' has been dismissed as an outmoded attempt to predicate essential features of social form upon what is seen as the purely technical business of bringing down wild animals of particular species in a particular environment. I want to insist, to the contrary, that only by virtue of their involvement in social relations of a certain kind can the practical activity of human beings be regarded as hunting; considered apart from these relations it is merely predation. When we speak of hunting societies, far from using technological or ecological criteria to characterize social forms, we are in fact recognizing that it is the social form of appropriation which characterizes the practical activity. Those who fail to recognize this are guilty of the greater error, namely one of divorcing social consciousness from productive work, relegating appropriation to the application of abstract, ideal rules, and reducing the labour process from a flow of purposive activity to a mere aggregate of behavioural executions or the mechanical operation of a system of forces.

II

Sharing and co-operation

What, then, are the social relations that characterize hunting as a form of appropriation? Part of the answer is hidden in the apparently purely technical observation that hunters procure 'wild' or *non-domesticated* resources as opposed to *domesticated* ones (Ellen 1982: 128). What do we mean when we say that an animal is wild rather than domestic(ated)? A wild animal is one that does not, in the living state, *belong to anybody*; that is to say, it is not 'engaged' by the structure of social relations of the human community. It has no place there, neither in direct, intersubjective relations with human domestic groups (as the animal which is tame), nor as the embodiment or vehicle of relations *between* particular persons or households. Thus in contrast to the wild, the process of domestication (often incorrectly rendered as 'breeding') refers to the social incorporation of successive generations of living animals.[2] Consequently, if we claim that hunters exploit wild animals whereas pastoralists exploit domestic(ated) ones, we are in fact basing our distinction not on the technical nature of the work, nor on the ecological association set up between human and animal populations, but on the *social* definition of the resource. The *objectives* of hunting and herding respectively follow from the social distinction: in the former case to bring animals down in order to share in a collective resource, in the latter case to tend and protect that segment of the animal population to which one alone has access, and which constitutes the foundation of domestic security in the fields of transport and subsistence. In short, hunting and herding have both to be regarded as the practical concomitants of determinate systems of social appropriation, one based on a principle of collective access, the other on a principle of divided access, to living animal resources (Ingold 1980: 3–5).

The principle of collective appropriation is summed up in the much used, and much abused concept of *sharing*. My purpose in the present section is to take a closer look at what is meant by this concept; and then to develop a contrast between sharing and co-operation, as one aspect of a systematic dichotomy of social and material relations. Having established the contrast, I shall show that it is homologous to the opposition, already elaborated, between hunting and predation. But to begin with sharing, our first concern is to identify the ontological level at which it operates. More specifically: is sharing a kind of *behaviour*, the spontaneous expression of innate dispositions fixed in the course of the phylogenetic history of the species? Or is it a *rule*, part of the imposed regulative order of culture in which are embedded the formal principles of abstract appropriation? Or again, is it an *experience* of total mutual involvement, an aspect of the intersubjective domain of social being as it is brought to bear in appropriative action?

The first view of sharing is most commonly encountered in discussions of the evolution of human subsistence patterns, which invariably draw on the possible comparisons and contrasts between the presumed practices of prehistoric hominid hunter – gatherers and those of contemporary non-human primates. There are conflicting claims regarding the incidence of sharing among the latter. Parker and Gibson (1979: 376) hold that with chimpanzees, 'active food sharing only occurs in the case of mothers giving hard-to-prepare [vegetable] foods during the period between weaning and self-sufficient feeding', and that among the earliest hominids – with a pattern of subsistence based on gathering supplement-ed by some small-game procurement – it would have been hardly less limited. However, a number of observers claim to have witnessed the widespread sharing out of meat by predatory chimpanzees (Teleki 1975: 151–5), as well as by baboons (Strum 1981: 278). Galdikas and Teleki have gone out of their way to stress the continuities in meat-sharing across a whole range of primate species: 'meat from vertebrate prey is *occasionally* distributed among some cercopithecids..., *routinely* dis-tributed among some pongids..., and *traditionally* shared among some hominids' (1981: 247). Despite such assertions, the distribution of meat by non-human primates does not appear to be at all like sharing by human hunters, since rather than manifesting a positive inclination or injunction to give, it seems merely to indicate the permissibility of others taking, or feeding simultaneously on the same carcass. Isaac has characterized this sort of behaviour as 'tolerated scrounging', and considers sharing proper to be a uniquely human trait, accompanying the development of the complementary specializations of gathering for postponed consumption and hunting large game. Together with the sexual division of labour, tool-making, language and bipedal locomotion, sharing is presented as one of a set of functionally interdependent components in the kind of socio-economic system postulated for early man, which are said to have emerged together in the course of gradual evolutionary change under natural selection (Isaac 1978: 90).

In the ongoing argument about the continuities and contrasts between human and non-human primate sharing, it is generally assumed that what is at issue is the presence or absence of a particular behavioural trait or attribute. But this is to reduce sharing to a thing that humans (and possibly other primates) 'have', and thus 'as much a part of our nature as is standing on two feet' (Ingold 1982: 163). Surely, however, there is more to sharing than intraspecific interactions (events of distribution), just as there is more to hunting than interspecific interactions (events of predation). This additional component is, of course, that of intentionality, the conscious control of self in dealing with the world of nature and with other persons. Sharing, we would argue, consists not in behavioural events whose consequence is the consumption of food by individuals other than the procurer, but in the wilful regulation of such events by the person or persons responsible. Thus, even if reports of meat-distribution among non-human primates prove to be well-founded, we would still not be entitled to conclude that food is being shared. The same goes for large social carnivores among which distributive behaviour has been conclusively documented (Schaller and Lowther 1969: 334–5). On precisely equivalent grounds, we have argued that we cannot infer, merely from observations of predatory behaviour, that animals are being hunted. What humans 'have', that raises predation to hunting, construction to tool-making, and distribution to sharing, is *self-consciousness*. And this, in turn, implies a corresponding temporal awareness: sharing, just like hunting and tool-making, depends upon the capacity of the subject to reflect upon his own existence in the dimension of time; or as Wilson has so persuasively argued, it 'incorporates an idea of the future of one's own condition' (1975: 12).

In apparent agreement with Isaac, Wilson asserts that human hunter – gatherers are distinguished from non-human primates 'by the fact of their *co-operation and sharing*' (1975: 12, 19 fn. 8). But the essence of sharing, he maintains, lies in the subjection of conduct to *rules*, rather than in the fulfilment of internal dispositions: 'the individual does not share "naturally" – it is the obligation to share that counts'. The obligation, however, is one that man has brought upon himself; like the promise, it is voluntarily entered into yet henceforth imposed upon the will of the subject. Human beings began to share, then, at the point when their interactive behaviour was placed under the direction of a design, 'social structure', of which they themselves were the authors.[3] Notice again the similarity with the argument for the origins of tool-making, which likewise lie in the authorship of a design that precedes and governs the subsequent execution. Another writer to have stressed the rule-governed character of human sharing, in the most forthright terms, is Fortes. The cohesion of hunter–gatherer communities, he writes, 'is based on the dominance of the rule of prescriptive altruism reflected in their ethic of sharing in all aspects of their social and economic life' (1983: 26). By 'prescriptive altruism', Fortes specifically has in mind acts that are 'culturally defined, rule-governed, intentionally exercised, perceived as moral obligations' (1983: 29). In these respects they stand in complete contrast to the kind of conduct generally defined as altruistic by students of animal behaviour, which issues spontaneously from the nature of individuals, and which is so regarded by virtue of its beneficial physical consequences for other individuals rather than on account of the intentions that motivate it.

These different notions of altruism underlie a certain misunderstanding between Wilson and Fortes, although their positions are otherwise remarkably congruent. Evidently adopting the biological definition of altruism, Wilson *contrasts* it with sharing, which 'does not constitute altruistic behaviour but is obligatory behaviour...sharing has the status of a rule in [hunter-gatherer] societies' [1975: 12]. Fortes, on the other hand, insists that sharing is an instance of altruism for the very reason that it is obligatory and not spontaneous (1983: 44–5 fn. 19). There is no real difference here, but the misunderstanding does serve to highlight the vital distinction between behaviour that distributes material means and the intentional regulation of such behaviour. If the notion of altruism has tended to slide over the distinction, the same is true of the notion of sharing. Likewise, as we have already seen, the concept of hunting tends to slide over the distinction between extractive behaviour and its conscious control (Figure 5.1).

Our own position as regards the nature of sharing, though apparently close to that of Wilson and Fortes, is not identical with it. The difference is summed up in our earlier distinction between *rule* and *experience*. We should note, first, that sharing does not imply any curtailment of the accountability, and hence also of the autonomy of the acting self: indeed it is the very condition of such autonomy (see Chapter 9). The more that conduct is attributable to impersonal rules, and the more that intentions can be offloaded from the particular person onto the imaginary agency of society, the less scope remains for the exercise of personal powers. In the extreme case the complete prescriptive altruist, entirely beholden to society, carries no responsibility for his actions at all. Sharing differs from prescriptive altruism in this: through mutual involvement a man loses nothing of himself, but incorporates into his person something of the other. Generalizing over the community at large, where the prescriptive altruist gives himself up for the whole, in sharing each person embraces the whole within himself. In other words, if altruism subtracts from the person, sharing augments it.

The idiom that best captures what we mean by the experience of sharing is one of *companionship*, or 'shared activity in itself' (Gibson 1985: 393). Basing his argument on material gathered among the Buid of the Philippines, Gibson shows that the idiom of companionship 'implies that social actors come together as autonomous agents to pursue a common goal'. In this it contrasts with the rules of kinship, which place people under *obligation*:

Among the Buid, a relationship based on kinship is involuntary, non-terminable and implies the dependency of one of the parties on the other. By contrast, a relationship based on companionship is voluntary, freely terminable and involves the preservation of the personal autonomy of both parties. (1985: 392)

Now for Fortes, the rule of prescriptive altruism is the very essence of kinship, which among hunter–gatherers is supposed to be generalized across the whole community. Our own view of sharing differs from Fortes's precisely as companionship differs from kinship, and by the same token we would conclude that one of the characteristics of hunter – gatherer communities is that they are *not* significantly structured by kinship relations. It should be noted that we are not limiting the objects of sharing to food, since food-sharing may itself be only an aspect of the sharing of activities and company. In a word, people share *each other*, and I believe that this is what is implied in the many ethnographic accounts that attribute the cohesion of hunter–gatherer communities to 'face-to-face relationships'.

Such relationships, binding the same people over an extended period of time, constitute in Price's (1975: 4) terms an 'intimate social group, . . . small in scale and personal in quality'. Moreover as he points out, in an intimate economy the experience of mutual 'face-to-face' involvement is intrinsic to productive activity as well as to distribution. We do not say that a man first goes hunting, expressing his nature as an isolated individual while executing certain *technical* rules, and then on return with his kill suddenly submerges his identity into that of the group, submitting to another set of *social* rules which govern the distribution of the meat. Rather, the distribution expresses the same set of intersubjective relations that constitute the hunter as a responsible agent, and that he takes with him into his hunting. He it is, in person, who both hunts and shares. Sharing and hunting, then, are two sides of the same coin; each implies the other. Because, through a history of sharing, each person encompasses all others and hence the collectivity, in his production he confronts nature as a domain of collective resources, whose appropriation for this reason takes the form of hunting.

Let me turn now from sharing to co-operation. It is possible to draw a distinction between solitary and co-operatively organized predation: solitary predators move alone or at most in pairs, usually relying on techniques of stalking and the use of portable implements to make their kills; whereas co-operative predation can involve many more individuals in the execution of complex sequences involving battue and ambush, often assisted by nets, pounds, or other relatively fixed facilities (Terray 1972: 107–9; Ingold 1980: 56–65; Meillassoux 1981: 15). As Steward originally demonstrated, in his classic application of the method of cultural ecology to so-called 'band societies', the extent and nature of co-operation can be derived from a consideration of environmental conditions, including the habits of the animal species being exploited, together with the instrumental devices available for exploiting them, the latter forming part of a received cultural tradition. Co-operative arrangements, then, are an aspect of 'the behavior patterns involved in the exploitation of a particular area by means of a particular technology' (Steward 1955: 40). They are, in other words, a part of the organization of work, laying down a programme to be followed in the course of extractive activity (Murphy 1970: 155). Within this organizational framework, which constitutes the 'band' as an effective subsistence unit, members are differentiated, if at all, by their respective roles in the process of extraction, and are bound by what Meillassoux has aptly called 'relations of adhesion' (1981: 17).

What is the nature of these relations, manifested in the co-operation of the band, and how do they differ from the relations expressed in sharing? That we are dealing with relations of fundamentally different kinds should be evident from the fact that the distinction between solitary and co-operative extraction has no bearing at all on the incidence of sharing. Wilson's (1975: 11) statement that 'whenever the hunting is co-operative, the catch is shared' is ethnographically without foundation. If kills are initially divided among those who have participated in the work of procuring them, this is only preliminary to a much wider distribution of meat prior to consumption, and the spoils brought back by hunters operating on their own are no less widely distributed (Woodburn 1972: 199). Sharing has its foundation in the social constitution of the agent, and not in the technical character of the labour process. Regardless of whether a man hunts alone or with others, he confronts nature as a subject of social relations, so that his hunting is a form of social action. And just as his life is produced through the activities of others, so the products of his activity are as much theirs as his. Not so, however, for non-human predators, from whom hunters are distinguished by their sharing but *not* (*pace* Wilson 1975: 12) by their co-operation. Patterns of co-operative behaviour in the conduct of predation have been widely observed among 'social' carnivores such as the wolf, wild dog, hyena and lion (Schaller and Lowther 1969: 330–3; Kruuk 1972: 274–83), and even among chimpanzees (Teleki 1975: 161–2), and these clearly have their analogues in human practices.

Before proceeding further, we need a working definition of co-operation, and we may as well begin with the one supplied by Marx:

When numerous workers labour purposively side by side and jointly, no matter whether in different or in interconnected processes of production, we speak of this as co-operation. (1930: 340)

Nothing in this definition rules out the co-operation of hunters, and indeed in a footnote, Marx suggests that perhaps 'hunting was the earliest form of co-operation' (1930: 350 fn. 1). But such co-operation, he maintains, is but primitive, and 'is sharply distinguished from capitalist co-operation'. We are to regard the difference, moreover, not merely as one of degree, in scale or complexity, but principally as one of kind. That said, Marx thenceforth disregards primitive co-operation altogether, reserving the term for the particular historical form taken by the labour process under capitalist relations of production. And this leads him to the somewhat bizarre conclusion that co-operation *originates* with capitalism (Marx 1930: 350–1; see Firth 1975: 39–40). A closer look at what Marx found so distinctive about co-operation in capitalist manufacture reveals that he is using the term in a special sense which is in no way implied in his initial definition, but which – curiously enough – allows us to speak of co-operative relations not only in human communities but also throughout the animal kingdom, for example among so-called 'social' insects which could not conceivably be said to *labour purposively* side by side at all.

The crux of the matter lies in the observation that workers who co-operate on the factory floor do so for no other reason than that they happen all to have contracted to the same employer, who commands the sum total of their labour-power. Only under capitalism, with the alienation by producers of their capacity to work, can the powers of a *plurality* of individuals be placed under the guidance and control of a *single* will. And it is this will, acting alone and not in consort, that combines and orchestrates the powers furnished by the workers it controls (Ingold 1983: 134–5). Whatever direct, intersubjective relations may exist between workers as persons are strictly extrinsic to the labour process. 'Their co-operation does not begin', Marx writes, 'till the labour process begins, but in the labour process they have already ceased to belong to themselves' (1930: 349). Here we find the sense of co-operative relations apparently specific to capitalism: they obtain not between *persons who co*-operate in production, but between *things which* are instrumentally co-*operated* in the labour process. And these things are none other than the faculties and powers – 'arms and legs, head and hands' (Marx 1930: 169) – constitutive of objective human nature, augmented of course by culturally acquired attributes such as knowledge and skills. Consider, for example, the detail worker of capitalist manufacture, programmed to execute repeatedly but one operation, and whose whole body – as Marx says – is converted into 'the automatic specialized instrument of that operation'. An aggregate of such bodies, with complementary specializations, constitutes what Marx calls 'the living mechanism of manufacture' (1930: 356). Co-operation, then, lies in the physical workings of this mechanism, in the functioning of a supra-individual system of productive forces. And if we state that co-operative relations exist between men, we must add the qualification that they do so only in so far as men themselves exist as corporeal components of the natural world, as individual organisms – albeit enculturated ones. Social relations of production, quite to the contrary, exist between men as persons, in so far as they transcend the world of nature: they are relations of control over the mechanism constituted by the aggregate of co-operating bodies, *and are no part of the mechanism itself.* The same dualism, between man as a working body, and as an agent who puts his body to work, will be recalled from our earlier discussion of Godelier's definition of production.

Now once co-operation is conceived in interactional terms, as the conjoint engagement of working bodies whose result, in terms of the extraction or transformation of environmental materials, exceeds the sum of the effects of each body working independently, it is not difficult to see how the same concept could be applied – say – to the behaviour of ants and bees. Indeed it could be argued that the organization of the insect community presents the closest analogue in the animal kingdom to the organization of detail workers on the factory floor, for the co-operation of individual natures estranged from the subjectivity of their bearers is no different in principle from the co-operation of individuals presumed devoid of subjectivity in the first place. In both cases, relations obtain only between objects and not subjects, though in manufacture the blueprint for co-operation is imposed by the 'alien will' of the capitalist rather than being part of an innate 'biogrammar' established in the course of natural selection, and therefore serves his (productive) interests and not the (reproductive) interests of co-operating individuals (Marx 1930: 347). It follows from the comparison that those patterns of human interaction comprised by the organization of work have their counterpart in what biologists commonly regard as the 'social organization' of insect communities, and that the sociobiological definition of society – 'a group of individuals belonging to the same species and organized in a co-operative manner' (Wilson 1980: 7) – could apply just as well to the association of workers in the factory as to the association of bees in the hive. Yet of the former, Marx tells us that they do not enter into *social* relations one with another at all (1930: 349). Thus the co-operative interactions that biology defines as social here stand *counterposed* to the social, pertaining to the forces rather than to the relations of production (Figure 5.2).

Human hunters, unlike insect predators, are not devoid of subjective intentionality, and unlike factory workers, they remain in command of their own labour-power. This does not mean, however, that they do not co-operate in the labour process. Several individuals, conjointly executing

Figure 5.2 Co-operation among insects, human hunters and on the factory floor.

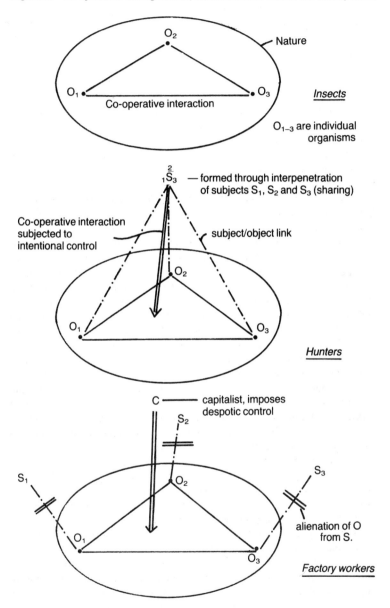

a plan of campaign, may have greater chances of success in making kills than if each were to act alone, so that co-operative tactics may readily be understood as part of a population's adaptive response to the environmental conditions of extraction, just as they may be among non-human predators (Schaller and Lowther 1969: 314–15). The association of co-operating individuals constitutes an effective mechanism of predation, the functioning of which is revealed in the manifest 'behaviour patterns' identified by Steward. These patterns, as we have already seen, are an aspect of the organization of work, whose blueprint is contained neither in the plan of a despotic authority, nor in the genetic constitution of the human organism, but in an acquired, *cultural* tradition. But if as individuals, members of a co-operating team are differentiated in their tasks, they are united as persons in a common purpose. And this unity is grounded in the relations of total mutual involvement which we recognize as sharing. These relations, moreover, which exist in respect of the mechanism of production as well as its products, are by the argument adduced above quite separate from the relations of co-operation that constitute the mechanism itself. The latter are of external, physical contact between discrete individuals; that is, they are relations of adhesion – to recall Meillassoux's expression. The former are relations of *interpenetration* of persons, founded upon their shared experience. In short, the purpose that controls the combined labour power of the severalty of individuals making up the hunting band is not that of an alien will to which they are commonly contracted, but the common purpose of the community embodied, through sharing, in each producer. And it is this purpose that puts the given innate and acquired capacities of individuals to work, engaging them in co-operative interactions one with another, and conjointly in extractive interactions with objects in the environment.

Now the distinction we have drawn between sharing and co-operation, having to do with the constitution of persons and the interaction of individuals respectively, can be precisely mapped onto another between *communion* and *communication* (Langer 1972: 202). Like sharing, communion suggests the interpenetration or fusion of conscious subjects, whereas communication refers to the exchange of units of information between individuals interacting as separate, objectively defined entities. There is no need to restrict the notion of communication, as Langer does, to 'the intentional transmission of ideas from one individual to one or more others' – a restriction that leads her to the extraordinary conclusion that non-human animals, without language, do not communicate at all. An organism communicates, in our terms, when as part of an end-directed performance it emits signals which influence the behaviour of one or more other organisms – usually conspecifics. In this sense, communication is virtually synonymous with co-operative interaction (Bastian 1968: 576), and in biological definitions of society the two are commonly linked: Wilson, for example, regards the essence of sociality as 'reciprocal communication of a cooperative nature' (1980: 7). Whilst for the individuals involved, patterns of communication – like those of co-operation – generally have adaptive consequences that have promoted their establishment under natural selection, nothing is implied here about intentionality (*pace* Burghardt 1970: 12). We have argued that the intentional component of action is derived from the *intersubjective* domain; that is to say, it has its foundation in communion, and is not an intrinsic property of communication any more than it is of co-operation or predation, all of which denote nothing more than teleonomic, behavioural executions. But by virtue of this communion, or intersubjective involvement, human beings do not just communicate with one another, they *converse*. And for just the same reason, they are not merely predators that co-operate, but hunters who share.

These observations have an immediate bearing on the thorny issue of the relation between hunting and the origins of language. In Chapter 3 we outlined two alternative positions on this issue. According to one, the primary function of language is to communicate information about environmental objects, conditions or circumstances, of strategic value in the conduct of co-operative foraging or predation. The other holds that language emerged as a vehicle for the management of intersubjectivity, for the identification of persons rather than things. In the first view, language is an instrument of co-operation, an auxiliary to the organization of work, belonging in that sense with the forces of production. In the second, it is a condition for the constitution of social relations of production, and of the persons bound by them. Whilst accepting that language *does* function instrumentally in extractive activity, we are inclined to the second view when it comes to accounting for its origination (see also Parker and Gibson 1979: 374). This is because non-human predators show themselves eminently capable of executing complex, co-operative sequences without the facility of language, co-ordinating their movements through the maintenance of visual contact. This is the case not only among carnivores such as wolves and lions, but also among non-human primates, above all, baboons and chimpanzees. As Teleki notes, 'many carnivores and both baboons and chimpanzees manage to pursue and capture prey without using purposive, directional patterns of communication' (1975: 165).

There is no reason why early hominids should not have been equally capable, and if language is inessential to co-operative predation, the benefits that accrue from co-operation cannot be assumed to have placed a selective premium on its emergence (Schaller and Lowther 1969:

333–4). It is moreover a fact that among contemporary hunters, language is very little used in the phases of pursuit and capture – which often take place in complete silence simply in order not to disturb the prey (see, for example, Silberbauer 1981: 209–11, on the G/wi Bushmen). In this context, Teleki's observation that among chimpanzees, apparently purposive vocalization is most evident in the course of meat distribution rather than predation, assumes a particular singificance. We may well speculate that the original adaptive function of language lay in its conferring on individual speakers the ability to cope with the conflicting demands of the distributive situation, through the construction and management of personal identity, and that only subsequently was it turned to account as a means of communication in the conduct of predation, possibly enhancing the efficacy of specific kinds of joint pursuit tactics (Teleki 1975: 165). This is to understand language not primarily as a highly elaborate system of communication but rather as the foundation for conscious self-awareness. It did not initially help man to become a predator, nor even – through co-operation – a more efficient predator. What it did do, however, was to turn the protohominid predator into a human hunter.

We began our discussion with the remark of Marx and Engels that men, unlike other animals, *produce* their means of subsistence, and that in so doing they 'are indirectly producing their actual material life' (1977: 42). Further on in the same work they go on to assert that 'the production of life... now appears as a double relationship: on the one hand as a natural, on the other as a social relationship' (1977: 50). Now this is an initial formulation of a dualism that pervades the entire Marxian paradigm, 'between *material and social relations of production*' (Cohen 1978: 92). On the face of it, the distinction would seem to be simply one between two kinds of interaction: interspecific, extractive ones and intraspecific, communicative ones. In the context of hunting, for example, it might be said that there are the relations between individual hunters and their prey, and among hunters as members of a local aggregate or band. And indeed, having established the natural/social dichotomy, Marx and Engels proceed to offer a definition of the social, as 'the co-operation of several individuals' (1977: 50), that could apply just as well to the organization of the hunting band as to that of an insect colony. However, in so far as human and non-human animals exist as components of the natural world, as organisms, *so also must the relations between them*. We have shown that relations of co-operation are essentially of this kind, constituting a system of forces that is supra-individual but *not* supra-biological. Thus the co-operative or 'work' relations linking individual conspecifics cannot be social at all, but are rather material (Cohen 1978: 111). That is why it is meaningless to speak of the social relations of hunting as 'band relations'. Social relations of production exist between persons who operate the system comprising the sum of productive forces, and not between the individual components (somatic and extrasomatic) of the system being operated. Amongst hunters they are relations of sharing, not of co-operation. In short, relations between men are both social and material: between persons they are social, between individuals they are material (Cohen 1978: 93).

Moreover a precisely equivalent dichotomy can be drawn between social action and material reaction, and in the first part of this essay we linked this to the distinction between appropriation and extraction, or more specifically, hunting and predation. Appropriative action has its source in the person who is a subject of social relations, extractive behaviour issues from the individual as a natural being. We can no more comprehend the confrontation between hunters and prey in exclusively material terms than we can comprehend the relations among hunters in terms that are exclusively social. Sharing is a social relation, but then so is hunting social action. Predation is a material reaction, but then so is co-operation a material interaction. If the essence of hunting is the intentionality that sets the body to work, through sharing the intentions are those of the collectivity. If the essence of predation is the work of the body, in co-operation a collection of bodies work conjointly with a concomitantly heightened effect. Putting all four terms together, we arrive at a summary formulation of the following kind: sharing constitutes the common purpose that, in hunting, engages human bodies in co-operative interactions whose material outcome is predatory extraction. Sharing, like hunting, pertains to the human history of nature; co-operation, like predation, pertains to the natural history of man.

All of this has an immediate bearing on how we draw the boundary between social and ecological systems. As an example of how *not* to draw the boundary, we have this assertion by Cook, purporting to reiterate the crucial message of Marx and Engels, 'that it is a mistake to allow an interspecific population focus to displace a concern with intraspecific relations and processes which facilitate man's *un-animal-like* manipulation and transformation of his natural environment' (Cook 1973: 42, see also Ellen 1982: 91). The alleged mistake is attributed to a once-fashionable brand of ecological anthropology that claimed to be able to comprehend the human economy entirely within an ecosystemic framework, using terms and concepts derived from animal ecology and population biology (Rappaport 1971). But there is nothing whatever 'un-animal-like' about patterns of intraspecific, co-operative behaviour in human populations, patterns which – for the greater part of human history preceding the origins of agriculture – facilitated thoroughly 'animal-like' processes of extraction, of raw materials from the environment. It is perfectly possible to examine both intra- and interspecific interactions within a naturalistic, ecological framework, and to compare the co-operative and extractive behaviour of man and other animals. It is *not* possible, however, within the constraints of such a framework, to grasp the character of the relations among men that we call social. Nor is it possible to grasp what *is* 'un-animal-like' in man's confrontation with objects of the natural environment, which lies not in their manipulation and transformation, but in their appropriation. For it is nature appropriated, and not necessarily transformed, that is engaged in social relations.

Both intra- and interspecific relations, then, have their social and ecological aspects. To place the boundary between the social and the ecological at the boundary of the human species, putting all intraspecific relations into the domain of the former, and all interspecific relations into the domain of the latter, is to miss the parallels between human and animal patterns of co-operation, as well as what is specifically human in the labour process. It will not do to set up a division of labour between economists who study intraspecific, distributive exchange and ecologists who study interspecific, trophic exchange (Lee 1969: 73). According to the view for which we have argued here, the domain of the social is the domain of human purposes, furnishing the intentionality that 'drives' productive action. The boundary between the social and the ecological corresponds to that between the intentional and the behavioural components of action. It marks the point, in human life, *where mechanism takes over from the ends of purpose*. Human beings are, of necessity, simultaneously involved in systems of both social and ecological relations, constituting them respectively as conscious persons and as individual organisms. That is to say, they could no more exist as persons outside of society than they could as organisms outside of the ecosystem. In production, I submit, we find the essential link between these two domains of human existence.

Notes to Chapter 5

1   Ellen (1982: 130–6) completely misunderstands the nature of ecological production, by rendering it as the production of *energy*. It is of course an elementary law of thermodynamics that energy is not produced, rather it is harnessed and transformed – whether by living things or inanimate machines. By 'producing energy', Ellen evidently has in mind the expenditure of subsistence effort, where the values of that effort (r) and of the food obtained (p) are measured in calorific terms instead of in terms of social costs and benefits. 'Ecological efficiency' is then defined (after Harris 1971: 203) as the ratio of these two values (p/r). Ratios of this kind, however, are quite meaningless, since no more of a relationship obtains between the effort expended in throwing a spear and the calorific yield of the hunter's kill than between the electric

current needed to trigger a thermostat and the heat output of the boiler it controls (Ingold 1979: 276). As understood by ecologists, production is an energy conversion process like any other (for example, the conversion of boiler fuel into heat), whose efficiency is given by the ratio of the energy content of each increment of organic growth to the content of the food ingested or synthesized during the same interval. In line with thermodynamic law, this ratio can never reach 100 per cent, and is usually a long way below, the balance of ingested energy not stored in living tissue having been either not assimilated or dissipated in respiration (Odum 1975: 65).

2   One of the very few archaeologists to have recognized this point is Ducos, who notes that 'all those features which distinguish the *domestic* animal from the wild one...stem not from the evolutionary dynamics of the animal but from those of the human society'. He goes on to offer a definition of domestication very close to our own:

'Domestication can be said to exist when living animals are integrated as objects into the socioeconomic organization of the human group, in the sense that, while living, those animals are objects for ownership, inheritance, exchange, trade, etc., as are the other objects (or persons) with which human groups have something to do' (Ducos 1978: 54).

3   Fried likewise declares that 'the paramount invention that led to human society was *sharing*' (1967: 106). But Wilson's position is rather that the invention which led to sharing was *society.*

References for Chapter 5

Bastian, J. 1968 Psychological perspectives. In *Animal communication*, ed. T.A. Sebeok. Bloomington: Indiana University Press.

Bourdieu, P. 1977 *Outline of a theory of practice.* Cambridge University Press.

Burghardt, G. M. 1970 Defining 'communication'. In *Communication by chemical signals* (Advances in chemoreception Vol. I) eds. J. W. Johnston Jr., D. G. Moulton and A. Turk. New York: Appleton-Century-Crofts.

Cohen, G. A. 1978 *Karl Marx's theory of history: a defence.* Oxford University Press.

Cook, S. 1973 Production, ecology and economic anthropology: notes towards an integrated frame of reference. *Social Science Information* 12: 25–52.

Ducos, P. 1978 'Domestication' defined and methodological approaches to its recognition in faunal assemblages. In *Approaches to faunal analysis in the Middle East*, eds. R. H. Meadow and M. A. Zeder. Harvard University, Peabody Museum of Archaeology and Ethnology, Bulletin 2.

Ellen, R. 1982 *Environment, subsistence and system: the ecology of small-scale social formations.* Cambridge University Press.

Engels, F. 1934 *Dialectics of nature.* Moscow: Progress.

Faris, J. C. 1975 Social evolution, population and production. In *Population, ecology and social evolution*, ed. S. Polgar. The Hague: Mouton.

Firth, R. 1975 The sceptical anthropologist? Social anthropology and Marxist views on society. In *Marxist analyses and social anthropology*, ed. M. Bloch. London: Malaby.

Fortes, M. 1983 *Rules and the emergence of society* (Royal Anthropological Institute Occasional Paper 39). London: RAI.

Fried, M. H. 1967 *The evolution of political society*. New York: Random House.

Galdikas, B. M. F. and G. Teleki 1981 Variations in subsistence activities of female and male pongids: new perspectives on the origins of hominid labor division. *Current Anthropology* **22**: 241–56.

Gibson, T. 1985 The sharing of substance versus the sharing of activity among the Buid. *Man* (N.S.) **20**: 391–411.

Godelier, M. 1972 *Rationality and irrationality in economics*. London: New Left Books.

Godelier, M. 1978 Infrastructures, societies and history. *Current Anthropology* **19**: 763–71.

Godelier, M. 1979 Territory and property in primitive society. In *Human ethology*, eds. M. von Cranach, K. Foppa, W. Lepenies and D. Ploog. Cambridge University Press.

Harris, M. 1971 *Culture, man and nature*. New York: Crowell.

Ingold, T. 1979 The social and ecological relations of culture-bearing organisms: an essay in evolutionary dynamics. In *Social and ecological systems*, eds. P. C. Burnham and R. F. Ellen (A.S.A. monogr. 18). London: Academic Press.

Ingold, T. 1980 *Hunters, pastoralists and ranchers*. Cambridge University Press.

Ingold, T. 1982 Review of *Omnivorous primates*, eds. R.S.O. Harding and G. Teleki. *Man* (N.S.) **17**: 162–4.

Ingold, T. 1983 Gathering the herds: work and co-operation in a northern Finnish community. *Ethnos* **48**: 133–59.

Isaac, G.L. 1978 The food-sharing behavior of protohuman hominids. *Scientific American* **238**(4): 90–108.

Kruuk, H. 1972 *The spotted hyena: a study of predation and social behavior*. University of Chicago Press.

Langer, S. K. 1972 *Mind: an essay on human feeling*, vol. 2. Baltimore: Johns Hopkins University Press.

Leacock, E. and R. B. Lee 1982 Introduction. In *Politics and history in band societies*, eds. E. Leacock and R. B. Lee. Cambridge University Press.

Lee, R. B. 1969 !Kung bushman subsistence: an input-output analysis. In *Contributions to anthropology: ecological essays*, ed. D. Damas. Bulletin 230, National Museums of Canada, Ottawa.

Lee, R. B. 1980 Existe-t-il un mode de production 'fourrageur'? *Anthropologie et Sociétés* **4**: 59–74.

Marx, K. 1930 *Capital*. London: Dent.

Marx, K. 1964 *Economic and political manuscripts of 1844*. New York: International Publishers.

Marx, K. and F. Engels 1977 *The German ideology*, ed. C. J. Arthur. London: Lawrence and Wishart.

Meillassoux, C. 1981 *Maidens, meal and money*. Cambridge University Press.

Moscovici, S. 1976 *Society against nature*. Brighton: Harvester Press.

Murphy, R. F. 1970 Basin ethnography and ethnological theory. In *Languages and cultures of western North America*, ed. E. H. Swanson, Jr. Pocatello: Idaho State University Press.

Odum, E. P. 1975 *Ecology.* New York: Holt, Rinehart and Winston.

Parker, S. T. and K. R. Gibson 1979 A developmental model for the evolution of language and intelligence in early hominids. *The Behavioral and Brain Sciences* **2**: 367–408.

Price, J. A. 1975 Sharing: the integration of intimate economies. *Anthropologica* **17**: 3–27.

Rappaport, R. A. 1971 Nature, culture and ecological anthropology. In *Man, culture and society* (revised edition), ed. H. L. Shapiro. London: Oxford University Press.

Saussure, F. de 1959 *Course in general linguistics.* New York: McGraw-Hill.

Schaller, G. B. and G. R. Lowther 1969 The relevance of carnivore behavior to the study of early hominids. *Southwestern Journal of Anthropology* **25**: 307–41.

Schmidt, A. 1971 *The concept of nature in Marx.* London: New Left Books.

Silberbauer, G. B. 1981 *Hunter and habitat in the Central Kalahari desert.* Cambridge University Press.

Steward, J. H. 1955 *Theory of culture change.* Urbana: University of Illinois Press.

Strum, S. C. 1981 Processes as products of change: baboon predatory behavior at Gilgil, Kenya. In *Omnivorous Primates*, eds. R.S.O. Harding and G. Teleki. New York: Columbia University Press.

Teleki, G. 1975 Primate subsistence patterns: collector – predators and gatherer–hunters. *Journal of Human Evolution* **4**: 125–84.

Terray, E. 1972 *Marxism and 'primitive' societies.* New York: Monthly Review Press.

White, L. A. 1959 *The evolution of culture.* New York: McGraw-Hill.

Wilson, E. O. 1980 *Sociobiology: the new synthesis* (abridged edition). Cambridge, Mass.: Harvard University Press.

Wilson, P. J. 1975 The promising primate. *Man* (N.S.) **10**: 5–20.

Woodburn, J. 1972 Ecology, nomadic movement and the composition of the local group: an East African example and its implications. In *Man, settlement and urbanism*, eds. P. J. Ucko, R. Tringham and G. W. Dimbleby. London: Duckworth.

6

Territoriality and tenure: the appropriation of space in hunting and gathering societies.

If we are to arrive at generalizations about the nature of human society on the basis of systematic comparison of ethnographically documented instances, we must at least be reasonably confident that we are comparing like with like. In a recent discussion of the phenomenon of territoriality, Dyson-Hudson and Smith complain that one major impediment to cross-cultural comparison lies in a lack of standardization in the use of terms to denote the appropriation of space by human groups. 'The term "territory" and "territoriality" tends to be applied to hunter–gatherers and pastoralists, while what may be equivalent behavior among agriculturalists is described in terms of land tenure systems' (1978: 25–6). It is indeed the case that in the apparently endless controversy over whether or not hunting and gathering bands 'own' the land they occupy, the object of such ownership has generally been conceived as a territory, whilst in accounts of agricultural societies this concept has more often been reserved to denote the wider domain of political sovereignty or jurisdiction rather than the particular blocks of cultivable land over which people may claim rights of use and disposal.[1] The reasons for this contrast are of some significance, and I shall touch on them shortly. However, I shall go on to argue that what has been described as land tenure very definitely does *not* connote the same kind of behaviour as that implied by territoriality, and that whilst we may legitimately inquire into the forms of both tenure and territoriality in hunting and gathering societies, it is absolutely essential to maintain the distinction between them.

My position, in brief, is that the opposition between the two terms corresponds to that between the social and material dimensions of human existence, an opposition that must be recognized in the analysis of *any* society, whether of agriculturalists, pastoralists or hunter–gatherers. Tenure is an aspect of that system of relations which *constitutes* persons as productive agents and directs their purposes, territoriality is an aspect of the means through which those purposes are put into effect under given environmental circumstances. After a review of the ways in which the concept of territoriality has been employed in studies of animal behaviour, I shall devote the major part of this essay to an elaboration of the distinction between territoriality and tenure. This will lead us, in the final part, to an exploration of the kinds of tenure we might expect to find in hunting and gathering societies, and to the question of whether or not we can regard the object of such tenure as land.

I

Most recent inquiries into human territoriality have taken their place as part of a wider debate about the behavioural continuities between man and other animals, and their possible hereditary basis. The study of contemporary hunters and gatherers has a special significance in the context of this debate, since it is supposed that they present us with the closest approximation we have to the conditions once obtaining throughout the long period of hominid evolution during which the fundamental phylogenetic adaptations of the species were taking shape under the pressures of natural selection (Wilson 1980: 292). When, therefore, it is claimed that a particular group of hunters and gatherers do or do not exhibit 'territoriality', as the case may be, the concept has evidently to be understood in one of the many senses employed by ecologists and ethologists. As is well known, the investigation of territorial behaviour in the animal kingdom began with the study of birds; not until well into the present century was it extended to mammals, and eventually to man. One of the first recorded observations of avian territoriality, interestingly enough, was presented in terms of a metaphor from land tenure: it was Willughby who, in 1622, described the place seized by the nightingale as its 'Friehold' (Nice 1933). The tendency today is somewhat the reverse, for having construed the natural order as a reflection of civil society, we are inclined to regard social relations of tenure as manifestations of a natural disposition towards territoriality. The resulting confusion, which it will be my primary purpose to dispel, exemplifies our susceptibility to what Sahlins has aptly called 'Scientific Totemism' (1976: 106).

The systematic study of territoriality in birds began in Germany with the work of Altum (1868). Long unknown to the English-speaking world, Altum introduced the definition of a territory as an area defended by its holder against intrusion, to ensure food and breeding space; and most importantly, he recognized the function of song as a means by which individual birds advertise their respective territorial positions. This latter point is of more than mere ornithological significance, since it focuses attention on the *communicative* aspect of territorial behaviour, an aspect that will be of crucial significance in the argument I am about to present.

The Irish naturalist, C.B. Moffat, emphasized the role of territorial competition in stabilizing the number of birds in an area around an equilibrium point, by excluding surplus individuals from reproduction (Moffat 1903). His remarkable anticipation of the theory of group selection, later to be expounded by Wynne-Edwards (1962), remained, like Altum's work, long unrecognized. It too had a significance that extends even to man, for as Carr-Saunders showed in 1922, if hunter–gatherer populations are to be regulated by a density-dependent mechanism around an environmentally determined optimum level, there must be a one-to-one association between band and territory (Carr-Saunders 1922: 202). Much of the effort devoted to the 'discovery' of exclusive territories, in the face of a good deal of plain evidence to the contrary, has been motivated by a commitment to the view that some such equilibrating mechanism exists. However, most claims to have established a mechanism of this kind are quite unfounded, resting as they do solely on the observation that women in hunting and gathering societies are usually constrained to space out successive births at intervals of four years or so (e.g. Birdsell 1958). For density-dependent control, it would be necessary for the average birth interval to vary directly with the size of the group exploiting a bounded territory. Absolutely no evidence has been presented to this effect. For this reason, I consider the argument to have reached a dead end, and do not intend to pursue it further here.

More than any other previous work, Howard's *Territory in bird life* (1920) established the concept of territoriality in the study of animal behaviour, serving to stimulate comparable investigations in other branches of the animal kingdom. Howard argued that holding a territory is the combined result of two dispositions, first 'to remain in a particular place in a particular environment' and second to defend that place against incursion by outsiders (1920: 18). Subsequent authors have tended to emphasize one of these dispositions at the expense of the other, generating much definitional confusion (Carpenter 1958). The criterion of boundary defence is most frequently stressed, as originally by Altum, and in Noble's (1939) minimal definition of the territory as 'any defended area'. Others, however, have laid greater weight on the attachment to place, regardless of whether or not an area is actively defended (Pitelka 1959, Kaufman 1971). One solution which has been widely adopted, following Burt (1943), is to distinguish between 'territory' and 'home range': the former denoting a defended area, the latter a region within which an individual or group habitually moves, possibly anchored on one or more central sites, but without rigidly defined boundaries. The distinction rests on the separation of the *behavioural* from the *ecological* component of territoriality, the one having to do with intraspecific aggression and defence, the other with the association between a population and its environmental resources (Peterson 1975: 55–6). It is of course possible for mobile individuals or groups to carry around with them portable 'fields', excluding others from coming within a certain fixed distance, without any recognized attachments to specific sites; just as attachments to place do not presuppose exclusive aggression or defence (Hinde 1956: 342, Tinbergen 1957).

Even if boundary defence is taken to be an essential attribute of territorial behaviour, little or no actual fighting need be involved. Aggression, as Kummer has pointed out, occurs during the initial establishment of territories, when individuals or groups may clash for occupancy of the best sites. But 'once this is settled, the movements of the owners become formalized and predictable; conflict is minimized' (Kummer 1971: 224). So long as everyone knows where the boundaries are, territorial behaviour will be limited to periodic but harmless ritualized posturing. The same point underlies Wilson's redefinition of the territory as 'an area occupied more or less exclusively...through overt defence or advertisement' (1971: 195). Defence presupposes the possibility of imminent attack, whereas through advertisement the individual or group periodically announces its position relative to those of its neighbours. The notion of 'advertisement' takes us back to Altum's original demonstration of the function of bird song; and since then many similar examples have been found in other branches of the animal kingdom, involving visual and olfactory as well as auditory signals. Taken together, they show that *territorial behaviour is basically a mode of communication*, serving to convey information about the location of individuals dispersed in space. By contrast, and to anticipate our argument somewhat, *tenure is a mode of appropriation*, by which persons exert claims over resources dispersed in space.

The criterion of boundary defence is not, however, a necessary concomitant of a 'behavioural' approach to territoriality. By relating territorial exclusion inversely to hierarchical dominance, it can be shown that complete boundary closure is a limiting case that occurs only when no party is prepared to accept subordination to another. Willis (1967: 102) recognizes the potential openness of boundaries by defining the territory as 'a space in which one animal or group generally dominates others which become dominant elsewhere'. Of two neighbours, the dominance of each grades off with distance from an occupied centre (Leyhausen 1965: 249), leaving an indistinct frontier region between their respective territories where neither has a clear priority. Silberbauer (1981) has applied Willis's definition to what he regards as territoriality among the G/wi Bushmen of the Kalahari, stressing the point that to adopt a view of this kind is to obviate any consideration of boundary defence. There is no necessary restriction of the flow of individuals across territorial boundaries, the only condition being that visitors accept a position subordinate to their hosts, and recognize the privileges of the latter (Eibl-Eibesfeldt 1979: 141). According to Silberbauer, among the G/wi 'a visiting band or a single visitor submits to the dominance of the host band by either waiting for an invitation or by seeking permission to enter and occupy the territory' (1981: 187). Myers depicts an exactly similar situation among Pintupi Aborigines of the Australian Western Desert. Movement is unrestricted, but 'when moving into another's range one should ask, or somehow announce one's presence, as a form of deference, usually with smoke'. Moreover, although visitors have the same rights of access to resources as their hosts, 'in decisions about where to go, or how to deal with disputes, they are clearly "second class citizens"' (Myers 1982: 185, 191).

There is a striking parallel here between the alleged 'ownership' of territory, and the 'ownership' of animal kills in hunter – gatherer societies, which cannot go unremarked. An owner is virtually obliged to distribute his spoils, just as he is to admit outsiders. It seems to be as rare, and to be regarded as equally reprehensible, for permission of entry to be refused as to withhold shares of meat. Either form of denial can precipitate disputes, as too can the taking of resources without first asking permission. As Williams states of the Yolngu, of northern Australia, 'one could say that to own is to have the obligation to share' (1982: 148). Though 'ownership' here refers to territory, this statement could likewise have been made about extracted produce. In both instances, the concept of ownership does not denote a real division of access to resources, but serves merely to effect an ideological separation between 'givers' and 'receivers' in the case of food-sharing, and 'hosts' and 'visitors' in the case of territorial admission. This separation is a necessary condition for the expression of generosity, and for the satisfaction and prestige that accrues to those who – from time to time – are in a position to play host to their neighbours (see Hiatt 1965: 27, for an example from the Gidjingali people of northern Arnhem Land, Australia). We return to this point in Chapter 9.

II

The concept of tenure, at least as it has been used in anthropology, has its source in the field of jurisprudence. The fact that this concept has been central to the analysis of social structure among agricultural peoples, whilst until recently it has been considered inapplicable to societies of hunters and gatherers, is surely symptomatic of a residual commitment to the comparative method of classical social evolutionism, according to which the hunter–gatherers of today are assimilated to a preconceived image of natural man at or near the absolute zero of cultural development. For tenure implies man's subjective *transcendence* of the natural world: one cannot appropriate that within which one's being is wholly contained. On the practical level, or so orthodox evolutionism had it, this transcendence was marked by the inception of 'food production' – cultivation, the domestication of plants and animals, man's *mastery* over nature (Childe 1942: 55, Engels 1934: 179–80, see Ingold 1979: 282–3). On the other hand, in so far as territoriality is supposed to issue from innate disposition, its manifestation in hunting and gathering societies is regarded as a consequence of man's original failure to transcend his *own* nature. Hunter–gatherers, it is often assumed, have yet to bend nature to a social purpose; wholly enmeshed within a web of material relations they are deemed to remain subservient to her demands – hence the persistent inclination to view hunting and gathering societies in terms that are exclusively ecological rather than social (Ellen 1979: 5).

For my part, as I have argued in Chapter 5, I would hold that man is everywhere both social subject and natural object. As an agent of production, a person, he stands apart from the natural world and acts purposively upon it; yet as an organic human being, a biological individual, he is an integral part of that world, confronting the components of the environment as one of nature's forces (Marx 1930: 169). We have therefore to separate the appropriation of nature by social persons from the patterns of associative interaction that are generated between individuals in the course of this appropriative movement. These patterns, which have their counterparts in the animal kingdom, constitute what the ethologist or sociobiologist typically regards as 'social organization'. Wilson, for example, takes a society to be a collection of co-operating individuals engaged in reciprocal communication, whose association is governed by a set of behavioural instructions contained in the biogram – or its cultural analogue. Territorial behaviour, as we have seen, presents one facet of this co-operation and communication, which is likely to surface in one form or another whenever it can be shown to confer an adaptive advantage upon each and every individual. Yet reductionist sociobiology is utterly blind to the intersubjective domain of human existence, and therefore can see no difference between tenure and territoriality. Thus Wilson (1980: 128) can assert that 'nearly all vertebrates and a large number of the behaviorally most advanced invertebrates, conduct their lives according to *precise rules of land tenure*, spacing and dominance' (my emphasis). Schaller and Lowther (1969: 319) likewise bring their discussion of home range and territoriality among social carnivores under the heading of 'land tenure system'. A similar reductionism underlies the suggestion of Dyson-Hudson and Smith, with which I began, that territoriality and tenure may be different terms for the same thing, conventionally applied to hunter–gatherers and cultivators respectively.[2]

In my view, the concept of tenure pertains to quite another domain of reality, and to an entirely different understanding of what is meant by social life. 'Being social', as I have argued in Chapter 2, 'implies not co-operation but *consciousness*,...the establishment of a dimension of intersubjectivity which is not reducible to the association and interaction of individuals defined in objective (organic or physical) terms.' In short, tenure is an aspect of relations between persons as subjects, territoriality relates individuals as objects. The former informs appropriative action, the latter is manifested in co-operative behaviour. Translating the opposition into a Marxian idiom, we would say that where territoriality belongs to the *forces* of production, laying down a template for the practical conduct of activity, tenure belongs to the *relations* of production regulating access to, and control over, the resources of nature.[3] Thus what Godelier defines as a 'territory', in a language much closer to jurisprudence than to ethology, is actually the object of tenure:

The term 'territory' is used to designate a portion of nature and space that is claimed by a given society, this society guaranteeing all, or only some, of its members stable rights of access to control and use of all or part of the resources found therein, and which it (the society) is capable of exploiting. (1979: 138)

The territory, in these terms, is a portion of *property*, whose concrete appropriation is jurally represented by abstract rules of 'ownership'. And as Godelier points out, in all societies the holding of property constitutes a relation between persons, so that the forms of ownership of territory function as social relations of production (1979: 144).

We have now established the poles of an essential dichotomy: *tenure engages nature in a system of social relations, territoriality engages society in a system of natural relations*. From this we can move on to a further contrast, that where tenure denotes a process that is continually going on, territoriality denotes a succession of synchronic states. It is a frequent observation in ethology that territorial behaviour can take multiple forms, even within a single population over time, and that it may be – so to speak – switched 'on' or 'off' according to current environmental circumstances (Hinde 1956: 342–3, Carpenter 1958: 229, King 1976: 327, Dyson-Hudson and Smith 1978: 23, Wilson 1980: 289). No more in animals than in man is territoriality, as often claimed, a 'fixed biological imperative' (Guenther 1981: 117). During the extraction of dispersed, predictable and sedentary fauna or flora, territorial compartmentalization may promote the even spread of population over common resources and hence their efficient exploitation. But when the same population turns to the pursuit of prey that is concentrated, mobile and unpredictable in location, territorial boundaries impede rather than facilitate resource extraction, and may very well be disregarded (Wilmsen

1973: 8–9). Moreover, a particular configuration of boundaries is rarely long-lasting; territories are likely to be renegotiated from one year or season to the next. Their size, too, will vary, depending upon the pressures on space – in Huxley's (1934: 227) metaphor they are compressible, like elastic discs. Nevertheless, despite all this variability, territorial behaviour results from the activation of a programme that is imprinted, either genetically or as part of a learned tradition, in the individuals of a population. In other words, it manifests the nature of those individuals regarded as discrete entities, or things.

Now tenure, as I have shown, is an aspect of social (that is, intersubjective) relations. Such relations, like the persons that they constitute, are processes in time. To find out about tenure, an anthropologist has to ask of his informants: 'who owns, or has rights over, this land?' The answer comes: a certain person, or maybe several persons with multiple, nesting or overlapping claims. To pursue his inquiry, he has then to discover who these persons are, and for this he can be satisfied with nothing less than a complete biography of each in their mutual relations (Luckmann 1979: 67). Every person *is* his past, a continuous, experiential trajectory described by the temporal unfolding of a total system of social relations of which he is but a particular point of emergence. In short, to understand persons, social relations and hence tenure we must adopt a perspective that is holistic and processual rather than atomistic and static, as adopted in the analysis of territorial interaction. Tenure is about the ways in which a resource locale is worked or bound into the biography of the subject, or into the developmental trajectory of those groups, domestic and otherwise, of which he is a member. For it is only by virtue of his belonging to the community that a person acquires a relation to a determinate portion of natural space, furnishing those material conditions of his social being 'which constitute, as it were, a prolongation of his body' (Marx 1964: 87–9) Through tenure, the locale stands to its holder in a relation of metonymy.

A perfect illustration of this point may be drawn from Myers's (1976) superb study of the Pintupi of Western Australia. What is held among the Pintupi is a 'country' (*ngurra*), a term which can refer just as well to a specific place of abode as to the familiar landscape around it with all its peculiar features. But a person identifies with a country only because of his involvement, during the various phases of his life from conception to death, with particular others who are known as his 'one country men': thus in talking about countries one is in fact talking about histories of interpersonal relations (1976: 162). Pintupi residential groups are extremely fluid, and in the desert environment people move around a great deal; therefore every individual is likely to number a different set of others among his one country men (1976: 331–2). Since it is through these others that he derives both his attachments to place and his social identity, it follows that *his* country will not be quite the same as that of anyone else, and indeed that the construction of the 'person' and the 'country' are – to all intents and purposes – the same. As Myers puts it: 'The countries with which [a person] identifies, therefore, constitute a kind of record of who he is, with whom he is identified or related, and where he has been' (1976: 392).

All this suggests an approach to tenure somewhat analogous to Mauss's (1954) celebrated treatment of the gift. What makes the gift more than an inert object is its capacity to convey or prolong the person of the giver beyond the spatio-temporal bounds of his own immediate self. As the material embodiment of an intersubjective process within which persons are constituted as purposive social agents, gifts are seen to be empowered with a creative principle. But the 'spirit' of the gift, its vital force or subjective load, exists – like the process it manifests – only in the current of time; outside that current the gift object reverts to its original condition as a static thing. That is why gift exchange has to be conceived as a linear projection of past into future, rather than as a sequence of isolable events each frozen in the instant of the present. Tenure, I believe, should be regarded in a similar way. Every claim is part of a continuous process, expressing an intention or promise for the future through the fulfilment of past obligation. Writing of land claims among the agricultural Kalanga of Botswana, Werbner observes that 'these claims are understood by the people themselves in terms of histories of past land-holding, so that a contemporary patch of land is seen as having a time dimension represented by ancestral estates' (1975: 119).

How different, again, this is from territorial behaviour, which presupposes no sense of past and future, no awareness of time, no commitments or intentions. The territorial configuration may be comprehended synchronically as a transient equilibrium, one of a diachronic sequence of such equilibria, manifested in isolated events of communicative behaviour. Indeed the comparison that de Saussure drew between language change and successive moves in a game of chess is also peculiarly apposite to the discussion of territoriality. To adopt his terms, as in chess each move on the territorial board 'is absolutely distinct from the preceding and subsequent equilibrium. The change effected belongs to neither state: *only states matter*' (de Saussure 1959: 89, my emphasis). In tenure, to the contrary, only process matters.

But to return to the analogy with the gift, not only does the object of tenure have a past, it is also conceived to be more than a passive container for exploitable resources. Recall that Mauss found the prototype for his notion of the animating principle of the gift object in a

Maori concept (*hau*) that pertains in the first place to the *land*, or more particularly, to the forest and its game (Mauss 1954: 8). Now as a spiritual quality, the *hau* of the land refers to its productiveness or fecundity (Sahlins 1972: 167–8); and if this is indeed similar to the spirit that animates the gift, then we must suppose that it is similarly derived, through a transferral of the creative movement of social life from personal subjects to material substance. Thus it seems that the country itself, or the nexus of locales within it, is imbued with the power that grows the men who hold it, a power that insistently demands periodic ritual renewal (as gifts demand repayment) if social life is to continue. This is a point that has received particular emphasis in much of the ethnography on Australian Aboriginal society. Munn (1970) has drawn attention to a pervasive theme of Aboriginal thought in the way that objects, or features of the landscape, are seen both to engender subjects in the form of living persons, and to be the congealed embodiments of the past creative activity of ancestral beings. The transformation of subjects into objects and *vice versa* is, as Munn recognizes, equally central to the Maussian understanding of gift exchange, in which things become 'parts of persons' and persons 'behave in some measure as if they were things' (Mauss 1954: 11, see Munn 1970: 142)

This native conception of the consubstantiality or interconvertibility of places and people, according to which each appears immanent in the other, has convinced many anthropologists that Aboriginal tenure is primarily spiritual in quality, rather than having anything specifically economic about it (e.g. Piddington 1971: 240). In a classic study of Aboriginal social organization, Elkin asserted that the bond to country 'is a religious one', based on deep-seated spiritual and emotional attachments:

From one point of view, the members who belong to the local group by birth, own their subdivision of the tribal territory. But it is truer to say that the country owns them and that they cannot remain away from it indefinitely and still live. (Elkin 1938: 40–1)

No one has expressed this interpretation with greater precision and economy than Mr Justice Blackburn, in his assessment of the anthropological evidence in support of Yolngu claims of land ownership in the celebrated Yirrkala case of 1971. 'The fundamental truth about the aboriginals' relationship to land', he wrote, 'is that whatever else it is, it is a religious relationship'; and moreover 'it seems easier, on the evidence, to say that the clan belongs to the land than that the land belongs to the clan' (cited in Williams 1983: 94–5).[4]

Implicit in this formulation is the notion that tenure must be *either* religious (as in the Aboriginal conception) *or* economic (as in the western conception), but cannot exhibit both aspects simultaneously. 'In studying

Aboriginal local organization', Hiatt has written, 'it is important to distinguish two kinds of relationship between people and land – ritual relationships and economic relationships. The ownership of land (if the term is to be used) must be understood in the light of this distinction' (1962: 284). On the basis of his own data on the Gidjingali, Hiatt found that the only ties of an exclusive nature between people and places existed in the ritual sphere (1965: 28). Rights of tenure were vested in patrilineal clans (or sometimes groups of two or three clans); the objects of tenure were so-called 'estates' consisting of clusters of sites and the surrounding country. In economic life, however, people moved quite freely over the terrain, unhindered by estates or their putative boundaries, and resided in loose-knit communities whose variable membership was drawn from several clans. We can refer to these communities as bands, and to the living area of each – in which it customarily hunted, gathered and camped – as its range (Stanner 1965: 2). Thus 'a clan has an estate, a band has a range' (Maddock 1982: 42); the relationship of clan to estate is religious in character, that of band to range is economic. About the latter, however, there was nothing exclusive, since the total range was open to all (see also Warner 1937: 379).

The separation of the economic from the religious, in this analysis, rests on a very narrow view of the economy, by which it becomes virtually coextensive with the field of material relations of co-operation (constituting the band as a unit of foraging) and of extraction (linking the band's population with the resources of its range). There is no way of comprehending, within the dichotomy of band and range, either the social relations of production, or their embodiment in the physical features of the landscape. Yet it is precisely these relations between persons with respect to place which, projected ideologically as religious relations between place and persons, furnish tenure with a spiritual dimension. There is no incompatibility between the statements, on the one hand, that as persons belong to clans so the locales constituent of estates belong to them; and on the other hand, that they belong to these locales, from which they are conceived to have issued and to have derived the substance of their being. As Williams writes, 'owning the land and being owned by it are not necessarily contradictory or mutually exclusive' (1983: 106–7). These are but two ways, more or less 'economic' and 'religious' respectively, of describing the same *social* relations of tenure. Indeed the distinction between religion and economy, upon which western legal and anthropological argument sets such store, has no meaning for native people. Seen through their eyes, 'at once the distinction is dissolved. The apparently non-economic aspect of the man-land relationship is only so to us...' (Hamilton 1982: 90). For the very provisioning of society is thought to depend upon the proper conduct of ritual activity, whose object is periodically to revitalize the environment, thereby securing the re-production of all animal and plant life.

It follows from these observations that the paired concepts of band and range, and of clan and estate, fall on either side of a division not between the domains of economy and religion, but much more fundamentally, between those of material (or ecological) and social relationships. Thus the band consists of an aggregate of individuals engaged in a common nexus of ecological relations through their exploitation of the range, the estate consists of a set of environmental locales engaged in a common nexus of social relations within and between clans, relations which may be viewed either in their economic or in their religious aspect. The same division, as we have shown, separates territoriality from tenure, and it is to this – following our Australian detour – to which we must now return.

'Social relations', including relations of tenure, '*are what they do*, or better still what they make men do' (Godelier 1979: 146). They are the locus of human intentions, of conscious agency. If, then, territorial behaviour has adaptive functions, these must lie in the implementation of social purposes under specific environmental conditions. In other words, territoriality is an *instrument* of the appropriative movement which we have subsumed under the concept of tenure, constituting one part of the complex apparatus that men interpose between themselves and the natural world in the realization of their objectives. To discover what the instrumental functions of territoriality are, and the circumstances under which it is more likely to represent a facility than a hindrance, we are well advised to turn to parallels in the animal kingdom. And the lesson that these parallels teach us, as we have already observed, is that territorial behaviour establishes a *form of co-operation*. By parcelling out a common range, the occupants of each block know with some precision where their neighbours are, and what particular resources they are exploiting. When resources are dispersed, and more or less fixed, this knowledge will be of benefit to everyone. When they are not, it may be more advantageous for individuals to concentrate in order to share knowledge about the location of prey, and to exploit it effectively. It is therefore no surprise to find that many species possess 'wired-in' territorial programmes that will be activated under conditions of the former kind, whilst remaining latent under the latter.

Nor is it any surprise to find analogous, culturally coded programmes in human populations. Thus according to Peterson, 'land ownership ideo-logies which exhaustively divide up people and place have adaptive consequences', since they allow people 'to predict where other groups are and which resources they are using' (1979: 121). Among the Pintupi, Myers writes, the members of local groups make no attempt to withhold environmental resources for their exclusive enjoyment, and always grant free access to visitors. Nevertheless, 'people still must know how many persons are exploiting an area and where they are in order to plan strategies of exploitation'. For this reason, it is only proper that visitors should announce their arrival and intentions; moreover they too are eager for whatever information their hosts can supply, simply in order 'to avoid coming upon a string of previously exploited areas' (Myers 1982: 184–6). Precisely the same point has been made by Tanner, with regard to the so-called 'family hunting territories' of the Mistassini Cree of the Canadian subarctic. 'The definition of a territory boundary', he explains, 'is not as often used in keeping outsiders off one's land, as it is in making sure in advance that the hunting and trapping activities of the group do not overlap with those of another' (Tanner 1973: 112). From data on the Kalahari Bushmen, Cashdan adduces similar instances in which hosts actively direct visitors on where best to go gathering or hunting, and sees in them examples of something much more general: 'the use of territoriality as a means of information exchange and resource allocation [which] appears to be widespread among human foragers in areas of sparse and unpredictable resources' (1983: 50).

Cashdan's argument warrants closer consideration at this point. She claims that human hunter–gatherers have two possible means available to them for 'excluding outsiders from territorial resources': by *perimeter defence* and by *social boundary defence*. The former, involving an actual policing of marked borders, is only feasible when the enclosed area is small, containing exceptionally dense and predictable resources. The alternative is to control entry to local groups, so that only those persons admitted to membership of a group can enjoy access to the resources of its territory. Drawing on Australian Aboriginal material, Peterson (1975: 60–2) has interpreted traditional greeting ceremonies as rites of entry in the context of a system of this kind, operating through the defence of social group boundaries. Yet Peterson's case for the functional analogy between greeting ceremonies and boundary defence leaves many questions unanswered. For one thing, ethnographic sources appear to be unanimous on the point that entry could not be denied to anyone who applied in the appropriate way. As Silberbauer states of the G/wi Bushmen, even unwelcome visitors had to be admitted; only subsequently might they gradually be 'eased out of the band' through the withdrawal of normal fellowship and co-operation (1981: 141, 189) As a mechanism of discretionary exclusion, local group entry formalities appear to have been singularly ineffective. But for another thing, one wonders – as does Cashdan – 'why should potential intruders ask to be included in the social group in the first place? Why trouble to cultivate rights of access if one can take resources without asking?' After all, if the territorial perimeter is neither marked nor defended, there is nothing to stop uninvited entry.

Cashdan's answer is that 'where territories are large and resources unpredictable, outsiders can minimize their foraging costs considerably if they obtain information from residents about the location of resources. They therefore have an incentive to seek access to the social group, since it is through the social interactions of these rituals that information exchange takes place' (1983: 50).

Evidently, the operation of the territorial system depends upon the willing collaboration of both visitors and residents in 'playing the game' in their own interests, the former by seeking entry to the local group, the latter by openly granting it. Cashdan's conclusions fully corroborate our own, that territoriality in human as in non-human populations furnishes a mode of reciprocal communication, conveying information about the locations of people and resources which is of mutual benefit to all parties. But by the same token, it has nothing whatever to do with the maintenance, through active defence, of exclusive access to resources by a social group. Our view is rather that territoriality is a means of effecting *co-operation* over an extensive but common range in an ecological situation (the exploitation of dispersed fauna or flora) which precludes regular face-to-face contact between co-operating units in the course of extractive activities. Quite simply, it prevents adjacent groups, ignorant of each others' positions, from traversing the same ground and thereby spoiling the success of their respective exploitative operations. The same general argument may be applied to the territorial division of grazing grounds in some pastoral societies. As Godelier notes, 'each group . . . *co-operates* with the others by *abstaining from presence* on the fraction of territory being exploited by the others. This is a form of indirect negative co-operation which implies an absence of personal relations with other groups while engaged in productive activities' (1979: 151). An alternative procedure is to parcel out time rather than space, such that different groups traverse the same pastures in a fixed sequence of rotation (Barth 1960, Carlstein 1982: 110–11). This, too, has its counterpart in the animal kingdom, as in Leyhausen's classic account of the movements of cats, whose regulation 'works very much like the section block signals on a railway' (1971: 26).

Our general conclusion from these observations is that territoriality is one aspect of the organization of work, governing not the social appropriation of land but the practical conduct of its exploitation. This, of course, supports our earlier assertion that, in orthodox Marxian terms, it pertains to the forces rather than to the relations of production. From this conclusion, we can derive one important corollary, which is that *territorial compartmentalization may be perfectly compatible with the collective appropriation of nature*. As evidence we could cite numerous instances from the ethnographic record of hunters and gatherers in which there is public recognition of demarcated territories but no conception at all of trespass in the form of taking resources from another's area. There can be no such offence as poaching when intruders have the same rights of access as anyone else. If a transgression occurs, it lies in not having asked before taking, not in the taking itself (Williams 1982: 148). Though territorial boundaries are generally open to movement across them, such movement should be publicized and not concealed: one does not arrive or leave without advertising the fact (Sutton 1978: 91–2). Among the Pintupi, as Myers reports, 'what makes people angry is unannounced travel, going in a secretive fashion' (1982: 185). The intentions of persons who do attempt to conceal their movements are bound to be suspect: the suspicion, however, is not that they are out to raid the territory's food resources but that they are planning an attack on members of the resident group (Hiatt 1965: 27). This suspicion, in turn, motivates the sometimes violent retribution meted out to such intruders.

But quite regardless of any possibly malicious purposes, interlopers whose entry and movements remain unannounced pose a potential threat in that they are liable to upset the labour process, perhaps quite accidentally, for example by disturbing the hunting or trapping sequence at a critical moment, and frightening off the game. This is the case among the Nganasan of the Taimyr Peninsula in northern Siberia, who hunt wild reindeer out on the tundra during the summer season within annually fixed territories. Every hunt is a delicate operation, requiring precise co-ordination, and it can take only a single intruder to cause the herd to stampede in the wrong direction and to be lost. Popov is quite explicit in his account that 'trespass', in this situation, lies not in poaching game to which one is not entitled, but in ruining the hunt for everyone present (Popov 1966: 56, see Ingold 1980: 292 fn. 2). Among hunters and gatherers generally, practical wisdom dictates that neighbouring groups should maintain a reasonable distance between their respective areas of exploitation (Tanner 1973: 112-13). As Silberbauer's G/wi informants explained: 'it is foolish to crowd the country when there are other campsites available, and...too many people in the same place will scare the game animals away. Mutual avoidance is, in this situation, a matter of amicable common sense' (Silberbauer 1981: 198).[5]

The danger from interlopers is not only that they might interfere with extractive activities. In Aboriginal Australia there is the much greater risk that they might unknowingly disturb some sacred site and hence jeopardize the ritual renewal of natural resources, not only for the particular group on whose territory the site is located, *but for the entire collectivity*. As Strehlow makes clear for the Aranda of central Australia, in looking after its sacred sites and conducting the necessary increase rituals every local group is 'believed to perform an indispensable economic service not only for itself but for the population around its borders as well' (1970: 102). It is therefore just as important for outsiders as for residents to ensure that no mishaps occur. The environment, to adopt the vivid metaphor of Verdon and Jorion (1981: 99), is like a mine-field, in which one must tread delicately and carefully. It is therefore best for everyone that it be reserved for those who know it well; and if others are to move in it is advisable that they should ask first and defer to their hosts on arrival. In their possible interference in the work both of resource extraction and resource reproduction, and its damaging conse-quences, lie the real reasons for the rules, so commonly encountered in hunting and gathering societies from all regions of the world, that new-comers must seek permission for entry into a band, and that visitors adopt a position subordinate to that of their hosts.[6]

Though there are many functional analogies between territoriality in man and in other animals, human beings are of course unique in their capacity for symbolic representation. Many species of birds, as Howard observed, adhere to territorial boundaries with remarkable precision, yet 'there is no necessity. . . for the bird to form a mental image of the area to be occupied and to shape its course accordingly' (1920: 19). It is simply, he argued, a matter of habit formation. The hunter–gatherer, however, *does* hold such an image, which is by no means confined to his immediate area of occupation but may cover an extensive tract of country occupied by a large number of other groups (e.g. Leacock 1969: 8, on the Naskapi). This is his conceptual map of the natural environment. Provided that the individuals of a population share a common conceptual map, it is possible for them formally to communicate their intended spatial positions, located in terms of the map, *prior to taking them up*. For example, the areas of exploitation for the constituent local groups of a regional band may be negotiated annually in the context of a public band assembly (Ingold 1980: 154). Alternatively, neighbouring groups may express their inten-tions through frequent mutual visiting and the formalities of 'asking permission' to which we have already referred.

Whatever the context of negotiation, it requires the definition in the imagination of territories and their boundaries in advance of their reali-zation through manifest behaviour; that is to say, we are dealing with a self-conscious process.[7] As Blundell argues, territorial organization can be viewed in terms of 'a set of ideas operating in the minds of the hunter–gatherers', which functions as a cognitive model or blueprint for behaviour (1980: 112). Similarly, Thornton maintains that 'what is essential in the definition of territory is that it is an image or icon, a symbolic representation'. Accordingly, he proposes the following, rather elaborate definition:

Territory is the symbolic differentiation of space (topologization) and the appropriation of this topological space into a structure of meaning by attributing shared and public values to places, directions, and boundaries such that it may be graphically, cognitively, or ritually represented as a coherent and enduring image. (Thornton 1980: 19)

There is no doubt that this kind of representational process depends upon the faculty of language, and particularly on its property of displacement, by virtue of which speakers can refer to persons and locales remote in time and space. Possessed of this facility, it is quite unnecessary for parties in face-to-face contact to define territorial boundaries by standing at them and emitting stereotyped audio-visual signals of the kind that, in the ethological literature, come under the rubric of 'agonistic display' or 'defence'. Cashdan (1983) is therefore wrong to characterize that mode of territorial demarcation unique to humans as 'social boundary defence'. For what many non-human animals achieve by defensive posturing, humans achieve by symbolic, linguistically mediated communication. The latter is not a form of defence at all (except perhaps of ideas); it is rather an alternative means to defence of exchanging information about the locations of individuals and resources, far less costly in terms of time and energy expenditure.

We have here a simple explanation of why it is that the forms of agonistic territoriality so common in the animal kingdom are virtually absent among human hunter–gatherers. There may be exceptions: thus on the basis of observations among the !Ko Bushmen, Heinz (1972) maintains that they are strongly and aggressively territorial, bearing witness to an 'intolerance confined to space' which he considers to be common to both human and non-human animals. But this is not a view that is widely shared (though see Eibl-Eibesfeldt 1979: 147), and Heinz's interpretation of the data on the !Ko has been challenged by Guenther (1981), who correctly points out that aggression and defence are not necessarily associated with territoriality. Though the association might hold for some non-human animals, it does not hold for man (1981: 117).[8] For the same reason, we cannot account for acts of aggression or the conduct of warfare in human societies by appealing to otherwise latent territorial instincts, since if any such instincts existed, they would be expressed in co-operation rather than competition, and in the opening rather than closure of channels of communication. If we are to discover specific parallels between the demarcation of territories by human and non-human animals, they should be sought not so much in defence as in 'advertisement', and particularly in those forms of advertisement (such as scent or scratch marking) where communicating parties are *not* in direct audio-visual contact. During those periods when individuals or groups are engaged in what Godelier calls 'indirect negative co-operation', they must perforce communicate by means other than speech, and must indicate territorial limits by resorting to the 'language' of signs. These signs have, as it were, to be 'written down' onto the landscape (or seascape) in the form of durable boundary markers of diverse kinds – notched trees, stone cairns, buoys, etc. – whose implicit message can be 'read off' on encounter by others.

Again, however, I must insist (*contra* Thornton 1980: 17) that neither the holding of a conceptual map, nor the erection of territorial signposts, amounts to the *appropriation* of resources in space. What is not contained in the opposition between mental image and behavioural event is the conscious purpose of the actor. So to the conceptual map of the environment and the events of territorial communication we must add the appropriative movement they convey; a movement that, as an unfolding of social relations of tenure, is apparent only in the dimension of time.

III

Let us admit that, besides the collective appropriation of nature by hunting and gathering societies, there is a level of tenure that relates to *specific* persons and groups within these societies. Our question now becomes: what manner of tenure is this? More particularly, is it possible to derive certain forms of tenure from hunting and gathering as modes of practice? Only if we can, will we be able to say anything general about principles of tenure in hunting and gathering societies.

To proceed, we need a set of terms to describe the geometry not of abstract, isotropic space, but of the substantial environment in which humans and other animals move, perceive and behave. Thus following Gibson (1979: 33–6), we speak of surfaces rather than planes, paths rather than lines, and places rather than points. Unlike a plane, a surface has only one side, not two; it is not an infinitely thin sheet but an interface between a medium (air) and a substance (earth). Likewise, whereas a line may be drawn between two points on a plane, a path is inscribed on a surface, and affords movement from one place to another. And a place, in Gibson's words,

is a location in the environment as contrasted with a point in space . . . Whereas a point must be located with reference to a co-ordinate system, a place can be located by its inclusion in a larger place . . . Places can be named, but they need not have sharp boundaries. The habitat of an animal is made up of places. (1979: 34)

Equipped with these terms, appropriate to the geometry of surfaces, we can begin by recognizing three logically distinct kinds of tenure: zero-dimensional (of places, sites or locations), one-dimensional (of paths or tracks) and two-dimensional (of the earth or ground surface). In what follows, I intend to show that tenure in hunting and gathering societies is zero- or one-dimensional, whilst two-dimensional tenure is a consequence of agricultural production.

In much of the existing literature, it is assumed that if tenure is exercised at all by particular persons or groups in hunter–gatherer societies, it must be of *areas* of land somehow cut out from the total surface extent of the country. Ethnographers who have attributed two-dimensional tenure to hunters and gatherers have generally done so in one of two ways. Either they have confused it with the demarcation of territories for practical purposes, or they have assumed that holding particular sites or paths is necessarily derived from possession of a determinate surface area around or on each side of them. Both approaches have created rather more problems of interpretation than they have solved. The first, as I have already indicated, flies in the face of evidence that the supposed 'owner' of a territory cannot refuse outsiders access to its resources, and that the offence of unannounced intrusion lies not in the suspicion of poaching but in the potential hazard it poses to successful foraging (Riches 1982: 114–15).

The second approach has been peculiarly prevalent in the ethnographic literature. Time and again it is asserted that the 'ownership' of sites or paths is conditional upon the recognition of a claim on the surrounding country, within a certain indefinite distance. This assertion appears to underlie the designation of the objects of tenure in Australian Aboriginal society as 'estates' (Stanner 1965). The controversy surrounding this notion has been amply reviewed elsewhere, and I shall only touch on it here (Hiatt 1962, 1966, Birdsell 1970, Peterson 1972, Verdon and Jorion 1981, Hamilton 1982). In his study of the Gidjingali of northern Arnhem Land, Hiatt adopts an explicitly two-dimensional idiom for the characterization of land tenure, speaking of the estates made up of clusters of sites (some but not all of which had totemic significance) as 'territorial possessions' that included the countryside surrounding each cluster. However, he goes on to say that these site clusters were not circumscribed by boundaries, and that since disputes over land never arose 'it was difficult to discover the attitudes of owners towards their estates' (Hiatt 1965: 14–16). There is clearly something rather paradoxical about this, for what is initially presented as the tenure of a land *area* eventually boils down to unenforced and unenforceable claims within unrecognized boundaries, which is surely an admission that land is not held in this form at all (Verdon and Jorion 1981: 98). Berndt's remarks on Aboriginal tenure in the Western Desert are similarly puzzling. He describes the local group of people having common ties to 'a given site or constellation of sites' as *land*-owning, but adds the rider that 'the local group country is defined not by boundaries explicitly demarcating it from similar units, but by the actual sites connected with the ancestral being and his acts' (1959: 98

and fn. 69, see Hamilton 1982: 99). This latter point is confirmed in Myers's account of the Pintupi, among whom country (*ngurra*) names 'refer to specific features [of the landscape] rather than to areas enclosed within spatial boundaries' (1976: 170).

If the object of tenure is an estate, and if each estate is one of a number of exclusive tracts into which the entire land surface is divided (Peterson 1976: 8), then it must be possible to tell at what point one is entering or leaving it, and at any moment, whose estate one is in. According to some accounts, estate boundaries are recognized in Aboriginal societies, though like central sites, they are generally marked by natural features such as hills, ridges, watercourses, or abrupt changes of gradient, soil or vegetation (Sutton 1978: 51–6, Williams 1982: 141–3). Strehlow reports that among the Aranda, the borders of estates are precisely defined in myths relating the travels of totemic ancestors, and mark the points beyond which estate-holders had to hand over the control of stories, songs and ceremonies pertaining to these beings to their next neighbours down the line of ancestral travel. 'This method of marking areas', he maintains, 'ensured that all border rockholes, springs and other waters were located within accurately described boundaries' (Strehlow 1965: 138). However, a series of such 'hand-over points', located on tracks converging on a ceremonial centre at the heart of the estate, do not in themselves constitute a boundary, for their function is not to divide a continuous surface into blocks but rather to divide continuous paths into lengths or sections. Among the neighbouring Pitjantjatjara, no points of this kind are recognized, nor is there any other basis for the definition of boundaries: 'in effect, each site has a circular zone of bush accessible to exploitation from it, and is linked to other sites by corridors along which people moved' (Layton 1983: 19).

By and large, when anthropologists have asked their native travelling companions to indicate whether they are in one estate or another, or to specify whereabouts the transition occurred, their inquiries have met with a blank response. Hiatt's Gidjingali informants admitted that they were in a new estate only when the first site of that estate's cluster was reached (1965: 16). Long before, Warner had reported the same experience. Each Murngin (Yolngu) clan's land is centred on a water-hole, but as you travel from one water-hole to another there is increasing doubt as to the possession of the intervening land. 'No native', says Warner, 'would bother himself about it' (1937: 18).[9] A parallel situation obtains among the Kalahari Bushmen, who refer to the object of local group tenure (with certain dialectal variations) by the concept of *n!ori*, literally connoting a place or location: 'a person will refer to a locality as *n!ori mima* = my place, meaning "the place where I belong" ' (Wilmsen 1980: 19). Among these desert hunter–gatherers, just as among their

Australian counterparts, the location generally corresponds to a water-hole; however Lee claims that the *n!ori* includes not just the hole but the block of land around it, from which a group draws its food. Logically, blocks should have boundaries, but Lee's expectations on this score were confounded by native opinion:

> In walking from one n!ore to another, I would often ask my companions, 'Are we still in n!ore X or have we crossed over into n!ore Y?' They usually had a great deal of difficulty specifying which n!ore they were in, and two informants would often disagree, one saying, 'We are already in Y'; the other saying, 'No, we are still in X'. (Lee 1979: 334)

Having defined the *n!ori* as a block, Lee has first to admit that its boundaries are somewhat indefinite, and is subsequently moved to suggest that there *are no* boundaries, that the people 'consciously strive to maintain a boundaryless universe' (1979: 335)![10]

The non-existence of boundaries is problematic for anthropologists, and not at all for the people with whom they work, only because they persist in using terms such as estate and block, whose primary reference is to a bounded *surface area*, for what is in fact the tenure of *place*. In other words, recalling our earlier distinctions based on Gibson's geometry of surfaces, two-dimensional concepts are being applied to describe zero-dimensional tenure. As Gibson recognized, places need not be externally bounded, and may be localized by their inclusion within larger places, in a nesting series. What appears, on one level, as a single large place, resolves on closer inspection into a cluster of smaller ones. This point is perfectly illustrated in Keen's account of the Yolngu, where he explains that the object of tenure for every land-owning group is a 'big-name' place, which incorporates a cluster of 'small-name' places each of which is a trace left by some Supernatural Being in the form of an outstanding feature of the landscape (Keen 1978: 47). Thus when it turns out, as among the Gidjingali, that a clan holds a cluster of sites, we do not have to suppose that this follows from their inclusion within a bounded area, which for some strange reason is not recognized by the people themselves. On the contrary, the surrounding country is held by virtue of its inclusion, in some sense, within the sites themselves. Land does not contain sites; rather the sites contain the land. How this is possible is a matter to which I shall return shortly.

We have given examples of the misapplication of ethnographers' two-dimensional concepts to zero-dimensional tenure. It is not difficult to find evidence of similar distortion in the ethnographic representation of one-dimensional tenure. A particularly revealing instance comes from Speck's classic account of alleged land-holding among Mistassini hunters and trappers in northeastern Canada. He writes that 'the Mistassini refer to their hunting grounds by using the term [meaning] "my path, or road", as though their business of life lay along the well-known track over which they pass in canoe and with sled in setting their traps and killing the meat- and fur-producing animals' (Speck 1923: 460). Among the more southerly groups, which lack dog traction, a term is used meaning 'my river'. Instead of taking native usage at its face value, however, Speck insisted on rendering the Mistassini appropriation of linear tracks and watercourses as instances of the tenure of land *areas*, despite the facts that no method existed for marking boundaries, and that no cases of trespass were known (Ingold 1980: 154). In her account of the Dogrib Indians of the Canadian northwest, Helm admits that whilst each regional band is 'defined in terms of the "road" (the main routes) of summer and winter movement', the tract enclosing these routes cannot be regarded as an object of tenure: 'it "belongs" to no group; any group is free to use its resources'. But the very existence of the tract remains something of an enigma in Helm's account, for centred on the band's road, it is said to have 'an axis rather than boundaries or edges' (Helm 1972: 76). This is rather like saying that all you need to define a circle is a centre. Where tracks freely criss-cross one another, as among the Alaskan Kutchin trappers described by Nelson, it is simply impossible to conceive of each as the axis of a discrete, block holding. Here, men 'own' their traplines, they can even rent them out. But yet again, this one-dimensional tenure of *paths* is rendered in two-dimensional terms as a claim to *areas*: 'traplines are areas in which individuals or families have exclusive rights to all furbearers'. Though each trapline is defined primarily in terms of 'a circuitous complex of trails', it is construed by the ethnographer to include 'a certain unspecified amount of surrounding territory', appearing schematically as a *strip* of land with the trail circuit as its centreline, whose borders are but 'hazily defined zones' (Nelson 1973: 156–8, see Figure 6.1).

These examples, as I have suggested elsewhere, make a good deal more sense if we recognize that hunting and trapping

appropriates nature vectorially, through the demarcation of points of interception and the lines connecting them, rather than through the imposition of a spatial grid. To 'own' a line is not to exercise any prior claim to the surrounding territory, nor to the resources upon it, but only to the animals whose tracks happen to cross the line itself and which consequently fall victim to the trapper. Likewise, the hunter appropriates only those animals whose path he succeeds in crossing. (Ingold 1980: 155)

This notion of one-dimensional tenure may also be applicable to Australian Aboriginal society, in cases where – as in the eastern part of the Western Desert– 'a person's primary affiliation to land is not to a

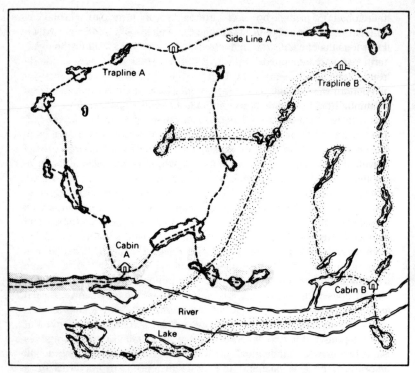

Figure 6.1   Schematic representation of two neighbouring traplines, as found among the Kutchin of Alaska, showing characteristic interdigitation. The diagram is reproduced from Nelson (1973: 157), who has depicted the lines as strips of land with a certain breadth (indicated by stippling and shading), with actual trails running down the centre of each. Copyright © 1973 by the University of Chicago. Reprinted by permission.

bounded territory, nor yet to a specific site within a bounded area. . . [but] comes about as a result of being born at a particular place, near a water-hole *on the track* of a particular totemic ancestor' (Hamilton 1982: 102, my emphasis). This gives him access to sites all along the track. And it is down these mythical tracks 'that contemporary people move in their quest for food and spiritual sustenance, because these two elements are irrevocably linked' (Berndt 1972: 187).

Indeed, the idea that the trajectory of a person's subjective life is *a passage along a well-established road* appears to be a pervasive one among hunters and gatherers, though it is by no means limited to them (Fernandez 1979: 41–2). It is worth noting that in agricultural societies, where objects rather than persons tend to move from place to place, it is these objects – propelled in acts of gift exchange – that may be conceived to have their particular paths. In that celebrated exchange of valuables known as the Kula, practised by the people of the Trobriand Islands, the term *keda* – meaning road, route, path or track – is 'used to describe the route along which kula shell valuables are exchanged', and by extension to connote 'the various "paths" along which participation in the kula leads' (Campbell 1983: 202–3). Every *keda*, like the valuables that flow along it, has a history constituted by past transactional sequences. Similarly in hunting and gathering societies, the road or track has a past, described by the people, ancestors and spirits who – in an unbroken succession – have travelled it and left their mark on the countryside (see Peterson 1972: 16, on the Murngin). Just as each mythic being, moving down its original track, left a part of its creative essence at successive points along it, so its living descendants, following the same route, perform an integrative movement, putting the parts together in the construction of their own being. Through such movement, paths in the terrain are caught up in the continuous process of social life, projecting an ancestral past into an unborn future.

Although the notion of the road of life is of course a moral and mystical one, it does happen to mirror the ways in which hunters and gatherers conduct themselves in practice in the course of their exploitative activities. From their point of view both moral and physical movement, the religious journey and the economic quest for food, are part of the same process: namely *living*. The difference, perhaps, is one of scale. The imprints in the landscape of the activities of mythic ancestors are gigantic compared with those left by ordinary humans, and likewise the principal paths that connect them encompass a myriad of tracks actually followed in food-procurement activities and other kinds of regular travel. What goes for places also goes for paths: a single major path reappears 'close up' as an array of minor paths, so that the movement along them seems more capillary than arterial. If every big place includes a cluster of actual sites, then every road includes a bundle of actual tracks.

Our provisional conclusion, then, is that tenure in hunting and gathering societies is not of surface area, but *of sites and paths within a landscape*. In agricultural societies, on the other hand, two-dimensional tenure does come into operation. The cultivator appropriates the land in *plots*, which may be relatively dispersed or consolidated, again within a landscape. The distinction between *land* and *landscape* is crucial, and requires some further elaboration. When we come to ask what, exactly, *is* land, the answer turns out to be highly elusive. We can observe soil, rocks, trees, vegetation, hills and valleys, lakes and rivers: together these add up to the landscape, but land is none of these things. Like the weight of physical bodies, and the value of commodities, land seems to be the common denominator of the natural world, inhering in all its multifarious manifestations but directly visible in none. The problem drove Marx to one of his occasional lapses into triviality, when he tried to show that land (in his terms, the earth) is man's universal instrument of labour 'since it provides the worker with the platform for all his operations, and supplies a field for the employment of his activity' (1930: 173). To put it more bluntly, man uses the land to stand on, or in Gibson's words, it 'affords support' (1979: 131). Without it, we would literally be nowhere.

Meillassoux (1972: 98–9) is more specific, when he argues that only with agricultural production (as opposed to hunting and gathering) does land become an instrument of labour. Even this marks a considerable departure from the concept of instrument *sensu stricto* as something interposed between the worker and the subject matter of his labour, and which serves 'as the conductor of his activity' (Marx 1930: 171). Territorial demarcation, as we have seen, functions instrumentally in this sense; but it is not the kind of instrumentality that Meillassoux attributes to land. His point, if I interpret him correctly, is that the agriculturalist does not adapt his purpose to the constraints of nature but actually *engineers* selected patches of nature to suit his purposes. Pursuing the same idea, I suggest that to turn a piece of the landscape into a field is to remove a covering of *specific things that grow*, leaving a *general potential for growth*. It is to this creative potential that the concept of land refers, and its appropriation is what we mean by land tenure.

Does this mean that there is no tenure of land in hunting and gathering societies? Certainly not; but to appreciate the nature of tenure in these societies we have to stop thinking about the land in exclusively two-dimensional terms, as surface area. Regarded as a generalized, creative potential, land may just as well be condensed within particular locales, or distributed along particular paths. That is to say, it remains embodied in the properties of the landscape. What agriculture achieves through the practical operations of ground clearance and preparation is the *separation* of the land from its embodiment in the landscape. Hunters and gatherers appropriate the land by holding the objects or features that originally contain it; agriculturalists appropriate the land by disconnecting it from those features so that it may be harnessed in the construction of an artificial, substitute environment. And because of the kind of mystical inversion which treats land as the source of a power that 'grows' the persons who hold it, ritual attention focuses in hunting and gathering societies on the constituent objects of the landscape in which that power is thought to reside, yielding a form of animism rather than a cult of the earth.

We can now begin to see how it is that land, as we asserted earlier, can be contained within sites. To complete our argument it is necessary to return to the question of the relation between places or paths and the surrounding country. My point, in brief, is that whilst every place has its own country, it is the country that constitutes the place. How should we describe the character of a place? Perhaps by some distinctive local feature such as a peculiar tree or rock formation, but also by the way the world looks from that place, by the vista it affords to someone standing there. Travel to another place some distance away and you will see the same world, but from another aspect, and it will look quite different. For things that loomed large or were strongly represented in the first view may now be on the periphery, if they have not retreated out of the field of perception altogether, and *vice versa*. When we say that a place enfolds the country around it, or that the country constitutes the place, we do not mean by country a part cut out from the whole, like a circle of given radius including the place at its centre, lying *outside* all other such countries and relating to them through contiguity along its external boundaries. A country is not a particular territorial division, a piece in a mosaic. It rather embraces the entire picture, but from a particular point of view within it. That is why it is absurd to ask at what point has a traveller moved from one country to another. Country X is the world as seen from place X, country Y is the world as seen from place Y. In between X and Y one can be in neither country, because one is in neither place. Only on arrival at a place has one fully arrived at its country. Likewise, when we say that a path includes a country, we do not mean by the latter an exclusive strip that includes the path (Figure 6.1), but the total landscape as it is experienced by someone moving down it.

'The real whole', wrote the philosopher Henri Bergson, 'might well be . . . an indivisible continuity. The systems we cut out within it would, properly speaking, not be *parts* at all; they would be *partial views* of the whole' (1911: 32). Here, in a nutshell, is the essence of the relationship between the total environment of hunters and gatherers and the countries that are held by local groups. Nature is indivisible and continuous; every country is not a part of the whole *containing* a specific place, it is rather a partial view of the whole *from* a specific place, or the whole as it is enfolded by that place. That is why the exercise of zero- or one-dimensional tenure by persons or groups is perfectly compatible with the collective appropriation of nature. In holding sites or paths, hunters and gatherers do not divide up the world among themselves, each group taking its own portion and looking after it exclusively. It would be more true to say that each takes hold of one aspect of the world, or one part of the creative essence that underwrites its total constitution. And in tending that essence, every group makes a vital, albeit partial contribution to the maintenance of the whole. For an illustration of this point we can return to Strehlow, who is speaking of the Aranda of central Australia. Members of the various Aranda clans, he explains, had the power to bring about the increase of plants and animals *throughout the entire country*, so that the existence of the Aboriginal population was believed to depend on the continued existence of *all* local groups within it. 'The religious acts performed by the totemic clan members of all the inland tribes at their respective totemic centres were regarded as being indispensable for the continuation of all human, animal and plant life in Central Australia' (Strehlow 1970: 103).

Let me finally come back to the distinction between tenure and territoriality. I have argued that sites and paths in hunting and gathering societies, and surface plots in agricultural societies (or all three in societies where agriculture is combined with hunting and gathering), embody the creative principle we call land, and in this capacity are objects of tenure. Territories, however, *are* parts or subdivisions of a landscape. Unlike holdings of land, which are defined in terms of places, paths and surfaces, a territory is necessarily defined by a perimeter boundary, so that whatever falls within the boundary is a part of the territory. There can, in theory, be no territories without boundaries, however blurred and indistinct they may appear in practice.[11] For this reason the territory is always a single, unbroken tract, whereas a land-holding can consist of many dispersed sites or plots without any clearcut boundaries of inclusion. It is noteworthy that this contrast applies with respect not only to the kinds of territories designed to regulate the practical conduct of foraging and predation, but also to those demarcated in politically centralized societies to indicate domains of sovereignty and jurisdiction. Such, for example, is the *icalo* among the Bemba of Zambia, meaning 'the district under the rule of a particular chief,... a tract of country with more or less definite boundaries'. When it comes to Bemba land tenure, however, 'a newcomer to the country notices at once the *lack of boundaries* between the garden beds round a village' (Richards 1939: 242–3, my emphasis).

Of course where two-dimensional tenure is the rule, areas of land may have boundaries too, but they are boundaries of a very different kind. They correspond to the limits of the person, not to a behavioural schedule. To draw a boundary across the landscape is to bring a territory into being; the land boundary, however, is the *result* of a concrete, appropriative movement. Territorial boundaries are open, indeed their very existence is predicated upon the possibility of movement across them.[12] Land boundaries, to the contrary, demarcate zones of exclusion: they are not there to indicate where people and resources are, but to keep other people off the resources. Therefore, if such boundaries are marked by artificial structures, we would expect their function to lie in physically *impeding* movement. Territorial boundary markers, by contrast, are more like signposts than fences, comprising part of a system of practical communication rather than social control.

To conclude, I have attempted to demonstrate that the phenomena of territoriality and land tenure are quite distinct. Whilst territorial demarcation among hunters and gatherers may be comparable in certain respects to territorial behaviour in other branches of the animal kingdom, its purpose among both men and other animals is essentially a practical one. Simply, it enables a dispersed population to forage more efficiently, by warding individuals off areas whose resources may have already been depleted by others, and by preventing disturbance by interlopers in the conduct of exploitative activities. Tenure, by contrast, has to do not with practical co-operation but with social appropriation. The tenure of plots · in agricultural societies is to be compared with the tenure, in hunting and gathering societies, of paths and locations in a landscape, but not with its territorial subdivision. All the essential attributes of tenure apply, regardless of whether the object of tenure is zero-, one- or two-dimensional. In all cases we find exclusivity of access devolving upon specific persons or groups, the casting of the object in a temporal continuum, the imputation to it of creative potency and, as a corollary, its position as the focus of regenerative ritual. It is surely better to recognize the nature of hunter–gatherer tenure for what it is than to distort it by a reductionist confusion with territoriality or by its assimilation to the agricultural tenure of surface area.

It is important to add one final comment. In most regions of the world, hunting and gathering peoples have been dispossessed of their land, either wholly or in part, by alien colonists and the states that represent them. One of the arguments used by the settlers to justify this usurpation was that the land was *terra nullius*, free for all, and that hunter–gatherers who merely wandered over it in foraging for food had no more rights to it than the wild animals that did the same. We have shown, to the contrary, that a form of tenure did exist in hunting and gathering societies, but that it did not amount to the tenure of the ground surface. Could it not, then, be argued that to satisfy traditional native claims, no more need be conceded than rights of access to protected sites, allowing the entire area not actually enclosed within these sites to be turned over to the State or to private commercial interests? The argument is invalid, for the simple reason that sites derive their identity and significance from their position within the total country. Cut out the country, leaving the site high and dry as an enclosed island, and it is no longer somewhere but nowhere, and thus utterly devoid of content. To take away a country is to extinguish the sites that enfold the country. Conversely, the systems of zero- and one-dimensional tenure that we have described can only work on the premise that the country as a whole is held in collective tenure by its entire native population. Yet to regain even a fraction of that country, native people have had to contend through a process of law for their title to exclusive blocks, cut out from the whole. In so doing, traditional principles of tenure have inevitably been compromised. Native claims to land come to rest on the notion of enclosure of sites within determinate, bounded tracts. And since the holders of sites are local groups, it follows that whatever areas are designated as aboriginal lands must be apportioned between them, so that each gains exclusive, corporate possession of a particular tract. Thus the very principles upon which indigenous hunter–gatherers have reclaimed their lands have, in their application, brought about the fragmentation of these lands and a corresponding fragmentation of native society into many and potentially conflicting proprietary interests.

Notes to Chapter 6

1 I shall not be dealing with the 'politico-jural' sense of territoriality in this essay (see Fortes and Evans-Pritchard 1940: 10–11). It would, however, be a fascinating project to trace the historical connections between this usage and the more modern 'ecological' usage. One suspects that the connections are close, indicating yet another instance of the transferral of concepts from the domain of society to that of nature.

2 Another example of the same confusion is contained in the following assertion: 'Nobody . . . seems to have taken issue with the idea that man has been a territorial animal, in the sense of defending areas of real estate, since the development of agriculture' (Peterson 1975: 56). We do, however, take issue with the idea that the tenure of land by agriculturalists is a manifestation of territorial behaviour.

3 I should confess, here, to having modified a view previously expressed. According to Ingold (1980: 152), 'the definition and defence of territories by human groups, if and where it occurs, is carried out by conscious intent, and therefore constitutes an aspect of the social relations existing between them'. My error lay in a failure to distinguish between the intent of social persons, and their conscious models of the procedures through which their purpose is translated into practical effect.

4 Bicchieri (1969: 68) makes a similar observation for the Mbuti Pygmies: 'a specific territory . . . "owns" its band . . . A specific band "belongs" to these *discrete* areas and acts as if it had the resources of the particular territory in stewardship.'

5 The same applies in the conduct of maritime fishing. Access to the fish resource is collective. Where territories are demarcated their purpose is to prevent the nets of different crews from getting entangled or fouled up. The interloper risks having his gear cut but his catch will not be confiscated – or if it is the confiscator will be regarded as the thief (Palsson 1982: 267). Acheson's account of lobster fishermen in Maine presents another example of the confusion of territoriality with tenure. Among Maine 'harbour gangs', he writes,

'informal norms about territoriality and hence ownership do exist' (1975: 184).
It appears, however, that these territorial norms form part of a practical
arrangement, 'connected to the technology in use', which demands of each
gang a detailed knowledge of the sea-bottom over a small area (1975: 192).

6 Examples in the literature are legion, and I can cite here only a few: on
Aboriginal Australia see Peterson (1975), Sutton (1978: 91–4), Myers (1976:
341–5; 1982), Williams (1982); on the Kalahari Bushmen see Marshall (1976:
187–90), Lee (1979: 337–8), Silberbauer (1981: 141, 194), Hitchcock (1982: 23),
Cashdan (1983); on northern hunter–gatherers see Riches (1982: 124). For one
further example, I cannot resist citing this extract from Drucker's work on the
Indian societies of the American northwest coast, on account of the
comparisons and contrasts it offers with Australian and African material:
'Characteristically, a man is said to have "owned" an economically important
tract. This "ownership" was expressed by his "giving permission", as the
natives usually put it, to his fellows to exploit the locality each season. At the
same time fellow members of his local group – his relatives – had an inalienable right to exploit the tract. The present writer time and again has heard
statements by informants from northwest California to Tlingit country to the
effect that a certain man "owned" a particular place, for example a fishing-site,
and that his permission was required before other members of his society
could use it. Nonetheless no instance was ever heard of an "owner" refusing to
give the necessary permission. Such a thing is inconceivable to the natives'
(Drucker 1939: 59).

7 One way in which territorial boundaries may be given conceptual recognition
is by the repetition of place-names between territories and their non-repetition
within them (Correll 1979: 173, see Riches 1982: 125–6).

8 As Lee has pointed out, 'culturally defined boundaries do not necessarily imply
sanctions against trespass...So if we find boundaries in a given case, we
should not commit the frequent error of assuming that they enclose a defended and exclusive territory' (in Lee and DeVore 1968: 157). See also
Williams (1982: 150).

9 Shapiro has expressed the same point as a general characteristic of Australian
Aboriginal local organization: 'Probably the most common arrangement is a
core area consisting of one or more sacred sites – natural features associated
...with mythical beings – surrounded by land whose identity is increasingly
uncertain with distance from the core. At its peripheries such an estate is all
but indistinguishable from lands associated with other ritual lodges [i.e.
estate-holding groups]' (1979: 17).

10 Evidence on this point is somewhat contradictory. According to Hitchcock
(1982: 25), each *n!ori* has boundaries demarcated on the basis of known
features of the landscape such as dunes or trees.

11 It would appear that in many cases, hunters and gatherers have been thought
to recognize boundaries, and hence territories, when in fact they do not. These
misunderstandings have arisen from inherent ambiguities in ethnographers'
questions and informants' responses. Thus Dixon writes: 'An aboriginal Australian's response "from Smith River to Jones Creek" is ambiguous – it could
mean either (a) from the south side of Smith River to the north side of Jones

Creek, or else (b) it could imply that the tribe lived on both sides of both streams, and also in the intervening territory...In many cases (a) must have been inferred by the ethnographer whereas (b) was intended by the informant' (1976: 208).

12 The same is true of ethnic boundaries (Barth 1969: 9). The parallel, suggested by the citations in Wilmsen (1973: 5), warrants further investigation.

References for Chapter 6

Acheson, J. M. 1975 The lobster fiefs: economic and ecological effects of territoriality in the Maine lobster industry. *Human Ecology* **3**: 183–207.

Altum, B. 1868 *Der Vögel und sein Leben*. Münster: Niemann.

Barth, F. 1960 The land use patterns of migratory tribes in south Persia. *Norsk Geografisk Tidskrift* **17**: 1–11.

Barth, F. 1969 Introduction. In *Ethnic groups and boundaries*, ed. F. Barth. Oslo: Universitetsforlaget.

Bergson, H. 1911 *Creative evolution*. London: Macmillan.

Berndt, R. M. 1959 The concept of 'the tribe' in the Western Desert of Australia. *Oceania* **30**: 81–107.

Berndt, R. M. 1972 The Walmadjeri and Gugadja. In *Hunters and gatherers today*, ed. M. G. Bicchieri. New York: Holt, Rinehart and Winston.

Bicchieri, M. G. 1969 The differential use of identical features of physical habitat in connection with exploitative, settlement, and community patterns: The BaMbuti case study. In *Contributions to Anthropology: Ecological essays*, ed. D. Damas. National Museums of Canada Bulletin 230. Ottawa: Queen's Printer.

Birdsell, J. B. 1958 On population structure in generalized hunting and collecting populations. *Evolution* **12**: 189–205.

Birdsell, J. B. 1970 Local group composition among the Australian Aborigines: a critique of the evidence from fieldwork conducted since 1930. *Current Anthropology* **11**: 115–31.

Blundell, V. 1980 Hunter–gatherer territoriality: ideology and behaviour in northwest Australia. *Ethnohistory* **27**: 103–117.

Burt, W. H. 1943 Territory and home range concepts as applied to mammals. *Journal of Mammalogy* **24**: 346–52.

Campbell, S. F. 1983 Kula in Vakuta: the mechanics of the keda. In *The Kula: new perspectives on Massim exchange*, eds. J. W. Leach and E. R. Leach. Cambridge University Press.

Carlstein, T. 1982 *Time resources, society and ecology, vol. I: Preindustrial societies*. London: George Allen and Unwin.

Carpenter, C. R. 1958 Territoriality: a review of concepts and problems. In *Behavior and evolution*, eds. A. Roe and G. G. Simpson. New Haven, Conn.: Yale University Press.

Carr-Saunders, A. M. 1922 *The population problem: a study in human evolution*. Oxford University Press.

Cashdan, E. 1983 Territoriality among human foragers: ecological models and an application to four Bushman groups. *Current Anthropology* **24**: 47–66.

Childe, V. G. 1942 *What happened in history*. Harmondsworth, Middx.: Penguin.

Correll, T. 1976 Language and location in traditional Inuit societies. In *Inuit land use and occupancy project*, ed. M. Freeman. Ministry of Supply and Services, Ottawa.

Dixon, R. M. W. 1976 Tribes, languages and other boundaries in northeast Queensland. In *Tribes and boundaries in Australia*, ed. N. Peterson. Canberra: Australian Institute of Aboriginal Studies.

Drucker, P. 1939 Rank, wealth and kinship in northwest coast society. *American Anthropologist* **41**: 55–65.

Dyson-Hudson, R. and E. A. Smith 1978 Human territoriality: an ecological reassessment. *American Anthropologist* **80**: 21–41.

Eibl-Eibesfeldt, I. 1979 *The biology of peace and war: men, and animals and aggression.* London: Thames and Hudson.

Elkin, A. P. 1938 *The Australian Aborigines.* Sydney: Angus and Robertson.

Ellen, R. F. 1979 Introduction: anthropology, the environment and ecological systems. In *Social and ecological systems*, eds. P. C. Burnham and R. F. Ellen (A.S.A. monogr. 18). London: Academic Press.

Engels, F. 1934 *Dialectics of nature.* Moscow: Progress.

Fernandez, J. 1979 On the notion of religious movement. *Social Research* **46**: 36–62.

Fortes, M. and E. E. Evans-Pritchard 1940 Introduction. In *African political systems*, eds. M. Fortes and E. E. Evans-Pritchard. London: Oxford University Press.

Gibson, J. J. 1979 *The ecological approach to visual perception.* Boston: Houghton Mifflin.

Godelier, M. 1979 Territory and property in primitive society. In *Human ethology*, eds. M. von Cranach, K. Foppa, W. Lepenies and D. Ploog. Cambridge University Press.

Guenther, M. G. 1981 Bushman and hunter–gatherer territoriality. *Zeitschrift für Ethnologie* **106**: 109–20.

Hamilton, A. 1982 Descended from father, belonging to country: rights to land in the Australian Western Desert. In *Politics and history in band societies*, eds. E. Leacock and R. B. Lee. Cambridge University Press.

Heinz, H. J. 1972 Territoriality among the Bushmen in general and the !Ko in particular. *Anthropos* **67**: 405–16.

Helm, J. 1972 The Dogrib Indians. In *Hunters and gatherers today*, ed. M. G. Bicchieri. New York: Holt, Rinehart and Winston.

Hiatt, L. R. 1962 Local organization among the Australian Aborigines. *Oceania* **32**: 267–86.

Hiatt, L. R. 1965 *Kinship and conflict.* Sydney: Angus and Robertson.

Hiatt, L. R. 1966 The lost horde. *Oceania* **37**: 81–92.

Hinde, R. A. 1956 The biological significance of the territories of birds. *Ibis* **98**: 340–69.

Hitchcock, R. K. 1982 Tradition, social justice and land reform in Central Botswana. In *Land reform in the making: tradition, public policy and ideology in Botswana*, ed. R. P. Werbner. London: Rex Collings.

Howard, H. E. 1920 *Territory in bird life.* London: John Murray.

Huxley, J. S. 1934 A natural experiment on the territorial instinct. *British Birds* **27**: 270–7.

Ingold, T. 1979 The social and ecological relations of culture-bearing organisms: an essay in evolutionary dynamics. In *Social and ecological systems*, eds. P. C. Burnham and R. F. Ellen (A.S.A. monogr. 18). London: Academic Press.

Ingold, T. 1980 *Hunters, pastoralists and ranchers.* Cambridge University Press.

Kaufman, J. H. 1971 Is territoriality definable? In *Behavior and environment: the use of space by animals and men*, ed. A. H. Esser. New York: Plenum.

Keen, I. 1978 *One ceremony, one song: an economy of religious knowledge among the Yolngu of North-East Arnhem Land.* Unpublished Ph.D. thesis, Australian National University, Canberra.

King, G. E. 1976 Society and territory in human evolution. *Journal of Human Evolution* 5: 323–32.

Kummer, H. 1971 Spacing mechanisms in social behavior. In *Man and beast: comparative social behavior*, eds. J. F. Eisenberg and W. S. Dillon. Washington, DC: Smithsonian Institution Press.

Layton, R. 1983 Ambilineal descent and traditional Pitjantjatjara rights to land. In *Aborigines, land and land rights*, eds. N. Peterson and M. Langton. Canberra: Australian Institute of Aboriginal Studies.

Leacock, E. 1969 The Montagnais-Naskapi band. In *Contributions to anthropology: band societies*, ed. D. Damas. National Museums of Canada Bulletin 228. Ottawa: Queen's Printer.

Lee, R. B. 1979 *The !Kung San.* Cambridge University Press.

Lee, R. B. and I. DeVore (eds.) 1968 *Man the hunter.* Chicago: Aldine.

Leyhausen, P. 1965 The communal organization of solitary animals. In *Social organization of animal communities*, ed. P. E. Ellis. Symposia of the Zoological Society of London, 14.

Leyhausen, P. 1971 Dominance and territoriality as complemented in mammalian social structure. In *Behavior and Environment: the use of space by animals and men*, ed. A. H. Esser. New York: Plenum.

Luckmann, T. 1979 Personal identity as an evolutionary and historical problem. In *Human ethology*, eds. M. von Cranach, K. Foppa, W. Lepenies and D. Ploog. Cambridge University Press.

Maddock, K. 1982 *The Australian Aborigines: a portrait of their society* (second edition). Ringwood, Victoria: Penguin.

Marshall, L. 1976 *The !Kung of Nyae Nyae.* Cambridge, Mass.: Harvard University Press.

Marx, K. 1930 *Capital.* London: Dent.

Marx, K. 1964 *Pre-capitalist economic formations*, ed. E. J. Hobsbawm. London: Lawrence and Wishart.

Mauss, M. 1954 *The gift.* London: Routledge and Kegan Paul.

Meillassoux, C. 1972 From reproduction to production. *Economy and Society* 1: 93–105.

Moffat, C. B. 1903 The spring rivalry of birds, some views on the limits to multiplication. *Irish Naturalist* 12: 152–66.

Munn, N. D. 1970 The transformation of subjects into objects in Walbiri and Pitjantjatjara myth. In *Australian Aboriginal anthropology: modern studies in the social anthropology of the Australian Aborigines*, ed. R. M. Berndt. Perth: University of Western Australia Press.

Myers, F. R. 1976 'To have and to hold': a study of persistence and change in *Pintupi social life*. Unpublished Ph.D thesis, Bryn Mawr College, Penn.

Myers. F. R. 1982 Always ask: resource use and land ownership among Pintupi Aborigines of the Australian Western Desert. In *Resource managers: North American and Australian hunter-gatherers* eds. N. M. Williams and E. S. Hunn (AAAS Selected Symposium 67). Boulder, Colorado: Westview Press.

Nelson, R. K. 1973 *Hunters of the northern forest: designs for survival among the Alaskan Kutchin*. University of Chicago Press.

Nice, M. M. 1933 The theory of territorialism and its development, in fifty years of progress of American ornithology. Lancaster, Pa.

Noble, G. K. 1939 The role of dominance in the life of birds. *Auk* **56**: 263–73.

Palsson, G. 1982 *Representations and reality: cognitive models and social relations among the fishermen of Sandgerdi, Iceland*. Unpublished Ph.D. thesis, University of Manchester.

Peterson, N. 1972 Totemism yesterday: sentiment and local organization among the Australian Aborigines *Man* (N.S.) **7**: 12–32.

Peterson, N. 1975 Hunter–gatherer territoriality: the perspective from Australia. *American Anthropologist* **77**: 53–68.

Peterson, N. 1976 Introduction. In *Tribes and boundaries in Australia*, ed. N. Peterson. Canberra: Australian Institute of Aboriginal Studies.

Peterson, N. 1979 Territorial adaptations among desert hunter–gatherers: the !Kung and Australians compared. In *Social and ecological systems*, eds. P. C. Burnham and R. F. Ellen (A.S. A. monogr. 18). London: Academic Press.

Piddington. R. 1971 A note on Karadjeri local organization. *Oceania* **41**: 239–43.

Pitelka, F. A. 1959 Numbers, breeding schedule and territoriality in pectoral sandpipers of Northern Alaska. *Condor* **61**: 233–64.

Popov, A. A. 1966 *The Nganasan: the material culture of the Tavgi Samoyeds*. Indiana University Uralic and Altaic Series 56, Bloomington.

Richards, A. I. 1939 *Land, labour and diet in Northern Rhodesia*. London: Oxford University Press.

Riches, D. 1982 *Northern nomadic hunter–gatherers: a humanistic approach*. London: Academic Press.

Sahlins, M. D. 1972 *Stone age economics*. London: Tavistock.

Sahlins, M. D. 1976 *The use and abuse of biology*. London: Tavistock.

Saussure, F. de 1959 *Course in general linguistics*. New York: McGraw-Hill.

Schaller, G. B. and G. R. Lowther 1969 The relevance of carnivore behavior to the study of early hominids. *Southwestern Journal of Anthropology* **25**: 307–41.

Shapiro, W. 1979 *Social organization in aboriginal Australia*. Canberra: Australian National University Press.

Silberbauer, G. B. 1981 *Hunter and habitat in the central Kalahari Desert*. Cambridge University Press.

Speck, F. G. 1923 Mistassini hunting territories in the Labrador peninsula. *American Anthropologist* **25**: 452–71.

Stanner, W. E. H. 1965 Aboriginal territorial organization: estate, range, domain and regime. *Oceania* **36**: 1–26.

Strehlow, T. G. H. 1965 Culture, social structure, and environment in Aboriginal Central Australia. In *Aboriginal man in Australia*, eds. R. M. Berndt and C. H.

Berndt. Sydney: Angus and Robertson.

Strehlow, T. G. H. 1970 Geography and the totemic landscape in Central Australia: a functional study. In *Australian Aboriginal anthropology: modern studies in the social anthropology of the Australian Aborigines*, ed. R. M. Berndt. Perth: University of Western Australia Press.

Sutton, P. 1978 *Wik: aboriginal society, territory and language at Cape Keerweer, Cape York Peninsula, Australia.* Unpublished Ph.D. thesis, University of Queensland.

Tanner, A. 1973 The significance of hunting territories today. In *Cultural ecology*, ed. B. Cox. Toronto: McClelland and Stewart.

Thornton, R. J. 1980 *Space, time and culture among the Iraqw of Tanzania.* London: Academic Press.

Tinbergen, N. 1957 The functions of territory, *Bird Study* **4**: 14–27.

Verdon, M. and P. Jorion 1981 The hordes of discord: Australian Aboriginal social organization reconsidered. *Man* (N.S.) **16**: 90–107.

Warner, W. L. 1937 *A black civilization: a social study of an Australian tribe.* New York: Harper and Row.

Werbner, R. P. 1975 Land, movement and status among Kalanga of Botswana. In *Studies in African social anthropology*, eds. M. Fortes and S. Patterson. London: Academic Press.

Williams, N. M. 1982 A boundary is to cross: observations on Yolngu boundaries and permission. In *Resource managers: North American and Australian hunter–gatherers*, eds. N. M. Williams and E. S. Hunn (AAAS Selected Symposium 67). Boulder, Colorado: Westview Press.

Williams, N. M. 1983 Yolngu concepts of land ownership. In *Aborigines, land and land rights*, eds, N. Peterson and M. Langton. Canberra: Australian Institute of Aboriginal Studies.

Willis, E. O. 1967 *The behavior of bicolored antbirds.* University of California Publications in Zoology, vol. 79. Berkeley: University of California Press.

Wilmsen, E. N. 1973 Interaction, spacing behavior and the organization of hunting bands. *Journal of Anthropological Research* **29**: 1–31.

Wilmsen, E. N. 1980 Exchange, interaction and settlement in northwestern Botswana: past and present perspectives. *Boston University, African Studies Center Working Papers* No. 39.

Wilson, E. O. 1971 Competitive and aggressive behavior. In *Man and beast: comparative social behavior*, eds. J. F. Eisenberg and W. S. Dillon. Washington, DC: Smithsonian Institution Press.

Wilson, E. O. 1980 *Sociobiology* (abridged edition). Cambridge, Mass.: Harvard University Press.

Wynne-Edwards, V. C. 1962 *Animal dispersion in relation to social behaviour.* Edinburgh: Oliver and Boyd.

7

Changing places: movement and locality in hunter–gatherer and pastoral societies

The mobility of persons and of property

The present essay has no grand theoretical pretensions; its principal aim is merely to introduce some order and coherence to what has become, in the literature, a thoroughly chaotic nomenclature for denoting the various forms of spatial movement encountered in human societies, and in particular those of hunter–gatherers and pastoralists. Such societies have often been called 'nomadic', but precisely what nomadism entails has remained far from clear, and it is indeed rather doubtful whether the notion has any analytic utility at all. Nomads are more usually characterized negatively, in terms of what they lack rather than what they have, namely some kind of fixed attachment to place, as well as the accoutrements of civilization that are supposed to go along with such attachment. But if, as we have argued, territoriality is to be distinguished from tenure, it is also necessary to distinguish their respective negations. This suggests at least two senses in which the notion of nomadism might be understood: in one, unfettered physical movement across the landscape in the course of the practical business of resource extraction (absence of territoriality); in the other, the non-engagement in social relations of sites, paths or surfaces (absence of tenure). The discrepancy between these two senses becomes particularly acute in debates first about whether or not nomadism is specifically associated with pastoralism as opposed to hunting and gathering, and secondly about the nature of the process known as 'sedentarization'. I shall begin by reviewing these debates, before turning, in subsequent sections, to consider the relation between impermanence of settlement and residential flux, and to formulate a systematic classification of patterns of spatial relocation in human populations.

Lee and DeVore classify the principal features of what they see as the hunting and gathering way of life under the rubric of the 'nomadic style'

(1968: 11–12). They assume that human hunter–gatherers have to move around a lot in order to procure their food, but note in addition that local groups 'do not ordinarily maintain exclusive rights to resources' and that frequent visiting 'prevents any one group from becoming too strongly attached to any single area'. These assumptions are certainly questionable, but to the extent that they hold, hunters and gatherers could legitimately be regarded as nomadic in both the senses adduced above: material (mobility in resource extraction) and social (non-appropriation of resource locales). The same could be said for non-human animals, if and when similar conditions apply. But where, in a hunting and gathering society, individuals or groups exert definite claims in respect of particular places to which they have strong ties of attachment, though they might otherwise wander quite freely in the course of normal foraging activities and could still be regarded as nomadic in the one sense, they certainly could not in the other, for social relations would be firmly anchored to the landscape. This kind of anchorage, in the form of what we have called zero- or one-dimensional tenure, seems in fact to be less the exception than the rule amongst hunters and gatherers. Consequently, if they are still to be classed as nomadic, our concept of nomadism must be limited to the material sense.

Given this limitation, nomadism signifies the mobility of persons in space quite regardless of their specific social and economic objectives. It has therefore to be distinguished from pastoralism, which refers to a determinate system of productive relations and practices, or rather more loosely, to an entire 'way of life'. Not all pastoralists are nomadic, and among the world's nomadic peoples are included not only certain hunter–gatherer and pastoral societies, but also a motley assortment of groups for whom travelling is a condition of livelihood – itinerant tradesmen, migrant labourers, merchant seamen, and so on. Might we not, as Salzman (1971: 193) suggests, learn more about the phenomenon of nomadism *per se* by comparing its manifestations among these very different categories of people? Dyson-Hudson argues rather similarly, but adopts a still more restrictive view of the concept of nomadism, which in any case he feels is less than helpful for analytic purposes:

For 'nomadism' immediately breaks down into two quite distinct sets of phenomena, *viz.*: livestock rearing and spatial mobility. Each of those sets of phenomena embraces conditions quite beyond 'nomadism' in its generally-accepted sense. Indeed, 'nomadism' is simply the area of overlap between the two. (Dyson-Hudson 1972: 23)

It is to some extent a matter of taste whether one prefers to follow Dyson-Hudson in abandoning 'nomadism', as traditionally conceived, in favour of the separate consideration of pastoral herd management and spatial mobility, or Salzman in retaining the concept, but realigned so as to be coterminous with the component of spatial mobility itself. Both are making essentially the same point: that whatever connections may exist between forms of resource extraction and patterns of spatial movement are a matter of empirical investigation rather than logical necessity (Salzman 1980a: 2).

If the distinction between mobility and extraction is as obvious as it appears, why should there be such a persistent tendency to regard the pastoralist as the archetypal nomad, and to disqualify the 'nomadism' of hunters and gatherers? Khazanov, for example, decries the application of the term 'nomads' to hunter–gatherers and other non-pastoral, mobile groups. For since, as he writes, pastoralists do not just extract but *produce* their food, 'their reasons for being mobile are different and the character of the mobility is different'. They have too little in common with hunter–gatherers to be bracketed with them under the same label. He recommends, therefore, that the term 'wandering' be applied to mobile hunters and gatherers, and that we return to the original Greek meaning of *nomados* which referred specifically to the pasturing of domestic stock (Khazanov 1984: 15–16, see Salzman 1967: 115). How we should classify mounted hunters, who employ domestic herds in the chase and for transport, is not at all clear (Ingold 1980: 124). One senses, in the reluctance to accept the nomadism of hunters and gatherers, an anthropological reflection of the very general contempt that pastoralists have for their hunter–gatherer neighbours. For the wanderer is not just one who moves about; if he differs from the nomad it is because he roams without aim or purpose, follows no course, knows no destination. The connotations here are moral as well as physical: thus the nomad, with his relatively complex culture and social organization, furthers the advance of civilization; whereas the wanderer, bereft of all but the rudiments of culture and having strayed from the path of progress, contributes little or nothing at all. Precisely the same sentiments led Kroeber (1952: 396–8) to distinguish 'pastoral nomads' from 'primitive nomads' – the latter including all hunter–gatherer bands.

We need not be detained by what is evidently a caricature of hunter–gatherer existence. There is a more serious, and valid, reason for the association of pastoralism and nomadism, which exposes an equally serious inadequacy in the views of Salzman and Dyson-Hudson discussed above. It lies in their reduction of pastoralism to the technical aspect of resource extraction, 'livestock rearing'. An error of presumption, shared even by opponents of the empiricist position which they adopt, is that there is nothing more to pastoralism than the applied science of animal breeding (Asad 1978: 58, Salzman 1980a: 4–5). Whilst the derivation of subsistence from animals is common to both hunters and pastoralists, the herds of the latter are said to be domestic rather than wild. Yet as we saw in Chapter 5, domestic animals are distinguished from wild ones in that they are, in the living state, 'engaged' by the structure of social relations of the human community. Thus what is essential to pastoralism, and erroneously designated by such terms as 'rearing' and 'breeding', is the *social appropriation*, by persons or groups, of successive generations of living animals (Ingold 1980: 133). And it is on this social level that the link between pastoralism and nomadism is to be found. That is to say, we have to understand nomadism in terms of resource appropriation rather than resource extraction, or social relations of tenure rather than physical patterns of movement. But in this case, nomadism connotes not the absence of tenure, but the fact that this tenure is of movable property instead of things fixed in the terrain. Animals do not, of course, represent the only kind of movable property, but they are the only kind for which movement is a condition of existence. If there is a sense in which pas-toralists are nomadic where hunters are not, it lies in the detachment of social relations from their anchorage in fixed points in the landscape made possible by the transfer of tenure from locales, where herds may be found or intercepted, to the herds themselves. The pastoral animal is a vehicle in a dual sense: not only does it transport its owner's effects, it carries around his social relations as well.

The contrast we have drawn here does not, in itself, imply anything about the relative extent to which hunters and pastoralists actually move about in the course of normal extractive activities. Among pastoralists this extent varies enormously, depending upon the nature of the environment, the needs of the animals, the mix of pastoral and non-pastoral activities, and a host of other factors. Indeed it is a frequent observation that the activities of so-called pastoral peoples are many and various; the fact that one of them happens to be animal husbandry appears at first glance to be almost incidental. Others include the cultiva-tion of fields, gardens and orchards, various forms of wage-labour, trading, raiding and smuggling. At least one author (Chatty 1980: 82) has introduced 'crop cultivation' into the very *definition* of pastoralism.[1] So when are people who husband both crops and animals to be regarded as pastoralists rather than agriculturalists with an economy of mixed farming? Only, I would argue, when both sets of activities are organized by social relations which are materially embodied through the possession of livestock. In other words, if the notion of pastoralism as a system of production is to have any meaning at all, it must imply that under such a system, social commitments established through the control and dis-position of animal property constitute the dominant structural framework within which practical extractive activity – including but not exclusively that of animal husbandry – is carried on.[2]

This point brings me to the question of what is meant by sedentarization. Depending upon the sense of nomadism from which we start, this
can imply either a reduction in spatial mobility, associated perhaps with a
shift in the balance of animal husbandry and cultivation, or a structural
transformation in the social relations of production involving a transfer of
tenure from animals to land. If nomadism and sedentism are understood
in behavioural terms, they could certainly be taken to denote poles on
a continuum, between which individuals, groups and communities are
continually oscillating back and forth. It is only to be expected that the
people of a pastoral society, in the course of time, will devote propor-
tionately greater or lesser attention to animal husbandry, cultivation and
ancillary activities as they adapt to the changing configuration of opportunities and constraints afforded by their environment; and that this may
lead to their movements being alternately more wide-ranging and more
confined. The process of sedentarization, in this sense, is typically rever-
sible (Salzman 1980b: 14). If, on the other hand, we mean by 'sedentism'
that dominant social relations are anchored by the possession of immobile, landed property rather than mobile animals, then what is regarded as sedentarization may well consist of an *irreversible* change,
not of degree but of kind, in the structural matrix of practical economic
activity – though one that does not necessarily entail any diminution in
physical mobility. The rancher, for example, is as much engaged in 'livestock rearing' as is the pastoralist, and his work may involve an even
greater degree of physical mobility. Yet the transition from pastoralism to
ranching is often taken as a case of sedentarization, on account of the
introduction of a social principle of exclusive tenure over bounded tracts
of land.

By isolating the two meanings of sedentarization outlined above, it may
be possible to clear up some of the confusion inherent in Khazanov's
recent attempt to construct a systematic typology of basic forms of
'pastoral nomadism' (1984: 17–25).[3] Without concerning ourselves with
the various subtypes, these forms are 'pastoral nomadism proper',
'semi-nomadic pastoralism', 'semi-sedentary pastoralism', 'herdsman-
husbandry' and 'sedentary animal husbandry'. Something is obviously
wrong with a classification of nomadism which includes sedentism as one
of its varieties; and as the middle terms reveal, the classification turns out
to be – at least in part – of the forms of pastoralism rather than nomadism.
Rewriting the first term accordingly, as 'properly nomadic pastoralism',
we are given three alternative states of the pastoral economy, such that
agricultural activities are entirely absent from the first, merely supple-
mentary in the second (semi-nomadic) and predominant in the third
(semi-sedentary). The continuum between nomadism and sedentism here
connotes the balance of herding and farming activities *within* a pastoral

system of productive relations. But with the final two terms of his classification, Khazanov abruptly switches from 'pastoralism' to 'husbandry', that is from the character of the total system embracing multiple activities (herding and farming in various combinations) to that of a particular activity within a total system. 'Herdsman-husbandry' and 'sedentary animal husbandry' represent two ways of integrating the management of livestock in the context of an overall system that, in terms of relations of tenure, is clearly *agricultural* rather than pastoral. They differ in that the first involves rather more movement, and usually rather more animals, than the second.

In Figure 7.1 we present a general model for the transition from pastoralism to agriculture that encompasses these variations.[4] In the pastoral society, people engage in the practical pursuits of both herding and farming, and may be more or less mobile (nomadic or sedentary) depending upon the fluctuating balance of the two and their mode of integration. But relations established through the social appropriation of animals dominate, and circumscribe, those established through the appropriation of land. In the agricultural society there is the same balance of practical activities (for agriculturalists usually herd animals just as much as do pastoralists usually cultivate crops) and the same variation in degrees of spatial mobility. However on the social level, the relative dominance of relations established in respect of animals and in respect of land is reversed, such that the latter circumscribe the former. And it is this reversal of dominance that is implied when the transition from pastoralism to agriculture is identified as a process of sedentarization. Strictly speaking, it is a process whereby land replaces animals as the material embodiment of the claims and counterclaims that persons exert over one another. Returning once more to Khazanov's typology, 'semi-nomadic' and 'semi-sedentary' pastoralism correspond to variants of the situation depicted on the left-hand side of Figure 7.1, whereas 'herdsman husbandry' and 'sedentary animal husbandry' denote the herding component of the agricultural economy depicted on the right-hand side of the figure. The conclusion to be drawn from our model is that whereas a transition, say, from semi-nomadic to semi-sedentary pastoralism is one of degree, a transition from pastoralism to an agricultural economy incorporating a herding component (such as 'herdsman husbandry') is one of kind.

Impermanent settlement and residential flux

In what follows, I shall confine my attention to the varieties of nomadism understood as patterns of spatial mobility. It is probably true to say that no human group has ever been *fully* nomadic in the sense that the move-

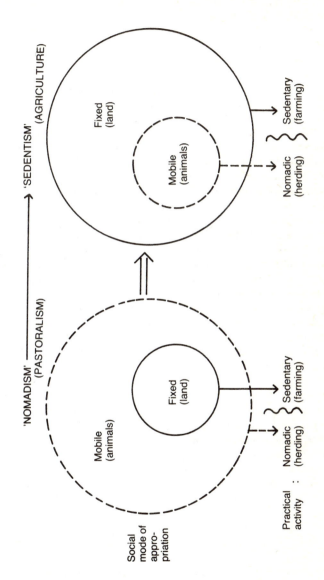

Figure 7.1 Nomadism and sedentism in the transition from pastoralism to agriculture.

ments of its members have had no reference whatever to place, and the same goes for most populations of non-human animals. Yet movement is surely the very condition – even the substance – of life itself: as Fernandez has succinctly put it, 'we move, are moved, or we die' (1979: 61). If we grant the universality of both movement and reference to place, it seems logical to look for the source of variation not in one or the other, but *in the relation between the two*. The key to this relation, I believe, is to be found in the scheduling of activities in time. Take any human being: there must be a fundamental alternation in his or her trajectory between periods at rest (sitting or sleeping) and periods of motion. Given the nature of the terrain and the prevailing mode of locomotion (whether on foot, horseback, or whatever), there is a limit to the distance the individual can travel during a normal day. If he plans to return to the same place in the evening from which he left in the morning, he cannot venture more than half that distance from the place. Plotting his movement in space against time, we arrive at the graph depicted in Figure 7.2a, which shows the maximum extent of a day's travel. Supposing, now, that movement is equally possible in all directions from the central place, we can imagine this figure rotated around the vertical axis, enveloping a region that looks like a double cone, whose upper half is the inverse of the lower half (see Figure 7.2b). Carlstein, from whose seminal study this way of representing the time constraints on spatial movement is derived, calls the double cone a *day prism*, and the volume it encloses a *prism habitat*. The individual, as he points out, is 'imprisoned' within the prism habitat 'by his own capabilities of traversing space as well as by his own decisional constraint to be back at a given time' (Carlstein 1982: 75).

   In practice, the constraints are liable to be somewhat greater than this model indicates. This is because extra time must be allowed for the food procurement activities which motivate the travel in the first place. Depending on their duration, the prism will be laterally truncated to a certain extent (see Figure 7.2c). The only way to reach resources situated further afield, beyond the maximum radius of the day prism, is to relax the requirement to return the same evening to the point of departure – unless alternative and faster means of transport are available. In Figure 7.3, we compare limiting trajectories, over a period of days, for a forager who always returns to the same place, and one who rests at a different place each night before coming back to his starting point. It is assumed that the durations of nocturnal rest, and of the diurnal extractive activities that interrupt travel, are the same for both. Even this simple comparison, which is of course grossly idealized, suffices to establish a point that is easily overlooked: the actual distance covered by the two foragers, over an equal number of days, is *identical*. Yet the first, if he kept up his pattern of daily return on a continuous basis, could hardly be called a

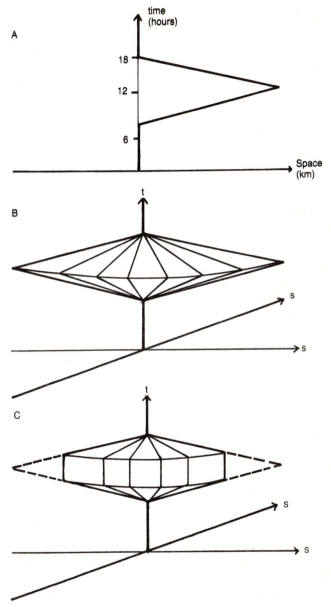

Figure 7.2 Limiting space–time trajectory for one day's travel with return (a), day prism (b) and truncated day prism (c).

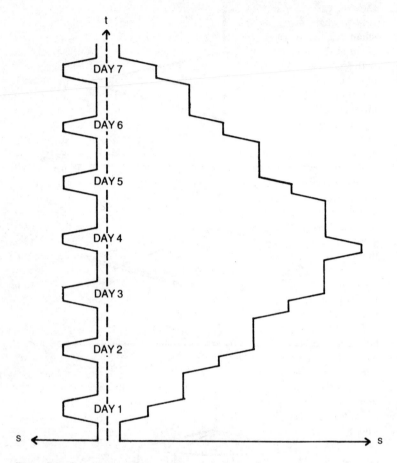

Figure 7.3 Comparison of space–time trajectories for two foragers, one who returns every day, the other who returns at the end of a week. The latter can travel further afield than the former, but the distance covered by both is identical.

nomad. Thus sedentary foragers, who maintain such a pattern, may travel just as much as – if not more than – nomadic ones whose pattern of return is less frequent and regular (Ingold 1982a: 531). The mere fact that most hunter–gatherers, as Lee and DeVore pointed out, 'have to move around in order to get food' (1968: 12), does not after all suffice to establish the nomadic character of their style of life.

A second glance at Figure 7.3 shows that the real distinction between the two cases lies in the *number of resting sites* and the *frequency of return*. These are inversely correlated such that, at the sedentary pole, a small number of sites is linked to a high frequency of return, and *vice versa* at the nomadic pole.[5] Evidently, the simple equation of nomadism with spatial mobility will not do, for in line with our initial conjecture, it is not the movement itself that counts, but the way this movement is oriented to place. This orientation, the fact that travel is towards an intended destination, makes the difference – as we have already seen – between nomadic movement and mere wandering. If we ask what moves, in a nomadic regime, that remains stationary in a sedentary one, the answer cannot be the individual – who moves as much in both – but his destination, which is moved 'in his mind' in advance of the journey itself. In its material aspect, nomadic movement is that component of actual 'on-the-ground' movement occasioned by the displacement of the point of arrival from the point of departure, and the nomadic track is a path connecting these points. Where the points of arrival and departure are the same, there is no nomadic movement, and no track. Now, since on arrival motion gives way to rest, and on departure rest gives way to motion, the punctuation of an overall itinerary by successive destinations corresponds to the temporal alternation of periods of motion and of rest. That is why this alternation, and not mobility *per se*, is fundamental to the definition of nomadism.

To rest in a place is, in a minimal sense, to 'inhabit' it, so that habitations may be defined as places from which people set out and at which they arrive. If the latter are spatially separate from the former, we may speak of shifts of habitation. Such relocations, as we have just shown, constitute the essence of nomadism in its material aspect. Hence there is much to commend Spooner's admirably simple definition of nomads as 'social groups with no permanent habitation' (1971: 198). That said, however, it is important to note that the 'permanence' of habitation is a matter of degree, for no human settlement is totally immune from the ravages of time. Moreover there is some ambiguity as to whether 'habitation', in Spooner's definition, refers to the site of settlement, the dwelling erected on that site, or the occupancy of that dwelling. For example, nomads may erect quite substantial and durable dwellings, but designed for temporary occupation in the annual round: their permanent habitations are not permanently inhabited. On the other hand, sedentary people may occupy makeshift dwellings that require periodic reconstruction, albeit on the same or a nearby site. There is an additional distinction to be made between nomads who carry along portable dwellings (or components such as wooden poles and lodge covers), and those who construct their dwellings out of materials available on the spot. Since the former requires an augmented transport capability, it is more typical of pastoral nomads or mounted hunters, whose domestic animals can be employed as beasts of burden.

In all human societies, for the majority of individuals during most of their lives, habitations are not just places at which they stop to cook, eat and sleep. They do so, nearly always, in the company of others, who together compose a micro-community that we call the domestic group. And as Carlstein remarks, 'most domestic units throughout the world consist of the same persons interacting with one another for hundreds or thousands of days' (1982: 71). When we plot the space–time trajectories of these persons, we find that they form a bundle whose various strands may tend to separate during periods of motion, but which converge, over and over again, during periods of rest. Orientation to place therefore goes hand in hand with an orientation to the company one expects to find there. Analytically, however, the *principle of reunion of persons* and the *principle of return in space* must be kept distinct (Carlstein 1982: 70), even though in many cases they are idiomatically merged in the notion of 'going home'. In what is often taken as the prototypical instance of nomadic movement, the entire domestic group – or even a whole community of such groups – makes a continuous series of site relocations, without ever splitting up. Pastoral migrations characteristically take this form, as amongst the Basseri of Iran, whose camp communities of 10–40 tents move in convoy, their members maintaining constant neighbourly relations one with another, 'while all other contacts are passing, ephemeral, and governed by chance' (Barth 1961: 125). Here there is an enduring union of persons without any return in space, until the same route is traversed on a subsequent migration.

On the other hand, one can envisage a situation in which fixed habitation sites (such as beside water-holes) are more or less continuously occupied, but in which there is so much coming and going of individual personnel between them that the social composition of the residents at any particular site is hardly the same from one day to the next. Yellen posits this kind of situation, on the basis of observations among !Kung Bushmen (Lee 1979: 51–5), as one that may have obtained quite generally among hunters and gatherers in relatively unpredictable environments. What looks, in the long term, like an 'almost random movement of individuals and families' generates a network of association that is *anucleate*, in that there are no enduring clusters of people whose commitment is exclusively to one another (Yellen 1977: 43–7). A comparison of the anucleate bands of hunter–gatherers like the !Kung with the highly nucleate camp-groups of pastoralists such as the Basseri, united by common interests in the defence of animal property, reveals the necessity of distinguishing between the physical impermanence of settlement and residential flux, or if you will, between changing places and changing company. The questions of *where* and *with whom* a person lives, that is, of his physical and social addresses, require different answers, and one kind of address can change without the other. Thus for the Basseri, Barth argues that the frequent relocations of settlement entailed in pastoral migration, far from being conducive to alterations in group membership and composition, provide almost daily occasions for the assertion of their constancy (1961: 46).

The tendency to conflate changes of place and company is exemplified in this composite definition of flux offered by Turnbull: 'the constant changeover of personnel between local groups and the frequent shifts of campsites through the seasons' (1968: 132). Though these do not necessarily go together, they may of course do so, particularly when no obvious motive for relocation can be found in the improvement of access to environmental resources. Among Hadza hunter–gatherers, for instance, people change camp sites on average about once a fortnight, but rarely shift more than a few miles, and quite often the distance between successive sites is less than a mile. If women cover three to four miles each day in their gathering activities, and if men venture even further in their hunting, it is difficult to see how such short relocations could have any significant effect on ease of access to food, especially when the environs of the new location are no better provided than those of the previous one. Moreover, the departure of one set of people from a particular site may be followed immediately by the arrival in the same vicinity of another, who may set up camp within yards of the previously occupied location (Woodburn 1972: 201–3). Even though moves sometimes *do* affect access to food, whether positively or negatively, their primary function – as Woodburn shows – lies in the opportunity they provide for Hadza men and women to rearrange their interpersonal relations. 'For, every time individuals move from one camp to another, they are associating themselves publicly with certain kin and affines and dissociating themselves from others' (1972: 205). In other words, they change place *in order* to change company, having no other particular reason for doing so.

Gulliver (1975) has argued along rather similar lines in discussing the causes of nomadic movement among the pastoral Turkana of East Africa. Although the needs of the herds for fresh pasture make it imperative to shift camp from time to time, every move allows individual herd-owners to choose between any number of prospective locations, all of which offer roughly comparable grazing in their vicinity. In deciding whether to go to this or that specific location, the first priority may be to get away from those with whom one is in dispute, and to join up with potential allies. Considerations of this kind may even motivate relocations that are detrimental to the immediate welfare of the herds. Movement, according to Gulliver, offers 'the continual possibility of association and dissociation with particular people...and can be used for personal and social purposes, expressing and effecting preferences' (1975: 379). When asked about the reasons for his move, it may of course be simpler and more expedient for the pastoralist to produce an answer couched in the language of environmental necessity, which does not implicate other people, and avoids touching on the more sensitive areas of interpersonal relations. In warning that anthropologists may be all too easily hood-winked by such rationalizations, Gulliver voices a general dissatisfaction with the tendency to understand nomadic movement solely in respect of its ecologically adaptive function for the population practising it. This dissatisfaction is echoed by Burnham, who likewise stresses 'the contingent quality of inter-personal and inter-group relations in spatially mobile societies', and finds the ecological approach unhelpful as a point of departure in their analysis (1979: 350). But this anti-materialist bias should not be carried too far. Though it is right to draw attention to the possible causes and consequences of impermanent settlement on the social level, in terms of the opportunities provided 'for continual choice and change in residential association' (Tapper 1979: 46), we should not ignore the fact that there are often compelling *practical* reasons to move, and that considerations of security may well put a premium on everyone's moving together. A key variable in this regard is the locus at which choices are exercised and decisions made: either by individuals of their own accord (Hadza), by heads of households (Turkana), or by leaders acting on behalf of the whole community (Basseri). Whether impermanent settlement does or does not entail residential flux must therefore depend to some extent on the political organization of the society in question.

In distinguishing between two kinds of impermanence, of individuals' co-occupation of a site and their co-residence with one another, we have the basis for making a further distinction between 'camp' and 'band', two terms commonly found in accounts of so-called nomadic peoples. Murdock (1949: 80) originally employed the concept of band to denote any nomadic or semi-nomadic communities, whether of hunter–gatherers or pastoralists, consisting of 'a number of families who habitually camp together'. In his terms, it was the physical impermanence of settlement that marked off the band, as a community-type, from the village or neigh-bourhood; whereas its membership was assumed to be fairly constant. Steward concurred, arguing that for a social aggregate to be classed as a band, it must have 'first, a fairly wide-ranging nomadism...and, second, permanent membership' (1969: 187). However, as one study after another demonstrated that such clearly bounded and enduring units were more the exception than the rule in hunting and gathering societies, the notion of band came to signify the very opposite of what it had meant for Steward, namely a transient association of individuals each of whom is normally free to choose between a whole range of possibilities of residential affiliation (Helm 1965: 378, Ingold 1978: 149–50). I would recommend that we continue to refer to associations of the latter kind as bands, when our purpose is to draw attention to the impermanence of their composition. But 'camp', a term traditionally favoured by students of pastoralism, is much more appropriate than 'band' for denoting the characteristic of temporary habitation.

Thus we could say of the Basseri community that it is a camp and not a village, because it occupies no fixed location, but that it is not a band, because it has a stable membership. The migratory units of Lappish reindeer pastoralists described by Pehrson (1957) are both spatially mobile and residentially fluid, and are therefore camps in one respect and bands in the other. Among hunters and gatherers, too, we can find communities that share both characteristics, and for which both terms are appropriate: we have seen an example of this from the Hadza. But in many cases it is the impermanence of residential composition rather than physical location which is the most striking feature (Ingold 1978: 147). Since we take the essence of nomadism to consist in frequent changes in place of habitation, or physical address, we cannot admit this residential flexibility – however typical it may be of hunter–gatherer social organization – as a component of their 'nomadic style' (*contra* Lee and DeVore 1968: 12). Nor, as we have previously argued, are hunters and gatherers necessarily nomadic merely because they move around a lot in the course of foraging activities: no human beings, even the most 'sedentary', can live limpet-like, permanently rooted to one spot. Nomadism, in short, is no more necessarily entailed in hunting and gathering than it is in pastoralism. In the following section, we shall introduce yet further restrictions on the applicability of the concept of nomadic movement, limiting it not just to changes of place, but to such changes as occur within a relatively homogeneous environment.

Towards a classification of forms of movement

'Nomadism' is not the only word encountered in the anthropological literature to describe more or less frequent shifts between settlement sites. Another is migration, sometimes regarded as a variety of nomadism, sometimes as a phenomenon of a quite different kind. One author to have taken the latter view is Krader, whose definition of nomadism is unusually restrictive. He considers nomads to be 'those people who have a fixed round of movement, whether seasonal, annual or multi-annual; they characteristically have a definite end-point to their movements over the surface of the earth, and a point of return' (1959: 499). Orientation to place is here the crucial factor, but instead of emphasizing *non*-return in the short term, Krader insists upon the principle of *return* in the long term. Nomadism, he writes, 'is a cyclical or rhythmic movement'; yet surely, cycles and rhythms characterize the life-process of virtually all human groups, including those we would normally regard as sedentary. Clearly, what is important in this context is the *periodicity* of the cycles, which could be ranged along a continuum from the diurnal, marking the pole of sedentism, through to the annual or multi-annual, marking the pole of nomadism. All are distinguished from non-cyclical or non-periodic movements, for which Krader reserves the concept of migration, citing as an example the movement of settlers from Old to New Worlds.

This is perhaps an extreme instance; at the other extreme are the rather frequent relocations of village sites made by pioneer swidden cultivators, which do not usually cover an immense distance. Writing of the Iban, notorious for their practice of this kind of cultivation, Freeman notes that they could almost be regarded as semi-nomadic, for in one generation they might advance 'over fifty to a hundred miles of territory, devouring virgin forest as they went. But *unlike true nomads, the Iban did not retrace their steps*; there was little inducement to return to inferior secondary jungle when virgin forest beckoned them on' (1970: 286, my emphasis). As this example suggests, the persistence of points of return in nomadic or 'long-cycle' movement, if measured on an absolute chronological scale, may be considerably greater than that for points in a sedentary 'short-cycle' regime, which places heavier demands on the limited resource potential of the local environment. Although sedentary farmers might return every evening, day in day out, from their fields to the village whereas nomadic pastoralists show up in a place only once or twice a year, the latter may have been doing so for a much longer period than the village even existed on that site, and may continue to do so long after it has disappeared, never to be rebuilt there. The implication is that in the long run, sedentary people may be characterized by a more pronounced 'shiftiness', or impermanence in their ties to specific locales, than are nomads. This point is represented schematically in Figure 7.4.

Apart from nomadism and migration, a third term figures prominently in Krader's discussion, namely 'transhumance'. He defines it as 'pastoralism under conditions of sedentary habitation, and as part of an economy mainly dependent on cultivation' (1959: 500). This is a rather loose description of a situation that commonly obtains (or used to obtain) in the mountainous regions of Europe and Asia, where farmers with permanent fields in fjord or river basins would take their livestock up to highland pastures for summer grazing. Khazanov, following established usage in Soviet anthropology, calls the same practice '*yaylag* pastoralism' (a variant of his 'herdsman husbandry'), after a Turkic word for summer pasture (1984: 23–4). Bearing in mind our comments, in the first part of this essay, on Khazanov's typology, it is debatable whether this should

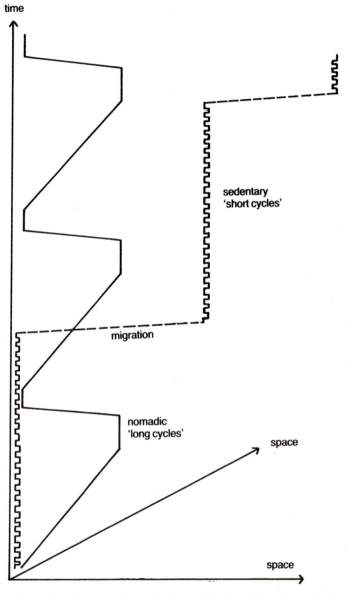

Figure 7.4   Schematic comparison of sedentary 'short cycles' and nomadic 'long cycles'. Krader's terms are used here; in our terms 'displacement' substitutes for 'migration', and 'transhumant migration' for 'nomadism'.

come under the rubric of pastoralism or agriculture. Either way, however, the implication is that 'transhumance' describes a specific economic form, and cannot therefore take its place alongside 'nomadism' and contingent terms in a general classification of patterns of movement. There could not, for example, be transhumant hunters and gatherers. We could, however, adopt the term in a much wider sense, to denote any movements of people occasioned by the seasonal exploitation of diverse ecological zones. A great many so-called nomadic peoples engage in seasonal movements of this kind, usually with well defined points of departure and return. The Basseri of Iran are one such people, the reindeer Lapps of northern Sweden are another, to take two familiar examples (Barth 1961, Manker 1953). In both cases the movements, which take humans and herds from lowlands to highlands and back again, occupy no more than a few months of the year, whilst for the remaining period people make only small local shifts within the particular seasonal range. The impression that they are constantly on the move from place to place, bolstered by their popular designation as nomads, is highly misleading.

Stenning has employed the notion of transhumance in just that broad sense suggested above, defining it simply as a pattern of 'regular seasonal movements' (1957: 58). His particular concern is to characterize the nomadism of the pastoral Fulani, who take their herds of cattle on an annual circuit southward in the dry season to more verdant pastures and northward in the wet in order to avoid the tsetse fly. Stenning calls this circuit the 'transhumance orbit'; it is of course identical to the kind of cycle that Krader takes to be specifically definitive of nomadism. Alongside transhumance, Stenning introduces the notions of 'migration' and 'migratory drift'. The latter is defined as the 'gradual displacement of transhumance orbits', something apparent only in the passage of time as an accumulation of very slight lateral shifts or lineal extensions at either end or in the middle of the transhumance orbit that may, in the very long run, lead to one range of seasonal grazing being relinquished piecemeal for another one. Migration, by contrast, refers to 'the assumption of new transhumance orbits by a sudden and often lengthy movement'. This occurs when, for such reasons as the outbreak of war or epidemic disease, people are compelled to abandon their former paths altogether, and to move to new and unfamiliar country (Stenning 1957: 58–9). This view of migration, as an irreversible, fugitive or colonizing movement, is close to Krader's, and there is no reason why we should confine its application to nomadic peoples alone.

A more elaborate classification of types of pastoral nomadic movement has been worked out by Johnson (1969: 165–76). The two major types are *horizontal* and *vertical* nomadism. In the first type, people remain at roughly the same altitude, but move to take advantage of areal variations in pasture abundance. These movements can appear quite irregular and erratic, but in arid regions may in fact be closely attuned to the incidence of rainfall. Seasonality is most apparent in the cycle of population concentration, for example around wells or water-holes in the dry season, and dispersal in the wet season to exploit areas otherwise inaccessible due to distance from water. Johnson distinguishes two subtypes of the horizontal type, which he calls 'pulsatory' and 'elliptical', depending upon whether the return route 'inwards' to points of dry season concentration retraces the 'outward' route of wet season dispersal, or whether the return follows a different path. Vertical nomadism, unlike horizontal, is geared to altitudinal variations in the seasonal occurrence of pasture and water, making use of different elevations in different seasons. One subtype, perhaps the most common, is 'constricted oscillatory nomadism', where the annual migration from lowland to highland and *vice versa* is funnelled along a confined linear path, at either end of which herding units fan out and disperse over the respective seasonal ranges. A second subtype, 'limited amplitude nomadism', refers to much shorter altitudinal movements within the confines of a single valley system. The third subtype, 'complex nomadism', is merely a catch-all for 'migration patterns that are so complex that it is impossible to classify them with any other pattern' (Johnson 1969: 175). Lacking any diagnostic features, this is not really a type at all, and the less said about it the better!

Bearing in mind that the object of classification is to facilitate rather than to impede comparison, I shall now venture to propose a scheme of my own which, although doubtless far from perfect, is in my view somewhat more satisfactory than its predecessors. I shall proceed by isolating three basic components of movement, which I shall call *nomadism* (in a limited sense to be defined below), *migration* and *displacement*. Each component can take various forms, and the combination of these forms, among different peoples in different environments, and during different periods of their history, yields the diversity of empirically observable patterns. That is to say, the pattern in any given case may be understood as the compound or resultant of a particular kind of nomadism, a particular kind of migration and a particular kind of displacement. It is possible, in addition, that one or two of these components may be absent altogether; for example we may find only migration, or only nomadism, with or without displacement. The null case, where all three components are absent, defines the extreme of absolute permanence of settlement.

Consider, to begin, a group of people moving at frequent intervals from one camp site to another within an environmental and climatic region that is relatively homogeneous – such as arid steppe, boreal forest or arctic tundra. Suppose that they are constrained neither by territorial divisions nor by the need to remain within reach of certain fixed locations. On a map, their path looks like a random walk, which is not to deny, of course, that their movements may be motivated by a rational assessment of such factors as local pasture or game abundance, or expected proximity to enemies and allies. Whether any human group is really so unconstrained in its movement is rather doubtful; however from what Woodburn has to say about the Hadza, who can apparently camp and forage just anywhere, they represent a close approximation (1972: 193). Among pastoral peoples, the Turkana are said to exemplify the condition of having 'no fixed residence, no location which is "home", and no interest in a determinate base' (Gulliver 1975: 370). More commonly, though, there exists some enduring central reference point. For the Karimojong pastoralists whose country adjoins that of the Turkana, this point is determined by the location of homesteads around which are situated cultivated fields. Whilst active men of herding age move about with the cattle, always alert to the indications of where fresh green pasture may be found, women, children and old people stay behind in the homestead. With domestic groups thus split in two, contacts must be kept up through periodic visiting trips between homestead and cattle camps, and this places a limit on how far the distance between them can be stretched. In Figure 7.5 we show the distribution of cattle camps used over a period of two years by a group of Karimojong households whose cultivations were all located in the nuclear area indicated with black hatching. The relocations of one particular herding unit over the same period are indicated by the lines connecting the camp sites. This unit travelled up to 55 miles from home, staying from a few weeks to two months at each site, but never using the same site twice (Dyson-Hudson and Dyson-Hudson 1969: 83).

We refer to such inter-site movement, within an ecological zone, as *nomadism*; and to the ideal typical situation of unconstrained movement as *full nomadism* (Gulliver 1975: 370). Where the mobility is tied down to a central place, as in the example just cited, we speak of *tethered nomadism* (Binford 1983: 341–3). Broadly speaking, both variants correspond to Johnson's category of 'horizontal nomadism'. The same zone may of course present radically contrasting aspects in different seasons: the winter snowfields of the Northern Shield become insect-infested swamps in summer, and ground that is utterly parched in the tropical dry season may be flooded in the wet. The human response to these variations very commonly takes the form of cycles of *concentration* and *dispersal*. The wide generality and profound social consequences of such cycles were first realized in the classic study of Mauss and Beuchat, on seasonal variations among the Eskimo (1979 [1905–6]). They are, however, as characteristic of tropical as of arctic populations (Lee 1979: 360–1): for example,

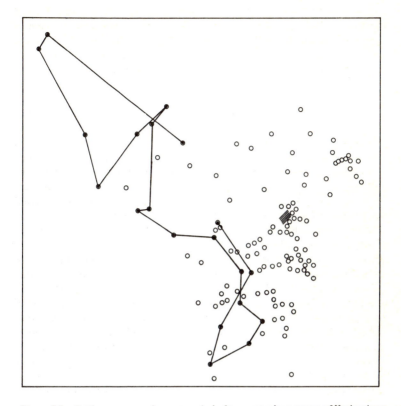

Figure 7.5 Cattle camps used over a period of two years by a group of Karimojong households, whose cultivations were located in the area marked with black hatching. Lines connect the successive camp sites of one herding unit (adapted from Dyson-Hudson and Dyson-Hudson 1969: 83). Original illustration Copyright © 1969 by Scientific American, Inc. All rights reserved. Reproduced by permission.

hunter–gatherers like the !Kung Bushmen of the Kalahari must congregate around permanent water-holes during the dry season but disperse during the wet. A material constraint, the scarcity of water, brings them together, whereas social forces – above all, the rising level of irritation and dispute in a large camp – drives them apart (Lee 1972: 181–2).[6] Among Karimojong pastoralists the reverse obtains: people and herds congregate in the neighbourhood of homesteads during the wet and disperse during the dry; the scarcity of pasture drives them apart, social forces bring them together, temporarily reuniting the members of domestic groups. Turnbull's study of Mbuti hunters suggests, however, that whilst the oscillation between concentration and dispersal is fundamental to the maintenance of social cohesion, allowing for the periodic defusion of interpersonal tensions, whether one season or another is adopted as the period of concentration is somewhat arbitrary. Mbuti net-hunters regard the honey season as a time of plenty, while archers see it as a time of scarcity. 'Each group takes appropriate measures to meet the perceived situation, the net-hunters splitting up into small units, and the archers congregating into larger ones!' (Turnbull 1968: 134). Turnbull's conclusions cannot nevertheless be accepted without some reservation, for as Abruzzi (1980) has shown, there are good ecological reasons – which Turnbull ignores – for these contrastive patterns of movement.

Seasonal cycles of concentration and dispersal are pronounced not only among tropical and arid-zone hunter–gatherers, but also among peoples of the boreal forest who practise hunting, trapping and fishing. Very often, however, their moves are made between a series of sites already marked by permanent or semi-permanent structures, perhaps containing stores of food, fuel and equipment left over from the previous phase of occupation on the expectation of a future return. Figure 7.6 shows the routes taken by the constituent households of the Skolt Lapp band of Suenjel in the period just before the outbreak of the Second World War, when these people still occupied their original homeland. The Suenjel Skolts at that time combined fishing and hunting with the management of small herds of domestic reindeer. They would reside from January to April in a concentrated settlement, from which they would then disperse radially, each household proceeding through customary spring, summer and autumn camp locations before congregating again in the central, winter village (Nickul 1948, Ingold 1976: 4). A number of distinctive features of the boreal forest environment promote the regular re-use of seasonal sites, as exemplified by the Skolt practice. First, relatively severe climatic conditions mean that more is required in the way of clothing and domestic utensils than in warmer regions. By establishing supply bases at a number of fixed points, less has to be carried around. Second, where timber is employed for fuel, it should be laid up in advance, during a previous occupation, so that it can dry out. Thirdly, winter dwellings – at least – must be fairly durable structures if they are to provide adequate shelter, and are not of the kind that can be knocked up in an hour or two. A fourth point is that marked variations in the availability of food, together with winter frosts, both necessitate and make possible extensive practical storage (see Chapter 8). And finally, the heavy reliance on fish and fur-bearers necessitates the regular use of fixed facilities such as nets and traps, rather than portable implements. These facilities cannot be set up just anywhere, but must be situated at carefully selected points whose location is determined by features of drainage and

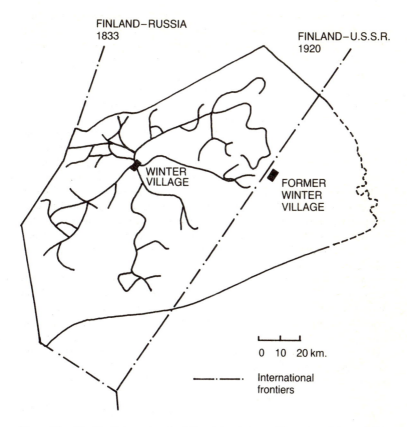

Figure 7.6 The Skolt Lapp band of Suenjel: winter settlement and household migration routes in 1938 (after Nickul 1948).

topography. Residential bases must likewise be located with a view to preserving access to these sites.

Though sometimes called 'semi-nomadism', I think it best to refer to the kind of logistically organized movement that has just been described as *fixed-point nomadism*. Thus the general category of nomadism, or within-zone movement, admits three varieties: full nomadism (no fixed locations), tethered nomadism (tied to a centre, but without regular re-use of peripheral locations) and fixed-point nomadism (tied to a centre, and with regular re-use of peripheral locations). In all three cases, the aggregate pattern may show seasonal cycles of concentration and dispersal. By contrast, we have to consider movement not within but *between* distinct ecological zones, designed to take advantage of the resources available in each zone at different times of year. I shall use the term *migration* to refer to such movement. Under this general category are subsumed the kinds of annual cycle that Stenning called 'transhumant', and while we follow his usage in this instance, our definition of migration is quite different from his, as indeed it is from Krader's. The implied distinction between nomadism and transhumant migration bears some resemblance to Johnson's between horizontal and vertical nomadism; however it should be noted that environmental transitions are not necessarily a function of altitude. If Lappish pastoralists can reach the tundra from the forest by moving *up* into the mountains, Chipewyan hunters reach it by moving *north* over monotonously flat terrain.

With this qualification, we would otherwise accept Goldschmidt's separation of 'true nomadism', involving free-ranging, horizontal movement over desert, steppe or tundra, from 'transhumance', involving periodic verticla shifts from winter to summer ranges (1979: 16–17). These are not, however, to be regarded as either/or alternatives, for a group may practise nomadism in one or the other, or both, of the zones between which it migrates. Gulliver, for example, has drawn specific attention to the combination of transhumance and nomadism among the Turkana, who periodically take their cattle up from plains to mountains, whilst leaving camels and small stock to browse at the lower level:

> It may be convenient to speak of the cattle following a system of transhumance between mountains and plains, *so long as that term does not obscure the movements within each region*. This may be contrasted with the *more truly nomadic movements* of the browse homesteads, which tend to move about all the year in response to gradually changing conditions of vegetation. (Gulliver 1955: 29, my emphases)

But when Jacobs speaks of 'transhumant herd and family movements' among the pastoral Maasai, who fan out from dry season pastures by rivers, wells or springs to outlying wet season pastures centred on rain ponds and other surface waters, he is confusing transhumance with the typical nomadic cycle of concentration and dispersal (Jacobs 1975: 417).

Besides the Turkana, we have already encountered several examples of peoples practising transhumant pastoralism: the Fulani, the Basseri and the Lapps. Could one equally find examples of transhumance among hunters? I think so, if the residential relocations of the human group are occasioned by seasonal migrations of the principal prey species. The Nganasan of the Taimyr Peninsula in northern Siberia make a return trip of some 800 miles between forest margins and tundra, keeping in step with the migratory herds of wild reindeer on which their livelihood depends (Popov 1966: 21–2). Similar migrations, if not quite so extensive, are made by many 'edge-of-the-woods' native peoples of the Canadian north, in their exploitation of the caribou (for examples, see Ingold 1980: 14–15). However, comparing the migratory movements of hunters and pastoralists, there are two important differences to note. The first is that hunters normally aim to *intercept* migrating herds at a series of points along their annual orbits, but not to follow them all the way. Indeed, to do so could be a sheer logistical impossibility (Burch 1972: 344–51, see Ingold 1980: 54–6). Pastoralists, on the other hand, must follow the herds

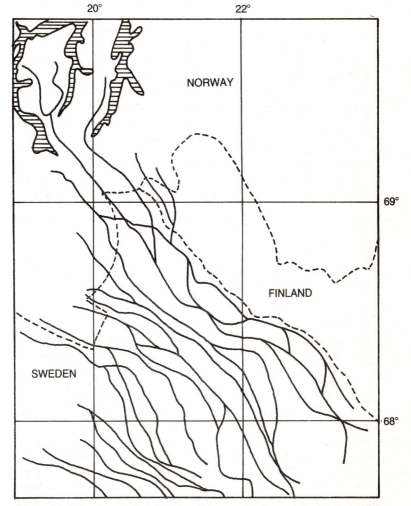

Figure 7.7   Migrations paths of the Swedish mountain Lapps (after Manker 1953).

for the full length of their migration, something greatly facilitated by their possession of draught, riding or pack animals. This continuous association between humans and herds is a necessary condition for their protection, which is the prime objective of the pastoral herd-owner for whom living animals are an embodiment of wealth and domestic security. Consequently, the pastoral transhumance orbit is likely to be much extended compared to that of hunters in an equivalent environment. Figure 7.7 shows the migration paths of Swedish mountain Lapp herding groups, as they existed in the 1940s, between lowland forest pastures in the southeast and highland mountain pastures in the northwest, occupied in winter and summer respectively. As can be seen, the range of each group takes the form of an elongated strip (Manker 1953).

A second difference between the migration of hunters and pastoralists, which also follows from the fact that living animals are not – for the former – a kind of property, is that among hunters the movement could just as well be from exploiting one species in one ecological zone to exploiting another species in another ecological zone. Indeed as a general rule, hunters will be more inclined to transfer from species to species than to pursue one species over its entire range, so long as adequate alternatives are available nearer at hand. To distinguish migrations occasioned by transfers between resources from those of the transhumant type, occasioned by the migration of a single resource, we refer to the first as *trans-resource* migrations. The Copper and Netsilik Eskimo, for example, oscillate between sea-mammal hunting off the arctic coast in winter and spring, and caribou hunting in the inland tundra in summer and autumn. The direction of these migrations is precisely the reverse of that of the caribou herds: south as the herds move north to the tundra, and north to the coasts as the herds retreat southwards to the forest, a zone which the Eskimo never penetrate at all. The contrast between the trans-resource migrations of the Eskimo and the transhumant migrations of such 'edge-of-the-woods' peoples as the Chipewyan and Dogrib is illustrated schematically in Figure 7.8. The latter, being harmonic if not coextensive with those of the migratory herds, are 'pre-adaptations' to pastoralism in a way that the former are not, and it therefore comes as no surprise that in northern Eurasia, among those peoples whose ranges have always straddled the forest/tundra divide, the transition from hunting to pastoralism has been realized to the fullest degree (Ingold 1980: 14–15).

The notion of trans-resource migration, though applicable to many hunting societies, was originally proposed by Salzman (1971: 192) to describe a move undertaken in the context of a pastoral economy. Among the Shah Nawazi Baluch of Iran, the biggest migration of the annual cycle, in late summer, involves a journey of about 100 miles from the zone of

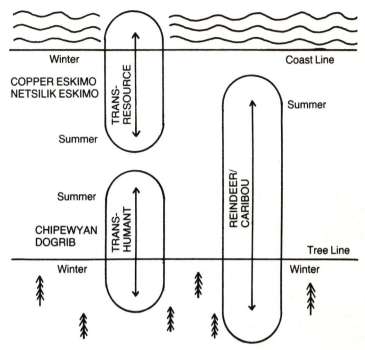

Figure 7.8   Transhumant and trans-resource subsistence cycles among arctic and subarctic wild reindeer/caribou hunters (adapted from Ingold 1980: 13). Original illustration Copyright © 1980 by Cambridge University Press. Reproduced by permission.

summer pastures for their flocks of sheep and goats to the zone of date cultivation, and must be made when the dates are ripe for harvest. What is significant here is that this move is not occasioned by the exigencies of herding, but by the concurrent scheduling of pastoral and non-pastoral activities in spatially separate locations. But unlike hunters, pastoralists do not have the option of leaving the herds to look after themselves whilst their attention is diverted to other resources, so that their trans-resource migrations cannot be socially all-encompassing. A few shepherds must be left behind to mind the flocks whilst everyone else is away. A reverse situation obtains in those societies practising what Krader called transhumance (Khazanov's '*yaylag* pastoralism'). Rather than a section of a predominantly pastoral people, as the Shah Nawazi Baluch, moving off to exploit a cultivated resource, among so-called transhumant farmers a section of a predominantly agricultural people moves off to exploit a pastoral resource. Both are really cases of trans-resource migration, by pastoralists and agriculturalists respectively, and there is no difference in principle between them.

Moreover, the actual distance covered is not at issue. One could, if need be, distinguish between long- and short-distance migration, as Johnson does in differentiating the subtypes of 'constricted oscillatory' and 'limited amplitude' vertical nomadism. But the distinction could only be a relative one. How far one has to travel to pass from one environmental zone to another depends upon the lie of the land: in mountainous country it may be very short, whereas on level ground the transition may be far more gradual. When sections of the population remain concurrently resident in both zones, this distance does have a bearing on the frequency of intervisiting and other forms of mutual contact. Such visits, involving the movement of individuals between sites without any total relocation of residence, may be called *trips* (Salzman 1971: 195). A further consideration concerns the possible superimposition upon the migratory oscillation, whether transhumant or trans-resource, of a seasonal cycle of concentration and dispersal. People may fan out at one end of the orbit and converge at the other, or fan out at both ends whilst converging in transit – as in Johnson's 'constricted oscillatory' type. These alternatives are illustrated schematically in Figure 7.9.

We have finally to introduce terms to cover the kinds of movement which Stenning designated as 'migratory drift' and 'migration'. Stenning's

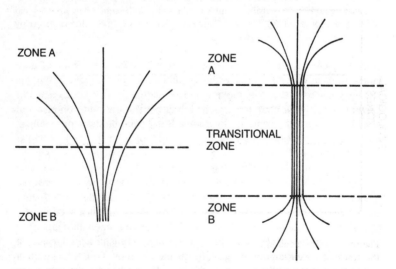

Figure 7.9   Convergence, divergence and constriction of migration orbits.

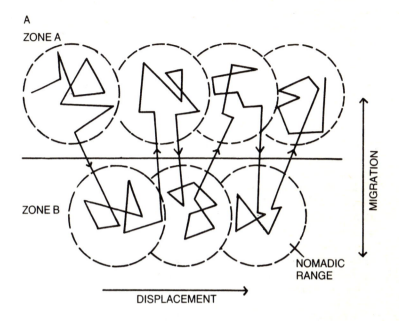

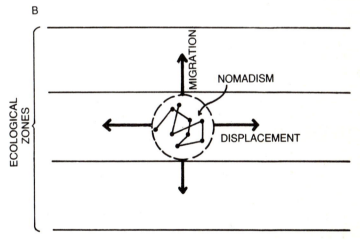

Figure 7.10   The combination of displacement with migration and nomadism. a: the track of a hypothetical household; b: a formal representation of the three components of movement.

usage is, I think, confusing, simply because it is so common to regard transhumant and trans-resource movements of a seasonal nature as the component 'migrations' of an annual cycle. I prefer to reserve the term migration for between-zone movements and nomadism for within-zone movements, contrasting both to the *lateral displacement* of nomadic ranges or migration orbits. The displacement may be gradual and cumulative, the outcome of a sequence of slight redirections in successive years. I see no objection to using the word *drift* to describe a process of this kind. For the more abrupt and wholesale shifts from one region to another, which Stenning calls migrations, I would suggest the term *dislocation*. Both dislocation and drift can affect otherwise sedentary communities: the resettlement of European farmers in the New World exemplifies the former, the pioneering movement into virgin forest of Iban cultivators exemplifies the latter. These are equivalent to what Krader called 'migration', whereas his 'nomadism' is equivalent to our 'transhumant migration' (see Figure 7.4). But displacement, whether in the form of drift or dislocation, can equally well combine with either or both of migration and nomadism. Figure 7.10a shows how this combination might be manifested in the residential track of a hypothetical household, followed over a number of years. It is assumed that the household migrates annually from zone A to zone B and back, and that within each zone it makes frequent moves to sites not previously used. Figure 7.10b is a more formal, schematic representation of the way in which our three major components of movement – nomadism, migration and displacement – are logically interconnected.

I conclude with a tabular presentation of our complete scheme for the classification of forms of movement involving the spatial relocation of settlement in human societies. No classification can be perfect, and there are bound to be instances which cannot easily be accommodated within the terminological framework suggested here. However, it does resolve some of the ambiguities that currently afflict the literature, especially of hunter–gatherer and pastoral societies.

Nomadism: within-zone movement
 (Johnson: 'horizontal nomadism')
(i) Full nomadism
(ii) Tethered nomadism
(iii) Fixed-point nomadism
Aggregate pattern may show seasonal cycles of concentration and dispersal.

Migration: between-zones movement
 (Stenning: 'transhumance', Johnson: 'vertical nomadism')

(i) Transhumant migration (Krader: 'nomadism')
(ii) Trans-resource migration (Krader: 'transhumance')
Aggregate pattern may show seasonal cycles of convergence and divergence of orbits.

Displacement: lateral shifts of sedentary settlements, nomadic ranges and/or migration orbits
    (Krader: 'migration')
(i) Drift (Stenning: 'migratory drift')
(ii) Dislocation (Stenning: 'migration')

Notes to Chapter 7

1 For other examples of the definitional pitfalls that attend the delineation of pastoralism *vis-à-vis* agriculture, and of nomads *vis-à-vis* sedentaries, see Monod (1975: 126–8).
2 The argument presented here is further elaborated in Ingold (1982b).
3 For an alternative typology, see Goldschmidt (1979: 17–18). Khazanov's contribution to the study of nomadism is reviewed in Ingold (1985).
4 The diagram is taken from Ingold (1984), where I have constructed an analogous model for the transition from hunting to pastoralism.
5 Binford notes that 'we may anticipate increasing repetition in the use of particular places when the system is becoming more sedentary' (1983: 370). Yet it is by the frequency of re-use that we *measure* sedentism. That is to say, it is an index, not an expectation.
6 It should be mentioned, however, that the cycle of concentration and dispersal among the G/wi Bushmen is the opposite of that among the !Kung: 'The Zhu/twasi [!Kung] aggregate in the dry season and disperse in the wet season, while the Central Kalahari Bushmen [G/wi] disperse in the dry season and aggregate in the wet season' (Barnard 1979: 140–1). Among both groups, however, seasonal cycles are primarily dictated by the availability of water.

References for Chapter 7

Abruzzi, W. S. 1980 Flux among the Mbuti Pygmies of the Ituri forest: an ecological interpretation. In *Beyond the myths of culture: essays in cultural materialism*, ed. E. B. Ross. London: Academic Press.

Asad, T. 1978 Equality in nomadic social systems? *Critique of Anthropology* **11**: 57–65.

Barnard, A. 1979 Kalahari Bushman settlement patterns. In *Social and ecological systems*, eds. P. C. Burnham and R. F. Ellen (A.S.A. monogr. 18). London: Academic Press.

Barth, F. 1961 *Nomads of South Persia*. Oslo: Universitetsforlaget.

Binford, L. R. 1983 *Working at archaeology*. London: Academic Press.

Burch, E. S. 1972 The caribou/wild reindeer as a human resource. *American Antiquity* **37**: 339–67.

Burnham, P. 1979 Spatial mobility and political centralization in pastoral societies. In *Pastoral production and society*, ed. Équipe écologie et anthropologie des sociétés pastorales. Cambridge University Press.

Carlstein, T. 1982 *Time resources, society and ecology Vol. I: Preindustrial societies*. London: Allen and Unwin.

Chatty, D. 1980 The pastoral family and the truck. In *When nomads settle*, ed. P. C. Salzman. New York: J. F. Bergin.

Dyson-Hudson, N. 1972 The study of nomads. *Journal of Asian and African Studies* **7**: 2–29.

Dyson-Hudson, R. and N. Dyson-Hudson 1969 Subsistence herding in Uganda. *Scientific American* **220**(2): 76–89.

Fernandez, J. 1979 On the notion of religious movement. *Social Research* **46**: 36–62.

Freeman, D. 1970 *Report on the Iban*. London: Athlone Press.

Goldschmidt, W. 1979 A general model for pastoral social systems. In *Pastoral production and society*, ed. Équipe écologie et anthropologie des sociétés pastorales. Cambridge University Press.

Gulliver, P. H. 1955 *The family herds*. London: Routledge and Kegan Paul.

Gulliver, P. H. 1975 Nomadic movements: causes and implications. In *Pastoralism in tropical Africa*, ed. T. Monod. London: Oxford University Press.

Helm, J. 1965 Bilaterality in the socio-territorial organization of the Arctic drainage Dene. *Ethnology* **4**: 361–85.

Ingold, T. 1976 *The Skolt Lapps today*. Cambridge University Press.

Ingold, T. 1978 The transformation of the siida. *Ethnos* **43**: 146–62.

Ingold, T. 1980 *Hunters, pastoralists and ranchers*. Cambridge University Press.

Ingold, T. 1982a Comment on Testart: 'The significance of food storage among hunter–gatherers'. *Current Anthropology* **23**: 531–2.

Ingold, T. 1982b Review of P. C. Salzman and contributors: 'When nomads settle'. *Nomadic Peoples* **10**: 61–4.

Ingold, T. 1984 Time, social relationships and the exploitation of animals: anthropological reflections on prehistory. In *Animals and archaeology (3): early herders and their flocks*. eds. J. Clutton-Brock and C. Grigson. Oxford: BAR (International Series 202).

Ingold, T. 1985 Khazanov on nomads. *Current Anthropology* **26**: 384–7.

Jacobs, A. H. 1975 Maasai pastoralism in historical perspective. In *Pastoralism in tropical Africa*, ed. T. Monod. London: Oxford University Press.

Johnson, D. 1969 *The nature of nomadism*. University of Chicago, Department of Geography, Research Paper No. 118.

Khazanov, A. M. 1984 *Nomads and the outside world*. Cambridge University Press.

Krader, L. 1959 The ecology of nomadic pastoralism. *International Social Science Journal* **11**: 499–510.

Kroeber, A. L. 1952 *The nature of culture*. University of Chicago Press.

Lee, R. B. 1972 Work effort, group structure and land-use in contemporary hunter–gatherers. In *Man, settlement and urbanism*, eds. P. J. Ucko, R. Tringham and G. W. Dimbleby. London: Duckworth.

Lee, R. B. 1979 *The !Kung San*. Cambridge University Press.

Lee, R. B. and I. DeVore 1968 Problems in the study of hunters and gatherers. In

Man the hunter, eds. R. B. Lee and I. DeVore. Chicago: Aldine.

Manker, E. 1953 *The nomadism of the Swedish mountain Lapps*. Nordiska Museet: Acta Lapponica 7. Stockholm: Hugo Gebers.

Mauss, M. and H. Beuchat 1979 [1905–6] *Seasonal variations of the Eskimo*. London: Routledge and Kegan Paul.

Monod, T. 1975 Introduction. In *Pastoralism in tropical Africa*. London: Oxford University Press.

Murdock, G. P. 1949 *Social structure*. New York: Macmillan.

Nickul, K. 1948 *The Skolt Lapp community Suenjelsijd during the year 1938*. Nordiska Museet: Acta Lapponica 5. Stockholm: Hugo Gebers.

Pehrson, R. N. 1957 *The bilateral network of social relations in Könkämä Lapp District*. Indiana University Research Center in Anthropology, Folklore and Linguistics, Publications 3. Bloomington.

Popov, A. A. 1966 *The Nganasan: the material culture of the Tavgi Samoyeds*. Indiana University Uralic and Altaic Series 56. Bloomington.

Salzman, P. C. 1967 Political organization among nomadic peoples. *Proceedings of the American Philosophical Society* **111**: 115–31.

Salzman, P. C. 1971 Movement and resource extraction among pastoral nomads: the case of the Shah Nawazi Baluch. *Anthropological Quarterly* **44**: 185–97.

Salzman, P. C. 1980a Is 'nomadism' a useful concept? *Nomadic Peoples* **6**: 1–7.

Salzman, P. C. 1980b Introduction: processes of sedentarization as adaptation and response. In *When nomads settle*, ed. P. C. Salzman. New York: J. F. Bergin.

Spooner, B. 1971 Towards a generative model of pastoralism. *Anthropological Quarterly* **44**: 198–210.

Stenning, D. J. 1957 Transhumance, migratory drift, migration; patterns of pastoral Fulani nomadism. *Journal of the Royal Anthropological Institute* **87**: 57–73.

Steward, J. H. 1969 Observations on bands. In *Contributions to anthropology: band societies*, ed. D. Damas. National Museums of Canada Bulletin 228. Ottawa: Queen's Printer.

Tapper, R. L. 1979 The organization of nomadic communities in pastoral societies of the Middle East. In *Pastoral production and society*, ed. Équipe écologie et anthropologie des sociétés pastorales. Cambridge University Press.

Turnbull, C. M. 1968 The importance of flux in two hunting societies. In *Man the hunter*, eds. R. B. Lee and I. DeVore. Chicago: Aldine.

Woodburn, J. C. 1972 Ecology, nomadic movement and the composition of the local group among hunters and gatherers: an East African example and its implications. In *Man, settlement and urbanism*, eds. P. J. Ucko, R. Tringham and G. W. Dimbleby. London: Duckworth.

Yellen, J. E. 1977 *Archaeological approaches to the present*. London: Academic Press.

8

The significance of storage in hunting societies

It is still customary in anthropology to divide the bulk of supposedly 'primitive' peoples into the categories of hunters and gatherers (or fishermen), agriculturalists and pastoralists. This classification, derived from the evolutionary schema of the nineteenth century, has long outlived the theories that gave rise to it, surviving as a set of 'odd-job' terms – useful enough for delimiting a field of interest, but of little theoretical significance. However, as social evolution has once more become a legitimate subject of anthropological inquiry, there is a growing concern to replace the old categories by an alternative set of terms which might point to critical transitions on the level of social relations rather than technical processes. Despite a lingering intuition that hunting and gathering societies do share certain characteristics which agricultural and pastoral societies lack, no one has been able to agree as to what these might be, and exceptions always come readily to hand.

In social terms, one important consideration lies in whether or not people are bound to one another by enduring relations in respect of the control and distribution of the means of subsistence. This consideration underlies two criteria by which hunting and gathering societies have commonly been distinguished. The first is that labour in such societies is not invested in the expectation of a delayed return (Meillassoux 1973). The second is that there is little or no storage of food, or otherwise expressed, that 'the environment itself is the storehouse' (Lee and DeVore 1968: 12, see Marx 1930: 171). These two criteria are, of course, complementary. The image is presented of foragers content to pluck what they will from an unmodified environment as and when they need it for immediate consumption, secure in the knowledge that food is all around them, so long as they are free to move and unencumbered with provisions (Sahlins 1972: 31–2). The husbandry of crops and herds, by contrast, involves time-lags both between the initial investment of labour and the realization of the product, and between harvesting and consumption.

These time-lags, it is supposed, create the basis for lasting mutual dependencies. Time ties people down.

It has since become apparent that the above criteria, whatever their social significance, do *not* distinguish the class of hunting and gathering societies. Ethnographic instances abound in which the extraction of food from the natural environment requires a considerable prior investment of labour, and in which extensive storage forms an integral part of the regular subsistence cycle. Thus Woodburn (1980; 1982) has argued that the most important distinction is between what he calls 'immediate-return' and 'delayed-return systems' of production. But he finds that the great majority of contemporary hunter–gatherer societies, and of course all agricultural and pastoral societies too, conform to the latter type. Only a handful of cases exemplify the former.[1] Indeed their number is so few, and their existence so hedged around by special circumstances, that doubts inevitably arise as to the significance of immediate-return systems as constituting the supposed 'baseline' of social evolution.

One manifestation of delayed return, with which I shall be primarily concerned in this essay, is represented by the *storage* of subsistence resources. Again we find that the absence of food storage, once held to be a major characteristic of any hunter–gatherer economy, is perhaps more the exception than the rule. We are obliged, therefore, to distinguish between hunters and gatherers who practise storage and those who do not (Testart 1981: 181–7; 1982: 523). In evolutionary terms, the potential significance of storage is considerable. First, by levelling out the effects of natural fluctuations in the availability of food resources, storage makes possible the support of greater concentrations of people over longer periods of time. Secondly, to the extent that people are immobilized by their supplies, storage fosters sedentism and inhibits residential flux. Thirdly, and perhaps most importantly, storage is a precondition for external trade, and hence for the integration of local societies of hunters and gatherers into wider systems of exchange and distribution.

Yet we have no reason to suppose that storage is the *cause* of demographic concentration, sedentism and trade. It could equally well be the consequence of an evolutionary movement with an independent, social dynamic. In other words, people may be required to lay up supplies by virtue of their involvement as members of self-perpetuating, solidary groups bound by relations of mutual interdependence. For the 'nomadic alternative', according to which security lies in the dispersal of population rather than the concentration of resources, entails the periodic dissolution of only temporarily constituted groups (Bailey 1981: 8). However, rather than trying to debate the chicken and egg question of whether storage is cause or consequence (Testart 1982: 524), I shall attempt to bring out certain ambiguities in the concept of storage itself, particularly with regard to its ecological, practical and social senses. The ecological sense will be discussed rather summarily, since it touches only marginally on my main argument, which has to do with the distinction between practical and social storage.

In brief, whereas practical storage is an aspect of the labour process in production, social storage is a concomitant of relations of distribution. Logically, the latter cannot be inferred from the former; empirically, each can occur both with or without the other. We must consequently introduce some conceptual refinement into the inclusive category of 'delayed-return' systems, in order to recognize the quite different kinds of time-lag associated on the one hand with the practical staggering of production and consumption schedules, and on the other with the deferment of access to socially appropriated resources. Though it is undeniable that, in many societies of hunters and gatherers, returns on labour are delayed, only when the initial investment of labour involves an appropriative movement does the delay serve to invest social relations with a quality of durability. Such investment, I maintain, is definitive of agricultural and pastoral production. In a purely extractive hunting and gathering economy, by contrast, whether or not it entails practical delays, social relations have the character of immediacy – in the sense that 'people are not dependent on *specific* other people for access to basic requirements' (Woodburn 1982: 434). In short, the much maligned category of 'hunting and gathering' may, after all, have some theoretical significance, denoting the practical concomitant of a system of social relations of production marked by *generalized* access, to which I have already referred as 'the collective appropriation of nature'.

Ecological storage

Every subsistence system serves to bring about a flow of energy and materials from select species of plants and animals to their human consumers (see Ingold 1979: 274–6). In ecological terms, storage represents an interruption of this flow, leading to a temporary accumulation. There are a number of points at which this interruption might occur, each point marking off a distinct phase in the physical metamorphosis and transport of food from its initial extraction to its eventual organic assimilation by the consumer population. In the beginning and final stages of this process, the store is an integral part of living nature: first in the form of the 'standing crop' of plants or animals, last in the human body itself. Indeed, when ecologists speak of 'storage' by plants or animals (including man), they are generally referring to the accumulation of materials and potential energy represented by living biomass, rather than the action of organisms in setting aside supplies of harvested food for future consumption. Similarly, the ecological concept of production refers to the formation of organic material *in* the world of living things as opposed to the extraction of material *from* it (Ingold 1979: 275–6). To be consistent, therefore, we should restrict the meaning of storage in its ecological sense to the concentration of nutrients at particular points in an ecosystem, as distinct from the actions which bring about these concentrations. Just as the ecosystem comprises a set of functional rather than spatial relationships, so the concentrations implied by the concept of ecological storage are not necessarily local, although they may be.

The obverse of ecological storage is waste – stuff thrown away, 'stored' if at all for posterity through the action of natural agencies rather than human design. The definition of waste is not without its problems. Thus, in non-industrial societies, the greater part of what is discarded in the various stages of production and consumption is returned to the natural environment for subsequent recycling. Indeed what is wasted from the point of view of the immediate needs of the human population may be crucial for the maintenance of other components of the ecosystem of which that population is a part, though depending, perhaps, on how narrowly the boundaries of the ecosystem are drawn. I think we may define waste in the context of the ecological concept of storage to represent not merely an interruption but a *deflection* in the flow of materials and energy from plants and animals to human bodies. Since the deflected flow may be taken up by non-human consumers (scavengers or decomposers), it is obvious that waste can only be specified in relation to the human population itself. Sometimes the deflection merely adds an extra 'loop' to a food chain that nevertheless concludes with man, as when reject tubers are fed to domestic pigs which convert them into meat for human consumption (Rappaport 1968: 58). Waste may be deliberately stored for recycling, for example as manure. Among some hunters and gatherers, materials initially dumped as waste may be reprocessed for consumption as emergency food, in the event that all other sources fail, so that the dump comes to function as a kind of store (e.g. Binford 1978: 146).

If we define waste as I have suggested, it is possible to identify as many potential points of waste as there are points of storage: in each case the waste component is that proportion of the food resource that is not only delayed but blocked, for whatever reason, from entering the subsequent stage in its passage from the environment to human consumers. We should not however assume that all of what is harvested is in fact convertible to edible foodstuffs. The components of waste consist of both edible and inedible parts. I imagine that from an archaeological perspective it would be important to examine at what points the various inedible parts are discarded – whether at harvest, before or after transport to the settlement, in the course of preparation, or whilst the prepared food is being actually eaten. It would then be possible to reconstruct the passage of food from extraction to consumption on the basis of the occurrence and distribution of successive inedible wastes.

But in addition, it would be necessary to take into account the possible uses of inedible parts for other purposes, such as bones for implements, skins for clothing and shelter, shells for containers, and so on. Indeed it has often been remarked of 'primitive' hunters, that there are few parts of their kills that do not have a use for some purpose or other. The contrast is with 'commercial' hunters who kill game only to obtain particular products such as furs or tusks with high market value, and obtain most of what they need by purchase. Despite this contrast, it would be wrong to suppose that where every part of an animal has a practical use there would be no waste, even if animals were killed only in response to immediate needs. This is because the different parts do not necessarily occur in nature in the proportions that are culturally required. For example, if so many animals have to be killed for their skins, to meet requirements for clothing and shelter, there may be a substantial wastage of edible meat. In short, the utilization of natural resources which is qualitatively complete may be quantitatively fractional.

Practical storage

It must not be forgotten that the storage of harvested produce for future consumption is not unique to man. Examples abound of the same kind of behaviour throughout the animal kingdom (Rindos 1980: 753, Stacey and Koenig 1984, Petter 1985). Nevertheless, compared with certain other animal species that have occupied similar ecological niches to man, of which perhaps the wolf is the best example (Hall and Sharp 1978), the capacity of the human body to store food already ingested is rather limited. Consequently, extra-corporeal storage becomes a necessary element of any subsistence system in which the supply of food from the natural environment is erratic. I refer to the purposive activity entailed in the formation of such stores as *practical* storage. I should stress that this is not equivalent to viewing storage as a technology, although that is how it is usually described in standard ethnographic accounts. Similarly, it is common to find hunting and gathering characterized by an inventory of the instruments employed. Clearly both hunting and gathering, and storage, regarded as aspects of a system of practical action, depend upon the application of a technology – including not only a set of artefacts but also the knowledge surrounding their manufacture and use. But such techniques should not be confused with the intentional activity which they conduct (Ingold 1979: 278; 1981: 123; see Chapter 5).

I am not concerned here with providing an inventory of the techniques of storage. An inventory of this kind, if attempted, would have to include procedures for stabilizing foodstuffs, such as salting, drying, freezing, smoking and pulverizing (O'Shea 1981: 169), and procedures for accommodating and protecting them, through the construction of storehouses, pits, cellars, chests, pots or whatever. It is perhaps on this level of technical procedure that storage by non-human animals is to be distinguished from storage by human beings. Such procedures amongst animals are largely programmed by heredity or conditioning, whereas amongst humans they follow a conscious blueprint or design, carried in the imagination of individuals and communicable symbolically. This design, of storage in its technical sense, is of course just one part of the overall pattern of cultural adaptation which enables a population to execute its social objectives under given environmental conditions. Naturally, the activity of practical storage will respond to variations in these conditions, even though the procedures for carrying it out are more or less fixed by cultural design.

Practical storage might best be regarded as a solution to the problems of activity scheduling (Flannery 1968: 75–6, see also Jochim 1976: 30–1, Torrence 1983). Suppose that throughout the year there is a continuous and fairly constant demand for certain foodstuffs, but that the procurement of each of these involves activities that are mutually exclusive. The producers must then divide their time between successive activities (Carlstein 1980: 26), taking into account variations in resource quality·and availability, and the amount of time required to obtain quantities of each in appropriate proportions. They may also have to make allowance for activities that, although part of the productive cycle, yield no immediate return in the form of harvested produce. Amongst hunters the construction and maintenance of facilities such as traps and surrounds can involve substantial inputs of co-ordinated labour. Likewise among swidden cultivators, the clearance and fencing of new plots may interrupt the harvesting of old ones. Moreover, a number of necessary activities may have to be scheduled in that suspend production itself, not only for particular individuals but also for the entire community. For example, everyone may congregate from time to time for major calendrical rituals, for public political negotiation and dispute settlement, and for inter-community trade, all of which may continue over prolonged periods.

Practical storage, then, is a response to the non-concurrence of production and consumption schedules. In the case of inter-community trade, it is additionally a function of the non-concurrence of production and exchange (of resources for export) and of exchange and consumption (of imported resources). For besides having a stock of food to consume for the duration of trading activity, the community must have resources harvested during one restricted period available for trade during another restricted period. And it will not consume immediately all that is received in exchange (Bahuchet and Thomas 1985: 19). My purpose in stressing these problems of scheduling is to bring out two points that are often overlooked.

The first is that the extent of storage is not simply determined by environmental fluctuations in the availability of resources for harvesting. Though it is obvious that storage helps to tide over lean seasons, we have also to consider what kinds of activities are involved in the exploitation of different resources, and whether they can be pursued simultaneously. For example, even where a number of resources (X, Y, Z) for which there is a continuous demand are continuously available in relative abundance, if the exploitation of one (X) means breaking off from the exploitation of any of the others (e.g. Z), some storage may be necessary (of both X and Z alternately, though not Y). To discover the magnitude and duration of this storage, a number of further questions must be answered. Does the exploitation of X require a long period of unbroken activity, or can it be done sporadically, in between other things? In other words, does it involve a few months of each year, a few days of each month, or a few hours of each day? Then, does it entail the simultaneous co-operation of all the producers of a local group in common tasks, or is each producer free to make up his own schedule? In the latter case, the need for storage may be obviated by injunctions to share. Thus, if one man has been concentrating on the exploitation of X and therefore lacks supplies of Z for immediate consumption, he may depend on receiving his needs from others who have been devoting their attention to the exploitation of Z, in his turn sharing with them his supplies of X. This would be impossible were everyone within the community of sharing engaged at the same time in the work of exploiting X. The same argument applies to productive activities on which the returns are not immediate. Sometimes these can proceed hand in hand with resource extraction, as with the tending and milking of cattle, or the weeding of a swidden plot and the daily harvesting of tubers. Even if they cannot, there need be no problem if different individuals are working to different schedules, and can receive assistance from each other. But projects involving communal labour, as in the construction of a hunting surround or in land clearance, may require that supplies of stored food exist to tide over the period of each undertaking. Again, when work is interrupted by non-productive activities, only those interruptions that cut across the whole society necessarily entail storage. For if they are scheduled for different individuals at different times, as when a man goes visiting his kin, each can rely on the hospitality of others until he is back to producing again.

The second point to emphasize is that the factors influencing practical storage are social as well as environmental. These social factors concern both how labour is allocated among different resources and consecutive stages of production, and the ways in which the resulting products are distributed. That social relations of distribution beyond the unit of domestic consumption can affect the pattern of storage has already been suggested: I have noted, for example, that within a community of sharing the scheduling of productive activities need not lead to storage, so long as concurrent schedules are out of phase with one another. Were every household ideally self-sufficient, the need for storage would be more acute. By contrast, inter-community trade may promote storage, not only because trading activities and the public celebrations that often accompany them interrupt production, but also because a quantity of goods has to be amassed for distribution within a limited period. However, if the exchange is of food surplus to the community's short-term needs for durable tokens of wealth – which may be exchanged back for food in future times of shortage – the need for long-term storage of food-stuffs may be eliminated (O'Shea 1981). In other words, the storage function is assumed by the exchange network (Bailey 1981: 8; the same is true of peasant marketing systems, see Belshaw 1965: 55), though always on condition that the productive schedules of the parties to exchange are out of phase.

The influence of the social division of labour upon the pattern of storage can be simply demonstrated, in the terms of our previous example, by considering the allocation of tasks between the sexes. Say only men harvest resource X, and only women Z, but both men and women harvest Y. In that case, the group may readily be supplied continuously with all three resources. But if X, Y and Z are all harvested by men, leaving women with the full-time job of processing the products for consumption, it may be necessary to store X and Z alternately, though to an extent depending on other conditions already outlined. In the first case, however, a different problem of activity scheduling is posed, concerning how the tasks of resource extraction are to be fitted in with those of preparation. If women are expected both to harvest and to prepare certain foodstuffs, they must have to break off from one activity to engage in the other. In theory, we might suppose this to lead to alternate storage of both raw materials and processed food. In practice, however, preparation normally entails a regular 'part-time' commitment, leaving some hours each day for extractive activities. There may consequently be no need to store prepared food for more than twenty-four hours at a stretch. Nevertheless, this does impose constraints on the kinds of resource extraction in which women can engage, quite apart from the possible additional constraints of child-rearing, for it excludes anything that demands prolonged and continuous activity.

We have still to consider the factor of transport. Besides being extracted and prepared, produce may have to be carried by some means from the site of exploitation to the site of consumption. This, too, takes time, and may interrupt other activities. The logistics of transport may have a critical bearing not only on whether produce is stored, but on where it is stored. If hunting, for example, involves a continuous period of unbroken activity, we would expect kills to be cached temporarily at the points where the animals were brought down, for subsequent collection and transport to the settlement. Moreover, just as the scheduling of re-source extraction must take account of seasonal fluctuations in supply, so the scheduling of transport may be critically influenced by environ-mental constraints such as seasonal flooding or snow and ice cover (Jochim 1976: 31). If the two schedules do not coincide – that is, if a resource is available only at a time when it is difficult to transport – har-vested produce will be deposited at the points of exploitation for the interval between extraction and transport. Naturally if supplies are not continuously being brought back to the settlement, there must be an element of storage at the point of consumption as well.

An alternative strategy is to move the settlement to the site of exploi-tation; though again, this may involve a temporary interruption of pro-ductive activity. I should stress here (*contra* Testart 1982: 524) that storage, even on a substantial scale and not merely of emergency rations, is by no means incompatible with nomadic movement. However the movement entailed is often a kind of 'fixed-point' nomadism (see Chapter 7) – a series of moves between pre-established locations, each conveniently situated for the exploitation of particular resources during particular periods. These locations may be marked by physical structures of a permanent or semi-permanent nature, including structures intended for storage. Rather than having to take all their supplies with them, people can then leave behind a reserve of stored produce on departure from each location, so that there is always something available on arrival the next time around (Binford 1978: 240–1). This is a common strategy in many northern hunting societies. Food may be cached at a great number of different points, dispersed widely over the landscape, so that the hunter can travel light and still be sure of finding something to eat (Roué 1985).

The introduction into hunting societies of domestic animals such as dogs, reindeer and horses, capable of acting as beasts of burden, may radically alter the logistics of transport, and indirectly the pattern of storage. Supplies can be moved around more easily, and in greater quan-tities,[2] leading to the relaxation of the 'fixed-point' constraint on nomadic movement (Carlstein 1980: 99–100). Moreover, the domestic animal itself represents a kind of living store, which can be killed for food in times of emergency. On the other hand, animals must be fed, and in this respect dogs differ profoundly from horses and reindeer. The latter, being her-bivores, can find their own food as and wherever they go (except on ice).

Dogs consume much the same kinds of food as humans, and are therefore as dependent on stored supplies, even though they help to carry these supplies about. Of course, as herds of domestic herbivores increase, they impose a requirement for unrestricted nomadic movement, on account of their needs for pasture. Dogs, on the contrary, may promote a degree of sedentism, for they can be kept permanently in one place, to which they can haul supplies of food from scattered sites of exploitation (see Jochelson 1908: 513 on the Koryak). Finally, we should note that the tendance of domestic livestock, in so far as it interrupts other productive activities, may introduce additional problems of scheduling which might have a bearing on practical storage.

Social storage

Apart from the practical and ecological senses of storage, the term has a quite distinct social sense which refers neither to the physical activity of setting stuff aside, nor to the organic accumulations that result, but to the *appropriation* of materials in such a way that rights over their future distribution or consumption converge upon a single interest. In this sense, the store has to be considered in its aspect as property or wealth, and storage as a concomitant of social relations of distribution. Although a store of wealth may be physically intact, this need not be so, and nothing in its definition stipulates that it should. However, a link between physical location and social appropriation may be established on the level of symbolic representation, by virtue of the classification of social space.

Evidently, there must be some accepted cultural code by which persons may be identified with their property. One way to achieve this is to imprint personal marks or emblems on the material items themselves. With harvested produce, such a procedure often presents difficulties of a technical nature, especially if its preservation entails the dismemberment, stripping or pulverization of the original items. Another way is to store the produce in containers, each bearing a personal imprint; these containers are portable and hence not tied to specific locations. But perhaps the most usual solution to the problem of identification is to deposit the produce in particular spaces symbolically associated with particular groups, particular sexes within each group, or particular individuals. In the mapping of social space, the plan of the dwelling, and of dwellings or hearths relative to one another in the camp or settlement, is generally of the utmost significance (e.g. Tanner 1979: 77–8). Beyond the settlement, in the bush or the forest, where the personification of space is not thus anchored but is open to continual reinterpretation, the symbolic plan (that is, the association of personal names with physical locations) may rest upon rather than underpin the practical arrangements of storage. Indeed, the location of stores beyond the settlement may be a secret known only to the possessor, whose aim in hiding his property is to protect it from theft.

The potential link that I have outlined between the physical location of stores and their social appropriation does not imply an additional constraint on mobility beyond those imposed by the technical conditions of transport. If the social map is anchored to portable dwellings such as tents, it can of course be established anew at each fresh camp site. However, in this context I should like to enter a few speculations on the significance of food containers. One is struck by the apparent paradox that, amongst hunters and gatherers, the elaboration and personification of portable food containers appears to be most characteristic of relatively *sedentary* peoples. This phenomenon may, I think, be related to the evolution of complex structures of distribution and exchange. Such structures accommodate regional variations in the supply of different environmental resources through the institution of trade between solidary local groups, rather than through the nomadic flux of personnel. The conduct of trade depends upon the carriage of produce into public arenas which are neutral as regards the personification of space. Where items of produce cannot by their nature be individually identified, the function of identification must be borne by containers, and a change of hands indicated either by transferring the produce from one container to another, or by changing the identification of the container – that is by 'relabelling' it.

Another possible function of food containers, which also relates to exchange and distribution, is that they allow the measurement of produce in standard units of volume. The significance of this function naturally depends upon the degree to which exchange involves the reckoning of strict equivalences. Thus, it will be of no consequence in a society of hunters and gatherers amongst whom all produce is freely shared out within and possibly beyond the co-resident band. Here there is no calculation of how much each individual has given to, or received from, the common stock; nor is the time-lag between giving and receiving of any concern. Sharing out food constitutes an aggregate of generalized reciprocities. However, as distribution comes to be constrained by the segmentary boundaries of a more rigid, 'tribal' structure, exchange across the boundaries assumes a more calculative character (Sahlins 1972: 228–9). Typically, such exchange is of relatively exotic, durable items rather than of foodstuffs, in which each segment is ideally self-sufficient. But this is not always so, particularly when different segments are associated with a range of variation in environmental possibilities, allowing each to specialize in particular branches of food production. Under just these conditions we would expect the role of food containers as units of measurement to be most significant (see Price 1962: 50 on the Washo).

This discussion leads us to the crucial issue of the relation between storage and sharing. At first glance these appear to represent the opposite poles of hoarding and giving stuff away (Lee 1969: 91). However, storage is equivalent to hoarding only in its social sense of the convergence of rights to specific resources upon a single interest. There is no necessary contradiction between storage and sharing if the former is conceived in its practical sense, occasioned by the non-concurrence of production and consumption schedules. In other words, the activity of practical storage does *not* constitute 'in the social order a transgression of the rule of sharing' (*contra* Testart 1982: 527). To appreciate this point, we must look more closely at the concept of sharing, whose significance is a good deal broader than that of the distributive concept of generalized reciprocity with which it is commonly confused. In most if perhaps not all hunting societies, it is axiomatic that subsistence resources are to be appropriated and enjoyed collectively. Yet in practice, the range over which food is distributed appears responsive to the kinds of game taken, and to ecologically induced fluctuations in the size of co-resident hunting units. The meat of large, rare animals is distributed widely, that of small, common animals is not. And naturally, if people periodically scatter in pursuit of a dispersed fauna, the scope of regular distribution is much reduced. In short, ecological considerations determine the extent to which hunters must share *out* the harvested produce in order that everyone should have a share *in* their collective resources. There need be no sharing out of resources to which everyone has direct and immediate access in nature. But these variations in the range of reciprocal distribution imply no curtailment of sharing as a *social principle of collective appropriation* (Ingold 1982: 532, see Chapter 9). Equally, if reserves of food have been set aside to tide over unproductive periods, there will be no sharing out of supplies as long as everyone can draw on adequate stocks for themselves. Yet if some run out, whilst others still have something left, the latter may be obliged to share out what they have with the former (Tanner 1979: 159). In other words, the fact that storage constitutes one element of a population's *practical* response to the conditions of its environment does not in the least imply a failure to share, even though – during the periods of living off supplies – food may be changing hands little or not at all.[3] *Social* storage, on the other hand, does represent the direct negation of sharing. As I have shown, this may impose a much stricter requirement for practical storage, since each producer is obliged to make separate provision for lean periods.

To this argument it might be objected that in most hunting societies, although there is no social division of access to living animals, kills of game are subject to rules of 'ownership' and hence – if set aside – would constitute the social stores of their respective proprietors. To counter this objection, I would emphasize that the owner of a kill has no more exclusive a claim to its eventual consumption than anyone else, though he may derive some indirect benefit from being in a position to distribute the meat (Dowling 1968: 505). Through his kills a man builds up a fund not of material wealth but of renown. In a society in which all material differentials are systemically eliminated, the renown accorded to the successful hunter may represent the major incentive without which a man would have little to hunt *for* (Endicott 1980: 657). It is in this connection that notions of 'ownership' should be understood. Far from reflecting a real division of control over material means, as in the pastoral 'ownership' of livestock, such notions serve to establish a conceptual foundation for the ascription of renown by effecting an ideological separation between the categories of 'givers' and 'receivers' of harvested produce. The principle of collective access to the means of subsistence, built into the productive relations of hunting, is 'mystified through the imposition of a concept of private ownership that renders obligatory distribution as enlightened generosity' (Ingold 1980: 160). In this way the ends of individuals are brought into line with those of the community.[4]

Harvesting and husbandry

I have argued that practical storage is a solution to problems of activity scheduling. Social storage, by contrast, is an aspect of the rationality of resource *husbandry*. The distinction may be illustrated by comparing the implications of the statements, commonly encountered in the literature, that for immediate-return hunter–gatherers 'the environment itself is the storehouse', and that pastoralists 'store on the hoof'. Both statements refer to reserves in the form of living plants and animals, but there is a subtle difference in connotation between them. In the first case, no intentional husbandry of resources is implied. The statement is rather an expression of the fact that, if all the resources necessary for subsistence are readily and continuously available in nature, and if the activities involved in their procurement can proceed simultaneously, there is no practical requirement to set aside harvested produce for future consumption. But when it is said that pastoralists store 'on the hoof', with the implicit connotation that hunters do not (despite their dependence on wild game that likewise exists 'on the hoof'), the definitive criterion is that the animal resource is husbanded. And this, in turn, implies that control over, or access to, the herds is divided between particular individuals or households. In this respect, the social relations of pastoral production are diametrically opposed to those of hunting, according to which there is no social appropriation of animals until they have been brought down. The pastoralist's 'store' is that particular section of the total animal population on which he can exert a direct claim, as against others in his society. It is, of course, a social store.

Husbandry always involves planning for the future, but the 'future' may be construed in a variety of ways, each of which has a bearing on the planning process. It may refer to a definite time or to a time interval, which may be closed or open-ended. The conditions of the future may be regarded as predictable or partially so, or wholly unpredictable. And the burden of the future may be faced collectively, or by individual persons or groups. Moreover, a distinction has to be drawn between the husbandry of living resources, which concerns the separation of a reproductive stock from that destined for consumption; and the husbandry of the consumption stock itself, which has to do with making the stock 'last out' over a given period.

Decisions relating to the former process may be taken after harvesting in those agricultural systems which involve the replanting of part of a stored crop,[5] whereas in pastoral systems they must be taken prior to harvesting, simply because 'dead animals do not reproduce' (Ingold 1980: 86–7). But whether by agriculturalists or pastoralists, the husbandry of reproductive stocks depends on the allocation of control over those stocks to distinct social persons or corporate groups in which the responsibility for decision making is vested. Furthermore, the objective is to provide for an indefinite future rather than a closed time interval. Just how this is done will depend upon perceptions of risk or uncertainty. For example, every pastoralist knows that the size of his 'minimum herd' – that is, the number of animals required to provide for his domestic group over an unlimited period – is not a fixed quantity, but depends upon environmentally induced fluctuations in the balance of natural mortality and natality in the herd, over which he has little or no control. Since these fluctuations are quite unpredictable, it is perfectly rational to seek to maximize herd size, by limiting the offtake for consumption to non-reproductive components of the herd, as a form of security for the indefinite future.

Turning to the husbandry of the consumption stock, the crucial factors are first whether the length of time over which the stock is to last is known or unknown, and secondly, whether the number of consumers is fixed or variable. Obviously a stock of resources, once withdrawn from the reproductive process, cannot be expected to last indefinitely. If the time period is known (allowing perhaps for a margin of safety), and the number of consumers fixed, the stock can be rationed through a division into equal parts per consumer per day. This, I take it, is how explorers ration their food when they go on expeditions. Subsistence hunters, for whom the 'expedition' is life itself, operate very differently. Life depends on killing game, but success in hunting is unpredictable. The hunter cannot say, after making a kill, 'this has to last me for so many days, so I and my family shall eat so much each day', for he cannot tell when he will make another kill. Moreover, others have equal and irrefutable claims on the meat, and he must never appear to be stingy. Better, then, to eat one's fill when there is meat to be eaten than practise unnecessary self-denial, for the very existence of the hunter rests on the assumption that more food will eventually be found. In short, the 'rationing' of stored supplies by hunters is a matter of making sure that everyone has their fair share of what food there is to hand, of making it 'go round', rather than the allocation of a daily quota, of making it 'last out'. For not only is the yield of hunting unpredictable, but also the number of potential consumers constantly varies as people come and go from camp. It is not surprising that many an explorer, measuring out his rations as he would count pennies, has expressed amazement at the apparent 'profligacy' of the native hunters he encountered. On the face of it, they appeared to share out and consume whatever they had without thought for the morrow, and were consequently branded as 'present-oriented' (Sahlins 1972: 30). They did not husband their resources.

The point I wish to emphasize here is that what has often been proposed as a contrast between 'present-orientation' and 'future-orien-tation' is really a contrast between orientation to two different *kinds* of futures. One is faced individually, and is of predictable duration. The other is faced collectively, and is of unpredictable duration (or more precisely, an uncertainty about when food will be found is contained within a certainty that it will be found). And although practical storage of the consumption stock may be an essential element of forward planning for both kinds of futures, only the first permits the conduct of husbandry. There is one other alternative, rather characteristic of agri-cultural societies and perhaps of some gathering societies which rely on highly predictable food staples. Here the future – that is the time until the next harvest – is of known duration, but the number of consumers varies markedly from day to day owing to the comings and goings of visitors and kin. The budgeting problem that this presents to the housewife in making her stocks of harvested produce last have been described with engaging sympathy by Audrey Richards. Writing of the Bemba, she shows that the solution is not to calculate on the basis of a fixed amount of food per person per day; but to cook 'more or less the same amount of porridge each day, however large the number of eaters' (Richards 1939: 152). Whether, at the end, one feels hungry or satisfied is supposed to depend on magical properties of the food, rather than on the quantity eaten (1939: 207).

To recapitulate: I have tried to show that whether harvested produce is set aside for future consumption, of what particular resources, and at what points in relation to the stages of transport and preparation, all depend on the conditions to which storage represents a practical response. But the *rationality* of resource management, whether of reproductive or consumption stocks, depends upon the allocation of social control in respect of those stocks. Assuming that the practical and social dimensions of storage can vary independently, we are presented with four possible combinations. First, there are peoples who produce only for immediate consumption and do not husband their resources: ideal-typical immediate-return hunter–gatherers for whom 'the environment is the storehouse'. Second, there are peoples who lay up stores of harvested produce, but who still do not husband their resources, whether these be a part of the environment or apart from it. Such are hunters who kill as and when the opportunity arises, living off supplies in the interim periods, and treating these supplies much as the first category of peoples would treat living resources. Third, there are pastoralists, in continuous association with their herds, whose resource extraction is geared to the satisfaction of immediate needs, but who husband their living property very strictly. I wish to stress here that this pastoral (social) 'storage on the hoof' has nothing at all in common with (practical) storage by opportunistic hunters. Pastoralists husband their resources, hunters do not; hunters set aside harvested produce for future consumption, pastoralists do not, or only to a very limited extent. Finally, typical of peasant agriculture everywhere is the combination of resource husbandry by individual domestic units of production with extensive storage (possibly subsumed by the market) to tide over the periods between harvests. In sum, whereas the husbandry of living or harvested resources is governed by the perception of their scarcity, scheduling – and the storage it entails – involves the budgeting not of resources but of *time* (Carlstein 1980: 26), and may 'actually be necessitated by a relative *abundance* (rather than scarcity) of provisioning opportunities' (Cook 1973: 44).

Time-lags and social integration

In this final section, let me return to the dichotomy between 'immediate-return' and 'delayed-return' systems of resource exploitation. To begin, we should recognize a number of different *kinds* of time-lag in the 'delayed-return' category. One kind is between the initial investment of labour in establishing the conditions for natural growth and reproduction of plant or animal resources, and their eventual harvesting. Another is between the construction of instruments of production and their use in resource extraction. And a third is between extraction or harvesting and consumption. Many systems which are 'delayed' in one respect are 'immediate' in another. For example, swidden horticulturalists often harvest from their plots continuously, gathering each day only what they need for immediate consumption, and without storing harvested produce at all. But there is naturally a time-lag between preparing and planting a particular plot, and the maturation of its crops.[6] Similarly, pastoralists who do not store produce derived from their herds to any significant extent may nevertheless experience delays between herding and resource extraction. Contrary examples are provided by hunting economies in which labour yields an immediate return in the form of kills but storage forms a part of the practical response to fluctuations in supply (Bailey 1981: 8). One reservation I have about the undifferentiated category of 'delayed-return systems' is that it lumps together such contrary situations as those outlined above, which appear to have nothing in common.

With regard to the time-lag between the construction and use of the instruments of production, I think it is helpful to introduce the distinction that Binford (1986) makes between implements and facilities. Implements such as bows and arrows or spears, which direct or translate the energy of men, may generally be easily made by individuals working alone, using raw materials readily available. Much effort, however, may be expended in conjunction with their use. By contrast, facilities such as nets, snares, pitfalls and surrounds, which interrupt the motion of animals, may involve a substantial investment of labour in construction and mainten- ance, but little or none in use, since the facility is 'operated' by its victim (Oswalt 1976, Torrence 1983). For example, the permanent drift fences and surrounds built by many reindeer- and caribou-hunting peoples represent a massive expenditure of labour, as well as a degree of advance planning and technical co-operation which bears comparison with the construction of irrigation works by agriculturalists (Woodburn 1980: 101, see also Meillassoux 1981: 14–15). My point in drawing out this contrast is to show that the proportion of labour invested in advance to that expended at the moment of extraction is likely to be high where hunting involves the construction of elaborate facilities, but low when it involves only the use of implements. Delays in the returns on labour in hunting will therefore be most significant in the former case.

Can we, then, establish any connection between the delay incurred in the construction and use of facilities, and that entailed by the practical storage of harvested produce? I do not think it would be hard to find instances where one kind of delay occurs without the other – that is, where the products of hunting and gathering with simple implements are stored, or where the 'catch' of facilities is allocated to immediate consumption. Nevertheless, the extensive use of facilities is typical of hunting regimes in which animal resources are both mobile and concentrated (Torrence 1983), and are intercepted rather than followed. In such regimes, the storage of kills may be vital for tiding over the periods between encounters with prey at successive points of interception. In other words, the construction of facilities and storage of produce may be integral components of a coherent response, at once practical and organizational, to the same set of environmental conditions.

By distinguishing between different kinds of time-lag, I do not mean to engage in an arid debate between 'lumping' and 'splitting'. My purpose is rather to cast doubt on some of the assumptions that 'lumping' implies. One is that 'those who consume most of their food on the day they obtain it and who are unconcerned about storage, also appear to be relatively unconcerned about conservation and about planned development of their resources' (Woodburn 1980: 101). This, of course, begs the question of what is meant by 'conservation' and 'planned development'. If an advance input of labour is implied, as in clearing plots, tending plants or herding animals, the assumption does not hold, for as I have already indicated, many horticulturalists and pastoralists do 'consume most of their food on the day they obtain it'. Of course, it might be argued that the horticulturalist 'stores' his tubers in the soil, prior to harvesting, and that the pastoralist 'stores' his animals on the hoof, but as I have stressed, storage in this form is *equivalent* to the planned conservation of a natural resource in the sense of *husbandry*. If storage is to be understood in this sense, the statement that people unconcerned about storage are unconcerned about resource conservation is simply tautologous.

It is important to be clear about this difference between the rationality of resource management and the labour involved in securing the reproduction of these resources in the natural environment: the former is an aspect of social relations of production, the latter is an aspect of the labour process. In the case of pastoral economies, this has been expressed by the distinction between husbandry and herding (Paine 1972: 79, Ingold 1980: 113–14). The same point is made by Bailey (1981: 6–8), where he distinguishes between 'controlled (vs. opportunistic) exploitation' and 'indirect (vs. direct) exploitation'. Obviously, the idea of a time-lag in the return on labour only makes sense in relation to the latter term of the distinction. Moreover, it should be apparent that the rationality of husbandry, or 'controlled exploitation', cannot logically be derived from aspects of the labour process (that is, whether it involves a direct or indirect return). I have shown that practical storage does not imply the husbandry of either living or dead resources. The same objection can be raised against the supposition that those who invest significant amounts of labour in the advance construction of facilities also conserve their animal resources. Again, the evidence from reindeer- and caribou-hunting peoples presents a picture entirely to the contrary (Ingold 1980: 69–71). However, the technical construction of the facility may *limit the possibility* of resource conservation. Pitfalls and snares, for example, cannot select the animals that run into them. When wild animals are caught in surrounds it is technically possible to select a proportion for slaughter and set others free,[7] whilst certain kinds of fishing net which catch larger individuals whilst allowing smaller fish to penetrate the mesh are automatically selective.

The dissection of the category of 'delayed-return' systems has led us to rather negative conclusions. To replace these with something more positive, we must return to the alleged *social* significance of the delayed return: that it leads to the establishment of lasting mutual dependencies and hence invests social relations with a quality of durability lacking from societies in which returns on labour are immediate. Now on purely logical grounds, a delay in the return on labour would only have social repercussions if the initial investment of labour entailed the appropriation of the resource; that is, if it made the resource the object of social relations both among those who can exert claims upon it and between those who can and those who cannot exert such claims. There is nothing in the arrangement of practical storage itself which specifies whether, for example, the store is to be appropriated individually or collectively. If practical storage is combined with the social principle of sharing, persons will be no more dependent on specific others than they are in an 'immediate-return' economy, similarly founded on a principle of collective appropriation. I do not mean that in such economies, people could necessarily survive on their own, but that their dependence on others is of a generalized kind (Ingold 1980: 273, see Woodburn in Lee and DeVore 1968: 91). The same applies to the construction of facilities: even if the facility is personally identified with its builders, this does not confer on them an automatic right to enjoy the products of its use, to the exclusion of others.

I should like to suggest that the particular conditions under which the initial investment of labour does entail the appropriation of the resource are definitive of pastoralism and cultivation as opposed to hunting and gathering. The implication of this suggestion, of course, is that there is something distinct about hunting and gathering societies in general. That is, they share the *social* character of immediate-return systems even though very often the returns on labour are *practically* delayed. I take it that this is what Meillassoux means to convey when, in belated recognition of the time-lag between the construction and use of instruments, he argues that 'if the returns [of hunting and gathering] are *instantaneous* ...they are not necessarily *immediate*' (Meillassoux 1981: 14, my emphases). To express a significant contrast by a pair of near synonyms is to invite confusion; nevertheless the meaning becomes clear when we recognize that one term of the distinction – instanteity – refers to a pro- perty of social relations of distribution, whereas the other – immediacy – refers to a property of the labour process in production. If this process entails practical delays, we cannot infer that persons are socially bound through the deferment of access to resources.

To substantiate my view, which is necessarily tentative, I would dis- tinguish between three qualitatively different kinds of labour that happen to correspond to the three kinds of time-lag already identified. The first is extractive labour: it creates nothing new, but merely effects a change of state, as from living to dead. Such labour yields a delayed return in the event that extracted produce is preserved for future consumption. The second is constructive labour: it builds things up out of raw materials, as in the manufacture of instruments, and yields a delayed return in their use. The third I would call appropriative labour: it establishes claims over resources growing and reproducing *in nature*. I have argued elsewhere that herding labour is essentially appropriative, for the animals actually do the work to support and reproduce themselves (Ingold 1980: 222–3). The extension of the argument from pastoralism to cultivation would entail a number of qualifications. We might have to distinguish such obviously appropriative activities as fencing, in which cultivators are evidently carving out islands of resources for themselves in opposition both to other persons or groups and to animal competitors, from the operations of ground-preparation and planting, in which they intervene *directly* in the processes of reproduction of those resources. There is a sense in which the latter lead to an embodiment of human labour in the resources themselves. Yet the establishment of such a physical link between labour and its subject matter carries an implication of social appropriation which is lacking when labour is merely embodied in the instruments by which resources are extracted. Thus where people neither appropriate nor intervene in the reproduction of living resources – that is in a purely extractive hunting and gathering economy – the appropriation of nature remains essentially collective: resources that belong to no one are available to all.

I conclude with an epilogue that adds a new twist to the problem, one that might commit much of what I have argued to irrelevancy. Up to now, my categories have been couched in purely 'etic' terms: real material distinctions between live resources and dead ones, and between resources and instruments of production. The problem becomes much more complicated, and perhaps more interesting too, if we take into account the categories of the people themselves. For example, do hunters conceive their kills to be 'dead'? In many cases, the killing of animals is believed to be a means of securing their future reproduction.[8] Hunting, as

Spencer remarks of the North Alaskan Eskimos, is a rite of renewal (Spencer 1959: 331). Thus, even if the labour expended in the hunt yields an immediate return in the form of kills (not necessarily for immediate consumption), that labour is conceptually equivalent to labour invested in establishing the conditions for the reproduction of the animal resource. In 'emic' terms, therefore, this is a 'delayed-return' system, for the returns on hunting in the present are viewed as the outcome of previous hunts in the past. Moreover, harvested and stored produce may be made conceptually equivalent to living resources in nature. For example, the Indians of the American northwest coast, notorious for invalidating practically every generalization that has ever been made about hunting and gathering societies, apparently considered the contents of their elaborately decorated storage boxes to be as much 'alive' as the inhabitants of their houses, the house itself being regarded as a large storage box, containing people (McDonald 1978). Thus the objective act of harvesting, or extraction of resources *from* living nature, is made equivalent to the appropriation of living resources *in* nature; and the objective act of consuming stored produce is made equivalent to harvesting. Conceptually, this amounts to the conversion of hunting and gathering into farming, and one cannot but wonder whether this has anything to do with the other supposedly 'tribal' features of Northwest Coast social organization. Perhaps it is some consolation to archaeologists that, lacking access to the conceptual schemes of the prehistoric peoples whom they study, they are spared from the challenge that such schemes present to anthropological attempts at theory-building!

Notes to Chapter 8

1 Woodburn (1982: 433) lists the following societies as falling into the 'immediate-return' category: Mbuti Pygmies (Zaire), !Kung San (Botswana, Namibia), Pandaram and Paliyan (south India), Batek Negritos (Malaysia) and Hadza (Tanzania).
2 For examples, see Popov (1966: 63–4) on reindeer among the Nganasan of northern Siberia, and Ewers (1955: 304) on horses among the Blackfoot Indians of North America.
3 This point has been recently confirmed by Binford, with regard to Nunamiut caribou hunters of Alaska. Most of the food procured goes into storage; and most of the time, consumption is out of stores. Yet a hunter's placing produce in storage is always conditional upon 'his judgement as to whether or not everybody already has meat'. Only if no household is without will he turn his kills over to his wife, who will preserve the meat for eventual serving to domestic dependants. If, however, some people are in need, food will be shared out immediately on the hunter's return to camp. Binford concludes that despite the extensive practice of storage, '*among the Nunamiut there is a strong sharing ethic*' (1984: 238–9, original emphasis).

4   I have discussed this point in greater detail elsewhere (Ingold 1980: 152–62). We return to it in Chapter 9.
5   There need be no physical separation of the portion destined for replanting and that destined for consumption. They may even be kept in the same vessel, from which seeds may be taken to cook or to sow as required (Richards 1939: 87).
6   In this connection, it is important to stress that post-harvest storage is not a *necessary* concomitant of agricultural production. Such vegetatively reproduced staples as taro and sweet potato may be cropped year-round for day-to-day needs, whilst their replanting merely involves the transference in space of cuttings from old plots to newly prepared ones (Clarke 1971: 123 n.2).
7   Such selection occurred in the 'cow-hunts' of early ranching (Osgood 1929: 28–9, 118) and the 'great hunts' for vicuña and guanaco of Inca Peru (Browman 1974: 194).
8   This is our principal theme in Chapter 10.

References for Chapter 8

Bahuchet, S. and J. M. C. Thomas 1985 Conservation des ressources alimentaires en forêt tropicale humide: chasseurs–cueilleurs et proto-agriculteurs d'Afrique Centrale. In *Les techniques de conservation des grains à long terme*, Vol. 3, Part I, eds. M. Gast, F. Sigaut and C. Beutler. Paris: Centre National de la Recherche Scientifique.

Bailey, G. N. 1981 Concepts of resource exploitation: continuity and discontinuity in palaeoeconomy. *World Archaeology* **13**: 1–15.

Belshaw, C. S. 1965 *Traditional exchange and modern markets*. Englewood Cliffs, NJ: Prentice-Hall.

Binford, L. R. 1968 Methodological considerations of the archaeological use of ethnographic data. In *Man the hunter*, eds. R. B. Lee and I. DeVore. Chicago: Aldine.

Binford, L. R. 1978 *Nunamiut ethnoarchaeology*. London: Academic Press.

Binford, L. R. 1984 Butchering, sharing and the archaeological record. *Journal of Anthropological Archaeology* **3**: 235–57.

Browman, D. L. 1974 Pastoral nomadism in the Andes. *Current Anthropology* **15**: 188–95.

Carlstein, T. 1980 *Time resources, society and ecology, Vol. I: Preindustrial societies*. London: Allen and Unwin.

Clarke, W. C. 1971 *Place and people*. Berkeley: University of California Press.

Cook, S. 1973 Production, ecology and economic anthropology: notes towards an integrated frame of reference. *Social Science Information* **12**: 25–52.

Dowling, J. H. 1968 Individual ownership and the sharing of game in hunting societies. *American Anthropologist* **70**: 502–7.

Endicott, K. L. 1980 Batek Negrito sex roles: behaviour and ideology. In *2nd International Conference on Hunting and Gathering Societies, 19 to 24 September 1980*. Quebec: Université Laval: Département d'Anthropologie.

Ewers, J. C. 1955 *The horse in Blackfoot Indian culture*. Smithsonian Institution Bureau of American Ethnology, Bulletin 159. Washington DC: US Government Printing Office.

Flannery, K. 1968 Archaeological systems theory and early Mesoamerica. In *Anthropological archaeology in the Americas*, ed. B. J. Meggers. Washington DC: Anthropological Society of Washington.

Hall, R. L. and H. S. Sharp 1978 *Wolf and man: evolution in parallel*. London: Academic Press.

Ingold, T. 1979 The social and ecological relations of culture-bearing organisms: an essay in evolutionary dynamics. In *Social and ecological systems*, eds. P. C. Burnham and R. F. Ellen. London: Academic Press.

Ingold, T. 1980 *Hunters, pastoralists and ranchers*. Cambridge University Press.

Ingold, T. 1981 The hunter and his spear: notes on the cultural mediation of social and ecological systems. In *Economic archaeology*, eds. A Sheridan and G. N. Bailey. BAR International Series 96. Oxford: BAR.

Ingold, T. 1982 Comment on Testart: 'The significance of food storage among hunter–gatherers'. *Current Anthropology* **23**: 531–2.

Jochelson, W. 1908 *The Koryak*. Jesup North Pacific Expedition, Vol. VI. American Museum of Natural History Memoir 10. Leiden: E. J. Brill.

Jochim, M. A. 1976 *Hunter–gatherer subsistence and settlement: a predictive model*. New York: Academic Press.

Lee, R. B. 1969 !Kung Bushman subsistence: an input-output analysis. In *Contributions to anthropology: ecological essays*, ed. D. Damas. National Museums of Canada, Bulletin 230. Ottawa: Queen's Printer.

Lee, R. B. and I. DeVore (eds.) 1968 *Man the hunter*. Chicago: Aldine.

Lee, R. B. and I. DeVore 1968 Problems in the study of hunters and gatherers. In *Man the hunter*, eds. R. B. Lee and I. DeVore. Chicago: Aldine.

McDonald, G. 1978 Paradigms of social/economic organization of hunting societies as provided by their art. Unpublished paper presented at the 1st International Conference on Hunting and Gathering Societies. Paris, 27–30.6.1978.

Marx, K. 1930 *Capital*. London: Dent.

Meillassoux, C. 1973 On the mode of production of the hunting band. In *French perspectives in African studies*, ed. P. Alexandre. London: Oxford University Press.

Meillassoux, C. 1981 *Maidens, meal and money: capitalism and the domestic community*. Cambridge University Press.

Osgood, E. S. 1929 *The day of the cattleman*. Minneapolis: University of Minnesota Press.

O'Shea, J. 1981 Coping with scarcity: exchange and social storage. In *Economic Archaeology*, eds. A. Sheridan and G. N. Bailey. BAR International Series 96. Oxford: BAR.

Oswalt, W. H. 1976 *An anthropological analysis of food-getting technology*. New York: Wiley.

Paine, R. 1972 The herd management of Lapp reindeer pastoralists. *Journal of Asian and African Studies* **7**: 76–87.

Petter, F. 1985 Le stockage de réserves alimentaires chez les animaux. In *Les techniques de conservation des grains à long terme*, Vol. 3, Part I, eds. M. Gast, F. Sigaut and C. Beutler. Paris: Centre National de la Recherche Scientifique.

Popov, A. A. 1966 *the Nganasan: the material culture of the Tavgi Samoyeds*. Indiana University Uralic and Altaic Series 56. Bloomington.

Price, J. A. 1962 *Washo economy*. Nevada State Museum Anthropological Papers No. 6, Carson City.

Rappaport, R. A. 1968 *Pigs for the ancestors*. New Haven, Conn.: Yale University Press.

Richards, A. I. 1939 *Land, labour and diet in Northern Rhodesia*. London: Oxford University Press.

Rindos, D. 1980 Symbiosis, instability, and the origins and spread of agriculture: a new model. *Current Anthropology* **21**: 751–72.

Roué, M. 1985 Techniques de conservation et rôle des réserves alimentaires dans les sociétés arctiques. In *Les techniques de conservation des grains à long terme*, Vol. 3, Part I, eds. M. Gast, F. Sigaut and C. Beutler. Paris: Centre National de la Recherche Scientifique.

Sahlins, M. D. 1972 *Stone age economics*. London: Tavistock.

Spencer, R. F. 1959 *The North Alaskan Eskimo: a study in ecology and society*. Smithsonian Institution Bureau of American Ethnology, Bulletin 171. Washington DC: US Government Printing Office.

Stacey, P. B. and W. D. Koenig 1984 Cooperative breeding in the acorn woodpecker. *Scientific American* **251**(2): 100–7.

Tanner, A. 1979 *Bringing home animals: religious ideology and mode of production of Mistassini Cree hunters*. London: C. Hurst.

Testart, A. 1981 Pour une typologie des chasseurs–cueilleurs. *Anthropologie et Sociétés* **5**: 177–221.

Testart, A. 1982 The significance of food storage among hunter–gatherers: residence patterns, population densities, and social inequalities. *Current Anthropology* **23**: 523–37.

Torrence, R. 1983 Time budgeting and hunter–gatherer technology. In *Hunter–gatherer economy in prehistory: a European perspective*, ed. G. N. Bailey. Cambridge University Press.

Woodburn, J. 1980 Hunters and gatherers today and reconstruction of the past. In *Soviet and Western Anthropology*, ed. E. Gellner. London: Duckworth.

Woodburn, J. 1982 Egalitarian societies. *Man* (N.S.) 17: 431–51.

9

The principle of individual autonomy and the collective appropriation of nature

Individuality in being and action generally increases to the degree that the social circle encompassing the individual expands.   (Simmel 1971 [1908]: 252)

Introduction

The opposition between individualism and collectivism, expressed in a variety of guises, is deeply rooted in anthropological thinking. Not only does it offer alternative points of departure for the construction of social theory, but also it provides a fundamental criterion by which the premises of our own society – variously designated as 'western', 'modern' and 'capitalist' – might be distinguished from all the others – 'non-western', 'traditional' and 'pre-capitalist'. One of the most sophisticated attempts at this kind of dichotomization is to be found in the writings of Dumont, where the opposition is expressed as between the *Homo hierarchicus* of the 'traditional' world (modelled on Indian civilization) and the *Homo aequalis* of the 'west'. (Dumont 1970; 1977). In the former conception, the particular man finds his being only in so far as he is positioned within a collectively ordered totality, 'society as a whole', which underwrites his destiny. In the latter, he is a self-contained individual, possessed of a fundamental autonomy, and free to pursue ends that are given to him by his inherent nature rather than coming to him from society. Thus in Dumont's categorical scheme, hierarchy is to equality as holism is to individualism (1970: 44).

It might readily be objected that these categories are altogether too vague to be of much service to our current concerns, which are not directly with Great Traditions of the East nor with Great Men of the West. They do, however, enable us to pose the problem which it will be my concern in this essay to solve. In most hunting and gathering societies, a supreme value is placed upon the principle of individual autonomy. Opportunities for the expression of hierarchical dominance are systematically denied, and equality is actively asserted (Woodburn 1982). Should we, then, classify hunters and gatherers as 'traditional' representatives of *Homo aequalis*? And if not, how are we to express the difference between their kind of individualism, and our 'western' kind? To anticipate our conclusion: it is that *theirs is an individualism grounded in the social totality*. In order to reach this conclusion, we have to show how the autonomy of the individual, far from being incompatible with a commitment to the whole, may in reality depend upon it. In the three sections that follow, I shall argue that this is so, first in the field of property rights and so-called 'ownership', secondly with regard to the practices of reciprocity, and thirdly as manifested in the organization of the band.

Property and ownership

In previous chapters, I have argued that implicit in the characterization of practical, food-producing activities as hunting or gathering is a social principle of collective appropriation, or undivided access to the means of subsistence in the form of living plants and animals. Yet individualistic property concepts, far from being unknown to hunters and gatherers, are a ubiquitous feature of their societies. So, too, are prescriptions that enjoin them to share whatever they may have procured with other members of the local group or band. These facts have inclined some observers to follow Morgan (1881: 63–78) in attributing the practice of 'communism in living' to hunter–gatherer societies, whilst others assert the contrary – that in these societies 'considerations of private property are supreme' (Herskovits 1952: 322). But as Herskovits goes on to point out, with good reason, the dichotomy between 'communism' and 'private ownership' is pretty meaningless unless the rights constitutive of property are more precisely specified, and these rights are known to vary quite substantially from one society to another (1952: 330). Our first task, therefore, must be to isolate the particular forms of possession that, in the ethnographic literature on hunting and gathering societies, have been rendered as 'ownership', and to compare them with what we, in our own society, commonly understand by the term. We have to consider the possession first of land, secondly of equipment, and thirdly of garnered plant and animal resources.

The question of hunter–gatherer land tenure has already been discussed at length in Chapter 6. I argued there that the division of the landscape into territorial compartments, far from defining zones of exclusive access to particular holders, actually serves to regulate the exploitation of dispersed resources over a common range, and that it should be seen as an aspect of practical co-operation rather than social competition. Under no circumstances can the land itself be alienated, and although a person could point to a tract extending from a place or on either side of a path as 'my country' and expect to be consulted by those intending to use its resources, he is not generally in a position to refuse access to outsiders. Possession, here, is a matter of looking after the country, or of tending the creative powers that are thought to reside in its core locales. So-called 'owners' are thus, in reality, no more than the custodians of parts of a world that belongs to all, and they exercise their rights and responsibilities on behalf of the collectivity.[1] In other words, what an owner possesses, *to the exclusion of others*, is the privilege of custodianship, not that which is held in custody. The contrast between this sense of ownership, and the legalistic, 'western' sense, was vividly demonstrated by the judgement of Mr Justice Blackburn, in a celebrated case involving a claim lodged by a group of Australian Aboriginal people whose country was threatened by an industrial mining project. Asserting that property 'implies the right to use or enjoy, the right to exclude others, and the right to alienate', Blackburn J. concluded that since Aboriginal custom did not countenance the exclusive use of land or the possibility of its alienation, the claim was invalid. Subsequent legislation, more favourable to the Aboriginal cause, has explicitly recognized the custodianship function in defining as 'traditional owners' those whose affiliations to a site on the land place them 'under a primary spiritual responsibility for that site and for the land'. But precisely what is entailed in this 'spiritual responsibility' remains far from clear, and is a hotly contested issue (Maddock 1983: 41–2, 86).

Perhaps the possession of tools and other equipment comes closer to our conventional notion of property (Service 1966: 22–3). Letourneau, who thought that the apparent universality of property concepts attested to the existence of a fundamental property-holding instinct common to both humans and non-human animals, saw in the manufacture of artificial instruments the genesis of an idea truly unique to man, namely that of *private* property. 'The articles', he wrote, 'have been in some sort confounded with their creator' (Letourneau 1892: 38–9). It is perfectly true that the tools which a man makes for himself, and constantly employs in the course of everyday life, may come to be treated as extensions of his person, just as do the songs, ceremonies and designs which may likewise be constitutive of his identity.[2] Yet it has also to be admitted that in our own 'modern' society, where manufactured commodities epitomize the category of wealth in general (Dumont 1977: 5–6), the extreme development of the concept of private property has gone hand in hand with the reduction of the bond between producer and product to a bare minimum (Herskovits 1952: 372). Most of what we own we have not produced ourselves. A moment's reflection shows that the hunter–gatherer's 'private ownership' of tools and our 'private ownership' of commodities represent diametrically opposed situations. In the first, we start from the premise of an intrinsic connection between subject and object, person and thing, and from the assumption that where everyone shares the skills and has access to the raw materials needed for manufacture, tools will tend to remain in the hands of their makers. If they change hands at all, they will do so as gifts, but once this happens their possession can no longer be exclusive. For as long as a vital link is maintained between the donor and the thing given (and it is because of this link that the thing counts as a gift), the 'hold' of the recipient will be added to that of the donor, but will not replace it. In a society already characterized by a complex division of labour, where much of what is needed must be obtained by exchange, exclusive 'private' ownership can only be the end result of the complete *severance* of the links between persons and things, which therefore count no longer as gifts but as commodities.

So these two kinds of individual possession are really quite different. One is founded on the non-exchange of objects positively attached to their makers, the other on the detachment of things from persons in the act of exchange. The latter, far from being a logical elaboration of the former, undercuts its very basis. Of course, not every element of the hunter's or gatherer's tool-kit is imbued with the same value as a marker of personal identity. Many items, casually made from raw materials available on the spot, and just as casually discarded, may be freely lent or borrowed apparently without thought of restitution in case of loss or damage (Ingold 1980: 156). The duration of such items, as between manufacture and discard, is generally negligible when set in the context of the life-span of the user. Where the bond between persons and things is so tenuous, it is scarcely appropriate to speak of their 'ownership' at all. And yet it is not uncommon for them to be embellished with property marks which apparently signify just that, namely their appropriation as the personal effects of particular individuals. The appearance, however, is deceptive. For what in fact are being claimed are not the tools themselves but the resources with which they come to stand in a relationship of physical contiguity. Consider the gold prospector, who establishes title to a site he has discovered by driving into the ground a wooden stake on which he has engraved his name. He is, of course, staking his claim, not claiming his stake! In itself, the stake is of no value at all, what is of value is the resource content of the site which it indicates. Likewise the arrow or harpoon point, bearing the personal mark of an 'owner', registers a claim over the animal struck, and in whose body it is lodged. A similar relation of contiguity exists between gathered fruits and the container that holds them, caught fish and the net in which they are enmeshed, and trapped game and the devices laid for it. In all these cases items of extractive equipment, besides discharging their technical functions in dispatching prey or transporting harvested produce, can simultaneously serve another purpose as vectors for a system of signs, establishing a set of relations between the persons signified and the resources with which they are brought into contact.

The possession of garnered plant and animal resources is thus, in a sense, 'encoded' by the instruments of hunting and gathering, and it is to this kind of possession that we must now turn. It is commonly assumed that whatever a hunter or gatherer takes from nature is initially his (or hers), regardless of what may subsequently happen to it prior to its eventual consumption. Does this not follow logically from the fact that only by dint of the procurer's own labour was it obtained for human use? Any discussion of this question must necessarily take as its starting point the capital disquisition of John Locke. The 'Law of reason', Locke argued, 'makes the Deer, that *Indian's* who hath killed it; 'tis allowed to be his goods who hath bestowed his labour upon it, though before it was the common right of every one.' The same applies to the products of the chase even in our own society: he who pursues and captures the hare, says Locke, 'has thereby removed her from the state of Nature, wherein she was common, and hath *begun a Property*' (Locke 1978 [1689]: 19). In another passage, in which he considers the fruits of gathering, Locke wonders at what precise point in the sequence from extraction to consumption does the moment of appropriation occur. The passage is worth citing in full:

He that is nourished by the Acorns he pickt up under an Oak, or the Apples he gathered from Trees in the Wood, has certainly appropriated them to himself. No Body can deny but the nourishment is his. I ask then, When did they begin to be his? When he digested? Or when he eat? Or when he boiled? Or when he brought them home? Or when he pickt them up? And 'tis plain, if the first gathering made them not his, nothing else could. That *labour* put a distinction between them and the common. That added something to them more than Nature, the common Mother of all, had done; and so they became his private right. (1978 [1689]: 18)

But the human gatherer, unlike most non-human primates, is not sustained solely by the produce he or she 'picks up' (see Chapter 4). Much of what is consumed has been gathered by others, and *vice versa*. Given the prevalence of food-sharing in hunter–gatherer communities, we are bound to reverse Locke's question: if the work of procurement makes the resource his who procures it, at what point does it *cease* to be his, reverting once more to the common? And by what right do those who have laboured not at all in the food quest claim their share?

The logic of Locke's argument, as it stands, is impeccable. As a man is the proprietor of his own body, so he is of the work the body performs, and hence also of the things with which he 'mixes' his labour. Property evidently begins within the individual, in the conscious control of self, and extends distalward in a chain of contiguities from the brain, through the hand and the instruments it manipulates, to the resources with which those instruments are brought into contact. But whence comes the individual? For Locke he is, apparently, a preconstituted entity, who comes into being already equipped with certain needs or desires and the bodily means to set about their satisfaction. Real people, however, are not like that at all. They come into the world as helpless infants, and for a very long period they are wholly or partially nourished by food procured through the labour of others. Do they not, then, 'belong' to these others by the very same token that their labour and its products 'belongs' to them? If that is so, the chain of property can neither begin with individuals nor end in the resources they procure; rather it must end where it began, in the community of nurture from which spring the producers and in which the food is consumed. To the extent that people are mutually involved in the production of each others' existence, the products of their respective labours are due to all. Thus what a man appropriates through his labour, he appropriates *on behalf* of the collectivity through which – and only through which – he finds his being. It may be exclusively his to dispose of, but it is not his alone to consume. As Dowling points out, on the strength of a long catalogue of ethnographically documented instances from diverse hunting societies, 'the rights and prerogatives entailed in ownership are primarily those of performing the distribution, not of deciding whether or not the animal will be distributed' (1968: 505).

.The possession of harvested produce, just like the possession of resource locales, turns out therefore to be a matter of custodianship. If the 'owner' of a locale can expect to be consulted about its use, so likewise the 'owner' of a slain animal – whether freshly killed or placed in storage – is entitled to take the initiative or to be asked in regard to its apportionment for consumption. In both cases manufactured objects function, *inter alia*, as insignia of ownership: ceremonial artefacts – sometimes regarded as the equivalent of our 'title deeds' (Peterson 1972: 15) – encode primary claims of spiritual responsibility for the country and its resources, just as hunting weapons encode claims of responsibility for the produce yielded. But neither to country and resources, nor to produce, can access be refused by those who carry the responsibilities and prerogatives of custodianship. It is not poaching or theft to exploit a place without permission, or to take food that has not been offered or formally requested, for when access is common such crimes are unknown. The misdemeanour is rather one of failing to recognize the owner's privilege of disposal, which is of course quite distinct from the privileges of use and consumption (Herskovits 1952: 325). But why should it be necessary for the custodianship of collective resources to be vested in particular persons? Why have notions of ownership at all? The answer, as I briefly hinted at in Chapter 8, has to do with their function in creating and upholding a distinction between the categories of givers and receivers, or granters and grantees. Without such a distinction, there can be no basis for the extension of generosity, nor for the influence and renown that flows from it. 'To give away', as I have noted elsewhere, 'one must first have, and others must not. A pretence of appropriation has therefore to be constructed ideologically, in order that it may be cancelled out socially' (Ingold 1980: 160).

Now an inherent problem of all systems in which access to resources is held in common, is that there is nothing to prevent a person from shifting onto others the burden of labouring to procure food, or of looking after the country by performing the necessary rituals of regeneration. However by superimposing, upon the principle of collective access, a system of individual privileges that afford esteem to those who, through the fruits of their labour, are entitled to enjoy them, this problem can be at least partially overcome. 'Ownership', as Fried puts it, 'really means that the man who fulfills the social requirements of "owner" is the one to whom prestige will accrue as the distribution proceeds' (1967: 66). One might suppose, then, that concepts of ownership would be most elaborate, and the pursuit of prestige most compelling, in those societies in which people are most likely to be chronically reliant on products which others have laboured to obtain, and whose procurement must be backed by strong positive inducements. This would particularly be the case when there is a primary dependence on wild game, whose pursuit is always an uncertain affair, but much less so when hunted produce supplements a staple diet of vegetable foods which are both abundant and predictable in their occurrence. A cursory reading of the literature on northern circumpolar hunters and tropical hunter–gatherers, which represent the extremes of reliance on hunted and gathered produce respectively, suggests that our supposition may indeed be borne out. For it is above all among the former that ideas of ownership are most explicit, and where intense competition to be able to own and thus to engage in prestige-conferring generosity has led to the proliferation of rules which serve to reduce the ambiguity in the ascription of ownership, and ensuing conflict, that can arise when more than one individual was concurrently on the scene of the hunt (Dowling 1968: 506).

Having reviewed the possession of each of land, equipment and resources in hunting and gathering societies, it is evident that in all three cases notions of personal property, far from being incompatible with the collective appropriation of nature, are in fact predicated upon it. In a discussion of the significance of property that, in many respects, remains unsurpassed, Hobhouse elucidates the minimal conditions under which man's control over things may be regarded as 'property' at all: 'it must in some sort be recognized, in some sort independent of immediate physical enjoyment, and at some point exclusive of control by other persons' (1915: 7). That is to say, my control is not property if others do not recognize it as a right, it is not property if I exercise my control only during those moments when I am using a thing, which at any different time others may use, and it is not property if there are no restrictions at all on who can use it. On these criteria, the only material items in a hunting and gathering society that constitute property are non-expendable, personalized implements. When it comes to resource locales and harvested produce, the things that a person acquires as a recognized, enduring and exclusive right are the practices or performances, together with the associated insignia (designs, songs, stories), that ensure the renewal of the country and the distribution of its yield. Far from exercising rights of enjoyment, *as against the world*, over the means of subsistence, as does the pastoralist in the possession of his flocks and herds or the agriculturalist in the possession of fenced-in plots, the hunter–gatherer enjoys exclusive rights to the *custody* of the means of subsistence, which he holds *on behalf of the world*. In short, the kind of individual possession that we have characterized more precisely as custodianship is possible, and indeed necessary, because the enjoyment of essential resources is common to an unbounded collectivity. And even the exclusive ownership of material equipment, based as it is on the intrinsic connection between items and their makers-cum-users rather than on the severance of such connections in exchange, is founded upon free and generalized access to the raw materials and skills of manufacture.

Reciprocity and sharing

These conclusions lead us to make some observations on the concept of reciprocity, particularly as it relates to sharing. It is nowadays commonplace to refer to the phenomenon of food-sharing in hunting and gathering societies by the term 'generalized reciprocity', originally introduced by Sahlins in a celebrated paper on primitive exchange (1972 [1965]: 185–275). With regard to such hand-to-hand movements by which foodstuffs initially held now by one person, now by another, are shared *out* among many, the term is perfectly acceptable – barring the possible confusion with Lévi-Strauss's category of 'generalized exchange', which denotes something quite different (Sahlins 1972: 193 n.4). However, it was brought in as part of a wider theoretical scheme about which I do have certain reservations, and which I believe has led to some confusion in the literature. First of all, it is never clear whether reciprocity is meant to refer to real material flows, or merely to an abstract, moral ideal. At one moment, Sahlins unequivocally specifies the former: 'It is notable of the main run of generalized reciprocities that the material flow is sustained by prevailing social relations' (1972: 195). Yet at another moment he speaks of the fragmentation into autonomous domestic units supposedly intrinsic to the productive infrastructure of every primitive society – whether of hunter–gatherers, pastoralists or agriculturalists, or a mixture of the three – being 'mystified by an uncritical ideology of reciprocity' (1972: 124). The latter assertion is, of course, adduced to support his well-known construct of the 'domestic mode of production' (DMP), according to which each and every household is primarily concerned to provision its own members. The consequent, and quite arbitrary exclusion from the infrastructural level of all relations of distribution beyond the household only compounds the confusion. If, instead, we ignore Sahlins's idiosyncratic way of drawing the boundary between infrastructure and superstructure, we are left with a concept of reciprocity which, like the notion of 'sociocultural system' also prominent in his account, totally fails to distinguish ideology from its foundations in social reality. This greatly reduces the utility of the concept to characterize the properties of a mode of production.

As regards hunting and gathering societies, the analysis of ownership presented above implies an inversion of Sahlins's argument. Whereas for Sahlins the fragmentation of the productive infrastructure into a multitude of separate proprietary interests is overcome through the public pressures of politics, law and morality, we have concluded – to the contrary – that the overt recognition of separate rights of possession in extracted produce is superimposed on an infrastructural principle of common access to living resources and the products obtained from them (Ingold 1980: 160). There is a way of testing Sahlins's argument, since it supposes that in times of extreme scarcity, normal reciprocal relations will break down, leaving every household to fend for itself if necessary through 'guile, haggle and theft' (1972: 214). I have discovered no reliable evidence, in the literature on hunting and gathering societies, that anything of the kind has ever occurred. To me, the material suggests that as a crisis becomes more acute, 'generalized reciprocity proceeds to the point of dissolution of domestic group boundaries' (1980: 149). Under such circumstances, I would predict that what Sahlins (1972: 195) calls 'negative reciprocity'[3] – that is, taking for nothing instead of giving for nothing – 'rather than closing in from beyond the frontiers of the household, will be expelled altogether from the wider social field, only to make its appearance within the heart of the domestic group itself' (Ingold 1980: 149). In situations of economic collapse, it is the intra-domestic relations between husband and wife, between mother and child, and between parent and grandparent, that take the strain. Thus the basic cleavages in the hunting and gathering society are not between domestic groups, but between the sexes, and between generations.

This brings me to another reservation about Sahlins's scheme, which concerns the way in which the concept of 'generalized reciprocity' is defined in relation to those of 'balanced' and 'negative' reciprocity. The problem lies in the imputed correlation between types of reciprocity and social distance, reckoned in terms of a model of society envisaged from the vantage point of the participating individual as a series of ever-widening social sectors to which he sees himself as belonging: household, lineage, village, tribe, etc. (Sahlins 1968: 16, 85, see Figure 9.1a).[4] At first glance, there would seem to be two quite different kinds of 'negative reciprocity': the one considered by Sahlins – feuding or raiding between segments widely separated by social distance; and the one we have noted above – the negation of 'caring' *within* the confines of the household, manifested at the extremes in such practices as infanticide and senilicide (Ingold 1980: 150). But then the correlation between social distance and the 'negativity' of reciprocity no longer applies. Likewise, both feuding or raiding and ceremonial gift-exchange (a form of 'balanced' reciprocity in Sahlins's terms) may take place between parties equally separated by social distance, representing 'negative' and 'positive' states respectively of the same relationship. In other words, to each of 'generalized' and 'balanced' reciprocities there corresponds a 'negative' counterpart, yielding the two kinds we have outlined (Figure 9.1b). In the case of the majority of hunting and gathering societies, which lack the segmentary rigidity of a 'tribal' structure, I would argue that the sectoral model is anyway invalid, so that in normal times we would expect 'generalized reciprocity' to extend across the board, reaching its limit only along the lines of contact with agricultural or pastoral neighbours.

It is in fact rather paradoxical that a notion of reciprocity brought into explicit correspondence with a tribal design, attributed in the main to agricultural and pastoral societies, should be adopted to characterize the distributive practices of hunters and gatherers who, with a few notable exceptions, have a far more flexible kind of organization marked by the absence rather than the proliferation of boundaries of exclusion.[5] Like any other kind of reciprocity, generalized reciprocity is conceived as a relation *between* economic identities, autonomous and discrete (Sahlins 1972: 94). In Sahlins's scheme, these units are households, each of which is credited with 'a certain autonomy in the realm of property', leading it to assign priority to its own particular interests (1972: 92). The agricultural

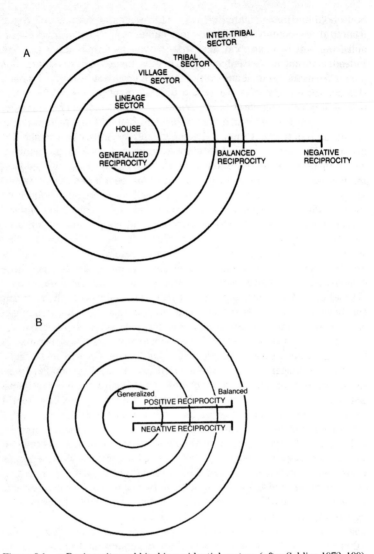

Figure 9.1   a: Reciprocity and kinship residential sectors (after Sahlins 1972: 199).
b: An alternative view of negative reciprocity, as forms on a continuum corresponding to the range of positive forms from generalized to balanced. At the pole
corresponding to generalized reciprocity is the negation of caring within the
household (in extreme circumstances, expressed in infanticide and senilicide); at
the pole corresponding to balanced reciprocity (such as ceremonial gift exchange)
is feuding and raiding between opposed tribal segments.

household has its fields and the pastoral household its flocks and herds, islands of resources to whose enjoyment it has the most immediate claim, and from which others may derive some benefit only at its discretion. Indeed it is no accident that we should associate the exploitation of *domestic* resources with a *domestic* mode of production, for the primary significance of domestication lies in the appropriation, by human households, of living plants and animals (Ducos 1978: 54), leading to the division of access to means of subsistence which is fundamental to the constitution of the DMP, and which the norm of reciprocity serves, in this instance, to override. In a hunting and gathering society, by contrast, where there is no such division, generalized reciprocity appears in quite another aspect: namely as a generalization across the collectivity of the kinds of relations that under a DMP are *internal* to the household (Service 1966: 24). When a hunter who has taken initial custody of a kill exercises his right in distributing the meat, he forgoes nothing, since he has no greater claim to its consumption than anyone else. Rather than sharing stuff out in spite of an entitlement to reserve it for his exclusive use, he shares it out because the right of enjoyment is lodged with the collectivity.

In order to clarify this contrast, it is important to recognize that sharing can be understood in two quite different ways: first, as a principle of generalized or unrestricted access whereby means of subsistence are enjoyed *in common*; secondly, as a distributive movement whereby stuff held at the outset by a single person is *divided up*, so as to be available for use by an aggregate of beneficiaries. We may distinguish these as sharing *in* and sharing *out* respectively. Since reciprocity is essentially a distributive concept, implying prestations of goods from hand to hand, a pattern of reciprocities can only be regarded as sharing if sharing is itself regarded in the second of the senses adduced above. We could equally well contrast the two senses in their respective negations. The opposite of sharing out, as generalized reciprocity, is negative reciprocity – a concept whose connotations have already been touched upon. As for the negation of sharing conceived as a principle of collective access, this is precisely equivalent to what we defined in the last chapter as 'social storage', marked by the convergence of rights to resources upon a single proprietary interest. Now it should become immediately clear that in the Sahlins treatment, where sharing is introduced as an indicative formula for generalized reciprocity (1972: 194), this sharing *out* is characterized by its transgression of the limits of sharing *in*. For these limits are narrowly set at the boundaries of the household, in its capacity as a resource-holding unit, whilst only those transactions that *cross* the boundaries are admitted as reciprocal. But if, as we believe appropriate for hunting and gathering societies, the limits of resource access are widened indefinitely

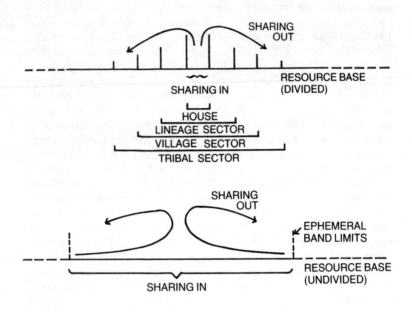

Figure 9.2 The relation between sharing in and sharing out, in a segmentary social order underwritten by a domestic mode of production (above), and in an incorporative social order underwritten by the principle of collective appropriation (below).

to embrace the entire collectivity, or if there are no limitations on access at all, it must follow that all sharing *out* – all generalized reciprocity – *must be underwritten by the positive principle of sharing in, and cannot override the boundaries set by its negation.* The contrast between this view of the relation between sharing *in* and *out*, and the one implicit in Sahlins's 'tribal' model, is indicated schematically in Figure 9.2.[6]

Bands and tribes

There is a well-established tenet of anthropological orthodoxy which holds that tribes emerged in the course of social evolution from what are known as 'bands', and represent a level of integration intermediate between those of the band and the chiefdom. Elman Service, whose *Primitive Social Organization* is devoted to an account of these three putative evolutionary stages, contrasts band and tribe in the following terms:

A band is only an association, more or less residential, of nuclear families. . . A tribe is an association of a much larger number of kinship segments which are each composed of families. They are tied more firmly together than are bands. . . A tribe is of the order of a large collection of bands, but it is not *simply* a collection of bands. (1971 [1962]: 100)

According to this formulation, the tribe is essentially an emergent entity, that increment by which the whole composed of a number of multi-family units exceeds the sum of its parts. The identification of this increment is not without its problems, and one could well follow Fried (1967: 165) in doubting its very existence, and by implication, the utility of 'tribe' as a concept of anthropological analysis. However, for Sahlins, whose phrasing of the band/tribe dichotomy virtually replicates Service, the crucial indicia of a tribal level of integration are so-called 'pan-tribal institutions', including systems of inter-group marriage, age grading, military organization and religious cults (Sahlins 1961: 325). 'Such institutions', he goes on, 'clearly demarcate the borders of a tribe, separating it as a social (and ethnic) entity', whereas intermarrying bands do not form discrete blocs, so that 'no one can say where one so-called "tribe" ends and another begins' (1961: 343 fn. 3).

Let us provisionally accept this view of the tribe, and ask: by what kind of relations is it constituted? If the essence of tribal integration lies in the institutional order that arises out of, and is superimposed upon, the aggregate of kin-based local communities, then the social relations out of which the tribe is built must exist between parts or positions as they are defined within this emergent institutional framework. That is to say, they are relations between *persons*, in the sense originally expounded by Radcliffe-Brown (1952: 193–4). Now compare them with the relations that constitute the band, which is generally conceived as a transient assemblage of co-resident individuals and families, its organization arising out of the practical exigencies of subsistence procurement under given environmental conditions (Steward 1955). If relations among band members are to be regarded as *social*, this is to understand the social in a sense quite different from that adduced above, for they are relations of interaction between particular human beings, not of differentiation between the components of an instituted order. To put it another way, when we speak of 'band society', we mean by 'society' an association of individuals acting together in work and distribution; when we speak of 'tribal society', the reference of society is to an entity that *transcends* the spontaneous association of individuals, having a corporate identity of its own that governs the life of its constituent elements. Where the band signifies a *mode of practical co-operation*, the concept of the tribe signals a *specific form of social consciousness*, by which persons are located within a structured system of segmentary opposition.

The two senses of society, corresponding to band and tribe respectively, are already familiar to us from our discussion in Chapter 2. It is noteworthy that whilst the former may be generalized across the animal kingdom, and is applicable wherever individuals of the same species are found to be 'organized in a co-operative manner' (Wilson 1980: 7), the latter is commonly reserved for human beings, who alone are considered capable of externalizing their shared, subjective experience on the level of ideas, and hence of forming collective representations. We seem here to have yet another instance of the transfer of a conceptual dichotomy originally drawn at the limits of humanity onto the boundary between agriculturalists or pastoralists and hunters and gatherers. Thus it is no accident that the distinction between band and tribe is conventionally mapped onto that between food *collecting* and food *producing*. Just as we were led, in Chapter 5, to seek a sense in which human hunter–gatherers, as self-conscious agents, produce their means of subsistence, so too we are now challenged to discover that form of social consciousness through which these agents are constituted as persons. Whatever this may turn out to be, it alone qualifies as a candidate for recognition as the true evolutionary antecedent of the tribe. And by the same token the candidature of the band, which is not a form of consciousness at all but an association of individuals, must be rejected. Since they are constituted by relations of such fundamentally different kinds, bands cannot turn into tribes.

The key to the difference between 'tribal' and 'pre-tribal' designs lies, I believe, in the demarcation of boundaries. Tribesmen, as Sahlins emphasized, see themselves as belonging to a distinct social and ethnic group, in a world that includes other such groups to which they stand opposed. From the start, then, personal identity is founded upon a principle of exclusion. But this very principle, that establishes the tribe in its external aspect as a monolithic entity, operates *within* the tribe to set up a nesting series of segmentary divisions, refracting – and eventually obscuring – the initial discontinuity into a multitude of progressively finer discriminations. But the collectivity to which hunters and gatherers belong is, for them, an *unbounded* one. If we may be permitted one generalization, it is that the internal differentiation of a society is a function of its external boundedness. Remove the external boundary, and its internal refractions must necessarily disappear as well. A person derives his sense of belonging, then, not through setting himself apart from others, but by drawing them into his own ambience; his position in the collectivity rests not on the successive differentiations of segmentary opposition but on the successive integrations of inclusive incorporation. There is no limit in principle (though obviously there is one in practice) to how far this incorporation can proceed: in a sense each person embraces within himself the whole of humanity. That is why people in hunter–gatherer societies so often refer to themselves by the term in their language which, literally translated, means mankind.

The distinction we have drawn between social orders founded on the logics of inclusion and exclusion, 'pre-tribal' and 'tribal' respectively, corresponds of course to the opposition drawn in the previous section between economies underwritten by the principle of sharing *in*, and by its negation. It is the latter that slices up the social field so as to give it the appearance – for someone located within it – of a series of progressively wider but externally bounded sectors. Now the band, as an association of locally co-resident individuals and families, is a unit of sharing *out*: food is widely distributed within local groups, but very rarely circulates between them. Thus when we argue that bands cannot be transformed into tribes, we are doing no more than to assert that tribal society rests on the negation of sharing in rather than sharing out, such that whatever reciprocal interactions do occur cease to be grounded in the collective appropriation of nature. We find in pastoral and agricultural societies, just as much as among hunters and gatherers, local communities whose members associate with one another both in production and distribution. The residential composition of these communities, particularly among some pastoralists, can be every bit as fluid as it often is in hunting and gathering societies. We could, then, call them bands. Were we, however, to follow conventional usage in equating the band with the 'pre-tribal' social order, we would finish up by discovering bands in 'post-band' society!

A vital corollary of the principle of unbounded inclusion, or sharing in, is the autonomy of the individual who, though dependent for his very existence on his involvement in the collectivity, depends on others *in general* rather than on *specific* others (Woodburn 1982: 448). A person is free to move from one local group to another, receiving his share wherever he goes. And he does so, in order 'not to maintain a wide range of specific reciprocal partnerships, but to *avoid* the curtailment of personal freedom that such partnerships would imply' (Ingold 1980: 273, see Henriksen 1973: 41–2). But as soon as the social order is internally differentiated, say according to the categories of a kinship system, the incumbents of one position or the members of one descent group are placed in a specific relation towards those of another, a relation that involves rights and obligations, or in a word, *mutual dependences*. Herein lie the foundations of hierarchy. Yet according to the argument advanced above, a prerequisite for differentiation is the external boundedness of that institutionally defined entity, 'society as a whole'. Thus hierarchy is not an automatic concomitant of a commitment to the collectivity, and only appears so when we restrict our attention to those 'traditional' societies where boundaries of exclusion are clearly recognized. Where they are not, individualism and collectivism are quite compatible: indeed it could be argued – as I have done elsewhere – that the principle of collective appropriation, 'far from limiting the scope for individual autonomy, in fact allows its fullest expression' (Ingold 1980: 273).

Conclusion

With that, we can return to the question that originally prompted our inquiry. How does the individualism of the hunter–gatherer differ from that of 'western' man? On the one hand, following Fried (1967), the transition from hunting and gathering to agricultural and pastoral pro-duction has been broadly correlated, on the sociopolitical plane, with a movement from 'egalitarian' to 'rank' societies. On the other hand, following Dumont (1970), the transition from a 'traditional' to a 'modern' kind of society has been linked with the replacement of the ideals and principles of hierarchy with those of equality. Have we then, in the west, arrived back at the point from which our original hunter–gatherer pre-decessors set out? The most obvious indication that we have *not* lies in the manifest inequalities of western society, inequalities that are conspi-cuous by their absence among assertively egalitarian hunters and gatherers. In a recent article, Béteille (1986) has dwelt at length on what (after Simmel 1971 [1908]: 274) he calls the 'individualism of inequality' so central to contemporary doctrines of libertarian capitalism. This forms the main plank of his criticism of Dumont's argument, in which individualism is tied to equality. Béteille's objection, however, carries force only in so far as inequality is equated with hierarchy. It seems to me, and from my reading of Dumont, that these are concepts of fundamentally different import, and that the difference lies in the contrast between atomistic and holistic conceptions of society.

Hierarchy, as Dumont shows, is a property of society regarded as a total institutional order, and not of its individual parts or components taken by themselves, since it inheres in the *relations between* these parts, constitutive of the whole. But inequality, as it is commonly conceived in the west, has its foundations in the supposed differential endowment – whether in physique or intellect – of unique, self-contained and mutually exclusive individuals. That is to say, it is a property of the parts which, statistically compounded, generate the aggregate known as 'society'. Likewise social inequality, or 'stratification', is understood to result from the compounding of individual differences, rather than from the determination of the whole. There is a correspondence, then, between atomistic individualism and the paradigmatic opposition equality/inequality. But if inequality is to be distinguished from hierarchy, as we have suggested, we can go on to ask whether there might exist *another* notion of equality, constituted by its opposition to hierarchy rather than inequality, and signifying not a quantitative identity in the 'natural' endowments of individuals occupying the same stratum, but an elimination of qualitative differentials in the relations between them. Indeed there is such a notion, and it corresponds to the equality of a social whole that is as yet unbounded and undifferentiated. It is in precisely this holistic sense that hunter–gatherer society is egalitarian; moreover this equality endures *despite* the clear and often explicit recognition of differences in ability as between one individual and another. Some men appear quick-witted, others slow; some make good hunters, others persistently fail. But where, in the west, such differences are popularly elevated as the root cause of social inequality, among hunters and gatherers they remain matters of idiosyncratic variation that in no way compromise the equality of relations founded in their commitment to the whole. As Woodburn puts it, 'equality is, in a sense, generalized by them to all mankind' (1982: 448).

We have shown, in the three sections of this essay, how the integration of the person within an unbounded and inclusive collectivity underwrites a particular kind of individual autonomy. This is evident first in the realm of property, which is held *on behalf of* the world of other persons rather than *as against* it; secondly in the pattern of generalized reciprocity or sharing out, which is practised not *despite* an exclusive entitlement to the stuff distributed, but *because* it is the world's to enjoy; and thirdly in the freedom of association manifested in the fluidity of composition of the band, by virtue of which people are able to shift their residential affiliations in order to *avoid* dependences rather than in order to *proliferate* them. How, then, are we to characterize this sense of individualism, corresponding to what might be called 'holistic egalitarianism'?

Let us say that, compared to the individualism of western man , the relation between part and whole has been turned outside in. In our own society we imagine every individual to be an exclusive being, a private subject locked up within the confines of a body, standing against the rest of the world consisting of an aggregate of other such individuals, and competing with them in the public arena for the rewards of success. But the dichotomy between public and private domains has no meaning for the individual in a hunting and gathering society. Far from standing opposed to others, he incorporates them into the very substance of his being. The people around him, the places he knows, the things he makes and uses, all are part and parcel of his own subjective identity. He pursues his interests, but these are not the sectional interests of a divided world, rather they are interests which both originate with, and seek fulfilment through, the collectivity. He enjoys an autonomy of intention and action, but this is not an autonomy preconstituted in advance of his entry into social relations, rather it is constituted by his involvement in the whole. For him there is no contradiction, no conflict of purpose, between the expression of individuality and his generalized commitment to others. Since the world of others is enfolded within his own person, these are one and the same. In short, if we wish to express the essential difference between the hunter–gatherers and ourselves, it is that whereas for us representatives of *Homo aequalis*, every individual is an independent element of the aggregate collectivity, for them the collectivity is present and active in the life of every individual.

Notes to Chapter 9

1 To cite just one example, from Sutton's study of the Aboriginal people of western Cape York Peninsula, Australia: 'owning' land, Sutton tells us, is spoken of by using the verb which means 'to look after, wait for, wait upon, guard'. Thus 'land tenure is more a type of established custodianship rather than inalienable or alienable possession' (1978: 57).

2 Service (1966: 23) has pointed out that there exists an ancient legal term, *personalty*, which is appropriate for items of this kind, that are 'private' by virtue of their indissoluble connection with their holders.

3 The term was originally Gouldner's. He speaks of 'the *negative* norms of reciprocity, that is . . . sentiments of retaliation where the emphasis is placed not on the return of benefits but on the return of injuries, and is best exemplified by the *lex talionis*' (1960: 172). Sahlins's usage is, in fact, a good deal more liberal, since it covers the infliction of injury on another party regardless of whether it is retaliatory, or of whether retaliation from the injured party will ever be forthcoming.

4 There is a precedent for this sectoral model in the work of Simmel. 'We are', he wrote, 'surrounded by concentric circles of special interests. The more narrowly they enclose us, the smaller they must be' (1971 [1908]: 261). But Simmel took a quite different view of the relation between reciprocity and social distance. In his view, altruism peaks at the two extremes of closeness and remoteness, but declines to a minimum in the intermediate zones. One sacrifices his interests for an immediate kinsman, or for a complete stranger who is still a fellow man. 'But a relative coolness . . . befits the person who is neither quite near to us nor unreachably far from us.' Being no stranger, he is also known as no friend (1971 [1908]: 267–8).

5 This paradox has given rise to such bizarre misinterpretations of Sahlins's scheme as that of Leacock, who thinks that he is positing generalized and balanced reciprocity as the definitive distributional modes of 'band societies'

and 'villagers' respectively (Leacock 1982: 159). In fact, of course, Sahlins has villagers primarily in mind in his formulation of both types of reciprocity. For according to his sectoral model, households that practise generalized reciprocity close to home also participate, only one step further afield, in a 'village sector'.

6 I believe that Price (1975) is getting at this contrast when he insists, *contra* Sahlins, that sharing should be distinguished from reciprocity (including even its generalized form), and that the former is the 'dominant mode of economic allocation', in band societies, the latter in tribal societies. His 'sharing' would correspond, in our terms, to the situation in which sharing out is underwritten by sharing in; his 'generalized reciprocity' to that in which sharing out overrides a division into discrete economic interests.

References for Chapter 9

Béteille, A 1986 Individualism and equality. *Current Anthropology* **27**: 121–34.

Dowling, J. H. 1968 Individual ownership and the sharing of game in hunting societies. *American Anthropologist* **70**: 502–7.

Ducos, P. 1978 'Domestication' defined and methodological approaches to its recognition in faunal assemblages. In *Approaches to faunal analysis in the Middle East*, eds. R. H. Meadow and M. A. Zeder. Peabody Museum Bulletin 2. Harvard University: Peabody Museum of Archaeology and Ethnology.

Dumont, L. 1970 *Homo hierarchicus*. London: Weidenfeld and Nicolson.

Dumont, L. 1977 *From Mandeville to Marx*. University of Chicago Press.

Fried, M. H. 1967 *The evolution of political society*. New York: Random House.

Gouldner, A. W. 1960 The norm of reciprocity: a preliminary statement. *American Sociological Review* **25**: 161–78.

Henriksen, G. 1973 *Hunters in the barrens: the Naskapi on the edge of the white man's world*. Newfoundland Social and Economic Studies 12. Institute of Social and Economic Research, Memorial University of Newfoundland.

Herskovits, M. J. 1952 *Economic anthropology*. New York: Knopf.

Hobhouse, L. T. 1915 The historical evolution of property, in fact, and in idea. In *Property, its duties and rights*. London: Macmillan.

Ingold, T. 1980 *Hunters, pastoralists and ranchers*. Cambridge University Press.

Leacock, E. 1982 Relations of production in band society. In *Politics and history in band societies*, eds. E. Leacock and R. B. Lee. Cambridge University Press.

Letourneau, C. J. 1982 *Property: its origin and development*. London: Walter Scott.

Locke, J. 1978 [1689] Of property. In *Property: mainstream and critical positions*, ed. C. B. Macpherson. Oxford: Blackwell.

Maddock, K. 1983 *Your land is our land: Aboriginal land rights*. Ringwood, Victoria: Penguin.

Morgan, L. H. 1881 *Houses and house-life of the American aboriginees*. (Contributions to North American Ethnology Vol. IV). Washington DC: Government Printing Officer.

Peterson, N. 1972 Totemism yesterday: sentiment and local organization among the Australian Aborigines. *Man* (N.S.) **7**: 12–32.

Price, J. A. 1975 Sharing: the integration of intimate economies. *Anthropologica* **17**: 3–27.

Radcliffe-Brown, A. R. 1952 *Structure and function in primitive society*. London: Cohen and West.

Sahlins, M. D. 1961 The segmentary lineage: an organization of predatory expansion. *American Anthropologist* **63**: 322–45.

Sahlins, M. D. 1968 *Tribesmen*. Englewood Cliffs, NJ: Prentice-Hall.

Sahlins, M. D. 1972 *Stone age economics*. London: Tavistock.

Service, E. R. 1966 *The hunters*. Englewood Cliffs, NJ: Prentice-Hall.

Service, E. R. 1971 [1962] *Primitive social organization: an evolutionary perspective*. New York: Random House.

Simmel, G. 1971 *On individuality and social forms*. Selected writings, ed. D. N. Levine. University of Chicago Press.

Steward, J. H. 1955 *Theory of culture change*. Urbana: University of Illinois Press.

Sutton, P. J. 1978 *Wik: aboriginal society, territory and language at Cape Keerweer, Cape York Peninsula, Australia*. Ph.D. thesis, Dept. of Anthropology and Sociology, University of Queensland.

Wilson, E. O. 1980 *Sociobiology* (abridged edition). Cambridge, Mass: Harvard University Press.

Woodburn, J. 1982 Egalitarian societies. *Man* (N.S.) **17**: 431–51.

10

Hunting, sacrifice and the domestication of animals

I

Sacrifice archetypically involves the ritual slaughter of a domestic animal. Among pastoral peoples who depend to a considerable extent on herds of domestic stock for their subsistence, the apparent demands of various spiritual agencies provide the most usual pretext for killing animals whose slaughter products are subsequently used to provision the human group. But hunting peoples, too, base their livelihood upon the products of slaughtered beasts. Moreover, the hunt, just like the sacrifice, is a drama often imbued with religious significance, involving some kind of exchange between mankind and the spirit world. The parallel seems to me to offer a possible approach to the problem of how to relate the origins of sacrifice to the domestication of animals. For we may ask: what, if anything, takes the place of sacrifice among hunting peoples without consumable domestic stock? Could the answer lie in the hunt itself? Could we, in other words, interpret the genesis of sacrifice as a corollary, on the religious plane, of the socioeconomic transformation from hunting to pastoralism? However this may be, to compare the religious aspects of the hunt with those of sacrifice would surely throw some light on the ways in which domestication affects man's perception of the world of animals, and of his relations with it. That, in brief, is what I attempt to do in this essay.

The idea of such a comparison came to me some time ago, as I was winding up a study of hunting, pastoralism and ranching among the circumboreal peoples of Eurasia and North America, all of whom rely for their livelihood, in whole or in part, on herds of reindeer or caribou. In an epilogue to this study, I speculated as follows:

Now if the slaughter of wild animals by hunters is a rite of renewal, so every slaughter of domestic or pastoral stock is an act of sacrifice, offered to the spiritual guardian of the herds in order to secure future prosperity. In each case, reindeer are being killed to provision human households, and in each, their correct ritual treatment in death is held to be necessary for the reproduction of the herds. Thus, the transfer of control over the disposal of animals from the supernatural 'Reindeer-Being' to human householders marks a ritual inversion rather than a trend towards the secular. In the hunt, a presentation of animals is made by the spirit to man; in the sacrifice, men present animals to the spirit. In both, the shaman intervenes as propitiator, 'calling' the spirit to *send* animals to the hunter, and to *accept* animals from the pastoralist. Whether hunted or sacrificed, reindeer are, of course, *consumed* by humans: so it is only the soul of the victim that is released to its spiritual 'master' in sacrifice, just as it is only the bodily substance of the wild animal that is released to man in the hunt. Where both wild and domestic herds exist side by side, we might even envisage a situation in which spiritual and bodily components pass in opposite directions, the sacrifice of a tame beast conveying an appeal to the spirit to reciprocate by sending game in the future. (Ingold 1980: 283)

I should now like to pursue these speculations, remaining with circum-boreal societies, and paying particular attention to the reindeer which is unique among the animal species of this region in constituting both the prey of hunters and the potentially sacrifiable property of pastor-ralists. It is hardly surprising that matters turn out to be a good deal more complicated than I had previously envisaged.

The data, unfortunately, are rather patchy, and rest in many cases on recollections of practices long extinct, preserved in early ethnographies or in the narratives of explorers and missionaries. The nature of the sources is such that a somewhat Frazerian treatment of the subject is almost unavoidable, which means reserving the right to draw on material now from this group of people, now from that, more or less as it suits the purposes of our exposition. Not that Frazer's own discussion of animal propitiation, which – like ours – builds extensively on northern North American and Eurasian ethnography, is to be underrated. For Frazer recognized full well that the 'savage', who purports to venerate the very animals that he commonly hunts, kills and eats, is no fool. Not only has he sound, practical reasons for acting in the way he does, but also in his conception of the animal as a being possessed of a free intelligence and an immortal soul, 'he is more liberal and perhaps more logical than the civilized man, who commonly denies to animals the privilege of immortality which he claims for himself' (Frazer 1957 [1922]: 679). If the belief in animal souls sounds odd, it is not half as odd as the western belief in a soul unique to humankind! And so we should not, Frazer warned, too hastily judge the savage 'as irrational and inconsistent, but must endeavour to place ourselves at his point of view, to see things as he sees them, and to divest ourselves of the prepossessions which tinge so deeply our own views of the world' (1957 [1922]: 679). This admirable advice was reiterated in what must now rank as a classic study by

Hallowell, of bear ceremonialism among circumboreal peoples. Noting that we observers are most inclined to be impressed by the mechanical ingenuity or technical skill of the primitive hunter, Hallowell stressed that the hunter 'finds himself in a radically different position with regard to the game he pursues than can be inferred from our own habits of thought. To him the animal world often represents creatures with magical or superhuman potencies, and the problem of securing them for their hide, meat or fur involves the satisfaction of powers or beings of a super-natural order. Consequently, strategy and skill are only part of the problem. Success or failure in the hunt is more likely to be interpreted in magico-religious terms than in those of a mechanical order' (Hallowell 1926: 10). It is with these magico-religious aspects of man's relations towards animals that we are concerned here.

II

Two key conceptions pervade the religious thought of all the societies that fall within our purview. The first is the belief in a veritable plethora of souls, normally invisible but not necessarily immaterial, inhabiting not only human bodies, but also those of many kinds of animal, as well as sometimes plants and things that we would regard as inanimate objects – both natural and artificial. The second is the idea that each recognized species or class of wild animals has what ethnography usually calls a 'spiritual owner', 'master' or 'guardian', who controls the disposition of the beasts within his domain either by withholding them from, or presenting them to, human hunters, as the case may be; and in the latter instance, demanding their correct treatment in death, consumption and subsequent deposition of the remains. The two conceptions, of individual soul and species guardian, are of course related, but not in any simple way. Our first task will be to clarify the nature of this relationship.

Let me begin with the soul. This comes in a bewildering variety of forms, to which an equally bewildering variety of labels have been attached. A cursory glance through the massive compendium of soul-conceptions among North American Indians by the Swedish scholar, Åke Hultcrantz (1953), reveals life-souls, body-souls, ego-souls, breath-souls, free-souls, guardian-souls, shadows and double-gangers. Hultcrantz's principal thesis, however, is that all this variety is underwritten by a basic dualism between the soul that animates or vitalizes the body, and the soul that can wander about outside the body and by this means observe from afar the living being which it normally inhabits. The distinction between these two kinds of soul is borne out in the experience of dreaming, for whilst the dreamer is unconscious – one of his souls having embarked on a journey to points remote in time and space – he remains alive and well, proof that the other soul is still active and in place (Hultcrantz 1953: 270–1; 1979: 131–2). However, if the wandering or 'free' soul is lost or abducted on its expedition, if it fails to return as expected to its normal abode, the days of its possessor are likely numbered, unless the aid of a shaman can be enlisted to recover and reinstal the missing soul. Death comes with the eventual departure of the 'body' soul, which is usually thought to flicker out along with the life of its possessor, unless it can find a new being to animate. Meanwhile the free-soul takes itself off to the land of the dead, where it continues its existence as a ghost in a world where, compared with that of the living, everything is inside-out or back-to-front. Not that it necessarily enjoys the ease of immortality; it is reportedly believed among the Ob Ugrians that just as a man's soul swells during his lifetime, so it shrinks after death as his former life is played back in reverse, ending up in the insignificant and ephemeral form of a small black beetle (Chernetsov 1963: 12–13).[1]

There are, then, three essential components to the ordinary living person: the physical body, the body-soul and the free-soul. This trichotomy admits of a great deal of further elaboration: for example the body-soul is almost infinitely divisible, such that there may be a separate bit for every organ. Any of these bits may inadvertently be mislaid or stolen, so that if – say – you were a Chukchi and prone to frostbite, you might claim to be short of the soul that inhabits the tip of your nose (Bogoras 1904–9: 332–3). Along with this conceptual dissection of the person goes the slicing of the picture of the world into a minimum of three horizontal layers. The upper layer is the sky, frequently divided into several storeys and supported from the middle layer, that is the inhabited earth of mortal men, by a vertical 'cosmic-pillar' (Holmberg 1964: 333–40, Hultcrantz 1979: 23–5). The lower layer is the inverted world of the dead whose feet, since they walk upside-down, are sometimes thought (as by the Lapps) to touch the soles of the living who walk upright (Holmberg 1964: 73). Often this underworld is conceived as aquatic, so that the three layers correspond to air, land and water respectively.

Whatever the variations, whose roots lie in both historical and environmental conditions, one common problem seems to worry all the peoples with whom we are concerned. It is that whilst life depends on the harmonious integration of the various components or levels of being, this can only be achieved at one locus by breaking things up at another. Thus, the hunter lives by killing and eating animals, which inevitably entails their dismemberment. Much of the ritual surrounding the treatment of slaughtered beasts, particularly concerning the careful preservation of bones and other inedible parts, and their deposition in the correct medium and in the precise order that they occur in the skeleton, is designed to assist the reconstitution of the animals from the pieces into which they have been broken for the purposes of consumption, thus ensuring the regeneration of that on which human life depends (Paulson 1968). Above all, nothing should be wasted, for this would indicate a casually destructive attitude to nature which would only offend the animal guardians (Speck 1935: 92, Martin 1978: 18, Nelson 1982: 219). But human beings, too, are fragile and temporary constructions that can all too easily fall apart, leading to sickness or even death. Finding all the pieces may require an arduous supernatural journey, usually undertaken by a shaman, who by way of the world-pillar can visit the several levels of the sky, or descend to the underworld, and bring back with him the lost souls of his patient. So as he conducts himself through life, a man must tread with caution, breaking as little as possible, doing what he can to mend what in nature must of necessity be broken, and warding off the equally inevitable and ultimate disintegration of his own person. For as surely as animals must die if he is to live, he must eventually die in his turn.

Now whilst it is clear that in the case of human beings, the free-soul belongs to the particular person, conferring upon him a unique identity, with animals the situation is rather more complicated. It is by no means true, as is sometimes asserted, that the hunter generally encounters animals as beings on equal terms with himself. In the majority of instances, individual animals are regarded merely as the manifestations of an essential type, and *it is the type rather than its manifestations that is personified.* In myths and stories, time and time again, a specific human being bearing a proper name that is all his own comes face to face with non-human persons who bear the names of species, such as Eagle, Fox, Hare and Reindeer (or Caribou). More precisely, the encounter (often in dream) is one between souls; thus the animal soul belongs to no particular beast but to an individuality of a higher order, represented by all the beasts of its kind. This, of course, is none other than the being whom we have already introduced as the animal 'master' or 'guardian'. Human beings, then, rank themselves with the masters, not with their animal charges, and together they compose the world of persons. As Hultcrantz has argued:

The guardian spirit of the individual becomes the guardian spirit of the species when the borderline between the individual and the collective is smudged out. The animal soul here manifests a greater flexibility than man's soul, because the transition from individual to species characterizes far more the animal than it characterizes man. . . . In the everyday world of practical reality man enters into contact with peers of individual character and shape. He experiences the animals in a totally different way: the animal is felt not only as an individual, but also as a type for its species; Reynard the Fox is both an individual and a type, representative for all foxes. (1953: 500)

In short, the animal guardian comes into imaginary being as a logical consequence of the transference of the free-soul from the individual to the collective. A nice illustration of this is furnished by a remark of Jetté, writing about the concept of free-soul or *yega* among the Coyukon of Alaska. 'It would seem', he observes, 'that whereas each individual has a *yega* of its own, in animals and things there is one *yega* for each species, but not for each individual' (1911: 101). The species concerned include all the usual fur-bearers, fish, and a number of kinds of birds.

Since they are conceived as 'other-than-human' persons, it is with the animal guardians, and not with individual animals, that human persons may enter into, and consummate, social relationships, Writing of the Ojibwa, Hallowell has provided an extremely sensitive account of the essential attributes of personhood in 'a world in which vital social relations transcend those which are maintained with human beings'. These attributes comprise on the one hand 'an inner vital part that is enduring', and on the other 'an outward appearance that may be transformed under certain conditions'. The former is an essence independent of its variable outward form, and is the locus of such powers as sentience, volition, memory and speech. All persons have these powers, and speaking as an Ojibwa, they 'are structured the same as I am'. Thus,

I can talk with them. Like myself, they have personal identity, autonomy, and volition. I cannot always predict exactly how they will act, although most of the time their behavior meets my expectations. In relation to myself, other 'persons' vary in power. Many of them have more power than I have, but some have less. They may be friendly and help me when I need them but, at the same time, I have to be prepared for hostile acts, too. I must be cautious in my relations with other 'persons' because appearances may be deceptive. (Hallowell 1960: 42–3)

The notion that personhood transcends the human/non-human dichotomy follows quite logically from the premise that humanity is an aspect of incidental form rather than essential content. The human being, to adopt Shirokogoroff's (1935: 190) apt translation of a Tungus concept, is but a 'placing' for a vital entity that can just as well be placed elsewhere. All persons are presumed to have the power to change their place, or form, more or less at will. To be sure, I appear to you now as a man, but you may have seen me the other day masquerading as an animal, though you might not have recognized me at the time. Similarly an animal guardian may appear under the guise of one of the animals it represents, but it may equally well assume the shape of some other beast altogether, or of a human being. Among the Ojibwa the Thunder-Birds, masters or guardians of the various species of hawk, are commonly held (as their name implies) to manifest themselves and to speak through thunder, but on other occasions they may appear as extraordinary birds or as human beings. Hence, 'their conceptualization as 'persons' is not associated with a permanent human form any more than it is associated with a birdlike form' (Hallowell 1960: 31–4).

There is, however, a fundamental asymmetry in so far as the human form is *always* occupied by a person of some sort (except when the free-soul is absent during sleep), whereas *ordinary* animals, encountered individually, are not. The difficulty is that when you meet an animal, you can never be quite sure whether it is ordinary or extraordinary. Appearances, as Hallowell says, may be deceptive; though the free-soul or guardian spirit that has accoutred itself in an animal garb is usually recognizable by virtue of its peculiar behaviour, deviating from the norm for the species in question. For example, if a bird that is normally shy of man comes to perch right beside you, it is likely to be the manifestation of some spirit or other, and should be addressed accordingly. But the spirit could be the free-soul of a living man who is asleep far away (in which case, when he wakes, he should recall having met you in his dream, and should be able to describe with precision what was going on in your place); it could be the soul of a man now deceased, paying a visit from the underworld; or it could be the guardian spirit of an animal species – though not necessarily of the species in the form of which it appears. Certain animals, however, are always regarded as extraordinary, and are invariably approached as one would approach other human beings, in the manner appropriate to particular persons. Chief amongst these is the bear, which for all circumboreal peoples – apparently without exception – is the object of special respect (Frazer 1957 [1922]: 662–78, Hallowell 1926, Karsten 1955: 113–22, Holmberg 1964: 85–98, Alekseenko 1968, Larsen 1970, Saladin d'Anglure 1980). Maritime hunters often accord equivalent rank to the walrus and whale, and other animals may also, under specific circumstances, receive similar treatment. I shall return shortly to consider these cases. First, however, I should like to give a few examples of native conceptions concerning the reindeer, and to move on from there to present an analogy between the 'mastery' by the animal guardians of their charges and by men of their domestic livestock.

III

Like other species of obvious economic utility to northern hunters, the reindeer is generally conceived to have a master or guardian who 'owns' the wild herds. Speck has provided a detailed account of this conception as it is held among the Naskapi. The master, known as Caribou-Man, dwells in a huge cavern within a hill, exercising his governance over a herd of many thousands of deer. From this cavern, reached through a narrow ravine, Caribou-Man dispatches his charges on their annual migrations, having already determined which animals, and how many, are to be taken by which particular hunters. After the hunt, the souls of slain animals return to base, where they are reincarnated in order to be dispatched again the next time round. The master, according to Speck's account, is visualized as a white and bearded human being, though he may also take the shape of an enormous caribou. His cavern, together with all the country round about, is strictly out-of-bounds to human hunters; those who have inadvertently strayed too close have returned with terrifying tales of a world where everything is of gigantic size and ferocious in appearance. Others have not returned at all (Speck 1935: 82–6).

The Quebec Eskimo described by Turner, who are neighbours of the Naskapi, entertain rather similar conceptions. Again the 'great spirit' who controls the reindeer inhabits a cavern under a hill, from where he commands the fortunes of the hunters and the spirits of animals that are slain. As among the Naskapi, the shaman can prevail upon the master to send deer to human communities that are suffering for want of food. Turner's account here contains a couple of interesting details that are worth noting. The shaman, he writes, informs the reindeer spirit 'that the people have in no way offended him, as the shaman, as a mediator between the spirit and the people, has taken great care that the past food was all eaten and that last spring, when the female deer were returning to him to be delivered of their young, none of the young (or foetal) deer were devoured by dogs' (Turner 1979 [1894]: 37). The reference to the complete consumption of previous provisions relates to the belief, already mentioned, that carelessly to waste food is to be disrespectful towards the providing spirit. It is also thought essential to restrain domestic dogs from touching the carcasses of slain deer, because they are liable to maul the bones whose perfect preservation is supposed to be a prerequisite for the regeneration of the herds (compare Tanner 1979: 166, on the Mistassini Cree). This rule, as Turner indicates, applies particularly to young and foetal animals, in other words to precisely that section of the herd on which future supplies depend. Fawns and pregnant does are of course hunted and killed along with the rest, and the foetus is a much-desired delicacy. But from the hunters' point of view their slaughter and consumption is an integral and necessary part of the creative cycle of renewal, releasing the vital essence of the animals so that they can be reclothed with flesh. Not only, then, do humans depend on the spiritual master of the deer for their supply of food, but also the master depends on the intervention of humans to perform the acts of killing which ensure the reproduction of his herds. This is a crucial point to which we shall return in a later section.

A further point of interest in Turner's account of Eskimo conceptions is that the great spirit of the reindeer is supposed to take the form of a huge white bear (1979: 36). As we shall see, on the mystical plane bear and man are interchangeable, so that the transformation of the giant, white and bearded Caribou-Man into an ursine equivalent is entirely comprehensible. But whilst the master is formidably powerful and masculine, the reindeer themselves are often seen as weak, vulnerable and feminine. The male hunter, approaching a reindeer with intent to kill, imagines himself on another level to be seduced by a beautiful girl, and the kill itself represents the consummation of sexual intercourse (Tanner 1979: 136–8). In this imagery the essential connection between killing and reproduction is once more apparent, for like intercourse its consequence is the conception of new life rather than its destruction.[2] There are many stories that tell of how the hunter, captivated by his female quarry, goes off to live with her, so that the animal master becomes his father-in-law. But by the same token, the master is somewhat enamoured of human girls and women, who run the risk of being raped if caught in a lonely spot. Thus, according to Saladin d'Anglure (1980), the Eskimo in the region where he worked regard the white bear as a lusty super-male, extremely dangerous to women. In virtually all circumboreal societies, women have to keep well clear when a slain bear is brought in, as it is supposed, on a ceremonial visit to the camp, and they are restrained from regarding him directly.

The ability of animal masters and other spirits to change not only their outward form but also their scale is a common theme among northern hunting peoples. A Chukchi shaman put it to Bogoras like this: 'you look at a *ke'le* [spirit], and he is smaller than a mosquito; again you look, and he is the size of an ordinary man, and then, behold! he is sitting on a cliff, and his feet touch the sandy beach below'. Moreover, whereas ordinary things look smaller, the farther you are away from them, spirits loom larger with increasing distance but are minute close-up (Bogoras 1904–9: 296). It seems that the factor of size is used to convey an impression of ferocity, thus the Caribou-Man is certainly a being to be greatly feared – only, however, if encountered on his home ground remote from human communities, where he appears as a terrible giant. But if the spirit enters the world of ordinary humans, the relation of scale is inverted, so that it is the latter who appear gigantic to the former. The huge and ferocious bear becomes a tiny mouse or shrew. The Coyukon of Alaska believe in the existence of a fabulous bear which is supposed to be 'exceptionally fierce, killing people and rushing upon them as though mad with fury'. Bears are rarely met with in Coyukon country, but the occasional encounter with a grizzly, Jetté suggests, may have been enough to call up this image of an ursine monster. The spirit is addressed, however, by a name that means 'the one which we call shrew', and is described as rather small in size (Jetté 1911: 108).

There is an extraordinary parallel between this Coyukon conception and that of the Chukchi, who regard the spiritual 'owner' of the wild reindeer, a character called Pičvu'čin, as being of diminutive size, 'not larger than a man's finger, and his footprints on the snow are like those of a mouse'. The mouse-like Pičvu'čin is everything that a man should be, except in miniature. He has a sledge made of grass, the domesticated reindeer that pull it are themselves either mice or roots of the plant *Polygonum viviparum*, and the great bear that he hunts is a lemming (Bogoras 1904–9: 287). Incidentally, the lemming is commonly selected as the miniature counterpart of the bear, apparently because of the shared capacity to stand erect, whilst the mouse is the counterpart of the man. According to the Chukchi, Bogoras explains,

> mice are people living in underground houses who use the root of *Polygonum viviparum* or *Polygonum polymorphum* as their reindeer, and have sledges of grass. By a sudden transformation they become real hunters with regular sledges, and hunt polar bears. When they want to carry the dead bear home, the sledge returns to its former size, and the bear turns into a lemming. (1904–9: 283–4)

From this it might seem that the Chukchi guardian of the wild deer is no formidable giant living under a hill, but a tiny mouse living in a hole. And yet perhaps the underground house is a great cavern after all, for its entrance is said to be reached through deep ravines near the forest border. 'From there he sends reindeer-herds to the hunters; but when he is angered he withholds the supply' (1904–9: 286).

I should like to draw attention to one further detail regarding the Chukchi conception that is most important to our argument. It is that Pičvu'čin is supposed himself to herd and to use the wild reindeer that he sometimes sends to man, both for pulling sledges and – in the case of the largest bucks – for riding. In other words the Chukchi are comparing Pičvu'čin's 'ownership' of the wild herds to the human ownership of domestic herds which are controlled and used in like manner, and on which Chukchi subsistence largely depends. As human persons stand to their domestic stock, so the spirit master of the reindeer stands to the wild herds – they are *his* domestic stock. Other spirits, all of which are denoted by the Chukchi term *ke'let*, keep domestic herds as well. Benevolent beings drive reindeer, though their form is often fantastical – as those of the sun, whose radiant deer, traversing the sky on their diurnal peregrinations, have antlers of burnished copper. But the reindeer of the evil spirits, which they drive and ride through the narrow passages of the underworld, is none other than the mammoth. The image is wonderfully appropriate, since in this region mammoths were often to be found encased and well preserved in the permafrost, with only their giant tusks protruding above the ground surface. The story is told of a Chukchi man who, looking at a pair of such protruding tusks, suddenly observed them to move. He caught such a fright that he subsequently went mad and died (Bogoras 1904–9: 305, 326–7). In fact, the idea of the mammoth as the domestic deer of the underworld is quite widely diffused in Siberia: it is, for example, represented among the Tungus with the antlers of a deer and· the tail of a fish – since in the Tungus conception the underworld is a watery one (Anisimov 1963b: 169).

Further confirmation of the point that the model for the man–animal relation in domestication is taken from the imagined relation between the spirit guardian and the wild herds under his dominion comes from Anisimov, in his work on the reindeer Tungus (Evenks). The relevant passage is worth citing in full:

> The beasts, fishes and birds which man hunts in order to live are for the spirits the same kind of herds as tame reindeer are for men. . . . In their [ruling spirits'] hands were all the sources of man's life. In order that man might exist, the spirits gave him a sufficient part of their innumerable herds of beasts. For this, man (said the shamans) must entreat the spirits and make sacrifices to them. Thus, we see that the herds of beasts were the property of the ruling spirits just as tame reindeer were of men. (Anisimov 1963a: 108)

This observation, in turn, offers a clue to the solution of a problem that long ago worried Czaplicka. She wondered 'why the reindeer, which plays such a unique role in the life of the Palaeo-Siberians, is neither worshipped nor venerated, and does not in any way enter into the religious life of the people *except as a sacrificial animal*' (1920: 495, my emphasis). An animal, quite simply, cannot simultaneously be the focus of veneration and an object of sacrifice, for towards the former man is the subordinate party, towards the latter he is dominant. Strictly speaking, of course, veneration is focused not on animals *per se* but on their spirit owners, and the owner of the wild reindeer is indeed revered, as we have already seen in the case of the Chukchi (Hallowell 1926: 81). But to the extent that guardianship over reindeer herds is transferred from the spirit owner to human persons, as in the transition from hunting to pastoralism, every man would be placed in the position of venerating something that, in effect, deputizes for his *own* spirit as a herdsman. That something, among the Chukchi and the neighbouring Koryak, is – as we shall see – the anthropomorphic fireboard.

A slight detour is necessary at this stage to obviate any possible mis-understanding. In emphasizing the parallel between the spirit mastery of wild herds and the human mastery of domestic ones I do not mean to suggest that the notion of mastery itself has its source in man's domesti-

cation of animals, or that its elaboration among hunting peoples has
something to do with their contacts with neighbouring pastoralists. When
it comes to the hunting societies of northern North America, who had
no such contacts until very recent times, any suggestion along these
lines would be patently absurd. To seek the origin of the idea of mastery
we have to look elsewhere, and the most likely place to find it is surely in
the structure of the human domestic group, and above all in the relations
between its male and female members. Though I cannot prove it, I would
speculate that hunting societies in which the sexual division of labour
contains a strong element of subordination of women to male heads of
households will also entertain ideas about (masculine) spirit masters who
are supposed to guard and control their (feminine) wild animal charges in
an analogous way. Certainly such subordination is rather characteristic of
the northern hunting societies with which we are concerned. Moreover,
as I have argued in another context (Ingold 1980: 151), the relation of
domination entailed in 'domestication' originally comes about through
the substitution of animals for subordinate humans within the domestic
division of labour of the hunting economy. Combining the analogy,
between human and spirit guardians as masters in their respective
households, with the substitution, of animal for female wards in the
human household, we obtain the parallel between spirit and human
mastery – of wild and domestic animals – by virtue of which each may
stand as a model for the other. Rather than the former being derived from
the latter, or *vice versa*, both are derived from a common source, having
their roots in the internal relations of the human family.

To return now to our main theme: among maritime hunters of the north
Pacific Coast, and throughout arctic and subarctic North America, the
only domestic animal of any significance is the dog. Yet we find here
precisely the same notion, that man's domination of his domestic chattels
is akin to that exercised by the spirit masters over the various wild
species, and as a corollary, that the ritual role of domestic animals is as
objects of bloody sacrifice. Evidence for the former assertion comes from
Tanner's recent monograph on the religious ideology of the Mistassini
Cree. To describe the relations of dominance and subordination between
the 'animal master' and the wild animal species it controls, the Cree most
commonly refer to individuals of the species as their masters' 'pets'. The
Cree term (*awhkaan*) used for 'pet' in fact refers to the whole class of
domesticated animals, but no other animal besides the dog is known to
have been kept in this way beyond recent times. The animal masters,
Tanner writes, 'are thought of as being in a dominant relationship to a
particular class of game animals. They both look after the animals and
influence their actions, *in the same way that a hunter looks after and
controls his own dogs*' (Tanner 1979: 139, my emphasis). If this is so, it

must follow that dogs – along with other domestic animals – have no 'other-than-human' guardian, and hence that they have no free-soul, either individually or collectively, as distinct from the souls of their respective human masters. Otherwise put, the spirit of the domestic animal is the soul of man, controlling the animal from without. It is difficult to find explicit confirmation of this point in the literature, one can only infer the absence of non-human guardians from the fact that they are never mentioned. I did come across a casual remark, in Spencer's ethnography of the North Alaskan Eskimo, that dogs lack souls, a remark that was presented as a statement of the obvious (Spencer 1959: 301). More significant perhaps is the reported belief of the Ojibwa that 'the dog was created especially for the purpose of sacrifice' (Vecsey 1983: 108). That is to say, its role in the overall scheme of things is to be disposed of by men, as wild animals exist to be disposed of by spirit masters.

As objects of bloody sacrifice, domestic animals of different species appear to be more or less interchangeable. The Tungus, according to Shirokogoroff, sacrifice only what is practically available; 'therefore it is likely that with the change of the domesticated animal, the one formerly used for sacrifice will be replaced by another one' (1935: 199). Thus, horse may substitute for reindeer, and *vice versa*. Yet no one would willingly sacrifice a good working animal in its prime, and this tends to place a limit on the frequency of sacrifice amongst those with only small herds, unless 'fresh blood' can be purchased from neighbours in the form of live domestic stock of other kinds, such as pigs or fowl. On the other hand, should a community run seriously short of meat, a pretext can always be found to slaughter a beast, perhaps to furnish an offering to the spirit who appears to be withholding the supply of game, and then everyone is invited in to share the food (Shirokogoroff 1935: 202, see Ingold 1980: 100–1). Bogoras makes it quite clear that among the Chukchi, 'strictly speaking, every slaughtering of a reindeer is a sacrifice', and likewise among the Koryak ritual and secular slaughterings are in practice indistinguishable (Bogoras 1904–9: 368, Jochelson 1908: 96).

Should occasions for bloody sacrifice arise when, with regard to the increase of the herd, it would be imprudent to slaughter, the Chukchi offer substitutes – crude models of reindeer fashioned from crushed leaves or snow, sausages made from the stuffed stomach of the deer, or by an intriguing double substitution, wooden models of such sausages (Figure 10.1). These offerings should be included within the category of bloody sacrifice because they are consciously treated as surrogates for reindeer, just as among the Nuer cucumbers are offered as surrogates for oxen. According to Bogoras, they are 'often stabbed with a knife to represent the slaughtering' (Bogoras 1904–9: 369, see Evans-Pritchard 1956: 203). The coastal Chukchi and Koryak slaughter dogs when reindeer

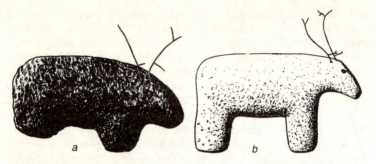

Figure 10.1   Chukchi sacrificial substitutes; small figures shaped like reindeer and made of pounded leaves (a) or snow (b). From Bogoras (1904–9: 369).

are unavailable, but whether they did so prior to the days when their inland neighbours had acquired domestic reindeer is not known for sure. Between reindeer sacrifice and dog sacrifice there is the important difference, noted by Jochelson, that whereas in the former case the owner sustains no material loss, since the slaughter products can all be consumed in the normal way, in the latter case the owner loses an animal whose value lay entirely in its working capacity, and whose slaughter products are practically worthless (Jochelson 1908: 90–1, 96). All such bloody sacrifices, whether of domestic animals or inanimate substitutes, must be distinguished from the bloodless offerings of things like tobacco, cooked food, sugar, flour and other exotic trade goods, and trinkets of various kinds. Though the ethnography often portrays these offerings as 'sacrifices', their significance is entirely different, as I shall shortly show. Only the bloody sacrifice can be regarded as the counterpart of hunting, since what is essential to both is the killing of beasts and the release of vital forces that this entails.

IV

The position so far is that we have established a homology between the disposition by spirit masters of wild animals and the disposition by human persons of domestic animals; we have seen that the latter normally takes the form of bloody sacrifice, and that – as persons – humans and animal masters rank on the same level. Contact between the two domains, of men and masters respectively, can be established in both directions. On the one hand the human community may call upon one of their number, especially credited with mystical power, to visit the spirit guardians of the animals, often with an appeal for help. This man is of course the shaman. On the other hand, the community may be visited by

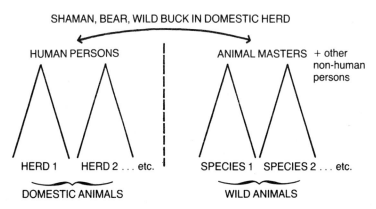

Figure 10.2   The domains of human persons and animal masters, and the contacts between them.

an emissary from the spirit world, and the usual form he takes is that of a bear (see Figure 10.2). Indeed to all intents and purposes, as far as the people are concerned, the bear *is* a shaman; or in other words, a shaman may just as well be a human masquerading as a bear, as a bear masquerading as a human. Thus, it is often said that the bear's face is like the vizor of a mask that could at any moment be raised to reveal the countenance of a man, terrifying to the beholder. The important point for our argument, which follows from this, is that the ursine form – just like the human form – is invariably considered to be occupied by a person. Hence also, every individual bear ranks in his own right as a being on a par with the animal masters, indeed he may as we have seen *be* a master, as of caribou. A perfect illustration of this point comes from Speck's account of the Naskapi. On inquiring from a religious man of the Mistassini whether, like caribou and fish, bears formed a tribe with an overlord, the answer came: 'No, every bear is a chief himself' (Speck 1935: 95).[3]

The fact that the bear, of all animals, is universally singled out for special treatment probably has less to do with its size and strength, or with the desirability of its meat, than with its extraordinarily anthropomorphic qualities. They are, like human beings, omnivorous. The traces they leave behind them, in the form of footprints and excrement, are much like those left by men. They are manifestly intelligent, and display very human-like bodily and facial expressions, even weeping when upset. Their sitting posture resembles that of a man, and so does their capacity to stand erect upon their hind legs. Almost without exception, observers have noted the remarkably human form and proportions of the bear's carcass after it has been skinned, lending credence to the idea that the animal is really a man in disguise. One is indeed inclined to wonder whether, if bears did not exist, men would nevertheless have conjured up in their imaginations a beast of almost identical kind. Be that as it may, my present concern is to examine some of the implications of the doctrine that all bears are persons.

The first is that the bear, who can of course hear and understand human speech, should always be referred to and addressed as one would other persons, that is by using a kinship term (such as 'grandfather' or 'cousin'), a pronoun (such as simply 'he' or 'him') or an endearing nickname (such as the Finnish *mesikämmen* meaning 'honey-paws'; a name, incidentally, that rests on the belief that the bear lives during its winter hibernation by sucking a nutritive substance from its feet). Although the languages of circumboreal peoples generally include species names for the bear, to use them in the animal's hearing would be as insulting as to refer to a known person as just another human being. Recalling that personhood comprises an inner vital substance clothed in a transient outer garb, it is evident that species terms for bears and human beings denote only the latter component, the objective placing, which is incidental, rather than its essential subjective incumbent. Only in reference to the animal guardians can species terms be used as proper names, to denote persons, for each is a singular incarnation of all the members of the type. Thus, when the shaman, among the Naskapi or Quebec Eskimo, encounters a person called Caribou or Caribou-Man, the name derives from the species he controls. But Caribou is not a caribou, he appears either as a white man or as a white bear.

A second implication of the bear's personhood is revealed in the custom that, once the animal has been cajoled from its den and killed, it is offered profuse apologies. The hunters generally try to make out that the whole thing was a tragic and unfortunate accident, for which neither they nor the bear itself can take any of the blame. Sometimes responsibility is shifted to evil spirits, or to malevolent strangers from another tribe, or in more recent times to non-native Russian or Euro-Canadian intruders. Of course no such evasion or apology is needed when ordinary wild animals are killed, since the assumption is that the spirit master of the victims had already intended their slaughter, and that the hunters are no more than the executors of his intent. In other words, masters may purpose the destruction of the wild animals they control, and men can purpose the destruction of their domestic chattels; but persons cannot legitimately purpose the destruction of other persons – be they human or animal – so that if a killing occurs it must be construed either as an accident, or as the work of amoral beings who chanced to appear on the scene.

The death of the bear marks its initial point of entry into the human community. Throughout the ensuing ceremonial, which centres on a communal feast, the animal is treated as an honoured guest. The butchering is always carried out so as to leave the whole skin still attached to the head and shoulders, which are left intact. This is then set up inside the dwelling, in a place of honour, so that the bear presides over a feast that consists largely of its own meat and offal. Certain parts, notably the blood, heart, liver, paws and other vital organs, are allowed only to men, and are considered a source of spiritual strength. The idea of communion is quite pronounced, as in the drinking of the blood, in the care taken to ensure that every participant tastes a bit of every part of the animal, and in what is often called the 'eat-all' feature of the feast – the prescription that, stomach-ache notwithstanding, everything edible should be consumed in one sitting. There is little doubt that quite unlike the meal following a sacrificial slaughter or a regular hunt, which is just like any other, the bear-feast involves the partaking of sacred substance, signifying the complete incorporation of the person of the animal into the human group, or the merging of the identity of the one with that of the other. More correctly, it is an identification only with the male members of the group, whose domination over their womenfolk is thereby rendered with powerful dramatic effect.

As all good things must come to an end, the time eventually arrives when the bear has to take its leave of the community and return to its kind. It is given a lavish send-off, laden with gifts, and with exhortations to come again next year. The expectation is that the bear, on reaching home, will tell its friends and relatives about the excellent hospitality it received, so that they may be encouraged to come along too. In practice what happens at the end of the feast is that there are placed before the bear's head offerings of cooked food which are conceived as provisions for its journey. The Koryak, for example, 'slaughter a domestic reindeer for the bear, cook all the meat, and pack it in a grass bag' (Jochelson 1908: 89). Though intended for the bear, the meat will of course be eventually eaten by humans. Various objects, regarded as gifts, may also be placed on the head, carcass or skin: this presentation is sometimes known as 'dressing' the bear. Then, after a suitable time has elapsed, the head with its associated paraphernalia is carried out into the forest, perhaps in a specifically auspicious direction, and deposited on a raised platform or in the cleft trunk of a tree, safe from the depradations of dogs. And there it remains for posterity.

A remarkable variant of this general format of bear ceremonialism has been recorded among the Gilyak and the Ainu (on the Ainu practice, see Seligman 1962: 169–71, Watanabe 1972: 74–7). They not only hunt and kill adult bears but attempt, where possible, to capture infant cubs. A cub thus taken is raised in the intimate setting of the domestic group, where it is suckled by the women and is a playmate for the children. When it has grown a little too large and its hug a little too tight for comfort, the bear is confined to a cage, where it spends the next two or three years being fattened up in preparation for ritual slaughter. After the killing, which is again accompanied by ample apologies and condolences, the bear is treated in exactly the same way as one killed in the wild, following the pattern already described. The curious practice of raising cubs for slaughter greatly intrigued Frazer, who went so far as to regard it as a representative instance of a special type of animal sacrament – what he called the 'Aino [Ainu] type'. By lavishing attention on select individual cubs, Frazer supposed, hunters offer atonement to the bear species for the losses they have inflicted on its number, acquiring thereby a licence to exterminate any remaining animals they can lay their hands upon (Frazer 1957 [1922]: 698–9). This explanation undoubtedly misses the mark; for one thing it rests on a grossly exaggerated view of the role of the bear in the subsistence economy of the peoples concerned, and for another it fails to account for the fact that other species of equivalent if not greater importance in this regard - such as deer or salmon (Watanabe 1972: 37) – are not accorded the same treatment.

I would be more inclined to view the rearing of cubs as an attempt to prolong a beneficial visitation from the spirit world beyond the narrow time interval between the slaughter of the beast and its consumption.[4] Killing, then, marks not its entry into the community but the imminence of its departure. What is especially interesting about the Ainu practice is that it entails a kind of domestication, but one that is utterly different from the kind that exists in man's relation to domestic chattels such as dogs or reindeer, whose reproduction is under human control. The bear is not a slave, to be commanded and disposed of at the will of its owner, but the temporary resident of a human household, lodged as an emissary and a guest. Towards the bear, man is not master but host. And for the same reason, its slaughter cannot be regarded as an act of sacrifice; not, at least, in the same sense as the bloody sacrifice of animals subject to human domination (Hallowell 1926: 108–9). For having once established a communion or fellowship between the human community and the spirit world, the beast returns whence it came. Moreover, the offerings which it is supposed to take home with it are in the nature of ordinary, material gifts; namely food and other objects which are in themselves inert. If these offerings are to be regarded as things sacrificed, their donation must again be clearly distinguished from the bloody sacrifice of domestic chattels.

Consider for example the Koryak custom of offering a cooked reindeer as travelling provisions to the departing bear. The slaughter of the deer may certainly be regarded as a sacrificial act, the effect of which is to release the life force or vital essence of the animal. I reserve discussion of the significance of this act to the final part of the essay, and merely note at this point that the cooked meat of the slaughtered animal is but a material residue that is already drained of the mystical power generally thought to reside in the blood and vital organs, and that is consequently no more sacred than ordinary food. This *residue*, normally retained for human consumption, is what is subsequently offered to the bear. The Koryak actually look for evidence, in the form of scratch marks, purporting to show that the bear has tasted the meat, before discreetly removing the rest for themselves. In the same category of material offerings should be included what are often called 'sacrifices' to the animal masters – little bits of cooked flesh or other delicacies usually dispatched to the spirit world by being thrown into the fire, whence they depart with the smoke through the roof of the dwelling. The idea is that the spirits may be persuaded to reciprocate by sending meat to the hunters (Speck 1935: 81, Tanner 1979: 165). The exchange, in short, is one of material substance only.

Among the maritime Koryak, the ceremonial which attends the successful killing of a whale is modelled precisely on the bear ceremonial, and the same goes for the walrus-hunting festival of the Chukchi (Jochelson 1908: 66–72, Bogoras 1904–9: 379). The reindeer-keeping Koryak stage an analogous ceremony to mark the dispatch of a wolf, though its message is a different one. Like the bear, the wolf is regarded as a formidable shaman, 'a rich reindeer-owner and the powerful master of the tundra'. But he is an evil and vengeful character who, as a major predator, has built his herds by pinching animals from human owners. Therefore the object of the ceremony is not to encourage the animal to return, but to appease it 'lest his relatives come and take revenge'. The meat of the wolf is *not* eaten, but the slain beast is offered food and entertainment before being taken out into the forest or tundra to be placed on a platform. Alongside it is placed the carcass of a sacrificed reindeer, offered not, however, to the wolf but to the Supreme Being, who is asked not to permit the wolf to return. The wolf itself is offered no equipment at all for its home journey (Jochelson 1908: 89–90). Bogoras mentions in passing that the inland Chukchi likewise celebrate the killing of wolves, as well as wolverine and elk, but he provides no details (1904–9: 381). He does, however, give a fascinating account of another Chukchi ceremonial modelled on the bear-feast, which is of particular interest to us. It accompanies the arrival, during the rutting season, of wild reindeer bucks amidst the pastoral herds.

Chukchi reindeer-owners have good reasons for desiring that wild bucks should enter their herds, for they derive a double benefit – as well as yielding a supply of free meat, the bucks serve the does of the pastoral herd. It is thought that the offspring of the cross between wild and domestic deer is superior in every respect, and such animals are particularly highly valued (Bogoras 1904–9: 74). In a sense, the wild bucks do for the domestic herds precisely what human hunters do for the wild herds, for as will be recalled, the hunter's killing of his prey is identified on another level with an act of sexual intercourse in which the reindeer appears to him as a beautiful girl whom he causes to conceive. So, too, do the does of the domestic herd appear to the wild buck who comes to impregnate them.[5] But the buck should not of course be dispatched until it has had full opportunity to render its sexual services, therefore it must be persuaded to prolong its sojourn in the domestic environment for as long as possible. This persuasion is effected by means of incantations which are supposed to make the wild animal tame.

Bogoras has recorded two examples of such incantations, which are so rich in meaning that their full elucidation would require a separate essay. I have space here to cite only a part of one of them:

When a wild reindeer-buck that has just shed his hair joins a domesticated herd, the owner says, 'Let us try it and make of him a tame reindeer! Let him create offspring for us!' He goes to the herd and pronounces an incantation. He talks to the Being of the Zenith. 'Listen to me, you there above! I am in great need. This one wants to go away, and he is the first of his kind that I have seen here. Give me your wooden stake! I will stick it into his foot and fasten him to the ground; I will thrust it in between his antlers; I will pierce his lower jaw, and bring it down to the level of the ground. With what else will I pin to the ground this fleet-footed reindeer-buck? I will gather boulders from all sides, and pile them up between his antlers. How will he move his head? I will wrap his ears with sod. I will gather withered sedge-grass and cover his nose with it...I make him into a fawn newly born... Let me get possession of him!...' (Bogoras 1904–9: 497)

The imaginery, here, is one not only of pinioning, but more significantly of *enclosing* the wild animal, with rocks and earthen sods, so that he is wrapped up like a foetus in the womb, to emerge new-born as a fawn.

The resemblance between this taming of the wild buck and the domestication of bear cubs among the Ainu and Gilyak is almost uncanny. In the latter case, of course, the animals are *actually* captured new or recently born, and are literally enclosed in a cage. In both instances, the taming is an attempt to prolong a beneficial visitation, knowing full well that the time will come when the animal-being must depart. And in both, the imminence of departure is marked by its ritual slaughter, followed by a communal, sacred meal of meat and blood from the slaughtered beasts. Offerings of cooked food are made to the buck as they are to the bear; its antlers – as Bogoras prosaically remarks – 'are adorned with festoons of sausages and dried guts', and the head, having been taken into the tent, is entertained with singing and drumming. The sausages are made from the

Figure 10.3 A Chukchi drawing representing the ceremonial accompanying the killing of wild bucks that enter the domestic herd. Bogoras supplies the following commentary: 'Four carcasses of wild reindeer are lying on the ground. The fifth one is that of a domesticated reindeer slaughtered in sacrifice. A small fire is burning between the carcasses and the house. Two men, one on each side of the house, throw sacrifice to the "directions". Two women adorn the antlers of the animals with sausage. A party of guests stand ready to rush on for sausage. The herd is lying on the ground not far off' (Bogoras 1904–9: 380–1).

meat of a domestic reindeer slaughtered in sacrifice, and at the end of the feast the participants can help themselves to whatever they can grab of these offerings, and to any other food that remains (Bogoras 1904–9: 380–1, see Figure 10.3). The explicit parallels between the buck-ceremonial and the bear-feast are such as to leave us in no doubt that the buck which visits the domestic herd, entering thus the domain in which man exercises mastery over animals, is considered to be no ordinary beast but, like the bear, a personal emissary from the spirit world of the wild animal guardians.

V

Killing the wild buck, as we have just described it, is a quite different affair from the usual hunting of wild herds out in the open tundra, and from the regular sacrifice, back at camp, of domestic stock. It is to the significance of the latter that we must now finally turn. In order to do so, it is necessary first to introduce a rather shadowy entity or force that seems to hover behind the religious conceptions of all circumboreal peoples, yet without receiving much explicit elaboration, namely the Supreme Being – or more simply, God. Considering whether the belief in such a being formed any part of aboriginal thought among the Naskapi, or whether it was imported by Christian missionaries, Speck was inclined to the latter view, and yet adduced one striking argument in favour of the former. It ran as follows:

In the native system of thought the various families and genera of animals constitute races and tribes among which the human is included. They are dominated by their spiritual overlords, who rule their destinies and govern reincarnation through succeeding generations of their kind. Conceive a similar hierarchy ruling the cycle of existence of man, and the positive indications would seem to be affirmed. Man, then, has his Owner, and this is the High God. As man comes first among earthly beings, his Owner is implied as dominating the theocratic forces. (Speck 1935: 38)

The logic of the argument can be clearly seen if we add one more level to our earlier diagram (Figure 10.2). Men, as we saw, stand on a par with the animal masters, so where stands the master of man? He must stand on that higher level, supreme over all beings, human and non-human, who are themselves masters of animals, domestic and wild respectively (see Figure 10.4).

Moreover, by the same logic, this Supreme Being must also be the master of bears, and as such must simultaneously embody the collective essence of both bearness and humanity. We find here an explanation of the fact, noted by Hultcrantz, that the cult of the bear 'commonly

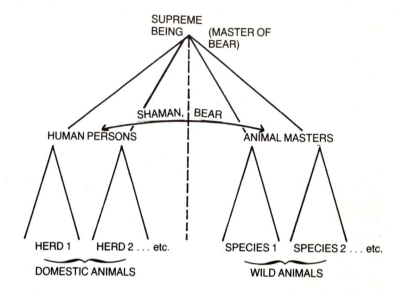

Figure 10.4   The position of the Supreme Being stands above the domains of both human persons and animal masters, and transcends the opposition between them.

addresses itself to the soul of the individual animal, less frequently to the bear guardian' (1961: 60). For the spiritual guardian of the bear, quite unlike that – say – of the wild reindeer or caribou, is none other than the Supreme Being or guardian of mankind as well, and less directly, of everything else that lives. And just as the concept of his supremacy may be derived by 'scaling up' from the supremacy of animal guardians over their charges, so the latter may be derived by a reverse 'scaling down'. To cite Hultcrantz again: 'The animal guardian owns and rules over animals in the same way as the Supreme Being rules over human beings, animals and the entire universe – the perception of dependence characterizing the religious feeling has here been transferred from the world of man to that of animals' (1961: 59).

Among the Tungus (Evenks), the Supreme Being has two aspects, never very clearly distinguished, but sometimes addressed by different names. In one aspect, as *Amaka*, he rules over everything pertaining to people; in the other somewhat subordinate aspect, as *Ekseri*, he rules over everything pertaining to the forest – including the spirit masters of wild animal species. So for example, *Ekseri* has the power to override the action of a spirit master in sending an animal to a particular hunter, if he considers the hunter unworthy of success. *Amaka* is depicted, just as we would expect from the foregoing argument, as 'a very old man dressed in resplendent fur clothing', or in other words as the archetypal, anthropo-morphic bear – indeed the word *amaka* is used synonymously for the Supreme Being and as a species name for the bear (Anisimov 1963b: 160–3). As we saw earlier, the species name can be used as a proper name for the master of the species who is, in this case, the Supreme Being. *Amaka*, moreover, is not only the ruler of people but also the originator of their herds of domestic reindeer. In this we have the explanation of a popular belief among the Tungus according to which the domestic herds sprang from the intestines and fur of a bear, for the bear is *amaka* (Vasilevich 1963: 71).

The Koryak also believe the Supreme Being to have been the source of their domestic herds. This Being, essentially benevolent, is only vaguely conceived, usually in anthropomorphic form. He does not reveal himself to man directly, but relies on a trickster character known as Big-Raven to translate the world-order he has created into a human reality. Thus, it was Big-Raven who brought domestic reindeer from the heavenly abode of the Supreme Being (Jochelson 1908: 18–25). Among the Chukchi, the conception of the Supreme Being is still more indefinite. He is referred to by terms translating as 'Upper Being', 'Merciful Being' and 'Life-giving Being'. There are also terms for 'Creator' and 'Luck-giving Being', but there is some confusion between these and the notion, perhaps borrowed from the Koryak, of Big-Raven. Of particular interest to us is the Chukchi conception of the 'Reindeer Being', who is supposed to look after the welfare of the domestic herds. The conception is again an indefinite one, and is interchangeable with two others: on the one hand with the Supreme Being in his guise as Creator or Merciful One, on the other hand with the anthropomorphic fireboard which, as we shall see, contains a kind of spiritual double of the human master of the herd. Whereas the Supreme Being offers a blanket protection over all herds, the fireboard of course only protects the domestic herd of its particular owner. In both these separate senses, the Reindeer Being has to be distinguished from the spirit master of the *wild* reindeer, Pičvu'čin, whom we introduced in an earlier section (Bogoras 1904–9: 314–15).

The various benevolent beings conceived by the Chukchi, including those just mentioned, are all denoted by the suffix *va'irgin*, which on its own simply signifies 'existence' or 'life force' (Bogoras 1904–9: 303). I do not think it would be a distortion of Chukchi ideas to equate this vital force, which flows through and animates the world of animals and men, with God. As Jochelson writes of the Koryak, whose religious concep-tions are very close to those of their Chukchi neighbours, they regard the

Supreme Being as 'the personification of the vital principle in nature taken in its entirety' (1908: 24). The benevolent spirits of the Chukchi and Koryak pantheons, then, embody many different facets of this total principle, of existence itself. To borrow Evans-Pritchard's felicitous term, they represent the one God 'refracted' along a number of different lines or directions (see Evans-Pritchard 1956: 107). Indeed, to every spirit there corresponds a direction of the compass, in which it is supposed to live, or more accurately, *the spirit is itself the direction* (Bogoras 1904–9: 303). Thus, the Chukchi *va'irgit*, benevolent beings, are vectors of God, and of existence. Moreover these beings, above all, are the recipients of bloody sacrifice, none more often than Zenith and Morning-Dawn, both regarded as particularly auspicious. The direction to which the sacrifice is made is always indicated by pointing the victim's head towards it, immediately after immolation (Bogoras 1904–9: 370). All sacrifices, then, are to God, but to God regarded and approached in particular ways. It is perhaps important to note at this juncture that the category of *va'irgit* is quite separate from that of *ke'let*, although both may be translated as 'spirits'. Where the former comprises the refractions of Being, the latter – as we have already seen (p. 252) – comprises all 'other-than-human' persons, including both the animal masters, who are generally harmless, and the whole panoply of evil spirits. As a general rule, *ke'let* may receive offerings of material substance, but are not overtly invoked in bloody sacrifice.

What do we learn from this of the significance of sacrifice? Recall that every slaughter of a domestic reindeer is a sacrifice to some *va'irgin* or other, and that the consumption of its slaughter products, quite unlike those of the bear or wild buck in the domestic herd, is an entirely secular affair. Therefore the essence of sacrifice must lie in the release rather than the absorption of vital substance, for assimilation by the invoked spirit. This substance, if not immaterial then at least volatile or fluid, is commonly identified with the blood (Bogoras 1904–9: 369–70, see also Shirokogoroff 1935: 199, Karsten 1955:96). There is a clear idea that if life is to continue, such substance must keep on flowing or circulating; for should the circulation be blocked, animals and then people will die. One does not, in sacrifice, contract with the *va'irgit* as one might with the *ke'let*, through material prestation and counterprestation; the *va'irgin* is not conceived like a person who, receiving with one hand, is obliged to give with the other, but rather as the fount of existence itself. So whatever its specific propitiatory purpose, sacrifice sends some of the vitality of the world along a particular direction to the source of creative regeneration, Supreme Being, whence it should return in the form of life and health to human beings, and the reproductive increase of their herds.

In this connection a few words should be said about the significance of

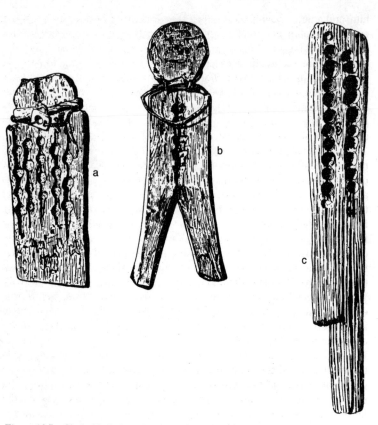

Figure 10.5 Chukchi fireboards, from Bogoras (1904–9: 350): (a) and (b) are
sacred fireboards – 'the holes made by drilling are considered the eyes of the
fireboard; and the squeaking noise produced by the drilling, its voice'; (c) is a
substitute fireboard made for regular, everyday use.

fire. Amongst the Chukchi every household has its own fire, and the
exchange of fire – for example by using in one hearth a piece of wood
already blackened in another – is strictly prohibited. However, this rule
applies only to 'genuine fire', that is the fire generated by means of a bow-
drill twisted on a wooden fireboard. The fireboard, roughly carved in
human form, is a precious family heirloom (Figure 10.5). Each board
goes with a particular reindeer brand, and is thereby associated with a
portion of the domestic herd. So when a boy is old enough to receive his
first reindeer, he gets with them a brand and a board (though if the
number of hereditary boards is insufficient, a new one will be made for

him, and a new brand established at the same time). When the household eventually splits up, each heir goes his separate way, taking his own herd, his own fireboard and his own fire. Now the board, as well as being the source of fire and in that sense a guardian of the hearth, is also a magical guardian of the herd. According to Bogoras, 'it is looked upon as a supernatural herdsman', the indispensable right-hand man of the human herd-owner (1904–9: 348–53). Jochelson, who records identical beliefs and practices among the Koryak, states that the sacred fireboard is actually known as the 'master of the herd' (1908: 32–6).

Both fire and fireboard play an important part in every sacrifice of reindeer. The blood of the slaughtered beast, collected in a ladle, is not only scattered in the direction of the spirit invoked in the sacrifice, but is also 'fed' to the fire, and smeared over the fireboard. In addition, during the early autumn ceremonial associated with the slaughter of reindeer fawns for their skins, members of the household paint designs on their faces with the blood of a slaughtered fawn. Each household has a design of its own which, with other sacred objects, is passed down the generations. The design is supposed to make the face of the wearer like that of the protective Reindeer Being (Bogoras 1904–9: 360–1, see Figure 10.6). When we recall that this Being is also identified with the fireboard, it is evident that the rite of face-painting serves to establish a complete identification between the human and the spiritual guardianship of the domestic herd. One could say that the master of the herd is in fact the Reindeer Being, but that this Being has a double aspect of which one is the fireboard and the other the human owner to whom it belongs. The principal purpose of the autumn ceremonial, however, is to celebrate the reunion of household and herd after the summer season, during which the herds roam on distant tundra pastures out of reach of the domestic environment (Bogoras 1904–9: 372, also Jochelson 1908: 86–7). By painting the fireboard and the faces of household members with blood, and by feeding it to the fire, the mystical bond between the human group, the hearth and the herd is dramatically reaffirmed.

Now fire comes from God, and its importance lies in the fact that it represents a concentration of vital power focused at the very heart of the domestic group, in the hearth, which is the sacred centre of every dwelling. Moreover, according to the Koryak view, fire 'signifies the source whence [domestic] reindeer originated', indeed legend has it that the Supreme Being pulled the first deer out of the fire (Jochelson 1908: 87). Yet fire itself springs from the fireboard, which is a human possession. Thus, I would argue that fire and fireboard serve to complete the cycle of creative regeneration initiated in sacrifice. The vital essence of slain beasts is thrown outwards, centrifugally, towards the various directions of the benevolent spirits, only to converge in a source of Being atop the

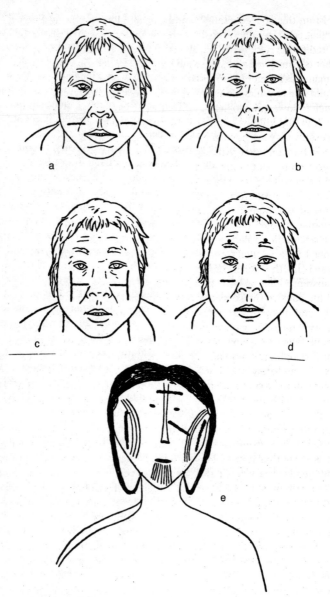

Figure 10.6 Chukchi face-painting designs, intended to make the face similar to that of the Reindeer Being. The lower drawing (e) reproduces a native sketch of the face of a tattooed woman with blood marks. From Bogoras (1904–9: 360).

world. From this source vitality returns, again along different directions, converging centripetally on the hearth where, by means of the fireboard, the sacred fire is rekindled. And the fire, in turn, recharges the domestic herd that is conceived to have sprung from it, under the watchful eye of the human master and his fireboard assistant. And so the cycle goes on.

I should like to conclude with a speculative leap which may seem rash, but which follows quite logically and naturally from all we have shown up to now. It is that killings of animals by human hunters *are* acts of bloody sacrifice; only they are ones in which the persons offering the sacrifice are other-than-human, namely the spirit masters of the wild herds. Hunting, as Spencer points out in his work on the North Alaskan Eskimo, is a rite of world renewal, so too is the sacrifice of domestic livestock (Spencer 1959: 331). But in the former case the cycle of regeneration begins and ends not in the human community but in the supposedly analogous communities of the spirits guarding each species of wild animal. With them is lodged the *intention* to present particular beasts for immolation. And when they are killed God takes the life, whence it returns to the spirit concerned in the form of the increase of the species under its guardianship. Again as with the sacrifice of domestic stock, should the flow of life back to the source of Being be blocked, animals will cease to multiply and people will starve. Thus, the Alaskan Eskimo tell the cautionary tale of a woman who, tired of processing her husband's bounteous kills of caribou, secretly placed a bucket over the unsevered head of a slaughtered animal, thereby obstructing the escape of its vital essence. Immediately the hunter's luck changed, and his family was soon reduced to starvation. Then one day the hunter saw the ghost of the caribou, still with the bucket on its head. He removed the bucket, and prosperity once more returned (Spencer 1959: 413–14).

If our interpretation be accepted, that the spirit master is understood to sacrifice beasts from his herd to God in order to ensure its renewal, then it is clear that human hunters offer a service to the spirit in performing the necessary acts of immolation. In return they receive, as a gift from the spirit, most of the meat and slaughter products – in other words the material residue of the sacrifice. As a token of appreciation, however, they return small counter-gifts in the form of material offerings, usually thrown into the fire. With the sacrifice of domestic stock, we see precisely the same pattern except with the positions of human and spirit masters reversed. It is true that the human herd-master can immolate his own animals, and does not need to call on spirit persons to do the job for him. However, the service that the spirit renders in appearing as a buck to impregnate the does of the domestic herd is strictly equivalent. It is also true that the slaughter products left over from sacrifice are consumed by humans, nevertheless at least some semblance is made of offering them to the spirit. And their apparent acceptance is taken as a pledge by the spirit to help man with gifts of meat and beneficial visitations in the future. Such visitations, the temporary incorporation of non-human persons within the human domain, are expressed in the idiom of eating and being eaten, as in the communion of the bear-feast. Gift offerings, on the other hand, connote the separation and departure of the non-human guest from the host community (similar offerings may of course be made to human guests from other communities).

Our argument, now complete, is summarized in Figure 10.7. From this diagram I think it can be seen that the entire structure of the sacrificial rite is already prefigured in native conceptions surrounding the conduct of hunting. All that is necessary to bring it out is to transpose mastery over herds from non-human to human persons, which is of course a corollary of their domestication, and marks the transition from a hunting

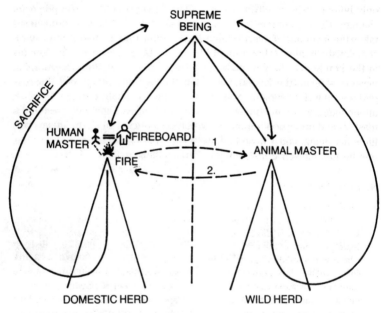

Figure 10.7   The sacrifice of animals by human and animal masters. When the sacrifice is made by an animal master, dashed arrow 1 connotes the immolation service performed by the human hunter, dashed arrow 2 connotes the gift of meat – the material residue of the sacrifice – from the animal master to man. When the sacrifice is made by a human master, arrow 2 connotes the sexual service performed by the animal master (as a wild buck in the domestic herd), arrow 1 connotes the gift of meat – the material residue of the sacrifice – from man to the animal master.

to a pastoral economy. Where once the hunter performed the immolation, and ate the meat, of animals owned and sacrificed by a spirit master, now – aided and abetted by a spiritual double such as the fireboard – it is *he* who purposes the sacrifice, both killing and eating the meat of his own animals. It is as though man has simply usurped the place of the spirit in the overall scheme of things. taking on both the powers of control over animals, and the responsibility for their renewal. One would not expect the spirit masters willingly to condone such usurpation of their powers, and the risk that they might retaliate by causing the wild herds to desert the hunting grounds may well have militated against human attempts to increase their holdings of domestic stock by the forcible abduction of wild animals caught alive (Ingold 1980: 282–3). Where men may struggle with one another for control over domestic herds through the direct use of physical force, coercion over the spiritual masters of wild animals can only be exercised by mystical means, through the offices of a powerful shaman. Hence, competition between men for control over wild herds takes the form not of overt raiding and counter-raiding, but of the covert, shamanistic contest (Hultcrantz 1978: 54–6). There are powerful shamans in the non-human domain too, out to seize the herds from their human masters – recall the Koryak view that the wolf is such a one. But it is perhaps as well to remember that although man may sometimes have the upper hand, and sometimes the lower, in his dealings with the animal masters and other non-human persons, this world in which he moves and finds his Being, and whose lineaments we have outlined in this essay, is one he has himself constructed.

Notes to Chapter 10

1 These beetles are actually seen coming from the woodwork of the box grave when it rots. As a curious piece of serendipity, we might note that Wittgenstein, in his *Philosophical Investigations* (1953: I § 294), chose the same imagery to depict one view of the relation between body and soul: 'Suppose everyone had a box with something in it: we call it a "beetle" '!

2 This imagined link between the death and regeneration of animals raises a number of questions that would repay further investigation. At what point is the animal considered to be actually dead? If the penetration of the animal by a hunter's weapon corresponds to intercourse, what corresponds to conception? Might the interval between intercourse and conception be likened to that between killing and consumption? In my reading for this essay, I did not come across anything that would help to resolve these questions; but no doubt there exists material from other ethnographic regions that might shed some light on them.

3 The Ainu of northern Japan, however, see things rather differently. In their view, bears are also organized into tribes with chiefs or headmen. However the latter are believed never to leave their abodes on remote mountain tops, and

so are never met by humans. These bear chiefs, it is supposed, send their subordinates on annual visits to Ainu communities. They are the individual bears encountered by Ainu hunters, which are received and 'sent off' with much ceremony (Watanabe 1972: 73–4, 154–5 fn. 63).

4   Watanabe (personal communication) has explained that the Ainu regard the captured bear cub as a kind of 'divine baby' which is fostered by its human captors prior to being returned to its proper parental home in the country of the bear spirit. It is not clear exactly what benefit this fostering is supposed to confer upon the human community. The logic of our argument, however, suggests connotations of fertility. If the killing of game by human hunters is metaphorically identified with acts of sexual intercourse, then the hunters must leave their own offspring in the care of animal guardians who sent the game to be killed (impregnated). Conversely, it might be supposed, on their visits from the spirit world to the communities of men, bears leave their offspring in the care of human persons.

. 5   This analogy could be pursued further. Since the spirit master of the wild reindeer is like a father to the animals in his charge (his 'daughters'), he requires an external agent – in the person of the hunter – to impregnate them, else the relationship between 'father' and 'daughters' would be incestuous. Likewise the human household head requires an external agent in the form of the wild buck to secure vigorous progeny for the does of his herd.

References for Chapter 10

Alekseenko, E. A. 1968 The cult of the bear among the Ket (Yenisei Ostyaks). In *Popular beliefs and folklore tradition in Siberia*, ed. V. Diószegi (Indiana University Uralic and Altaic Series 57). Mouton: The Hague.

Anisimov, A. F. 1963a The shaman's tent of the Evenks and the origin of the shamanistic rite. In *Studies in Siberian shamanism*, ed. H. N. Michael (Arctic Institute of North America, Anthropology of the North, Translations from Russian Sources No. 4). University of Toronto Press.

Anisimov A. F. 1963b Cosmological concepts of the peoples of the North. In *Studies in Siberian shamanism*, ed. H. N. Michael (Arctic Institute of North America, Anthropology of the North, Translations from Russian Sources No. 4). University of Toronto Press.

Bogoras, W. G. 1904–9 *The Chukchee*. Jesup North Pacific Expedition VII (3 parts), American Museum of Natural History Memoir 11. Leiden: E. J. Brill.

Chernetsov, V. N. 1963 Concepts of the soul among the Ob Ugrians. In *Studies in Siberian shamanism*, ed. H. N. Michael (Arctic Institute of North America, Anthropology of the North, Translations from Russian Sources No. 4). University of Toronto Press.

Czaplicka, M. A. 1920 Siberia, Sibiriaks, Siberians. In *Encyclopaedia of religion and ethics* XI, ed. J. Hastings. Edinburgh: T. and T. Clark.

Evans-Pritchard, E. E. 1956 *Nuer religion*. Oxford University Press.

Frazer, J. G. 1957 [1922] *The Golden Bough* (abridged edition). London: Macmillan.

Hallowell, A. I. 1926 Bear ceremonialism in the northern hemisphere. *American Anthropologist* **28**: 1–175.

Hallowell, A. I. 1960 Ojibwa ontology, behavior and world view. In *Culture in history: essays in honor of Paul Radin*, ed. S. Diamond. New York: Columbia University Press.

Holmberg, U. 1964 *The mythology of all races IV: Finno-Ugric, Siberian*. New York: Cooper Square.

Hultcrantz, Å. 1953 *Conceptions of the soul among North American Indians* (Ethnographical Museum of Sweden Monograph Series No. 1). Stockholm.

Hultcrantz, Å. 1961 The owner of the animals in the religion of the North American Indians. In *The supernatural owners of nature*, ed. Å. Hultcrantz (Stockholm Studies in Comparative Religion No. 1). Stockholm: Almqvist and Wiksell.

Hultcrantz, Å. 1978 Means and ends in Lapp Shamanism. In *Studies in Lapp shamanism*, by L. Backman and Å. Hultcrantz (Stockholm Studies in Comparative Religion No. 16). Stockholm: Almqvist and Wiksell.

Hultcrantz, Å. 1979 *The religions of the American Indians*. Berkeley: Univeristy of California Press.

Ingold, T. 1980 *Hunters, pastoralists and ranchers*. Cambridge University Press.

Jetté, J. 1911 On the superstitions of the Ten'a Indians (middle part of the Yukon valley, Alaska). *Anthropos* **6**: 95–108.

Jochelson, W. 1908 *The Koryak*. Jesup North Pacific Expedition VI, American Museum of Natural History Memoir 10. Leiden: E. J. Brill.

Karsten, R. 1955 *The religion of the Samek: ancient beliefs and cults of the Scandinavian and Finnish Lapps*. Leiden: E. J. Brill.

Larsen, H. 1970 Some examples of the bear cult among the Eskimo and other northern peoples. *Folk* **11–12**: 27–42.

Martin, C. 1978 *Keepers of the game*. Berkeley: University of California Press.

Nelson, R. K. 1982 A conservation ethic and environment: the Koyukon of Alaska. In *Resource managers: North American and Australian hunter–gatherers*, eds. N. M. Williams and E. S. Hunn (AAAS Selected Symposium 67). Boulder, Colorado: Westview Press.

Paulson, I. 1968 The preservation of animal bones in the hunting rites of some North-Eurasian peoples. In *Popular beliefs and folklore tradition in Siberia*, ed. V. Diószegi (Indiana University Uralic and Altaic Series 57). Mouton: The Hague.

Saladin d'Anglure, B. 1980 Nanuq super-male – L'ours blanc dans l'espace imaginaire et le temps social des Inuit de l'Arctique Canadien. In *2nd International Conference on Hunting and Gathering Societies, 19–24 September 1980*. Québec: Université Laval, Département d'Anthropologie.

Seligman, B. Z. 1962 Appendix II: The bear ceremony. In *Ainu creed and cult*, by N. G. Munro, ed. B. Z. Seligman. London: Routledge and Kegan Paul.

Shirokogoroff, S. M. 1935 *Psychomental complex of the Tungus*. London: Kegan Paul, Trench and Trubner.

Speck. F. G. 1935 *Naskapi, the savage hunters of the Labrador peninsula*. Norman: University of Oklahoma Press.

Spencer, R. F. 1959 *The North Alaskan Eskimo: a study in ecology and society*. Smithsonian Institution Bureau of American Ethnology, Bulletin 171. Washington, DC: US Government Printing Office.

Tanner, A. 1979 *Bringing home animals: religious ideology and mode of production of the Mistassini Cree hunters*. London: Hurst.

Turner, L. M. 1979 [1894] *Indians and Eskimos in the Quebec–Labrador Peninsula: Ethnology of the Ungava District, Hudson Bay Territory.* Québec: Presses Coméditex.

Vasilevich, G. M. 1963 Early concepts about the universe among the Evenks (Materials). In *Studies in Siberian shamanism*, ed. H. N. Michael (Arctic Institute of North America, Anthropology of the North, Translations from Russian Sources No. 4). University of Toronto Press.

Vecsey, C. 1983 *Traditional Ojibwa religion and its historical changes* (American Philosophical Society Memoir 152). Philadelphia: American Philosophical Society.

Watanabe, H. 1972 *The Ainu ecosystem: environment and group structure.* University of Tokyo Press.

Wittgenstein, L. 1953 *Philosophical investigations.* Oxford: Blackwell.

Index